DATE DUE

			PRINTED IN U.S.A.

Authors & Artists for Young Adults

ISSN 1040-5682

Authors & Artists for Young Adults

VOLUME 14

E. A. Des Chenes
Editor

 Gale Research Inc.

An International Thomson Publishing Company

I(T)P

NEW YORK • LONDON • BONN • BOSTON • DETROIT • MADRID
MELBOURNE • MEXICO CITY • PARIS • SINGAPORE • TOKYO
TORONTO • WASHINGTON • ALBANY NY • BELMONT CA • CINCINNATI OH

E. A. Des Chenes, *Editor*

Joanna Brod, Thomas F. McMahon, and Diane Telgen, *Associate Editors*

Mindi Dickstein, David P. Johnson, Ronie-Richele Garcia-Johnson,
Marion C. Gonsior, Helene Henderson, Janet L. Hile, Laurie Collier Hillstrom,
Tom Pendergast, Nancy E. Rampson, Megan Ratner, Susan M. Reicha,
Tracy J. Sukraw, Laura M. Zaidman, *Sketch Contributors*

Victoria B. Cariappa, *Research Manager*
Mary Rose Bonk, *Research Supervisor*

Reginald A. Carlton, Frank Vincent Castronova, Andrew Guy Malonis, and
Norma Sawaya, *Editorial Associates*
Laurel Sprague Bowden, Dawn Marie Conzett, Eva Marie Felts, Shirley Gates,
Sharon McGilvray, Dana R. Schleiffers, and Amy B. Wieczorek, *Editorial Assistants*

Margaret A. Chamberlain, *Picture Permissions Specialist*
Susan Brohman, Pamela A. Hayes, Arlene Johnson, Keith Reed, and
Barbara A. Wallace, *Permissions Associates*

Mary Beth Trimper, *Production Director*
Catherine Kemp, *External Production Assistant*

Cynthia Baldwin, *Product Design Manager*
Sherrell Hobbs and C. J. Jonik, *Desktop Publishers/Typesetters*
Willie Mathis, *Camera Operator*

The paper used in this publication meets the minimum requirements of American National Standard for Information Sciences—Permanence Paper for Printed Library Materials, ANSI Z39.48-1984. ∞™

Library of Congress Catalog Card Number 89-641100
ISBN 0-8103-5730-5
ISSN 1040-5682

10 9 8 7 6 5 4 3 2 1

Printed in the United States of America

Published simultaneously in the United Kingdom
by Gale Research International Limited
(An affiliated company of Gale Research Inc.)

I(T)P™ Gale Research Inc., an International Thomson Publishing Company.
ITP logo is a trademark under license.

Authors and Artists for Young Adults

TEEN BOARD

The staff of *Authors and Artists for Young Adults* wishes to thank the following young adult readers for their teen board participation:

Contents

Introduction xi

Ansel Adams 1
Renowned American photographer acclaimed as a pivotal figure in the evolution of modern photography.

Dave Barry 13
Pulitzer Prize-winning humorist whose books include *Homes and Other Black Holes* and *Dave Barry Is Not Making This Up*.

Peter Benchley 23
Novelist and screenwriter best known for his novels such as *Jaws* that mix monstrous terror with the wonders of the deep.

Tim Burton 33
Film writer, producer, and director whose efforts include *Pee Wee's Big Adventure, Beetlejuice, Batman,* and *Ed Wood*.

Barbara Corcoran...............................43
American author of mysteries, historical romances and other tales for young adults that convincingly explore coming-of-age feelings and concerns.

Richie Tankersley Cusick 55
Horror novelist who revels in exploring the dark side of human nature in works such as *The Lifeguard, Silent Stalker,* and *Scarecrow*.

Frank Deford 65
Award-winning sportswriter, biographer and novelist whose works often draw upon the author's twenty-seven-year career as feature writer for *Sports Illustrated*.

Arthur Conan Doyle 75
Prolific novelist, essayist, short-story writer and historian who is best remembered as the creator of famed detective Sherlock Holmes.

Roddy Doyle 93
Booker Prize-winning Irish novelist whose "Barrytown trilogy" and *Paddy Clarke Ha Ha Ha* offer keen and often humorous insight into the daily lives of working class families in modern Ireland.

Danny Elfman 99
Composer and musician who has been a member of the group "Oingo Boingo" since 1979, as well as the creator of award-winning scores and theme songs for popular films such as *Beetlejuice* and *Darkman* and for television series such as *The Simpsons*.

Frank Frazetta 107
Hugo Award-winning cartoonist and illustrator whose work is noted for its colorful images and attention to detail.

John Grisham 115
Bestselling attorney–turned–author , whose legal-themed novels include *A Time to Kill, The Firm, The Pelican Brief,* and *The Client*.

James S. Haskins 123
Author of nonfiction studies on subjects ranging from teenage alcoholism and the Vietnam War to such well-known figures as Kareem Abdul-Jabbar, Malcolm X, and Martin Luther King, Jr.

Will Hobbs 135
Award-winning author of suspenseful coming-of-age stories such as *Beardance* set in the mountains, canyons, and wilderness regions of the American Southwest.

Dorothea Lange 143
Celebrated American photographer whose large body of work encompassesa wide variety of American experience, including the economically depressed 1930s.

H. P. Lovecraft 151
Popular author of science fiction and supernatural tales who expanded the scope of the horror genre by mixing Gothic themes with cosmic terror.

Patricia McKillip 163
World Fantasy Award-winning fantasy and science-fiction writer whose works such as *Forgotten Beasts of Eld* incorporate colorful characters and fantastic adventure.

Andre Norton 169
Prolific Nebula Grand Masters Award-winner whose popular science fiction and fantasy works including the "Witch World" and "Time War" series often feature rite-of-passage themes.

Joan Phipson 181
Australian author of young adult suspense novels that feature authentic outback and urban-Australian settings.

Edgar Allan Poe 189
Innovative author credited with inventing the modern detective tale in "The Murders in the Rue Morgue," refining the Gothic horror story in tales like "The Pit and the Pendulum, and composing critically-acclaimed poetry, including "The Raven."

Harold Ramis 203
American director, producer, writer and actor who has parlayed a finely-honed sense of humor into a string of highly successful screen comedies, including *Caddyshack* and *Groundhog Day*.

Rod Serling 215
Six-time Emmy-Award-winning television writer, producer, and narrator best remembered as the creator of *The Twilight Zone*.

Leslie Marmon Silko 225
Pushcart Prize-winning American poet, novelist and short story writer whose collections *Storyteller* and *Laguna Woman* vividly depict the author's experiences as a woman of Native American ancestry.

Timothy Zahn 235
Hugo Award-winning science-fiction author of popular books like *Deadman Switch* and the "Star Wars" series.

Acknowledgments 245

Author/Artist Index 251

Introduction

Authors and Artists for Young Adults is a reference series designed to serve the needs of middle school, junior high, and high school students interested in creative artists. Originally inspired by the need to bridge the gap between Gale's *Something about the Author,* created for children, and *Contemporary Authors,* intended for older students and adults, *Authors and Artists for Young Adults* has been expanded to cover not only an international scope of authors, but also a wide variety of other artists.

Although the emphasis of the series remains on the writer for young adults, we recognize that these readers have diverse interests covering a wide range of reading levels. The series therefore contains not only those creative artists who are of high interest to young adults, including cartoonists, photographers, music composers, bestselling authors of adult novels, media directors, producers, and performers, but also literary and artistic figures studied in academic curricula, such as influential novelists, playwrights, poets, and painters. The goal of *Authors and Artists for Young Adults* is to present this great diversity of creative artists in a format that is entertaining, informative, and understandable to the young adult reader.

Entry Format

Each volume of *Authors and Artists for Young Adults* will furnish in depth coverage of twenty to twenty-five authors and artists. The typical entry consists of:

—A detailed biographical section that includes date of birth, marriage, children, education, and addresses.

—A comprehensive bibliography or filmography including publishers, producers, and years.

—Adaptations into other media forms.

—Works in progress.

—A distinctive essay featuring comments on an artist's life, career, artistic intentions, world views, and controversies.

—References for further reading.

—Extensive illustrations, photographs, movie stills, cartoons, book covers, and other relevant visual material.

A cumulative index to featured authors and artists appears in each volume.

Compilation Methods

The editors of *Authors and Artists for Young Adults* make every effort to secure information directly from the authors and artists through personal correspondence and interviews. Sketches on living authors and artists are sent to the biographee for review prior to publication. Any sketches not personally reviewed by biographees or their representatives are marked with an asterisk (*).

Highlights of Forthcoming Volumes

Among the authors and artists planned for future volumes are:

Chinua Achebe	Keith Haring	Joyce Carol Oates
Ben Bova	Stephen Herek	George Orwell
Ray Bradbury	Patricia Hermes	Stella Pevsner
James L. Brooks	David Hockney	Chaim Potok
Brock Cole	Zora Neale Hurston	Philip Pullman
Roald Dahl	Magic Johnson	Robert Redford
Linda Ellerbee	Barbara Kingsolver	Ann Rinaldi
M. C. Escher	Tanith Lee	Zilpha Keatley Snyder
Alan Dean Foster	Patricia MacLachlan	Oliver Stone
W. Michael and	Lurlene McDonald	Yoshiko Uchida
Kathleen O'Neal Gear	Larry McMurtry	John Waters
Genaro Gonzalez	Arthur Miller	William Wegman

The editors of *Authors and Artists for Young Adults* welcome any suggestions for additional biographees to be included in this series. Please write and give us your opinions and suggestions for making our series more helpful to you. Direct your comments to: Editors, *Authors and Artists for Young Adults*, Gale Research, Inc. , 835 Penobscot Building, Detroit, MI 48226-4094.

Authors & Artists for Young Adults

Ansel Adams

■ Personal

Born Ansel Easton Adams, February 20, 1902, in San Francisco, CA; died of heart disease, April 22, 1984, in Carmel, CA; son of Charles Hitchcock (in business) and Olive (Bray) Adams; married Virginia Best, January 2, 1928; children: Michael, Anne Helms. *Education:* Tutored privately at home; studied piano in San Francisco, 1914–27. *Politics:* Democrat. *Religion:* "No formal religion."

■ Career

Professional pianist and teacher, 1920–30; professional photographer, 1927–84. Photography correspondent, *Fortnightly Review,* 1931; founding member, Group f/64, San Francisco, CA, 1932; director, Ansel Adams Photography and Art Gallery, San Francisco, 1933–34; instructor in photography, Art Center School, Los Angeles, CA, 1939–42; director of photography department, Golden Gate International Exposition, 1940; vice–chair of photography department, New York Museum of Modern Art, 1940–42; photo–muralist, U.S. Department of the Interior, CA, 1941–42; photography consultant, Office of War Information, Los Angeles, 1942–44;

founder and director of photography department, San Francisco Art Institute (formerly California Institute of Fine Arts), San Francisco, 1946–49; consultant to Polaroid Corporation, Cambridge, MA, 1949–84; founding instructor, Ansel Adams Annual Photography Workshops, Yosemite Valley, CA, 1955–84. Appeared in instructional television series, *Photography: The Incisive Art,* National Educational Television (NET), 1959. *Exhibitions:* Include M. H. de Young Memorial Museum, 1932; An American Place, New York City, 1936; Art Institute of Chicago, Chicago, IL, 1951; Smithsonian Institution, Washington, D.C. (toured the U.S.), 1952; Boston Museum of Art, Boston, MA, 1967; San Francisco Museum of Art, San Francisco, 1972; Metropolitan Museum of Art, New York City, 1974; and Museum of Modern Art, New York City, 1979. *Member:* American Academy of Arts and Sciences (fellow), Photographic Society of America (fellow), Royal Photographic Society of London (fellow), Sierra Club (member of board of directors, 1934–71; honorary vice–president, 1978–84), Friends of Photography, Carmel, CA (founder and chair of the board), Old Capital Club (Monterey, CA).

■ Awards, Honors

Guggenheim fellowships, 1946–47, 1948–49, and 1959–61; Brehm Memorial Award, Rochester Institute of Technology, 1958; John Muir Award, Sierra Club, 1963; Conservation Service Award, U.S. Department of the Interior, 1968; Progress Medal, Photographic Society of America, 1969; special citation, American Institute of Architects, 1971; first

Ansel Adams Award, Wilderness Society, 1980; U.S. Presidential Medal of Freedom, 1980; Hasselbad Gold Medal (Sweden), 1981; Legion of Merit (France), 1982.

Honorary degrees from numerous universities and colleges, including University of California, Berkeley, 1961; Occidental College, 1967; Yale University, 1973; University of Massachusetts, 1974; University of Arizona, 1975; Harvard University, 1981; and Mills College, 1982.

■ Writings

Parmelian Prints of the High Sierras, [San Francisco], 1927.

Making a Photograph: An Introduction to Photography, Studio, 1935.

The Four Seasons in Yosemite National Park: A Photographic Story of Yosemite's Spectacular Scenery, Times Mirror, 1936.

Sierra Nevada: The John Muir Trail, The Illustrator, 1938.

(With wife, Virginia Adams) *Illustrated Guide to Yosemite Valley*, Crocker, 1940.

(With V. Adams) *Michael and Anne in the Yosemite Valley*, Studio, 1941.

Born Free and Equal: Photographs of Loyal Japanese–Americans at Manzanar Relocation Center, Inyo County, California, U.S. Camera, 1944.

Yosemite and the High Sierra, Houghton, 1948.

My Camera in Yosemite Valley: Twenty–four Photographs and an Essay on Mountain Photography, Houghton, 1949.

My Camera in the National Parks: Thirty Photographs with Interpretive Text and Informative Material on the Parks and Monuments, and Photographic Data, Houghton, 1950.

Yosemite Valley, Five Associates, 1959.

(With Nancy Newhall) *This Is the American Earth*, Sierra Club, 1960.

These We Inherit: The Parklands of America, Sierra Club, 1962.

(With Robert Baker) *Polaroid Land Photography Manual: A Technical Handbook*, Morgan & Morgan, 1963.

(With V. Adams) *Illustrated Guide to Yosemite: The Valley, the Rim, and the Central Yosemite Sierra, and Mountain Photography*, Sierra Club, 1963.

(With Newhall) *Fiat Lux: The University of California*, McGraw–Hill, 1967.

(With Newhall) *The Tetons and the Yellowstone*, Five Associates, 1970.

Ansel Adams: Images, 1923–1974, New York Graphic Society, 1974.

Singular Images, New York Graphic Society, 1974.

A Yosemite Album: Fifteen Photographs, Five Associates, 1974.

(With Laurence Clark Powell) *Photographs of the Southwest*, New York Graphic Society, 1976.

Yosemite and the Range of Light, New York Graphic Society, 1980.

Examples: The Making of Forty Photographs, Little, Brown, 1983.

Ansel Adams: An Autobiography, Little, Brown, 1985.

(With James Alinder) *Ansel Adams: Classic Images*, Little, Brown, 1986.

Also author, with James Alinder, of *Ansel Adams: Fifty Years of Portraits*, 1979.

PORTFOLIOS

Portfolio I, National Parks and Monuments, 1948.

Portfolio II: The National Parks, National Parks and Monuments, 1950.

Portfolio III: Yosemite Valley, Sierra Club, 1960.

Portfolio IV, Varian Foundation, 1961.

Portfolio V, Parasol Press, 1971.

Portfolio VI, Parasol Press, 1973.

Portfolio VII, Parasol Press, 1976.

The Portfolios of Ansel Adams (contains *Portfolios I–VII*), New York Graphic Society, 1977.

"BASIC PHOTO" SERIES

Camera and Lens: Studio, Darkroom, and Equipment, Morgan & Morgan, 1948, revised edition published as *The Camera*, New York Graphic Society, 1980.

The Negative: Exposure and Development, Morgan & Morgan, 1948.

The Print: Contact Printing and Enlarging, Morgan & Morgan, 1950.

Natural Light Photography, Morgan & Morgan, 1952.

Artificial Light Photography, Morgan & Morgan, 1956.

ILLUSTRATOR

Mary Hunter Austin, *Taos Pueblo*, [San Francisco], 1930.

Austin, *The Land of Little Rain*, Houghton, 1950.

Nancy Newhall, *The Pageant of History in Northern California*, [San Francisco], 1954.

Newhall, *Death Valley*, Five Associates, 1954.

Newhall, *Mission San Xavier del Bac*, Five Associates, 1954.

Edwin Corle, *Death Valley and the Creek Called Furnace*, Ritchie, 1962.

Newhall, *The Eloquent Light: Ansel Adams,* Sierra Club, 1964.

Edward Joesting, *An Introduction to Hawaii,* Five Associates, 1964.

(With others) David Ross Brower, editor, *Not Man Apart: Lines from Robinson Jeffers,* Sierra Club, 1965.

(With others) Harvey Manning, *The Wild Cascades: Forgotten Parkland,* Sierra Club, 1965.

Ann and Myron Sutton, *The American West: A Natural History,* Random House, 1969.

Liliane De Cock, editor, *Ansel Adams,* Morgan & Morgan, 1972.

(With others) Patricia Maye, *Fieldbook of Nature Photography,* Sierra Club, 1974.

Mary Street Alinder, *Ansel Adams: Letters and Images, 1916–1984,* Little, Brown, 1988.

Peter Wright, *The Mural Project: Photographs by Ansel Adams,* Reverie Press, 1989.

Andrea G. Stillman, editor, *The American Wilderness,* Little, Brown, 1990.

William A. Turnage, editor, *Ansel Adams: Our National Parks,* Little, Brown, 1992.

Harry M. Callahan, editor, *Ansel Adams in Color,* Little, Brown, 1993.

Also illustrator of Edward Joesting's *The Islands of Hawaii,* 1958.

■ Sidelights

On June 30, 1916, fourteen–year–old Ansel Adams took a vacation with his family that would determine the course of his life and dramatically alter the history of photography. "The splendor of Yosemite burst upon us and it *was* glorious. Little clouds were gathering in the sky above the granite cliffs, and the mists of Bridal Veil Fall shimmered in the sun," as he described their arrival at the northern California National Park in *Ansel Adams: An Autobiography.* "One wonder after another descended upon us; I recall not only the colossal but the little things: the grasses and ferns, cool atriums of the forest. The river was mostly quiet and greenish–deep; Sentinel Fall and Yosemite Falls were booming in the early summer flood, and many shining cascades threaded the cliffs. There was light everywhere!" Adams received his first camera on this trip and proceeded to become one of the most popular and acclaimed photographers ever.

"Adams was an undisputed master of the natural landscape. With clarity and precision he portrayed and heightened the spectacular vistas and rich native details of the western United States. Rivers, mountains, valleys, orchards, deserts, and sea—all are chronicled, and fused with his poetic vision and his conservationist instincts," Judy Dater explained in *Contemporary Photographers.* "As technical wizard he was possibly unsurpassed, both in his work and in his writings on the craft of photography," Dater continued. "His ability to convey the monumentality of landscape was unique, communicating a sense of space and scale distinctively American, a celebration of the untamed wilderness and the distant frontier," stated a writer for *Annual Obituary.* "In a period when most ambitious photographers have felt fortunate to win the support of one parochial segment of the total audience, Adams has been admired by a constituency so large and diverse that it could, one would have assumed, agree on nothing," John Szarkowski noted in his introduction to *The Portfolios of Ansel Adams.*

In addition to his accomplishments as a photographer—which came at a time when photography was just beginning to be recognized as a legitimate art form—Adams was also known for his eloquent and effective defense of the environment in the early days of the conservation movement. For these efforts he received numerous awards, including the Presidential Medal of Freedom—the highest civilian honor in the United States. The

In 1916, carrying a Brownie box camera, Adams made his first visit to Yosemite National Park in California, where he would eventually take his most famous photographs.

citation for the medal, presented by President Jimmy Carter in 1980, stated: "At one with the power of the American landscape and renowned for the patient skill and timeless beauty of his work, photographer Ansel Adams has been visionary in his efforts to preserve this country's wild and scenic areas, both on film and on earth. Drawn to the beauty of nature's movement, he is regarded by environmentalists as a monument himself and by photographers as a national institution. It is through his foresight and fortitude that so much of America has been saved for future generations."

A Wild Child

Adams was born on February 20, 1902, in San Francisco, California. His father built their family home on a sandy hillside overlooking the Golden Gate—a narrow passage connecting San Francisco Bay to the Pacific Ocean, which later became the site of the famous bridge. Adams described the idyllic view from his bedroom window in his autobiography: "I could see the Golden Gate from the north window and the cypress trees and rolling dunes around the old Chinese cemetery in what is now Lincoln Park to the west. I could also gaze well out to sea, beyond Point Bonita and the white glimmer of the Cabbage Patch, a dangerous shoal. I could watch ships of every description enter and leave the embrace of the Golden Gate." He spent much of his childhood exploring the woods, streams, and beaches around his home and developing a deep appreciation for wilderness.

A highly memorable experience for Adams was the San Francisco earthquake and fire of 1906. He remembered being awakened in the early morning by the violent shaking of his house. Both of the stone chimneys collapsed and all the windows were broken, but otherwise the structure was sound and no one in his family was seriously hurt. However, Adams did suffer one lasting effect from the earthquake: "I was exploring in the garden when my mother called me to breakfast and I came trotting. At that moment a severe aftershock hit and threw me off balance. I tumbled against a low brick garden wall, my nose making violent contact with quite a bloody effect. The nosebleed stopped after an hour, but my beauty was marred forever—the septum was thoroughly broken," he noted in his autobiography. "When the family doctor could be reached, he advised that

my nose be left alone until I matured; it could then be repaired with greater aesthetic quality. Apparently I never matured, as I have yet to see a surgeon about it." His crooked nose remained a distinguishing feature throughout his life.

Adams's parents came from wealthy families but suffered a series of misfortunes and eventually struggled to make ends meet. Adams recalled in his autobiography that his father "simply was not a good businessman and he could not cope with the deviousness that confronted him at most every turn" during various jobs in lumber, chemicals, insurance, and a merchant's exchange. A major blow came when the uncle whom Adams was named after, Ansel Easton, profited from the sale of his stake in a family business at Adams's father's expense. This betrayal led Adams to drop his middle name in 1934. Adams was also disappointed that his mother became depressed and "simply gave up" at a time when his father "desperately needed support and cheer."

Although he was frequently bedridden due to illness, Adams described himself as a hyperactive child. He always travelled around town at an all-out run, pestered adults with endless questions, and enjoyed all kinds of sports and activities. He found it impossible to sit still for any length of time and was impatient with school. His parents tried enrolling him in several different schools, but Adams could not adjust to institutional learning. "Each day was a severe test for me, sitting in a dreadful classroom while the sun and fog played outside. Most of the information received meant absolutely nothing to me," he stated in his autobiography. "One day as I sat fidgeting in class the whole situation suddenly appeared very ridiculous to me. I burst into raucous peals of uncontrolled laughter; I could not stop. The class was first amused, then scared. I stood up, pointed at the teacher, and shrieked my scorn, hardly taking breath in between my howling paroxysms. To the dismay of my mother I was escorted home and remained under house arrest for a week until my patient father concluded that my entry into yet another school would be useless. Instead, I was to study at home under his guidance."

Adams's father tutored him in French and algebra and encouraged him to read the classics of English literature. The highlight of his education came in 1915, when his father presented him with a year's pass to the Panama–Pacific International Exposition in San Francisco. Adams continued with

Adams and members of the Le Conte family travelled through Giant Forest in Kings Canyon, California, in 1925.

a few basic lessons at home, but spent part of each day touring the exposition. The exposition featured exhibits of industries and fine arts, pavilions from exotic countries, and concerts and other entertainment. This experience provided Adams with exactly the kind of education he needed, as he recalled in his autobiography: "I often wonder at the strength and courage my father had in taking me out of the traditional school situation and providing me with these extraordinary learning experiences. I am certain he established the positive direction of my life that otherwise, given my native hyperactivity, could have been confused and catastrophic. I trace who I am and the direction of my development to those years of growing up in our house on the dunes, propelled especially by an internal spark tenderly kept alive and glowing by my father."

Another important element of Adams's childhood was his early interest in music. He studied piano intensively with a number of teachers beginning when he was thirteen, and later credited music

for teaching him discipline and the value of creative expression. "The world of music was an immediate contrast to my undisciplined life and unsuccessful performance in school," Adams commented in his autobiography. "My scatterbrained existence was gradually being tuned to accuracy and musical expression." For several years he entertained hopes of a career as a concert pianist, but eventually decided that his hands were probably too small: "My style and repertoire were therefore constrained by my physical limits. I did develop an unusually beautiful touch and musical quality. I do not think I could have achieved much notice as a concert pianist, but . . . I could have become a performer of a limited repertoire, an accompanist, and teacher." Photography would soon replace music as his preferred medium of creative expression.

Revelations at Yosemite

Adams underwent a dramatic shift in focus following his first trip to Yosemite in 1916. Although he had enjoyed exploring the wilderness throughout his childhood, the natural wonders of the park completely overwhelmed him. His parents gave him his first camera shortly after their arrival, and he immediately began trying to record his experiences in snapshots. "A few days later, with my usual hyperactive enthusiasm, I climbed an old and crumbling stump near our tent to get a picture of Half Dome. I perched on top of this relic of arboreal grandeur with my camera and was about to snap the shutter when the stump gave way and I plummeted to the ground. On the way down, headfirst, I inadvertently pushed the shutter," Adams related in his autobiography. When he received his prints, the developer could not believe his story of how the picture came to be upside-down. "I do not think he was ever certain of my normalcy from then on. The negative is reasonably sharp and one of my favorites from this, my first year of photography," Adams continued.

Adams returned to Yosemite every year thereafter. In 1919 he joined the Sierra Club and took a job for the next four summers as custodian of the group's Yosemite headquarters, the LeConte Memorial Lodge. His duties included answering visitors' questions and leading tour groups on excursions into the wilderness. He also continued exploring the park on his own and with friends, and collected numerous tales about being invaded by ants in the middle of the night, being stranded at high elevations by unexpected heavy snowfalls, and barely avoiding disastrous falls during ill-advised rock climbs. As Adams expressed in his autobiography, "It is easy to recount that I camped many times at Merced Lake, but it is difficult to explain the magic: to lie in a small recess of the granite matrix of the Sierra and watch the progress of dusk to night, the incredible brilliance of the stars, the waning of the glittering sky into dawn, and the following sunrise on the peaks and domes around me. And always that cool dawn wind that I believe to be the prime benediction of the Sierra. These qualities to which I still deeply respond were distilled into my pictures over the decades. I *knew* my destiny when I first experienced Yosemite."

During one of these early summers at Yosemite, Adams looked for a place to practice piano and was directed to the home of Virginia Best, whose father owned Best's Studio, a craft and souvenir shop in the park. "We found considerable mutual interests in music, in Yosemite, and, it turned out,

in each other," Adams wrote in his autobiography. "From our first years of friendship, I felt a rightness about the two of us. We were comfortable together. My letters of the period express a calflike wonder and an introspective analysis at a simple, but deeply felt level." The couple was married in 1928 "after years of procrastination," with the bride in "her best dress, which happened to be black" and the groom in "knickers and my trusty basketball shoes." They eventually had two children, Michael and Anne—both of whom arrived early and caught their father on an excursion in the Yosemite high country.

Over the years Adams continually refined his photographic technique. He began by simply recording his experiences in a "snapshot diary," but gradually started to use the photographic medium to express his feelings about the world around him. He claimed in his autobiography that the precision and discipline he acquired through his musical training helped in his development as an artist: "I applied the axiom of 'practice makes perfect' to my photography. Mastering the craft of

The natural wonders of Yosemite, as seen in this 1936 work, *Juniper Tree, Crags under Mount Clark,* drew Adams to the park year after year.

photography came through years of continued work, as did the ability to make images of personal expression. Step by inevitable step, the intuitive process slowly became a part of my picture making." Adams's only formal photographic training came during a 1917 apprenticeship in a San Francisco photo–finishing business, where he learned the basics of darkroom work.

Although he was pleased with the results of some of his early efforts, Adams considered his photographic breakthrough to be *Monolith, The Face of Half Dome,* taken in Yosemite in the spring of 1927. He carried forty pounds of camera equipment on a hike with Virginia and some friends, intending to photograph the huge granite cliff known as Half Dome from the top of a nearby mountain. On the way there he used most of his film, saving only two exposures for his main objective. For the first shot, he set up his camera as usual and composed what he thought would be a good picture, using a conventional yellow filter. "As I replaced the slide, I began to think about how the print was to appear, and if it would transmit any of the feeling of the monumental shape before me in terms of its expressive–emotional quality. I began to see in my mind's eye the finished print I desired: the brooding cliff with a dark sky and the sharp rendition of distant, snowy Tenaya Peak. I realized that only a deep red filter would give me anything approaching the effect I felt emotionally," Adams recalled in his autobiography. When he developed the film, he realized the significance of this final exposure: "I had achieved my first true visualization! I had been able to realize a desired image not the way the subject appeared in reality but how it *felt* to me and how it must appear in the finished print. . . . It rests in my vault, still printable, and represents a personally historic moment in my photographic career."

Since photography usually was considered a hobby rather than an art form at this time, Adams initially was reluctant to commit himself to making a career of it. In 1926 Albert Bender, an influential San Francisco business person and patron of the arts, had published his first portfolio, *Parmelian Prints of the High Sierras,* in a limited edition of one hundred copies. Nevertheless, for the next few years Adams continued to juggle photography and music. By 1930 he realized that he needed to make a decision. While on a photographic project in New Mexico, Adams met fellow photographer Paul Strand, who was just gaining prominence, and viewed some of his recent negatives. He re-

called in his autobiography that the power of Strand's work convinced him once and for all which profession to choose: "My understanding of photography was crystallized that afternoon as I realized the great potential of the medium as an expressive art. I returned to San Francisco resolved that the camera, not the piano, would shape my destiny. Virginia was very supportive of my decision; my mother and aunt reacted differently, pleading, 'Do not give up the piano! The camera cannot express the human soul!' I replied, 'Perhaps the camera cannot, but the photographer can.'"

Photo–Finishing

With Adams's commitment to photography as a career came his association with a number of other artists. In 1932 he joined such well–known photographers as Imogen Cunningham and Edward Weston to form Group f/64, "the now legendary group that promoted the principles of sharp focus and pure, powerful form," Richard Lacayo noted in *Time.* While most creative photography up to this point had featured blurred images that imitated impressionist paintings, this group originated the idea that clear, realistic photographs could be an art form. The M. H. de Young Memorial Museum in San Francisco, which held an early exhibition of the group's work, "received many letters of protest, mostly from artists and gallery people, complaining that valuable space in a public museum had been given to photography, *which was not Art!,*" Adams remembered in his autobiography. Although Group f/64 existed for only two years, critics agreed that its impact on photography was immense.

Adams also formed personal relationships with a number of prominent artists during this period. Lacayo claimed that Adams "possessed a rare talent for winning the friendship of brilliant but difficult men and women." In 1933, for example, he went to New York City to meet a man he considered to be "the greatest photographic leader in the world," Alfred Stieglitz, and was offered an exhibition at Stieglitz's prestigious gallery, An American Place. Adams also became close friends with Stieglitz's wife, the famous painter Georgia O'Keeffe, and produced several well–known portraits of her over the years. In 1935 he began a long association with art historian Beaumont Newhall and his wife Nancy, who collaborated with Adams on several books. In 1948 he befriended Edwin Land, who invented the Polaroid Land instant photographic process. Adams eventually became a consultant to the Polaroid Corporation and assisted in the development and testing of new photographic technology. He noted in his autobiography that each of these personal relationships had an important influence on his work.

At the same time, Adams continued to refine his photographic technique and his ability to use photography as a form of expression. However, he stressed in his autobiography that he rarely planned his best photographs ahead of time: "I cannot command the creative impulse on demand. I never know in advance precisely what I will photograph. I go out into the world and hope I will come across something that imperatively interests me. I am addicted to the found object." Occasionally something Adams had seen would stick in his subconscious mind and torment him until he captured the image on film. Once, while driving home from an exhibition in Santa Barbara, Adams caught a glimpse of an interesting old fence out of the corner of his eye. The image grew stronger until he finally had to turn the car around and return to the scene to make a photograph.

Adams felt that technique and expression were intimately related—a strong understanding of technique enabled a photographer to transcend how the image actually appeared and capture its essence or feeling. He explained in his autobiography that his photographs enhanced reality: "As with all art, the photographer's objective is not the duplication of visual reality. Photographic images cannot avoid being accurate optically, as lenses are used. However, they depart from reality in direct relation to the placement of the camera before the subject, the lens chosen, the film and filters, the exposure indicated, the related development and printing; all, of course, relating to what the photographer visualizes. The exhilaration, when anticipation, visualization, mind, equipment, and subject are all behaving, is fantastic."

Moonrise, Hernandez, New Mexico

One photograph in which Adams perfectly achieved his artistic vision was *Moonrise, Hernandez, New Mexico*. In 1941 he received an assignment from the U.S. Department of the Interior to provide photographs from a number of National Parks to decorate the government offices in Washington, D.C. As he did for many assignments, Adams drove around the country in an old station wagon with a camera platform on top to collect the images. He was enroute to Carlsbad Caverns in New Mexico one late afternoon when he noticed a spectacular scene unfolding before him. The moon had appeared on the horizon, just as the setting sun illuminated white crosses in an old cemetery and snow–capped mountains in the distance. Adams swerved off the road and scrambled to get his camera ready in time, even estimating the exposure settings when he could not find his meter. "I knew it was special when I released the shutter, but I never anticipated what its reception would be over the decades. *Moonrise, Hernandez, New Mexico* is my most well known photograph. I have received more letters about this picture than any other I have ever made, and I must repeat that *Moonrise* is most certainly not a double exposure," he stated in his autobiography. Since he never concerned himself with dates, for many years Adams was unable to recall in what year the famous photograph was made—to the frustration of art collectors and historians. However, many years later an astronomer friend fed the moon's elevation and azimuth into his computer and was able to determine the photograph's origin to within five minutes. "It is too bad I can never date so exactly my thousands of moonless pictures!," Adams commented.

In 1943, Adams had a similar experience while on a wartime assignment documenting the life of Japanese–Americans held at the Manzanar War Relocation Camp in California. After the attack on Pearl Harbor during World War II, many U.S. citizens of Japanese descent were detained by the government because they were perceived as a threat to national security. While he was at Manzanar making photographs for his book *Born Free and Equal*, Adams also pursued some creative photographs in his free time. One cold morning he and Virginia drove to a nearby city to watch the sunrise over the mountains, and again an incredible scene developed. As Adams described it in his autobiography, "Beams of light began highlighting the brushy trees in the foreground of my composition; they also illuminated the rear end of a horse as it calmly grazed in front of the trees. Frustrated, I watched as the light appeared, just as I had hoped. Serendipitously, the horse momentarily turned to profile and I made the exposure. Within seconds, the tonal variety that created the mood of the scene was destroyed by a flood of even sunlight." This picture, *Winter Sunrise, The Sierra Nevada*, became another of Adams's best–known works.

This 1960 photograph entitled *Moon and Half Dome* captured one of Adams's favorite subjects, a huge granite cliff in Yosemite known as Half Dome.

As photography gained acceptance as an art form and Adams perfected his own technique, he also began to teach photography in universities and private workshops. In order to make his teaching easier, in 1940 he began to write down many of the principles he had used over the years. Eventually his writings were published as the "Basic Photo" series, which became an important reference for would–be photographers. Adams claimed that the starting point for a successful creative photograph was the photographer's visualization of the desired final image. Then the photographer could work backward to determine the technical settings—such as lighting, film, lens–stop, and exposure—needed to achieve the visualization. Adams invented the Zone System to help his students improve their technical control of film exposure. As he explained to Victoria and David Sheff during an interview for *Playboy*, "The Zone System enables a photographer to anticipate and control the tonal range of a print. The zones are essentially shades of gray ranging from black, which is zero, to white, which is ten. They correspond to exposure settings on the camera and can be used to identify the relative brightness of separate parts of the subject being photographed as

they will appear in the print." He first taught the Zone System at the Art Center School in Los Angeles, California, and later used it in annual workshops held at Yosemite.

Adams took his responsibility as a teacher of photography very seriously. He remembered how important the support and advice of other photographers had been to him in the early stages of his career, and he tried to be a positive influence on others. Hopeful young photographers often brought their prints to him, and he always tried to react appropriately. Adams also expressed his support for artists who tried to explore new directions in creative photography, and even encouraged them to use his work as a starting point. Upon his death in 1984, all of his negatives became the property of the Center for Creative Photography at the University of Arizona. He hoped that serious students would make their own prints from his negatives and go beyond his original creative expression, perhaps through computer enhancement."Photographers are, in a sense, composers and the negatives their scores," he noted in his autobiography. "They first perform their own works, but I see no reason why they should not be available for others to perform."

A Force for Nature

During his lifetime, Adams witnessed the beginning of the conservation movement in the United States and became one of its most influential promoters. Growing up surrounded by natural beauty had instilled in him a sense of appreciation and responsibility for the environment. But Adams's commitment went beyond trying to preserve the wilderness for future generations to enjoy—he believed that connecting with nature was a vital part of the human experience. As William Turnage, the executive director of the Wilderness Society, remarked in his preface to *Ansel Adams: Our National Parks*, "Adams's parks philosophy was rooted in his deep belief that nature and beauty, particularly as symbolized by wildness, were essential elements of the human soul. The intensity of this concept can be comprehended only by spending time with his photographs, as it is not something expressible in words."

Adams was highly sensitive to the impact of man on the environment. He spoke out frequently and eloquently against the damage he observed—in books, interviews, and public appearances. For example, in his introduction to *Our National Parks* he described the drastic changes that had taken place within his lifetime: "By the turn of the century the Nation came into its adult strength, industrialization had launched its triumphant final campaign, and men turned upon the land and its resources with blind disregard for the logic of ordered use, or for the obligations of an ordered future. The evidence is painfully clear; entire domains of the Pacific Northwest—once glorious forests—are now desolate brushy slopes. Thousands of square miles of the Southwest, once laced with green–bordered streams prudently secured by the groundcover of ample grass, are now a dusty phalanx of desert hills, starving the pitiful sheep and their shepherds that wander over them. We all know the tragedy of the dustbowls, the cruel unforgivable erosions of the soil, the depletion of fish and game, and the shrinking of the noble forests. And we know that such catastrophes shrivel the spirit of the people."

Adams also made his views known through endless letters to public figures over the years. He managed to express his strong opinions with wit and objectivity, and thus gained the respect of many of his opponents. "In these letters, Adams exhorted, suggested, inspired, implored, scolded—but was unfailingly cordial, no matter how intense the debate or disagreement," Turnage explained. "His letters were always interesting, often brilliant, containing insights and analyses that were frequently unique—sometimes startlingly so. He was remorseless in his insistence on a higher standard of care for nature and concern for the spiritual–emotional aspects of the visitor experience." Adams's prominence as an artist and position as a director of the Sierra Club gained him an audience with several presidents and numerous members of congress. After one interview where he was particularly outspoken regarding his opposition to "one of the most dangerous government officials in history," Secretary of the Interior James Watt, Adams received an invitation to speak with President Ronald Reagan at the White House. "It did not, to Adams's satisfaction, bring the president closer to a meaningful understanding of how you go about caring for the nation's natural heritage," Joseph Mathewson noted in Horizon. "But the fact that the meeting took place at all is an index both to the photographer's immense prestige and to the size and power of the conservationist constituency he had come to represent."

Although Adams was passionate in his defense of the environment, he also came to believe that it was important to communicate and share the wilderness experience. He felt that educating young people about nature would encourage them to protect it. "I passed through the messianic period, battling the implacable devourers and mutilators of wilderness, and gradually I entered a more philosophic–humanistic stage where I was able, in some small way, to separate personal euphoria from impersonal appraisals of the rights of man to participate in the bounties of the environment," as Adams described his philosophy in his foreword to Yosemite and the Range of Light. "But the most dedicated and gentle human feet, if there are enough of them, will wear down the sternest stone, strangle the near–surface roots of the giant sequoias, and flatten meadows into hardened promenades. The preservation and, at the same time, the human use of wild places present a mind– and spirit–wracking challenge for the future." This dilemma eventually led him to advocate a balanced approach to conservation, which would preserve some areas untouched for spiritual enrichment and make others available for recreation.

By most measures Adams's efforts to protect the environment were highly successful. For example, he was instrumental in convincing President Franklin Roosevelt to make Kings Canyon in California a National Park in 1940, and he received every major conservation award during his lifetime. Ironically, however, Adams's own photographs may have accelerated the decline of some of the wild areas he cherished by increasing their popularity. Enormous numbers of people responded to his work and wanted to experience the wilderness for themselves, with unexpected results. "It was not foreseen that the people, having saved it, would consider it their own, not that a million pink–cheeked Boy Scouts, greening teenage backpackers, and middle–aged sightseers might, with the best of intentions, destroy a wilderness as surely as the most rapacious of lumbermen, who did his damage quickly and left the land to recover if it could. It has developed, in other words, that to photograph beautifully a choice vestigial remnant of natural landscape is not necessarily to do a great favor to its future," Szarkowski commented. "In these terms Adams's pictures are perhaps anachronisms. They are perhaps the last confident and deeply felt pictures of their tradition. . . . If this is the case, his pictures are all the more precious, for they then stand as the last records, for the young and the future, of what they missed."

Timeless Images

From the time he made his first photograph at Yosemite in 1916, Ansel Adams rose to become one of the most renowned photographers of all time. He was widely acclaimed for the emotional power and technical excellence of his work, as well as for his tireless efforts to protect the environment. He achieved a lasting influence through his dozens of published books and the thousands of students who attended his courses and workshops, and even had a mountain at Yosemite named in his honor. By all accounts he maintained a remarkable enthusiasm and energy throughout his life. "He was a bluff, hearty extrovert who threw himself into causes with a zest that he had the basic good sense to recognize as occasionally comic. His letters to close friends are warm and wonderful; reading them, one frequently feels . . . what a marvelous thing it would have been to have him for a friend," Robert M. Adams commented in the *New York Review of Books.* "The wild streak in Ansel Adams was what vibrated against the wildness of the high country; the miracle is that he was able to crystallize so much of that wild energy in the austerity of his photographs."

Summing up his life's work in his autobiography, Adams stated: "My approach to photography is based on my belief in the vigor and values of the world of nature, in aspects of grandeur and minutiae all about us. I believe in people, in the simpler aspects of human life, in the relation of man to nature. I believe man must be free, both in spirit and society, that he must build strength into himself, affirming the enormous beauty of the world and acquiring the confidence to see and to express his vision. And I believe in photography as one means of expressing this affirmation and of achieving an ultimate happiness and faith."

■ Works Cited

Adams, Ansel, "Foreword," *Yosemite and the Range of Light,* New York Graphic Society, 1980, p. 9.

Adams, Ansel, *Ansel Adams: An Autobiography,* Little, Brown, 1985.

Adams, Ansel, "Introduction," *Ansel Adams: Our National Parks,* Little, Brown, 1992, p. 7.

Adams, Robert M., review of *Ansel Adams: Letters and Images, 1916–1984, New York Review of Books,* February 16, 1989, p. 34.

Annual Obituary, 1984, St. James Press, 1985, p. 188.

Dater, Judy, "Ansel Adams," *Contemporary Photographers,* St. James Press, 1988, p. 9.

Lacayo, Richard, "Closing Accounts" (review of *Ansel Adams: An Autobiography), Time,* January 20, 1986, p. 70.

Lacayo, Richard, "The Man Who Captured the Earth's Beauty" (review of *The American Wilderness), Time,* September 3, 1990, p. 62.

Mathewson, Joseph, "Picturing Ansel Adams," *Horizon,* March 1986, p. 9.

Sheff, David and Victoria, interview with Ansel Adams, *Playboy,* May 1983.

Szarkowski, John, "Introduction," *The Portfolios of Ansel Adams,* New York Graphic Society, 1977, p. vii.

Turnage, William, "Preface," *Ansel Adams: Our National Parks,* Little, Brown, 1992, p. 7.

■ For More Information See

BOOKS

Alinder, Mary Street, *Ansel Adams: Letters and Images, 1916–1984,* Little, Brown, 1988.

Contemporary Authors, New Revision Series, volume 10, Gale, 1983.

Current Biography Yearbook, Wilson, 1977.

Newhall, Nancy, *The Eloquent Light: Ansel Adams,* Sierra Club, 1964.

OTHER

Ansel Adams, Photographer (videotape; produced by Andrea Gray and John Huszar; directed by Huszar), Filmamerica, 1981.*

—Sketch by Laurie Collier Hillstrom

Dave Barry

■ Personal

Born July 3, 1947, in Armonk, NY; son of David W. (a minister) and Marion Barry; married Elizabeth Lenox Pyle, 1975; children: Robert. *Education:* Haverford College, B.A. (English), 1969.

■ Addresses

Office—*Miami Herald,* 1 Herald Plaza, Miami, FL 33123– 1693. *Agent*—Al Hart, Fox Chase Agency, Public Ledger Bldg., Room 930, Independence Sq., Philadelphia, PA 19106.

■ Career

Daily Local News, West Chester, PA, 1971–75, began as reporter, became editor; worked for Associated Press, Philadelphia, PA, 1975–76; lecturer on effective writing for businesses for R. S. Burger Associates (consulting firm), 1975–83; free–lance humor columnist, 1980—; *Miami Herald,* Miami, FL, humor columnist, 1983—.

■ Awards, Honors

Distinguished Writing Award, American Society of Newspaper Editors, 1986; Pulitzer Prize for distinguished commentary, 1988.

■ Writings

The Taming of the Screw: Several Million Homeowners' Problems Sidestepped, illustrations by Jerry O'Brien, Rodale Press, 1983.

Babies and Other Hazards of Sex: How to Make a Tiny Person in Only Nine Months, with Tools You Probably Have around the Home, illustrations by O'Brien, Rodale Press, 1984.

Dave Barry's Bad Habits: A 100% Fact Free Book, Doubleday, 1985.

Stay Fit and Healthy until You're Dead, illustrations by O'Brien, Rodale Press, 1985.

Claw Your Way to the Top: How to Become the Head of a Major Corporation in Roughly a Week, illustrations by O'Brien, Rodale Press, 1986.

Dave Barry's Guide to Marriage and/or Sex, illustrations by O'Brien, Rodale Press, 1987.

Dave Barry's Greatest Hits, Crown, 1988.

Homes and Other Black Holes: The Happy Homeowner's Guide, illustrations by Jeff MacNelly, Fawcett/Columbine, 1988.

Dave Barry Slept Here: A Short History of the United States, Random House, 1989.

Dave Barry Turns Forty, Crown, 1990.
Dave Barry Talks Back, illustrations by MacNelly, Crown, 1991.
Dave Barry's Only Travel Guide You'll Ever Need, Fawcett, 1991.
Dave Barry Does Japan, Random House, 1992.
Dave Barry Is Not Making This Up, Crown, 1994.
Dave Barry's Gift Guide to End All Gift Guides, Crown, 1994.

■ Adaptations

Dave's World, a television sitcom broadcast on Columbia Broadcasting System, Inc. (CBS– TV), beginning in 1993, and starring Harry Anderson as Dave Barry, is based on Barry's writings.

■ Sidelights

When syndicated humor columnist, author, and Pulitzer–Prizewinner Dave Barry discusses his motivations for writing about everyday life in the modern world, he could tell his audience that he does it as a public service to point out the flaws in contemporary American society, or he might say he does it to make other people laugh, or simply because he enjoys writing. But, then again, Barry believes in honesty. "I do it to make money," he revealed to *Contemporary Authors* interviewer Jean W. Ross. This ambition aside, Barry is known for being a truthful journalist, always providing his audience with the hard facts, such as the time he published a book on American history in which all the important events occur on October 8 (his son's birthday), or when explaining technical terms like "volts," which he defines in *Homes and Other Black Holes* as "little tiny pieces of energy shaped like arrows so you can tell which direction they're moving in science class diagrams." It is this kind of tongue–in–cheek writing that has made Barry what he is today, a popular journalist whose ambition, as he reemphasized to Ross, is to "make money without having to do anything useful."

Barry's stellar career has its beginnings firmly rooted in middle–class America. The son of David, a Presbyterian minister, and Marion Barry, the future columnist, according to *New York Times Book Review* writer Alison Teal, grew up in an "all–WASP upper–middle–class neighborhood, played Little League baseball, mowed his parents' lawn and . . . attended Episcopalian Church." He also studied at a New York school with the very Americana name of

Pleasantville High School, where he was elected Class Clown.

"As a kid," reported Peter Richmond in the *New York Times Magazine,* "his horn–rimmed glasses, home–sheared haircuts and wax–bean physique forced Barry to hone his sense of humor—largely out of self defense." In an interview published in *Crown News,* Barry elaborated with this description of himself as a child: "[I was a] geek with a real high forehead. Real high. You could have rented out advertising up there. In fact, there are certain board games you could have played on my forehead, no problem. Basically, though, things were pretty much OK until the summer of the fifth grade. The girls all went away to summer bosom camp. . . . And the guys started catching up. The other guys. I kept waiting for puberty to strike. One by one, it would strike my friends, but not me. They were all turning into men and I was still a little boy. I don't even think I've gone all the way through puberty yet. I still don't have any hair on my arms, and I worry about that."

Pursuing a Career in Journalism

In high school Barry wrote for his school's newspaper. The desire to be a writer was already strong in him, but, as he told Ross, "it just never occurred to me that you could have a job that didn't involve any actual work. When I wrote . . . I pretty much made stuff up—lied, that's what I did; I lied. I felt it would be fun to have a job like that where you could make stuff up and be irresponsible and get paid for it."

Barry continued to pursue journalism in college, where he developed other interests as well. Growing up in the '60s, Barry was naturally influenced by the culture of his time, becoming an avid fan of rock bands like the Beatles and the Rolling Stones and even forming his own blues band, the Federal Duck, while attending Haverford College. Barry played lead guitar, and the band slowly improved over time from being terrible to becoming just plain awful. As he commented to *Newsweek* contributor Harry F. Waters, "People were always throwing up on our amplifiers." In *Dave Barry's Greatest Hits* he describes the band's members as "extremely white suburban–style college students whose only actual insight into the blues came from experiences such as getting a C in Poli Sci."

After graduating from college in 1969 with a

bachelor's degree in English, Barry "spent two years doing conscientious objector duty for the Episcopal Church in New York," according to Richmond; he then found his first journalism job working for the *Daily Local News* in West Chester, Pennsylvania, where the hot topic on everyone's mind was not the Vietnam War, the women's liberation movement, or the sexual revolution, but sewage and zoning. "Sewage was even hotter than zoning when I was there," Barry noted to Ross. "I never realized how much people could care about it. It also didn't occur to me at the time that only a few people did, namely the people who were actually involved in it, who were the government people. The result was that I wrote several years' worth of stories that nobody read but me, and sometimes even I didn't read all the way to the end of them."

Eventually, Barry moved up from reporter to editor. It was at this point that he gained some first-hand experience with the ire of the reading public, as he recalls in one of his syndicated columns, "Customer Service, or Else": "[One] spring day, I made the editorial decision to put a photograph of some local ducks on the front page. At least, I thought they were ducks, and that's what I called them in the caption. But it turns out that they were geese. I know this because a WHOLE lot of irate members of the public called to tell me so. They never called about, say, the quality of the schools, but they were RABID about the duck–vs.–goose issue. It was almost as bad as when we left out the horoscope." Although the job wasn't glamorous, it wasn't all bad, either. Barry further remarked to Jesse Birnbaum in *Time,* "It was classic small town journalism, and I really loved that job."

Barry nevertheless gave up his post at the *Daily Local News* in 1975 for what looked like a better opportunity working for the Associated Press in Philadelphia. It wasn't. The job "was very restrictive," he told Ross. "It wasn't even as interesting as sewage." So Barry quit and earned his living by teaching a writing seminar to businessmen. As he described the work to Birnbaum, for eight years he lectured "a bunch of chemists or engineers about the importance of not saying `It would be appreciated if you would contact the undersigned by telephone at your earliest possible convenience,' and instead saying `Please call me as soon as

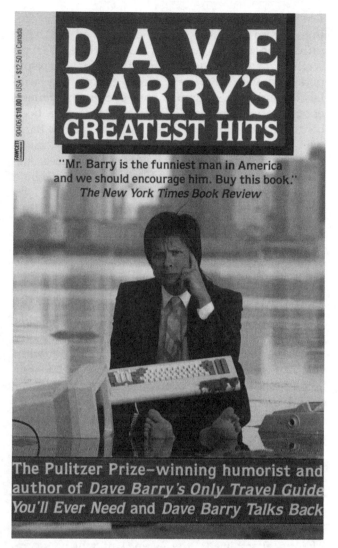

The best of Barry's tongue-in-cheek observations on modern life are collected in this 1988 volume.

you can,' which was revealed wisdom to these people."

Becoming a Pulitzer Prize Winner

By the early 1980s, Barry had a house, a family, and a son, Robert. Wondering what to do next, he decided there was nothing to lose in trying to pursue his lifelong dream: writing a humor column. Because his lecture schedule wasn't too hectic, Barry felt he had plenty of time to write a column, so he took the idea up with the *Daily Local News'* life–style editor. This wasn't too difficult a task, since the editor was also Barry's wife, Beth, who had already suggested he write the column. She agreed to run his column for twenty–two dollars a week. Although getting published in the *Daily*

Local News wasn't a great challenge, becoming a syndicated columnist proved to be a much more arduous task. Over time, Barry's writing began to appear in other small newspapers and then in papers across the country with larger and larger circulations, eventually gaining enough attention that he was able to sign a book contract with Rodale Press. At this point, Barry was earning enough that he could quit his teaching job and write full time. His new career became even more secure when the *Miami Herald* offered him a position. As he told Ross, the *Herald* "didn't even ask me to move to Miami, just said they would hire me. So I accepted and finally did move to Miami, possibly because of brain damage."

In 1986, before his move from Philadelphia to Miami, Barry had gotten offers from the *Washington Post* and *Los Angeles Times* to join their staffs, but, as Richmond wrote, "Barry is no deal–maker, and, confronted with a path directly into the white burn of fame, he recoiled. The Post, he feared, would want to rein him into the tight political world that lies within the Beltway, and the Times signified the land of sushi, the very mention of which brings to his face the cast of a fish's underbelly." Unlike many journalists, Barry does not revere the fourth estate, and so his rejection of positions with major national newspapers was a natural development in his career. Indeed, Richmond said, Barry demonstrates a "willingness—no, eagerness—to deflate the self–puffery of the craft of journalism itself, 'the essence of which,' he recently wrote, 'is writing authoritative stories about things you don't actually understand. I can remember, as a young reporter, writing lengthy, disapproving analyses of international banking practices at a time when my personal investment portfolio consisted entirely of discount pizza coupons.'"

Switching to humor columns was not, however, a complete success for Barry at first. "The outrage was tremendous at the beginning," Gene Weingarten, the *Miami Herald*'s former editor recalled in Richmond's article. "There was an unrelenting avalanche of letters from humorless people. Now, though, the humor–impaired no longer read him, and the rest get the joke, so [negative mail has] slowed to a trickle." By the mid–1980s, Barry was becoming as big a household name as Ronald Reagan or Kleenex. People around the country were reading his columns and buying his books, including *Babies and Other Hazards of Sex, Stay Fit and Healthy until You're Dead,* and *Dave Barry's Guide to Marriage and/or Sex.*

Some of Barry's most valuable pearls of wisdom are collected in *Dave Barry's Greatest Hits,* in which he offers clever insights into a wide range of topics, such as the important link between the airline industry and earwax: "When you talk about the post–deregulation airline industry, the three issues that inevitably arise are smoking, fog, and earwax. Follow me closely here. You know those little earphones they give you on airplanes so you can listen to old Bill Cosby routines? OK, let's assume that 20 million people have flown on earphone flights in the past 15 years. Let's further assume that each person leaves one–sixteenth of an ounce of earwax on these phones (this is an average, of course; Nancy Reagan leaves much less). This means that in the last 15 years alone, the airlines have collected nearly 600 tons. Do you have any idea how large a blob that makes? Neither do I, so I called the folks at the Miami Public Library, who did a little research and informed me that it was the most disgusting question they had ever been asked."

It was revealing commentary such as this that helped Barry win the Pulitzer Prize in 1988. No one was more shocked than Barry himself. "Let's be honest," he said to Birnbaum. "Nothing I've ever written fits the definition 'distinguished commentary.'" Barry rationalizes the prize committee's decision by explaining that the members must simply have been tired of reading "hundreds of heavy, huge entries, every one of them earthshakingly important. And that makes them very hostile toward journalism in general. . . . So they gave me the prize for distinguished commentary. . . . Not that I'm giving it back."

One of the articles that the Pulitzer committee noted specifically, and which has garnered Barry a great deal of fan mail, was titled "Can New York Save Itself?" With typical flair, Barry lambastes the Big Apple on a variety of subjects, including the subway system: "Although it was constructed in 1536, the New York subway system boasts an annual maintenance budget of nearly $8, currently stolen, and it does a remarkable job of getting New Yorkers from point A to an indeterminate location somewhere in the tunnel leading to point B"; Times Square: "Although this area is best known as the site where many thousands of people gather each New Year's Eve for a joyous and festive night of public urination, it also serves

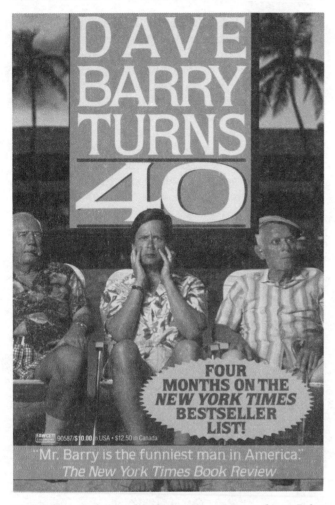

The author balances his humorous pieces about Baby Boomers' midlife crises with a serious glimpse of his own family in this 1990 work.

as an important cultural center where patrons may view films such as *Sex Aliens, Wet Adulteress,* and, of course, *Sperm Busters*"; and then–mayor Ed Koch, "the feisty, cocky, outspoken, abrasive mayor who really gets on some people's nerves, yet at the same time strikes other people as a jerk."

Sources of Inspiration

When asked by Ross where he gets his wry, tongue–in–cheek sense of humor, Barry names several sources of inspiration. "The . . . biggest inspiration to me was [American humorist] Robert Benchley. My father was a big fan of Benchley and [British humorist] P. G. Wodehouse and had a bunch of their books. When I was a kid, I read them all—I was a big reader. I loved both of them, but I especially loved Benchley because it didn't seem possible that a grownup could be that silly and get away with it. I was smitten by his writ-

ing and his attitude toward writing. Very definitely he's always been my idol." Later in the interview, the columnist also mentioned other influences. "I'm a big fan of Roy Blount; I like P. J. O'Rourke a lot; he's also a friend of mine. I like Art Buchwald, though he's not of my generation."

Yet there was someone else who had an even more profound effect on Barry's life: his mother. "My mom was the funniest person I've ever known," Barry told Waters. Barry's close relationship with his mother and the idealistic setting of his childhood didn't last forever, however. As Waters noted, the "humorist's background is rife with tragedy. Barry's father . . . and brother were alcoholics. His sister is an institutionalized schizophrenic. And his mother, who suffered from chronic depression, committed suicide." Taking an overdose of alcohol and Valium, Barry's mother died a few years after her husband's death from a heart attack, which was followed by the passing of her brother–in–law Frank, with whom she had also been close.

In *Dave Barry Turns 40,* Barry recalls the last time he saw his mother. Barry and his brothers, Phil and Sam, had convinced her to sell her house after their father had died, after which she had spent her days staying with one or the other of her sons, never really settling down. Under pressure from her family to find a new place to live, she asked Barry to help her look for apartments in Essex, Connecticut. "It was a bad time for me," Barry wrote, "but of course I said yes, because your mom is your mom. I met her in Hartford and rented a car." But since nothing but the return to the way things were with her husband in her old house would satisfy her, the search for an apartment was fruitless, and, by the end of the visit, Barry was "relieved" that she was leaving. Less than two weeks later, Barry's brother Phil called to tell him of the overdose. "The doctors want permission to turn off the machines," Barry remembered. "They say there's no hope. It's the only logical choice."

"The last thing I saw my mother do, just before she went down the tunnel to her plane," Barry continued, "was turn and give me a big smile. It wasn't a smile of happiness; it was the same smile I give my son when he gets upset listening to the news, and I tell him don't worry, we're never going to have a nuclear war. I can still see that smile anytime I want. Close my eyes, and there it is. A mom, trying to reassure her boy that everything's going to be okay." In a *People* review of *Dave Barry Turns 40,* Ralph Novak commented on this passage: "It's impossible to drop something like this into a humor book without its bringing things to a grinding halt, but Barry manages the process relatively gracefully."

Aside from the heartfelt passages about his mother, however, *Dave Barry Turns 40* is a humorous lament for the middle–aged. Drawing on articles he wrote for the *Miami Herald* around the same time he won the Pulitzer, Barry reworked his material and added new chapters to complete his personal survey of the wonders a Baby Boomer experiences as he slowly realizes he's no longer the spry hipster he once considered himself to be. The book offers several useful chapters on such topics as "Your Disintegrating Body," "The Midlife (Yawn) Marriage," "Planning Your Male Midlife Crisis," and "Wise Financial Planning for

In his 1989 book the humorist presents his own version of American history, in which everything takes place on October 8th.

Irresponsible Scum Such as Yourself." The book received a number of positive reviews from critics like Carl Sommers, who wrote in the *New York Times Book Review* that *Dave Barry Turns 40* "is like going through the humor section of a greeting card store, except there are more laughs here."

However, some reviewers didn't feel that this collection was as strong as *Dave Barry Slept Here,* the humorist's earlier work that spoofs American history. For example, Novak wrote that *Dave Barry Turns 40* didn't achieve the "triumph of concept and execution" that the earlier book did. In *Dave Barry Slept Here,* as Richard Lingeman explained in a *New York Times Book Review* article, Barry takes "pity on the droves of students who find American history boring" by simplifying over two hundred years of battles, treaties, and social change using two handy techniques. First, Barry declares that all important events in U.S. history occurred on October 8; second, all the boring stuff is cut out completely, which, Lingeman noted, "results in a very short book." Lingeman concluded that "Barry should be praised for his irreverent eye and his witty word processor." And A. J. Anderson observed in a *Library Journal* review that the book does have one problem that the reader must strive to overcome: "how to read it in public without laughing out loud."

A World Traveler

One of the greatest advantages to being a nationally syndicated columnist, author, and prize winner, Barry has discovered, is that publishers will offer to pay all the expenses for a writer and his family to travel abroad for the expressed purpose of writing about the experience later. The result of Barry's publisher's largesse has been a number of articles and the books *Dave Barry's Only Travel Guide You'll Ever Need* and *Dave Barry Does Japan.* As usual, the humorist's insights have been flavored with his unique perspective. Of a recent trip to England, for example, Barry happily observed in a 1994 column entitled "Runway Bombs, Rushdie Qualms," that "the British still speak in British accents, so that no matter what they say, it sounds really intelligent to Americans; and they still really say things like `bloody' and `smashing.'"

In order for Barry to write *Dave Barry Does Japan,* Random House offered to pay for the humorist and his family to go to Japan and record his thoughts about the culture of the Japanese people.

The resulting book provides a wide variety of information for anyone interested in that country. For example, about their Japanese food experience, Barry wrote: "As bold culinary adventurers, we experimented with all kinds of Japanese food for about fifteen minutes, then spent the rest of our trip looking for Kentucky Fried Chicken. Of course, sometimes we had to order Japanese food, in which case we would order the most Western–looking thing on the menu, such as spaghetti. But you never knew what you'd find in there. Corn kernels, for example, popped up everywhere, including in the spaghetti sauce, fried eggs, and one item I ate that was supposed to be a hamburger."

Barry also remarks humorously about the incredible efficiency of Japanese service, and how seriously people take their jobs in Japan. Relating a minor incident when Barry noticed that the bathroom in his Hiroshima hotel room didn't have any hot water, the humorist recalls how the bellman and two other men, were sent to his room in a matter of minutes. One man went to work on the sink, while the "sole function of the other one, as far as we could tell, was to apologize to us on behalf of the hotel for having committed this monumentally embarrassing and totally unforgivable blunder. . . . The bathtub was fixed in under ten minutes, after which all three men apologized extravagantly in various languages one last time, after which they left, after which I imagine that the hotel's Vice President for Faucet Operations was taken outside and shot. No, just kidding. He probably took his own life. That's how seriously they take their jobs over there." In a Chicago *Tribune Books* review, Clarence Petersen called this type of observation sophomoric, "but Barry does sophomoric better than anyone else."

Although most of the book is written along the same tongue–in–cheek lines, as with *Dave Barry Turns 40, Dave Barry Does Japan* also has its serious moment. In this case, it's when Barry and his family attend the annual memorial ceremonies at Hiroshima, one of the two cities on which the United States dropped nuclear bombs toward the end of World War II. While acknowledging the horror of the nuclear attack on Hiroshima, Barry became frustrated at the Japanese people's refusal to fully recognize the actions on the part of Japan that led to the attack. "I don't know if it's possible to justify what happened to Hiroshima—I certainly wouldn't try to justify it to the victim's families," Barry says in reaction to his visit to a Hiroshima museum. "But I found myself wanting

to shout to the other museum visitors: Do you know WHY my country did this? Do you wonder what would make a civilized country do such a thing? I'm not sure that *I* know the answer, but the museum doesn't even address the question. And I don't think that just saying `No more Hiroshimas' over and over again, like a mantra, is enough to guarantee that it will never happen again." Of the chapter on Hiroshima, Robert J. Collins commented in the *New York Times Book Review* that it is "as fine a commentary on the atomic bomb, Japan and America as we'll see in the lifetimes of the remaining survivors of World War II."

TV Phenom, Rock 'n' Roll Hipster

But Barry doesn't necessarily feel compelled to travel to distant lands to find material—humorous or serious—for his writing. As he told Birnbaum, his adopted hometown of Miami is as culturally diverse as England or Japan. "It's just a bizarre mixture of cultures," Barry remarked. "There are evidently cultures [in Miami] where it is considered basically good etiquette to keep your left–turn signal on at all times. Then there are people who feel it's important to buy the largest possible car, the kind you can land aircraft on top of with no problem, and they drive them incredibly slowly."

A television producer apparently found Barry's life in Miami fascinating enough—or at least profitable enough—to use it as the basis for a television sitcom entitled *Dave's World*, which stars comedian Harry Anderson. Although not a completely faithful to Barry's life—in the show "Dave" has two sons and a dog, while the real Barry has one son and two dogs, Earnest and Zippy—the program is otherwise completely based on Barry's writings, which are, of course, unquestionably based on autobiographical facts.

Barry is not only a name in television, but also in the music world. In a flashback to his days with the Federal Duck, Barry became part of a new band in 1992 called the Rock Bottom Remainders, which includes best–selling horror novelist Stephen King on guitar, *The Joy Luck Club* author–turned–vocalist Amy Tan, humorist Roy Blount Jr., cartoonist Matt Groening, and rock critics Dave Marsh and Joel Selvin. Occasionally, out of sympathy for fellow music lovers, the band will allow amateur musicians to play at one of their gigs, such as the time Bruce Springsteen sang

DAVE BARRY
デイブ・バリーが
DOES JAPAN
"日本をする"

THE AUTHOR OF *DAVE BARRY TURNS FORTY*
AND *DAVE BARRY SLEPT HERE*
EXPLORES THE MYSTERIOUS EAST

Following a trip to Japan, Barry recorded his unique perspective on Japanese food, culture, and history in 1992.

"Gloria" with them at the Hollywood Paladium. Originally formed by real singer Kathi Goldmark, the Remainders appear at American Booksellers conventions, playing favorites like "Wooly Bully," "Leader of the Pack," and "Louie, Louie." In a *Detroit Free Press* article, columnist/musician Mitch Albom described the band in which he once appeared as guest pianist: "the Rock Bottom Remainders [are] a merry band of authors who all share the following: 1) a love of old rock and roll, 2) working knowledge of the `E' chord, 3) enough book sales to keep from being laughed at too loudly, at least by publishing types."

Despite his public visibility and a growing number of fans (of his writing, if not of his musical talent), Barry is a private person who shies away from the suggestion that his columns are a venue for the voice of America. "I'm no one's spokesman," he told Richmond, later adding: "In no sense do I think of myself as any kind of phi-losopher. I hate self–importance. All I ever was was a guy making jokes. I like it when people tell me I'm funny, but I'm extremely uncomfortable when people go beyond that and attach social significance to it."

This fear of being taken seriously has led to his becoming as private a person as possible. The real Dave Barry is not a walking, talking stream of wisecracks and witty satire. "I very rarely go out in my normal life making sophomoric jokes," he told Richmond. The nutty columnist that many people see when Barry is recognized in public—like the little boy who became the class clown years before—throws up a barrier of laughter to protect himself. "I use humor partly as a defense, a way to keep people from getting too close. If I walk into a room and everyone knows I'm Dave Barry . . . , then I'll be Dave Barry for them, because it's a very easy way to relate."

Like his character on television, Barry is very casual and nonchalant about his work. In his office at the *Miami Herald,* he can often be found with his bare feet propped up on his desk, and he still sports a shaggy haircut more suitable to his sixties youth than to a nineties professional journalist. None of this means, however, that Barry doesn't feel a certain responsibility towards his audience, and he knows not to carry his license to satirize too far. As he tells Ross, there are certain subjects he stays away from: "I wouldn't write about rape," he asserts. "I wouldn't write about kids being killed. There are lots of subjects that just aren't funny. There are subjects that in themselves are not funny, but the way people deal with them can be funny. Death. There's a lot of humor in death if only because of the way we act about it. . . . There's a lot of humor around the edges of even the darkest subjects. This is certainly not my original idea, but I believe with all my heart that humor is the most essential way we deal with really terrifying and awful things."

Many of the ideas that Barry uses for his column and books come from the over four hundred letters he gets each week from his fans. Readers clip items from their local newspapers—bizarre tidbits such as snakes slithering through people's house plumbing and ending up in their toilets where they bite their unsuspecting victims in sensitive places, or news about the dangers of frozen waste falling from passing aircraft and plunging through people's roofs—and send them to Barry, who, due to the nature of his column, feels obligated to preface these news items by assuring his audience he isn't making these stories up. Such stories have become the basis for one of his more recent books, *Dave Barry Is Not Making This Up.*

Keeping his work in perspective, Barry realizes that as a syndicated columnist he is in a position to influence people with his opinions and philosophy. "People are always asking me what my political philosophy is, and don't I sometimes try to persuade people about something or why don't I use what I do for good," Barry commented to Ross. "My answer is always, I'm an entertainer, I'm strictly an entertainer. That's how I view myself. I'm much closer in some ways to being a stand-up comic than any kind of journalist." The humorist later added that his work does have a positive effect for his audience. "A lot of people are happy that there's someone else who's as weird as they are. My theory is that everyone is very weird, and that all humorists do is come out and admit it and reveal their weirdness, and then these readers say, Oh, I thought I was the only one with a mind like that. . . . I think that there's a vast untapped vein of weirdness and that it's probably a really good thing that a lot of us are afraid to show it."

"[W]riting is very important to me," Barry said to Richmond. "Writing columns is very important to me. I can't imagine doing anything else. It pays well, it's fun and I feel it validates me. So far it seems like the best job I could possibly have." Famous for littering his prose with such things as boogers, gerbil "doots," and bat urine, the famous columnist pensively concluded, "I'm just worried that there aren't enough bodily fluids to sustain my career."

■ Works Cited

Albom, Mitch, "Baby, We Were Born to Jam," *Detroit Free Press,* June 1, 1994, Section E, pp. 1–2.

Anderson, A. J., review of *Dave Barry Slept Here, Library Journal,* May 15, 1989, pp. 67–68.

Barry, Dave, interview with Jean W. Ross, *Contemporary Authors,* Volume 134, Gale, 1992, pp. 20–25.

Barry, Dave, *Dave Barry's Greatest Hits,* Fawcett, 1988.

Barry, Dave, *Homes and Other Black Holes: The Happy Homeowner's Guide,* Fawcett/Columbine, 1988.

Barry, Dave, *Dave Barry Turns 40,* Crown, 1990.

Barry, Dave, interview in *Crown News,* 1990.

Barry, Dave, *Dave Barry Does Japan,* Random House, 1992.

Barry, Dave, "Runway Bombs, Rushdie Qualms," *Detroit Free Press Magazine,* May 1, 1994, p. 17.

Barry, Dave, "Customer Service, or Else," *Detroit Free Press Magazine,* May 8, 1994, p. 4.

Birnbaum, Jesse, "Madcap Airs All," *Time,* July 3, 1989, pp. 68–69.

Collins, Robert J., review of *Dave Barry Does Japan, New York Times Book Review,* October 25, 1992, p. 17.

Lingeman, Richard, "Why July 4 Falls on Oct. 8," *New York Times Book Review,* June 18, 1989, p. 11.

Novak, Ralph, review of *Dave Barry Turns 40, People,* July 23, 1990, pp. 19–20.

Petersen, Clarence, review of *Dave Barry Does Japan,* Chicago *Tribune Books,* September 5, 1993, p. 8.

Richmond, Peter, "Loon Over Miami," *New York Times Magazine,* September 23, 1990, pp. 44, 64–67, 95.

Sommers, Carl, review of *Dave Barry Turns 40, New York Times Book Review,* July 1, 1990, p. 15.

Teal, Alison, review of *Dave Barry's Greatest Hits, New York Times Book Review,* October 9, 1988, p. 14.

Waters, Harry F., "He Can't Make This Up," *Newsweek,* December 16, 1991, pp. 60–61, 63.

■ For More Information See

BOOKS

Bestsellers '90, Issue 4, Gale, 1990, pp. 7–8.

PERIODICALS

Los Angeles Times Book Review, June 11, 1989, p. 6; June 10, 1990, p. 10; May 5, 1991, p. 14; November 1, 1992, p. 6.

New York Times Book Review, April 28, 1985, p. 25; May 13, 1990, p. 38.

People, March 14, 1988; September 11, 1989; November 9, 1992.

Publishers Weekly, September 4, 1987, p. 65; May 27, 1988, p. 48; July 22, 1988, p. 54;

April 21, 1989, p. 78; May 4, 1990, p. 45; May 3, 1991, p. 51; August 30, 1991, p. 75; August 24, 1992, p. 68.
Sports Illustrated, May 11, 1987.

Tribune Books (Chicago), June 21, 1987, p. 5; June 26, 1988, p. 9; October 2, 1988, p. 8; June 18, 1989, p. 9; May 19, 1991, p. 8; May 24, 1992, p. 2.
USA Today, October 3, 1985, p. 85.

—*Sketch by Janet L. Hile*

Peter Benchley

■ Personal

Full name, Peter Bradford Benchley; born May 8, 1940, in New York, NY; son of Nathaniel Goddard (an author) and Marjorie (Bradford) Benchley; married Wendy Wesson, September 19, 1964; children: Tracy, Clayton, Christopher. *Education:* Phillips Exeter Academy, 1953–57; Harvard University, B.A. (cum laude), 1961. *Hobbies and other interests:* Diving, tennis, wildlife, the theater, films.

■ Addresses

Home—Princeton, NJ. *Agent*—International Creative Management, 40 West 57th St., New York, NY 10019.

■ Career

Novelist. *Washington Post,* Washington, DC, reporter, 1963; *Newsweek,* New York City, associate editor, 1964–67; The White House, Washington, DC, staff assistant to the president, 1967–69; freelance writer and television news correspondent, beginning 1969. Host of television series, "Expedition Earth," ESPN, 1990–93; host/narrator/writer of more than a dozen wildlife/adventure television shows. *Member:* Coffee House, Century Association.

■ Writings

NOVELS

Jaws (also see below), Doubleday, 1974, abridged edition published as *Selected from Jaws,* Literacy Volunteers of New York City, 1990.
The Deep (also see below), Doubleday, 1976.
The Island (also see below), Doubleday, 1979.
The Girl of the Sea of Cortez (also see below), Doubleday, 1982.
Q Clearance, Random House, 1986.
Rummies, Random House, 1989.
Beast (also see below), Random House, 1991.
White Shark, Random House, 1994.
Three Complete Novels (contains *Jaws, Beast* and *The Girl of the Sea of Cortez;* twentieth anniversary edition), Wings Books, 1994.

SCREENPLAYS

(With Carl Gottlieb) *Jaws* (based on his novel of the same title), Universal, 1975.
(Coauthor) *The Deep* (based on his novel of the same title), Columbia, 1977.
The Island (based on his novel of the same title), Universal, 1980.

OTHER

Time and a Ticket (nonfiction), Houghton, 1964.
Jonathan Visits the White House (juvenile), with foreword by Lady Bird Johnson, McGraw, 1964.

Contributor to numerous periodicals, including *Holiday, New Yorker, New York Times,* and *National Geographic.*

■ Work in Progress

Writing the screenplay for *White Shark,* based on his novel of the same title.

■ Sidelights

"The great fish moved silently through the night water, propelled by short sweeps of its crescent tail. The mouth was open just enough to permit a rush of water over the gills. There was little other motion: an occasional correction of the apparently aimless course by the slight raising or lowering of a pectoral fin—as a bird changes direction by dipping one wing and lifting the other. The eyes were sightless in the black, and the other senses transmitted nothing extraordinary to the small, primitive brain."

The great white shark Peter Benchley describes in this introductory passage to his enormously popular first novel, *Jaws,* is just one of several extraordinary inhabitants of the deep that await the reader of the novelist's maritime adventures. While Benchley drew on his immense knowledge of the sea to provide the backdrop for his first four novels, his experiences as a speechwriter for President Lyndon Johnson and in the publishing world provided material for his 1986 novel, *Q Clearance,* and *Rummies,* published in 1989. These humorous narratives, which follow the exploits of a White House speechwriter and an alcoholic book editor, respectively, revealed a lighthearted side to Benchley's writing that was previously concealed. Although both books met with a measure of critical and popular approval, they were followed by two more high seas thrillers, *Beast* and *Great White.* But even if he had never written another novel, the phenomenal success of *Jaws*—and the movie of the same title for which Benchley cowrote the screenplay—was enough to link Peter Benchley's name forever with the aquatic, the terrifying, and

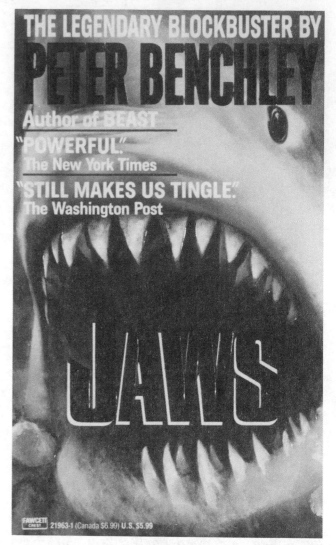

THE LEGENDARY BLOCKBUSTER BY

PETER BENCHLEY

Author of BEAST

"POWERFUL."
The New York Times

"STILL MAKES US TINGLE."
The Washington Post

JAWS

FAWCETT CREST 21963-1 (Canada $6.99) U.S. $5.99

A product of Benchley's childhood fascination with sharks, this extraordinarily popular 1974 thriller—and the equally acclaimed film—launched a nation-wide craze known as "Jawsmania."

the unexpected.

"Jawsmania" Sweeps Country

His seaside best–seller, *Jaws,* "made [Benchley] the most successful first novelist in literary history" noted Jennifer Dunning in the *New York Times Book Review.* Even before the book's February 1, 1974, publication date, lucrative deals had been struck for rights to the paperback reprints of the novel, several book club editions, and a movie version to be penned by Benchley. The novel was, according to *Time,* "a best–seller of numbing durability" and appeared on the *New York Times* list of top–selling titles for over forty weeks. Less than a year and a half after the initial printing of 35,000 copies, there were more than five and a half million copies of *Jaws* in print.

When *Jaws* the movie was released during the summer of 1975, a fearsome head of a great white shark with jaws opened wide lunged out from the cover of *Time* and the issue's lead story declared "The Summer of the Shark." A month later *Newsweek* dubbed the nationwide rage for sharks and everything to do with the movie or the book, "Jawsmania." In a case of life imitating art, the book so captured the imagination of the American public that shark sightings increased around the country—even in landlocked Nebraska. In a self–reflective passage from *Beast,* a more recent title, Benchley has one of his characters comment on the unusual effect *Jaws* had on some of those who read it. "He had been in his teens when *Jaws* swept the States," the character recalls, "and he had vivid memories of parents refusing to let their children get their feet wet, of beaches being closed and of otherwise rational adults declining to swim in water over their heads . . . in lakes."

While phenomenally strong first novels are not unheard of, they are rare, but in Benchley's case such success might have been predicted based on nothing other than his literary heritage. Born into a family that included both Peter's grandfather, Robert Benchley, a great American humorist, and Peter's father, Nathaniel Benchley, a novelist, this third–generation author grew up in a atmosphere where writing seemed the natural thing to do. In a *Palm Springs Life* interview with Roy Newquist, Peter recalled, "At home there was always such an assemblage of really great people, most of them writers or artists. . . . I guess it was inevitable that I should end up a writer." As a teenager, Benchley was already contributing freelance articles to magazines, and by his early twenties he had an agent representing him from the same agency that promoted his father's works. If Tom Congdon, the Doubleday senior editor who nurtured Peter's first novel from idea to publication, had any doubts about the salability of the work, they were diminished by the young author's literary ancestry. "I didn't realize it at the time," Congdon admitted to a *Miami Herald* interviewer, "but Benchley did have a track record—his father and his grandfather."

The Story of a Best–Seller

While Benchley first mentioned the idea for *Jaws* to Congdon over lunch in June of 1971, it had been planted in the author's imagination long before that. Benchley credits many boyhood fishing excursions off Nantucket Island with his father and other family members with initiating his interest in sharks and his fascination with the sea. As he explained in a *New York Times Magazine* interview with Ted Morgan, he would occasionally haul in sharks when the family was out fishing for swordfish. "I'd take them home and cut the jaws out," recalled Benchley, "and be left with 150 pounds of rotting meat on the lawn. I was struck by their inherent menace. They are prehistoric eating machines that have not evolved in 30,000,000 years." As an adult, Benchley worked on an article about sharks for *Newsweek* during his brief stay at that magazine in 1963. The idea for the novel finally jelled the following year when Benchley happened upon a true story about a 4,500–pound great white being caught off Long Island. From those bare details Benchley conjured up the yarn that would cause such a sensation.

Jaws tells the story of Amity, a fictional Long Island resort town that suddenly finds its economic fortune tied to a demonic, twenty–foot long great white shark hovering offshore. The struggle that ensues between man and fish is echoed in a similar conflict that takes place between the police chief, Martin Brody, and the town. When Brody is forced to keep the beaches open after the first apparent shark attack to avoid losing the tourist trade, the shark attacks again and then again. Finally, Brody decides he must take action, and the hunt for the enormous creature begins. Meanwhile the chief's wife, Ellen, tries to recapture her lost youth by arranging a tryst with Matt Hooper, the ichthyologist hired by the town to help in the investigation. The book's climatic final chapter pairs husband and lover in the same boat, accompanied by a harpoon–wielding fisherman named Quint, setting out to do battle with the shark.

While from the public standpoint *Jaws* made for an exciting read, many critics were not so enthusiastic. Some reasoned that the malevolent nature of the shark, its white color, and the almost obsessive way it is finally hunted down with a harpoon all pointed to an attempt by Benchley to retell the classic fish tale *Moby–Dick*. Melville's nineteenth–century novel featured a confrontation between the huge white whale of the title and the maniacal Captain Ahab, whose crew included a harpooner named Queequeg. Although Benchley denied the comparison in *Palm Springs Life,* his words couldn't convince the critics.

In *Time,* John Skow wrote: "Nothing works. Not a hokey assignation between [the police chief's] wife and a predatory ichthyologist, and especially not an eat–'em up ending that lacks only Queequeg's coffin to resemble a bathtub version of *Moby Dick.*" In *Newsweek* Peter Prescott pointedly characterized the novel as "*An Enemy of the People* meets *Moby Dick.*" "Passages of hollow portentousness creep in," claimed Andrew C. J. Bergman in his *New York Times Book Review* critique of the book, "as do clattering allusions—perhaps inevitable—to the Great American Fish Felon, Moby Dick." Bergman was not entirely displeased with the Benchley's work, however, and called the great white shark of the novel "an embodiment of imagined malignity" and praised the scenes in which it appeared. Other critics such as John Spurling complimented the novelist on his portrait of the underwater villain. "The shark, . . .

is done with exhilarating and alarming skill," Spurling wrote in the *New Statesman,* "and every scene in which it appears is imagined at a special pitch of intensity."

Celebrated by *Time* as a "hit right in the collective unconscious," the movie version of Benchley's best–seller became an instant success. After its June 22, 1975, release date, it became the fastest moneymaker in motion picture history up to that time, earning more than $124 million in eleven weeks. Benchley produced three complete drafts of the screenplay, with his final version reworked by several other writers, including Carl Gottlieb, who received coauthorship billing and even changed some material as filming progressed.

The screenplay remained faithful to the book, but to heighten suspense it focused primarily on the offshore action. Benchley even appeared in the film in a small role as a television reporter. The direc-

The 1978 sequel to *Jaws* lured viewers with its ominous slogan: "Just when you thought it was safe to go back in the water. . . ."

tor was the relatively unknown, but promising, twenty–six year old Steven Spielberg, who had at the time but one feature film, *Sugarland Express,* to his credit. So many problems developed during the filming of the movie—including dealing with three one and a half ton mechanical sharks that sometimes malfunctioned—that Spielberg told *Time,* "*Jaws* should never have been made. It was an impossible effort." The success of the *Jaws* movie led to three sequels, including *Jaws II* and *Jaws the Revenge.*

More Thrills

Following the impact of his first novel, Benchley's second fictional effort was widely anticipated. Again, before the book hit the bookstores both paperback and movie rights had been sold, this time commanding much higher fees than before. The idea for this novel, entitled *The Deep,* had come to Benchley during the writing of *Jaws.* While on a month–long diving expedition in the waters off Bermuda researching a *National Geographic* story about shipwrecks, he had become fascinated by the marine archeology of the area. Further research in the field led to the development of the novel. Although a work of fiction, the book contains, according to the "Author's Note" at the end, "many . . . facts about Bermuda, about shipwrecks, and about the Spanish trade with the New World . . . gleaned from historical sources."

Unlike *Jaws,* the bad guys in *The Deep* are humans not sea creatures, but the sea plays an even more important role in the book's action, for nearly all of it takes place underwater. The novel begins with a flashback to the sinking of a ship carrying ammunition and medical supplies to be used in World War II. After this introduction, chapter one returns the reader to the present day, opening in typical Benchley fashion with the first of many factual explanations woven into his fictional narrative. In a few short sentences Benchley manages to suggest the danger awaiting the reader on the pages to come and anticipates the end of the novel: "In sea water more than a few feet deep, blood is green. Water filters the light from above, seeming to consume the colors of the spectrum shade by shade. . . . In the twilight depths—180, 200 feet, and beyond—blood looks black." Before the story is over, the sea would be filled with blood.

The Deep tells the story of honeymooners Gail and David Sanders, who are diving to the sunken wreckage of the World War II– vintage ship. When they attempt to bring up valuables from the hulk, they suddenly become entangled with vicious drug traffickers and sinister treasure hunters. Things get nasty when the Sanders are threatened with death after refusing to hand over the items they have uncovered.

While not as popular with readers as *Jaws,* many critics thought the book compared favorably with Benchley's first effort. In *Time,* for example, Paul Gray found "*The Deep* . . . a better book—more cleverly plotted, less awkward when it ventures on land" than *Jaws.* Both Gene Lyons in the *New York Times Book Review* and Walter Clemons in *Newsweek* noted Benchley's exceptional use of factual information to lend realism to his story and praised this latest work. "Benchley's plot is tightly constructed and yields the maximum in suspense," Lyons remarked. "His style is for the most part unaffected and clear: it offends less often than it pleases. Many readers will feel improved by the constant flow of sheer information the book contains on such pertinent topics as the . . . flora and fauna of the sea, skin diving, treasure hunting and underwater salvage. Benchley obviously knows what he is talking about and incorporates it smoothly into his story." Clemons called the book "a neat adventure" and observed, "Benchley clearly loves underwater exploration. He conveys its alarms and beauty with joyous physical enthusiasm." The critic added: "There is sufficient expertise and underwater chill in *The Deep* to make it satisfying beach– bag cargo."

Kidnapped in the Caicos

Benchley's next novel, *The Island,* again involved a good deal of research on the part of its author. The idea for the book came nearly a decade prior to its publication when Benchley discovered Coast Guard statistics indicating that in three years more than six hundred sea–going vessels had mysteriously vanished with nearly two thousand people aboard. *The Island* is his attempt to answer the "why" behind the disappearances. In the book Benchley's main character, Blair Maynard, an editor at a weekly news magazine, comes across the same figures that had so intrigued Benchley. As if trying to put together pieces of a puzzle, Maynard follows a trail of clues first to Washington, DC, then Miami, and then to the Caicos, a small group of islands southeast of the Bahamas. Maynard's twelve–year–old son, Justin, accompanies his father on his journey. The two are kidnapped by members of a gruesome pirate society that has been responsible for the disappearing ships and crews, and their terrifying struggle to survive makes up the rest of the story.

Just as in *The Deep,* in *The Island* Benchley supplies plenty of details to lend a factual basis to his fiction. In an "Author's Note" appearing at the end of the novel Benchley writes: "In the course of preparing *The Island,* I consulted scores of books, and while I have endeavored to avoid any resemblance to real characters, I have tried equally hard to be faithful to historical reality." His efforts paid off, at least in the eyes of *Chicago Tribune Book World* contributor Lloyd Sachs who wrote: "Benchley has certainly done his homework on pirate lore—his portrait of the murderous but honorable buccaneer Jean– David Nau and his tenth– generation pirates, who are on the brink of extinction, is convincing and entertaining and more than a little affecting. Benchley succeeds in making their plight touching and funny with one small detail: that they have come to prize 6– 12 insect repellant more than just about anything."

Because *The Island* was Benchley's third adventure novel centered around the sea, some critics complained about similarities between the three books. In the *New York Times Book Review,* Jack Sullivan referred to the work as "Benchley's latest variation on *Jaws*" in which "bloodthirsty buccaneers" replaced the shark of the previous novel, but found "its individual episodes of violence . . . grimly persuasive." In *Best Sellers* F. T. DeAndrea claimed that Benchley "seems to have gotten himself in a rut," while noting that *The Island* "succeeds in turning the stomach, but it fails to get the reader involved." The *Washington Post*'s Joseph McLellan was a bit more positive about the novel, suggesting that Benchley "writes according to a formula. The formula moreover is a simple one: take a lot of salt water and put into it something unexpected and menacing. Anybody can do it, and in the wake of *Jaws,* quite a few have tried. The problem (the writer's problem, not the reader's) is that nobody seems to do it quite as well as Benchley." Another favorable review appeared in *Library Journal,* in which M. A. Pradt called *The Island* "an action–packed, cinematic novel."

Lyrical Interlude

In 1982, Benchley began his second decade as a novelist with publication of *The Girl of the Sea of Cortez,* his fourth novel. The book marked a de-

parture from his usual high seas adventure. The rapid, often bloody action of the other novels is replaced with tranquil, lyrical prose, and, instead of a rough–and–tumble, ready–for–adventure male lead, Benchley chooses a quiet, sixteen–year–old girl. Through the eyes of Paloma (whose name means "dove" in Spanish), the author describes the beautiful Sea of Cortez, which separates the peninsula of Baja California from the mainland of Mexico. Paloma's love for the natural world which she learned from her father, the deceased Jobim, leads her to shun the traditional tasks of the village women and spend nearly every day out on the water. Her special place, a seamount, a submerged volcanic peak teeming with every variety of sea life imaginable, is her refuge from the taunts of her younger brother and his friends. Most of the action of the novel centers around Paloma's relationship with the underwater creatures she encounters, her recollections of her father's wisdom, and her final defense of her seamount—aided by a gigantic manta ray—from the intrusion of her brother.

Some critics, such as Lola D. Gillebaard in the *Los Angeles Times Book Review,* thought the book moved too slowly. "This could be a refreshing deviation [from the style of his previous novels]," Gillebaard wrote, "but Benchley doesn't tell a story. His words describe rather than dramatize. Though his descriptions are often lyrical, this reader yearned for more conflict, more 'and then what happened?'" *Washington Post Book World* contributor Thomas Gifford similarly found aspects of the book worthy of praise but wanted more action. "When Benchley sticks to the manta ray, the girl, and the memories of her late father . . . ," Gifford maintained, "he is often effective, even poignant, moving. But out of water he is quickly beached and gasping his last. The problem is the plot."

One characteristic of the novel that made it similar to previous Benchley writings is the enormous amount of information about the sea which fills the narrative. In Mel Watkins's *New York Times Book Review* critique of the novel, he found the factual portions of the novel actually buoyed up what he saw as a skimpy plot. "The narrow story line is buttressed by the author's detailed descriptions of aquatic life," Watkins commented, "as well as an underlying conservation theme." Diane Casselberry Manuel, writing in *Christian Science Monitor,* claimed that the book was "packed with plenty of fascinating sea lore" but felt that Benchley's prose improved when he dealt with

THREE MONTHS ON THE *NEW YORK TIMES* BESTSELLER LIST

PETER BENCHLEY
Author of JAWS

BEAST

"Entertainingly scary...
Vivid and exciting."
The New York Times

22089-3 (Canada $6.99) U.S. $5.99

The author included an environmentalist theme in his 1991 novel about a giant squid that devours human prey.

less realistic themes. "When *The Girl of the Sea of Cortez* leaves fact behind and cruises into uncharted realms of human relationships and ancient superstitions," Manuel observed, "it sparkles like a parrotfish."

Two Comedies Break the Mold

As he did with *The Girl of the Sea of Cortez*, Benchley abandoned his adventure novel mold with his two other books that were published during the eighties: *Q Clearance* and *Rummies*. For his 1986 novel, *Q Clearance,* Benchley drew on his experiences as a White House speechwriter to bring to life the story of his fictional presidential speechwriter, Timothy Burnham. The novel opens as Burnham is given "Q clearance" because of a

promotion. His new status gains him his own personal document shredder and access to secret documents he cannot understand. In the wake of his promotion he becomes President Benjamin T. Winslow's chief confidant, is kicked out of his house by his liberal wife, and arouses the interest of a team of Russian spies.

Benchley's attempt to portray the humorous side of political life was roundly applauded by critics, many of whom asked themselves, like Donald Morrison in *Time*, "Where did a onetime spinner of sea–horse operas learn to write comedy?" One scene relates Burnham's makeshift repair with a stapler of a split in his pants just before he goes to talk to the President, but humor infuses every page. Reviewers pointed most frequently to Benchley's character portrayals in the novel as the book's strong point. "[Benchley] keeps the dialogue crackling with wit," declared Maria Gallagher in the *New York Times Book Review*, "and sketches even his cameo characters in wonderfully wicked detail." Calling the book "a very readable and thoroughly entertaining spy thriller," in *Library Journal*, Brian Alley also referred to Benchley's "skillfully drawn characters in an intriguing plot."

Critics and readers alike also found fascinating characters in Benchley's next novel, *Rummies*, in which he uses a gathering of recovering alcoholics and drug addicts in a rehabilitation center to explore a multitude of different personalities, including a movie star, a professional athlete, and a salesman who shows up at the center dressed as a rabbit. To avoid a threatened divorce by his wife and termination by his employer, Scott Preston, an alcoholic editor for a major New York publishing house, travels to New Mexico's famous Banner Clinic, founded by Western movie idol Stone Banner. Reluctant at first to admit he has a problem or anything in common with the other people at the clinic, Preston becomes involved with them only after one of the clinic's graduates is murdered, and several other incidents occur that start him wondering if Banner is truly as noble–minded as the aging star would like everyone to believe.

Rummies was commended for being an extremely funny book filled with witty characterizations of a variety of individuals. Critics especially seemed to be fascinated by Benchley's Scott Preston character, whose metamorphosis from addict to recovering alcoholic constituted what Dan Wakefield called in the *Washington Post* "the real drama" of the novel. "His evolution from a know–it–all, above–it–all, self–deluding lush to a vulnerable human being . . . is told in moving passages," Wakefield continued. "Preston is made miserably aware," *Los Angeles Times* contributor Elaine Kendall noted, "that all differences of education and background vanish in the brotherhood of addiction." While critic Anne Tolstoi Wallach wished that the novel had included a little more "hope and realism," in her *New York Times Book Review* essay on the novel, she praised Benchley as "a terrific writer of stripped–down prose, [and] a funny, literate man." Reviewing *Rummies* for the *Chicago Tribune*, David E. Jones asserted that "Benchley's credentials as a storyteller . . . are only reinforced by this effort, which may be his most ambitious adventure to date."

Tentacles, a Beak, and Slithering Arms

With the twentieth anniversary of the publication of his blockbuster first novel approaching, Benchley again turned to his fictional roots in two more high seas adventure novels, *Beast*, published in 1991, and *White Shark*, published three years later. As with his other thrillers, both books were compared with *Jaws*, and several critics suggested that either one or the other of Benchley's newer novels could easily be turned into suspenseful motion pictures with the simple addition of appropriate theme music.

The beast of Benchley's novel of the same title is less familiar to readers than the great white shark of *Jaws* and much more primitive. Introduced in short chapters told from its own point of view, this beast is a 100–foot long *Architeuthis dux*, or giant squid, complete with two probing tentacles, a beak for a mouth, and eight slithering arms lined with pointed hooks. Forced to come to the shallower coastal waters of Bermuda from its usual deep water home due to human devastation of its natural feeding grounds, the animal takes one after another victim, leaving mysterious clues as to its identity.

No intervention takes place until the squid devours the twin offspring of American cable television magnate Osborn Manning. When a woman onshore witnesses the boat from which the Manning children were diving go to pieces before her eyes and demands answers from local authorities, the story hits the newswires. Herbert Talley, a Canadian expert on squids and other cephalopods, reads the news reports of the monster's attack and decides to contact the youths' wealthy father as a way to get funding for his research on the gigantic creatures. Eventually, the two go to Bermuda and use extortion to force Whip Darling, the island's most experienced fisherman, to accompany them in a hunt fueled by Manning's obsessive desire to avenge the death of his children. The men are also joined by Liam St. John, Bermuda's egotistical self–proclaimed minister of cultural heritage, and Stephanie Carr, who plans to take photographs of the squid from inside a small submersible.

Based on the plot, comparisons with *Jaws* were inevitable, and reviewers were quick to make them. Calling *Beast* "Benchley's return to the devil–in–the–deep theme" in his *New York Times Book Review* evaluation of the book, Bill Kent found *Beast* compared favorably with Benchley's first novel. Noting that various elements that serve to move the plot of *Beast* along also add "consistent and compelling" tension to the story, he continued: "Unlike *Jaws*, in which the great white

With a revised perspective, Benchley focuses on the need to protect sharks from humans in this 1994 work.

shark represented nature at her most elementally cruel, the huge ammonia–reeking squid of *Beast* is driven by alternating fits of hunger and delight in killing—a crude simplification of the way humans exploit marine life. The book's environmental subtext . . . saves this novel from being too much a copy of his earlier success." In *School Library Journal* John Lawson similarly praised Benchley's effort, noting that the author "combined interesting, colorful characters with a sure–fire plot" and delivered "another of the well–written . . . sea adventures at which he excels." But Lawson and other reviewers felt the similarities between *Beast* and *Jaws* were detrimental to the newer book, thinking perhaps, as Elsa Pendleton did in her *Library Journal* review, "If this were more original, it would be lots more fun."

Another Shark Sighting

In *White Shark*, published in 1994, Benchley again writes about the great white shark, just as he did in his first novel. While Benchley's *Jaws* had itself been responsible for a type of mass hysteria and a lot of the fear of sharks people felt when the novel was first published, in the years since, the creature has become one of the most studied of all inhabitants of the sea, and thinking on it has changed. Now, the feeling is that sharks are not so much the evil monsters they were once thought to be, but important parts of the ocean's delicate chain of life. Sharks, it is said, need to be protected just like any other of the earth's creatures.

Simon Chase, the protagonist of *White Shark*, does just that for a living as founder and chief scientist of the Osprey Island Marine Institute, a private marine research center off the coast of Connecticut. Originally concerned about keeping a great white he has implanted with a telemetric sensor device out of the grasp of a dull–headed, deep–sea fisherman looking for a trophy, Chase worries even more when victims of a more fearful adversary start showing up. This time the monster doing the killing is a left–over Nazi experiment—an amphibious supersoldier—that had been holed up in a sunken U–boat recently uncovered in an Atlantic trench. The band of adventurers that join Chase on his quest to kill the monster include his twelve–year–old son, Max, an Native American named Tall Man, and Amanda Macy, a marine biologist.

Benchley is just as concerned in this novel as in his previous works with providing his readers

with good fiction as well as accurate scientific fact. "My hope is I'll give you a good time, . . . but I'm going to force you to learn something, too," he acknowledged to Craig Wilson in the *Detroit News*. "It doesn't bother me if you want to call it a good beach read, but if I heard from a scientist that I've made a mistake in there, *that* would bother me." Though in the *New York Times Book Review* Timothy Foote acknowledged that "Benchley has long been a graceful explorer of the deep in fact as well as fiction," he concluded that "this time out, the ghosts of clunky movie scripts past, present and to come seem to haunt his plot and prose." Elsa Pendleton, writing in *Library Journal*, found "the marine animals and the details of shipboard life are appealingly portrayed," while *Booklist* contributor Ray Olson noted that "Benchley . . . relays bits of natural history and environmental concern, before he and we readers get caught up in his latest soggy suspenser's action."

Whether writing about the horrors of the deep or the comic absurdities of contemporary life, Benchley has given his readers novels that have proven not only entertaining but informative, too. His gift for storytelling has earned him a wide audience, one that has come to expect a good scare or exciting adventure each time they open a new Benchley thriller. As Lyons observed, "What one gets from Benchley, and this, I think, is the essence of his commercial genius, is *escape*."

■ Works Cited

Alley, Brian, review of *Q Clearance*, *Library Journal*, July, 1986, p. 104.

Benchley, Peter, *Jaws*, Doubleday, 1974.

Benchley, Peter, interview with Ted Morgan, *New York Times Magazine*, April 21, 1974, p. 10.

Benchley, Peter, interview with Roy Newquist, *Palm Springs Life*, April, 1975.

Benchley, Peter, *The Deep*, Doubleday, 1976.

Benchley, Peter, *The Island*, Doubleday, 1979.

Bergman, Andrew C. J., review of *Jaws*, *New York Times Book Review*, February 3, 1974, p. 14.

Clemons, Walter, "Chilly Waters," *Newsweek*, May 10, 1976, pp. 109, 111.

Congdon, Tom, interview with *Miami Herald*, *Miami Herald*, June 8, 1975.

DeAndrea, F.T., review of *The Island*, *Best Sellers*, August, 1979, p. 155.

Dunning, Jennifer, *New York Times Book Review*, July 8, 1979.

Foote, Timothy, review of *White Shark*, *New York*

Foote, Timothy, review of *White Shark, New York Times Book Review,* June 5, 1994, p.22.

Gallagher, Maria, review of *Q Clearance, New York Times Book Review,* July 27, 1986, p. 9.

Gifford, Thomas, review of *The Girl from the Sea of Cortez, Washington Post Book World,* June 13, 1982, p. 11.

Gillebaard, Lola D., review of *The Girl from the Sea of Cortez, Los Angeles Times Book Review,* August 22, 1982, p. 11.

Gray, Paul, review of *The Deep, Time,* May 17, 1976, p. 80.

"Jawsmania: The Great Escape," *Newsweek,* July 28, 1975, p. 16– 17.

Jones, David E., review of *Rummies, Chicago Tribune,* November 17, 1989.

Kendall, Elaine, review of *Rummies, Los Angeles Times,* November 24, 1989.

Kent, Bill, "What's 100 Feet Long and Has Suckers?," *New York Times Book Review,* July 7, 1991, p. 7.

Lawson, John, *School Library Journal,* review of *Beast,* November, 1991, p. 155.

Lyons, Gene, review of *The Deep, New York Times Book Review,* May 17, 1976, p. 8.

Manuel, Diane Casselberry, review of *The Girl from the Sea of Cortez, Christian Science Monitor,* July 9, 1982, p. 14.

McLellan, Joseph, review of *The Island, Washington Post,* April 30, 1979.

Morrison, Donald, review of *Q Clearance, Time,* June 23, 1986, p. 82.

Olson, Ray, review of *White Shark, Booklist,* January 15, 1994, p. 875.

Pendleton, Elsa, review of *Beast, Library Journal,* July, 1991, p. 130.

Pendleton, Elsa, review of *White Shark, Library Journal,* February 1, 1994, p. 109.

Pradt, M. A., review of *The Island, Library Journal,* May 1, 1979, p. 1075.

Prescott, Peter, review of *Jaws,* February 4, 1974, p. 73.

Sachs, Lloyd, *Chicago Tribune Book World,* May 13, 1979.

Skow, John, review of *Jaws, Time,* February 4, 1974, p. 76.

Spurling, John, review of *Jaws, New Statesman,* May 17, 1974, p. 703.

Sullivan, Jack, review of *The Island, New York Times Book Review,* May 13, 1979, p. 22.

"Summer of the Shark," *Time,* June 23, 1975, pp. 42– 45.

Wakefield, Dan, review of *Rummies, Washington Post,* October 19, 1989.

Wallach, Anne Tolstoi, "Escape from Rehab," *New York Times Book Review,* December 17, 1989, p. 21.

Watkins, Mel, review of *The Girl from the Sea of Cortez, New York Times Book Review,* May 9, 1982, p. 14.

Wilson, Craig, "Fish Tale," *Detroit News,* June 29, 1994.

■ For More Information See

BOOKS

Authors in the News, Volume 2, Gale, 1976.

Contemporary Literary Criticism, Gale, Volume 4, 1975, Volume 8, 1978.*

—Sketch by Marian C. Gonsior

Tim Burton

■ Personal

Born in 1958, in Burbank, CA; son of Bill (a parks and recreation department worker) and Jean (a gift shop proprietor) Burton; married Lena Gieseke (an artist; divorced), February, 1989. *Education:* Studied animation at California Institute for the Arts on a Walt Disney fellowship.

■ Addresses

Agent—c/o Creative Artists Agency, 9830 Wilshire Blvd, Beverly Hills, Ca 90212.

■ Career

Film director, producer and writer. Worked as an artist/animator for films released by Walt Disney Studios, including *The Fox and the Hound,* 1981, and *The Black Cauldron,* 1985; animation designer, *Amazing Stories,* National Broadcasting Company, Inc. (NBC–TV), 1987; also director and producer of works for television, including the animated series *Beetlejuice,* American Broadcasting Companies, Inc. (ABC–TV), 1990, and *Family Dog,* Columbia Broadcasting Systems (CBS–TV), 1993.

■ Awards, Honors

Chicago Film Festival Award, 1982, for *Vincent;* NATO/SHO West Award, director of the year, National Association of Theatre Owners West, 1989, for *Batman;* Emmy Award (with others), outstanding animated program, 1990, for *Beetlejuice.*

■ Writings

Alfred Hitchcock Presents (anthology series; also see below), NBC–TV, 1986.
(Story editor with Caroline Thompson) *Edward Scissorhands* (also see below), Twentieth–Century Fox, 1990.
My Art and Films, HarperCollins, 1993.
The Nightmare Before Christmas (also see below), Hyperion, 1993.
The Nightmare Before Christmas Pop–Up Book, Mouse Works, 1993.
(Author of introduction) Matthew Rolston, *Big Pictures,* Bullfinch Press, 1991.
(Author of forward) Frank Thompson, *Tim Burton's "Nightmare before Christmas": The Film, the Art, the Vision,* Hyperion, 1993.

FILM DIRECTOR, EXCEPT WHERE INDICATED

Vincent (animated short subject), Buena Vista, 1982.
Frankenweenie (short subject), Buena Vista, 1984.
Pee Wee's Big Adventure, Warner Bros., 1985.
Beetlejuice (also see below), Warner Bros., 1988.

Batman, Warner Bros., 1989.

(And .producer with Denise De Novi) *Edward Scissorhands,* Twentieth–Century Fox, 1990.

(And producer with De Novi) *Batman Returns,* Warner Bros., 1992.

(Production supervisor) *Tim Burton's Nightmare Before Christmas,* Walt Disney, 1993.

Ed Wood, Touchstone, 1994.

TELEVISION DIRECTOR

Alfred Hitchcock Presents, NBC–TV, 1986.

"Aladdin and His Wonderful Lamp," *Faerie Tale Theatre,* Showtime, 1986.

Beetlejuice, ABC–TV, 1990.

Family Dog, CBS–TV, 1993.

Also director of "Hansel and Gretel," *Faerie Tale Theatre,* Showtime.

■ Work in Progress

A documentary about the career of actor Vincent Price.

■ Sidelights

First, a few scenes: A little boy named Vic Frankenstein secretly tries to resurrect his dead dog using a motley collection of household appliances. . . . Possessed dinner guests do a weird dance to ghostly calypso music. . . . The whizzing of blades and a shower of green leaves signal that a scissor–handed wizard is at work . . . A mysterious "caped crusader" prowls the dark streets of a rotting metropolis. . . . Ghouls and goblins cavort amongst the happy trappings of the Christmas season. . . . Now the test: If a person were asked to pick director Tim Burton out of a line–up—with nothing more to go on than this group of scenes—chances are good that they could do it. Burton's the tall, thin one dressed in black clothes with skeleton emblems dotted here and there, the man with the face capable of a wide, wide grin (a little bit Tom Petty, a little bit Jack Skellington) and the dark, electric–shock hairdo (a *lot* Edward Scissorhands). He's the guy flailing his arms as he talks, having a hard time finishing sentences. Joe Morgenstern, writing in the *New York Times Magazine,* suggested that Burton's "wild black hair, his vagrant's wardrobe and his California space cadet's demeanor" are not reasons to write him off as merely a strangling; rather, in these trappings the reviewer finds "a visionary artist" and "Hollywood's most original

young director."

"Tim Burton, like his work, is a wonderful mess," wrote David Breskin in *Rolling Stone.* "He's falling–apart funny and completely alienated; he's morbid and ironic; he's the serious artist as goofball flake. A self–described `happy–go–lucky manic–depressive,' he's like a bright flashlight in a very dark place: the grim factory of Hollywood." Both Burton's colleagues in the movie business and reviewers of many stripes—even those who find his work flawed—echo this praise. And the money Burton's movies earn at the box office backs up the talk.

Burton manages to make *his* kind of movies—beginning with *Pee Wee's Big Adventure* and extending through more recent works such as *The Nightmare Before Christmas*—and still appeal to both juvenile and adult audiences. It all comes back to the director's vision. David Ansen commented in *Newsweek* that Burton's "bold neoprimitive graphic style was evident from the start, along with a macabre streak of humor and an uneasy sense that the surface gregariousness of middle–class life can quickly turn threatening. But though there are dark intimations in all his work, Burton's vision is essentially comic." And how does the filmmaker view himself? Burton has said more than once that he doesn't consider himself a director. "I'm very split," he told Morgenstern, "a bit like an optimistic pessimist."

Strange and Unusual in Suburbia

Reflecting on his childhood, Burton said to Breskin, "This is funny, but I think I've always felt the same. I've never felt young, like I was a kid. I've never felt like I was a teenager. I never felt like I was an adult. . . . I guess if there was a flavor, I guess childhood was a kind of surreal, bright depression. I was never interested in what everybody else was interested in. I was very interiorized. I always felt kind of sad." Born in Burbank, California, Burton grew up with his brother Daniel in a middle–class suburban environment that at first glance seems a far cry from the worlds of the director's movies. Burton's father Bill worked for the Burbank Parks and Recreation Department, while his mother Jean had a gift shop called "Cats Plus" which specialized in items depicting cats.

For unspecified reasons, Burton is not close to his family. "It's been a source of confusion. I'm just something of a remote person in some ways. I've had an incredible desire to get out of the house from an early age," he admitted to Morgenstern. Added to the strain of family relationships was Burton's sense of alienation from his surroundings. He saw his suburban neighborhood as something other than a haven of normalcy and comfortable predictability; instead, it seemed like a blank facade hiding odd, even menacing things. He explained to Frank Rose in *Premiere:* "When you're a kid, you think everything is strange, and you think *because* you're a kid, everything is strange. Then when you get older, you realize it *is* strange."

As a child, Burton took refuge in strange and unusual things. He liked to play in the local cemetery and masterminded imaginative, elaborate pranks; he also made home movies of items like monster Christmas trees. Burton's off–center fascination was fed by a heavy diet of horror movies, particularly a series of films produced in the 1960s by Roger Corman featuring actor Vincent Price. "Vincent Price helped me get through childhood," Burton told Morgenstern. "I saw all of his horror movies on TV. A lot of them were based on Edgar Allan Poe short stories. There's something about those Poe melodramas that's very cathartic: unseen demons, dying alone, going insane, being trapped and tormented in a rear room."

While these types of tales don't fit a well–defined "happily–ever–after" scheme, when tipped upside down and looked at through the Burton lens, they don't seem so far off the fairy tale mark after all. "All monster movies are basically one story," the director remarked to Breskin. "It's *Beauty and the Beast.* Monster movies are my form of myth, of fairy tale. The purpose of folk tales for me is a kind of extreme, symbolic version of life, of what you're going through. . . . And I linked those monsters and those Edgar Allan Poe things to direct feelings. I didn't read fairy tales, I watched them."

Young Burton was also very taken with art and drawing. From an early age, he created cartoons and elaborate doodles, which Morgenstern described as "windows into other worlds." Burton told Breskin that he first had the impulse to draw "when it started for everyone. I'm just lucky that it wasn't beaten out of me. I was very lucky that I maintained a

passion for it and didn't give a fuck what my third–grade teacher thought of it."

Out of the "Factory" and into Films

After graduating from high school, Burton attended the California Institute of the Arts on a Disney fellowship. It was at the Institute that he learned the basics of animation, drawing his own characters and background designs, creating his own storyboards and shooting his own scenes— all without the competitive industry pressure of traditional film schools. After attending CalArts, Burton returned to Burbank to work as an apprentice animator at Walt Disney Studios. Burton's years there, working on projects like *The Fox and the Hound* and *The Black Cauldron,* proved torturous for the aspiring filmmaker, who found himself unsuited to drawing cute cuddly animals on demand. "The unholy alliance of animation is you are called upon to be an artist, but on the other hand, you are called upon to be a zombie factory worker. And for me, I could not integrate the two," Burton explained to Breskin.

The silver lining in the dark cloud of Burton's experience at Disney came when the studio, perhaps not knowing what else to do with the young animator, gave him the go–ahead—and the money—to do a project of his own. The result was *Vincent,* a six–minute animated short narrated by Burton's hero, Vincent Price. The film depicts a boy whose dark imagination belies his otherwise normal surroundings. Wrote Morgenstern, "Here was the first of Tim Burton's surreal landscapes, drawn with charming precocity in the style of such classic German expressionist films as *Metropolis* and *The Cabinet of Dr. Caligari*—tilted horizons, walls converging in forced perspective, stairways curving infinitely upward." Vincent Price himself was quite taken by the young director: "I was so struck by Tim's amateur charm. I mean amateur in the French sense of the word, in love with something. Tim was in love with the medium, and dedicated to it."

Burton's next original project at Disney was *Frankenweenie,* a twenty–nine–minute live action film, that—like the director's experience at Disney itself—proved to be a mixed blessing. On the one hand, the short piece almost didn't see the light of day; and on the other, it led to bigger things for Burton. Filmed in black and white in a manner that, according to Morgenstern, "might have

Burton's first directorial effort--the story of a budding scientist's attempts to bring his dead dog back to life--was an homage to James Whale, director of the 1931 classic, *Frankenstein*.

looked like a 1960's television sitcom in the hands of another director," *Frankenweenie* is about a boy who, after seeing his dog Sparky run over in the street, is overtaken by grief that transforms him into the "little mad scientist in the attic." Vic is successful at resuscitating Sparky's exhumed body, only to find that he must attempt it again after hysterical neighbors, thinking Sparky is some kind of monster, form a mob and chase the dog to his second death in a burning miniature golf course windmill.

Burton told Morgenstern that, as a kid, he always found more humor in horror than in comedy. He described one of his favorite scenes from the original *Frankenstein* movie, "where we have this hunchbacked, twisted man with an absurdly short cane walking up this expressionist stairway and, halfway up, he stops to pull up his sock." As morbid and grim as the plot of *Frankenweenie* may sound, it is full of jokes of just this sort; for example, in a striking scene set after Sparky's death, Vic stands gloomily by a window, watching rain fall against the glass. As

the camera moves back, the audience discovers that the "rain" is actually coming from a misdirected hose held by Vic's mother in a distracted attempt to water the yard. Despite (or perhaps because of) this type of humor, the film was deemed inappropriate for young audiences, got a PG rating, and was never released in theaters. (Fortunately for Burton fans, *Frankenweenie* is now available on video.)

Big Adventures on the Way to Gotham

Private screenings of Burton's short piece *within* the film industry, however, won the director some "insider" fans. One of those was Paul Reubens—Pee Wee Herman himself—who was looking for someone to direct what would become *Pee Wee's Big Adventure*. "I watched the first minute and said `Okay, this is my guy,'" Ruebens recalled to Morgenstern. *Pee Wee's Big Adventure* is essentially a road movie: Reubens's character (that strange but endearing bow–tied, man–boy who experiences the world with the passion of a child but who has the autonomy of an adult) has an incredible bicycle. The bicycle is eventually stolen, leading Pee Wee to set off on his own recovery mission. In the process, Burton takes the audience on a carnival ride that includes a frightful hitch with a ghostly story–telling trucker named Large Marge; an escapade in a biker bar, in which Pee–wee does a wild shoe dance to the tune of "Tequila"; and a hilariously heroic attempt to save a menagerie of creatures from a burning pet store.

"This cartoon without cels, one of the most un–selfconciously surrealistic works to have ever have been issued from Hollywood, was at one with its hero, able to wink at the grown–ups without condescending to the kiddies, and delivering a cornucopia of pleasant surprises to all," wrote Luc Sante in *Vogue. Pee Wee,* which was made for $7 million, delivered perhaps the biggest surprise of all. Despite the fact that most critics either ignored it or didn't "get" it, the movie brought in young audiences to the tune of $40 million at the box office. Speaking to Breskin, Burton described Pee Wee

as a "weird, alternative character who's protecting—who's fighting off things in the world—and has mutated into something that's separate. . . . It had less to do with his bike than it did the idea of passion about something that nobody else cares about. I kind of feel that way about . . . *the movies!* I make these things that are very hard to make—that are not pictures with a message by most people's standards—so I identify with a character that is passionate about something that nobody else really cares about."

Impressed by the success of *Pee Wee,* Warner Brothers allowed Burton the challenge of bringing movie–goers yet another wildly unusual character, the creepy, otherworldly Beetlejuice. "It was totally opposite from everything else I'd read," the director told Rose. "It had no structure, no plot, randomly weird ideas—it just had a weird quality that I loved. So we made the movie." Described by David Handelman in *Vogue* as a "nearly plotless gem," *Beetlejuice* revolves around

Armed with a new image, the caped crusader battles the Joker in Burton's wildly successful directorial feat, *Batman.*

As producer, director, and story editor, Burton had a close personal involvement with *Edward Scissorhands,* a 1990 fairy tale about a young man whose ability to sculpt hedges with his bare hands results in his being treated as an outcast.

the Maitlands, a nice young couple who are killed early in the movie when their car goes off a bridge. After death, the duo returns to their country home (which was in the process of being renovated at the time of the crash). Now ghosts, the Maitlands spend the bulk of the film trying to get rid of the fractious family from the city who has moved into the couple's house and turned it into a horrible modern art monstrosity. Since the neophyte ghosts are not very good at being scary, they resort to calling up the spirit Beetlejuice—a spectral gun for hire who specializes in getting rid of the living using any means necessary (including possession and the summoning of ghastly apparitions).

Like *Pee Wee, Beetlejuice* did not receive much favorable notice at first. Critics seemed to have a hard time keeping up with the movie's pace as it jumped from one world to the next, becoming frustrated when they discovered that there was essentially no plot in the pot at the end of the wild rainbow. Nevertheless, *Beetlejuice* brought in a huge profit for it's parent studio. Burton remarked to Breskin that *Beetlejuice* made him "feel very good, that the audience didn't need a certain kind of thing. Movies can be different things!" David Denby, in spite of the very mixed review he gave *Beetlejuice* in *New York,* concluded that the film "is probably the wildest movie

to become a smash hit in years, a happy event that suggests the big audience has a lot hipper taste in comedy than it does in action and drama."

The next stop for Burton was Gotham City, home of the Caped Crusader. Having obtained the character rights for the "Batman" character from DC comics, Warner Brothers hired a number of writers to try and come up with an appropriate script; eventually, studio executives approached Burton for both his input and a possible directing job. At the time, Burton was still at work on *Beetlejuice* and had only the success of *Pee Wee* to his credit. The executives were convinced, however, that not only did Burton have a real passion for the Batman character, but he was also willing to take the caped crimefighter in a different direction— away from the goody–two–shoes superhero of the comic books in favor of a solitary, damaged character trying to function for good in a dark and damaged world. In Burton's scheme, the conflict would develop out of the existence of an alter ego—the Joker—functioning for evil on the same dank plane.

Because Burton had no experience with action movies, he was given a top–flight technical crew able to execute Batman's escapes, rescues and breathtaking midnight batmobile rides ("Where does he get those wonderful toys?" the Joker muses after one such escape.) One of these notable set pieces revolves around Batman's final confrontation with the Joker, who has taken Bruce Wayne/Batman's love interest, reporter Vicky Vale, hostage. The action takes place seemingly hundreds of feet from the ground in the bell tower of a deserted cathedral, where the two foes battle for supremacy using all the tools in their respective arsenals.

An element of the *Batman* phenomenon that was impossible to ignore at the time of the film's release was Warner Brothers' monumental merchandising effort to encourages moviegoers to buy everything from posters and t–shirts to batmobiles, lunch boxes and action figures. Even Burton couldn't escape the hype. "It was so weird," he told Handelman. "To be working on something— it's your baby, you get very emotional about it, and then you keep hearing about it. You go, `God, enough about this damn thing!'" All told, the movie made $425 million worldwide; with the video release and merchandising added in, the figure reportedly soared above $1 billion.

Did critics feel that the film measured up to expectations? Anne Billson, writing in *New Statesman & Society,* called *Batman* "an art movie disguised as a blockbuster." The *New Yorker*'s Terrence Rafferty commented that Burton "managed to give the material a luxurious masked–ball quality and a sly contemporary wit without violating the myth's low, cheesy origins. . . . The genius of Burton's approach to *Batman* was that it revelled in impurity, celebrated the anything–goes recklessness of comic–book art, and made that quality seem as beautiful—as right, in its way—as the honed, shapely narrative power of the most affecting fairy tales."

Other critics, however, seemed to want exactly that—a honed and shapely narrative—and were not satisfied with the way the film moved from one striking "picture" to the next; still others were disappointed at the story's lack of exposition. Burton, speaking to Breskin, suggested that he's willing to live with those kinds of gaps: "If Batman got therapy, he probably wouldn't be doing this, he wouldn't be putting on this bat suit, and we wouldn't have this weird guy running around in a cape. . . . There is a charm about characters that know [understand] what they do, but do it purely." The director agreed, however, that *Batman* was a mixed bag; in fact, he once characterized

his creation as (much more a cultural phenomenon than a great movie"). "The movie that I feel the least close to has made the most money. It's odd. It's not something to think too much about, because what does it say about what it is that I want to do?," Burton mused for Handelman.

A Fairy Tale Cut From the Heart

The commercial success of *Batman* undoubtedly gave Burton the freedom to choose a project closer to his heart. Since it's release in 1990, *Edward Scissorhands* has been described by many critics as Burton's most personal project. The movie is about a young man created in a Gothic castle–laboratory. When the boy's inventor/father dies before he can finish his creation, Edward is left alone with two sets of shears for hands. One day, an intrepid lady selling Avon products makes her way into the castle, discovers Edward, and brings him home to live with her family in a suburban neighborhood. At first, Edward is a marvel to all. He quickly becomes the neighborhood hero when he displays his skills at sculpting hedges and hairdos; he later falls in love with the Avon lady's blonde cheerleader daughter. Even with these accomplishments, however, Edward is misunderstood

Burton directing Michael Keaton in the 1992 sequel, *Batman Returns,* which focused on the imaginative interplay between the characters.

by many in the community. He becomes a scape-goat for teen–age pranksters, is labeled a general threat, and eventually gets chased by an angry neighborhood mob back into the solitary confinement of his castle.

Breskin described *Edward Scissorhands* as "a simple fairy tale gift–boxed in a sophisticated design package. . . . Yearning and sentimental, the movie felt like Burton's ache." Burton acknowledged his personal connection to Edward as the lonely artistic outsider who can't touch. "There was a long period of time when I just hadn't been able to connect with anybody or have a relationship. Everybody goes through periods like that—the feeling that you can't connect, you can't touch," Burton explained to Rose. Relating that to Edward and the reason why he gave his character scissors for hands, the director explained that the film "was a visual representation of what's inside. I've always felt, just for me, for some reason, it encompassed a lot about how I feel about things."

Burton Meets Batman, Again

Burton surprised a great many people in the film industry when he agreed to direct *Batman Returns*. It wasn't the typical sequel pressure many directors feel after a box office hit—or even the lure of big money—that led Burton to take on the project. Rather, he was interested in having another chance at making a "Batman" movie that focused less on the elements of the action genre and more on the personality dynamics of a new crop of twisted characters. With a control over script, characters and design that was missing in the first *Batman*, Burton was able to realize his unique vision. "It is a funny, gorgeous, midsummer night's Christmas story about . . . well, dating, actually. But hang on. This is the goods. . . . Accept no prequels," raved Richard Corliss in *Time*. Corliss was referring to the batty, catty relationship between Batman and Catwoman, the warped, wild nighttime persona of the used and abused Selina Kyle, secretary to evil moneyman Max Shreck. Thrown into the mix is the Penguin, born deformed and rejected by his wealthy parents. Left for dead, the foundling is raised by a group of penguins who live in the city sewers. As an adult, the Penguin meets both Batman and Catwoman when he returns topside in a bizarre bid for mayor.

Stanley Kauffmann of the *New Republic* wrote that "like its predecessor, this isn't a film, it's a display—of action episodes and, chiefly, of production design. The plot doesn't matter, which is a good thing because it's murky." Rafferty, however, felt it's all an elusive matter of taste: "Burton's narrative technique seems more confident this time around, his rhythms smoother. The story doesn't go flat in the intervals between its showpiece sequences, as *Batman* did. The herky–jerky storytelling of *Batman* made a fascinating contrast to the picture's sleek design; in *Batman Returns*, the pace is even but the settings have a funky, irregular quality. The balance of incongruity comes out about the same, and preferring one kind of contrast to the other is strictly a matter of taste, or mood: a dark bat symbol against a light background, or vice versa." Reflecting on *Batman Returns*, Burton remarked to Handelman: "I like this *Batman* better, but on every movie, until the day it opens, I've felt it could easily go either way, I would understand. That's why I never get egotistical or confident. . . . Of course, I'd much rather things work out, and I've been very lucky."

A Christmas Trick or Treat

Burton's next movie, *The Nightmare Before Christmas*, brought the director's career nearly full circle. To make the film, Burton returned to the place where his professional life began: Disney Studios. *Nightmare* was based on a spoof of Clement Moore's poem that the director had written as a young Disney apprentice. At the time Burton's piece was written, "you couldn't give it away," the director told Jay Carr of the *Boston Globe*. The "ghosts" of Christmas haunt all of Burton's movies in some form or another, with Santa, sleighs, reindeer, and other trappings of the holiday season popping up everywhere. But, with the possible exception of scenes from *Edward Scissorhands*, *Nightmare* is the only Burton film that's really *about* Christmas. In a *People* article by Tom Gliatto and Lynda Wright, Burton commented on growing up in Burbank, where "there's no weather or seasonal changes, no emotional or visual stimulus. You looked to the holidays to give you a sense of ritual. . . . Kind of sad, really, the way [people] experience the seasons in California, walking down the aisles at Thrifty's."

Influenced in part by Dr. Seuss's *How the Grinch Stole Christmas* and the television perennial *Rudolph the Red–Nosed Reindeer*, *Nightmare* is a stop–action animated fable about Jack Skellington, popular resident of Halloweentown, who happens to step through a magical doorway into the land

The most joyous and most frightening of holidays come together in the highly inventive 1993 stop-action fantasy film, *Tim Burton's Nightmare Before Christmas.*

of Christmas. Completely enchanted, Jack returns home and begins a passionate plan to become the current year's purveyor of Christmas. In order to carry off his idea, however, he must enlist the help of Halloweentown's ghosties and ghouls. Sally— the rag–doll creation and slave of a duck–like mad scientist with a flip–top skull—senses that Jack hasn't quite got the hang of Christmas, but is unable to stop him before Santa is kidnapped and the faux St. Nick is on his way to deliver disastrous and frightful surprises to the world's good girls and boys.

"This giddily imaginative stop–motion animation musical is so stuffed with visual delights you won't want to blink," enthused Ansen. Those delights were the result of two years and $20 million worth of technical wizardry. Jointed figurine– type puppets with molded pop–in faces depicting different facial expressions were created from Burton's drawings and then posed and photo-

graphed over and over again. "There's something very primal about stop–action. It really is breathing life into something that doesn't have life," Burton related to Gliatto and Wright. "When I think of the process and how it turned out, I start laughing. It's a miracle." Peter Travers, reviewing the movie in *Rolling Stone,* agreed: "Tim Burton's *Nightmare Before Christmas* restores originality and daring to the Halloween genre. This dazzling mix of fun and fright also explodes the notion that animation is kid stuff. . . . It's seventy–four minutes of timeless movie magic." *Entertainment Weekly*'s Owen Glieberman found *Nightmare* less entertaining, commenting that Jack is "a technical achievement in search of a soul. And so is the movie. I'm not sure I've ever seen a fantasy film that's at once so visually amazing and so emotionally dead." But other critics felt that Burton's attempt to mix technical expertise with holiday whimsy worked very well indeed. Concluded Ansen: "Chances are, [*Nightmare*] will be around for many Halloweens to come."

Burton followed *Nightmare* with *Ed Wood,* a film about one of the most inept directors Hollywood ever produced. With movies like *Glen or Glenda* and *Plan 9 From Outer Space,* Wood used a roster of (largely) awful actors, terrible sets, and nonsensical scripts to create films with a truly unique vision. In *Ed Wood,* Burton concentrates not only on these aspects of Wood's unique working environment, but on his long personal and professional association with actor Bela Lugosi as well. The result was widely applauded by critics. Ansen called the movie "sweet, sad, and very funny," a crazily entertaining celebration" of Wood's career. Gleiberman agreed, terming *Ed Wood* "funny" and "bizarre." He closed by saying that the "beauty of [the film] is that Burton loves these losers for who they are."

If there's anything that scares Tim Burton, it seems to be the unreality of being big in Hollywood, a place where he's always lived but never felt fully at home. The same applies to the director's relationship with the film industry. "It's a business of sociopaths. If this were organized crime, most of us would be out in the East River by now. Where else can you get such a collection of people who couldn't have regular jobs? It's a big nuthouse," Burton remarked to Handelman. As an antidote, he stays busy with a slew of different projects, including a documentary about Vincent Price. He continues to draw and paint, and has completed a coffee table book about his work. Burton once said that he is glad that he never had a particular goal in life, suggesting that by not pursuing *one* thing, he's been able to do all kinds of things. "The tricky thing about being in the entertainment industry," Burton told Handelman, "is that basically no matter how much money is involved, how good the life is, the thing that still compels you is that thing inside. . . . It's so weird—you remain the same, and yet all around you, things just get jacked up. . . . Everybody's got it all figured out, and you're sitting here in the dark as usual, fumbling through."

■ Works Cited

Ansen, David, "Tim Burton Looks at Holiday Hell," *Newsweek,* November 1, 1993, p. 72.

Ansen, "Kitsch as Kitsch Can," *Newsweek,* October 10, 1994.

Ansen, David with Donna Foote, "The Disembodied Director," *Newsweek,* January 21, 1991, pp. 58–60.

Billson, Anne, "Blade Runner," *New Statesman & Society,* July 26, 1991, p. 32.

Breskin, David, an interview with Tim Burton, *Rolling Stone,* July 9–23, 1992.

Carr, Jay, "Tim Burton's Big Adventure," *Boston Globe,* October 17, 1993, pp. A9, A11.

Corliss, Richard, "Battier and Better," *Time,* June 22, 1992, pp. 69–71.

Denby, David, review of "Beetlejuice," *New York,* May 2, 1988, p. 95.

Gliatto, Tom and Lynda Wright, "And to All a Good Fright," *People,* November 22, 1993, pp. 73–74.

Gleiberman, Owen, "Halloween," *Entertainment Weekly,* October 22, 1993, p. 82.

Gleiberman, review of *Ed Wood, Entertainment Weekly,* October 7, 1994, p. 56.

Handelman, David, "Heart and Darkness," *Vogue,* July 1992, pp. 142–145, 194.

Kauffmann, Stanley, "The Odd Couple," *New Republic,* July 27, 1992, pp. 46–47.

Morgenstern, Joe, "Tim Burton, Batman, and the Joker," *New York Times Magazine,* April 9, 1989, pp. 45–46, 50, 53, 59–60.

Rafferty, Terrence, "The Current Cinema: Masked Ball," *New Yorker,* June 29, 1992, pp. 71–72.

Rose, Frank, "Tim Cuts Up," *Premiere,* January 1991, pp. 96–100.

Sante, Luc, "The Rise of the Baroque Directors," *Vogue,* September 1992, pp. 304, 319, 322, 324, 330.

Travers, Peter, review of "The Nightmare Before Christmas," *Rolling Stone,* November 11, 1993, pp. 80–81.

■ For More Information See

PERIODICALS

Entertainment Weekly, June 26, 1992, pp. 77–78.

Life, November, 1993, pp. 103–104.

New Republic, July 31, 1989, p. 24.

Newseek, June 26, 1988, p. 72–73.

New York, July 13, 1992, pp. 63–64.

People, July 3, 1989, p. 13; July, 8, 1991, p. 14.

Premiere, October, 1990, p. 73.

Time, April 11, 1988, p. 69.

Wilson Library Bulletin, November, 1988, pp. 100–101.

OTHER

Freaks, Nerds and Weirdos (special), MTV, 1994.*

—*Sketch by Tracy J. Sukraw*

Barbara Corcoran

■ Personal

Also writes under pseudonyms Paige Dixon and Gail Hamilton; born Barbara Asenath Corcoran, April 12, 1911, in Hamilton, MA; daughter of John Gilbert (a physician) and Anna (Tuck) Corcoran. *Education:* Wellesley College, B.A., 1933; University of Montana, M.A., 1955; University of Denver, post graduate study, 1965 66. *Politics:* Democrat. *Religion:* Episcopalian.

■ Addresses

Home—P.O. Box 4394, Missoula, MT 59806.

■ Career

Worked at a variety of jobs in New York City and Hamilton, MA, 1933–40, including writing for the Works Progress Administration, working as a theatre manager, and working as a playwright and free lance writer; Celebrity Service, Hollywood, CA, researcher, 1945–53; Station KGVO, Missoula, MT, copywriter, 1953–54; University of Kentucky, Covington, instructor in English, 1956–57; Columbia Broadcasting System (CBS), Hollywood, researcher, 1957–59; Marlborough School, Los Ange-

les, CA, teacher of English, 1959–60; University of Colorado, Boulder, instructor in English, 1960–65; Palomar College, San Marcos, CA, instructor in English, 1965–69; author of books for children and young adults, 1967—. Austin Community College, instructor in expressive writing, 1983; Women's Center, University of Montana, Missoula, instructor in writing for children, 1984—. *Wartime service:* Worked as a Navy inspector at a proximity fuse factory in Ipswich, MA, and for the Army Signal Corps in Arlington, VA, 1940–45. *Member:* Authors League of America, PEN.

■ Awards, Honors

Samuel French Award for original play, 1955; children's book of the year citation, Child Study Association, 1970, for *The Long Journey;* William Allen White Children's Book Award, 1972, for *Sasha, My Friend;* outstanding science trade book for children citations, National Science Teachers Association, 1974, for *The Young Grizzly,* and 1977, for *Summer of the White Goat;* Pacific Northwest Book Sellers' Award, 1975; Merriam Award, University of Montana, 1992; award from Western Writers of America, 1994, for *Wolf at the Door;* National Endowment of the Arts fellow.

■ Writings

JUVENILE NOVELS

Sam, illustrated by Barbara McGee, Atheneum, 1967.

(With Jeanne Dixon and Bradford Angier) *The Ghost of Spirit River*, Atheneum, 1968.

A Row of Tigers, illustrated by Allan Eitzen, Atheneum, 1969.

Sasha, My Friend, illustrated by Richard L. Shell, Atheneum, 1969, published as *My Wolf, My Friend*, Scholastic, 1975.

The Long Journey, illustrated by Charles Robinson, Atheneum, 1970.

(With Angier) *A Star to the North*, Thomas Nelson, 1970.

The Lifestyle of Robie Tuckerman, Thomas Nelson, 1971.

This Is a Recording, illustrated by Richard Cuffari, Atheneum, 1971.

A Trick of Light, illustrated by Lydia Dabcovich, Atheneum, 1972.

Don't Slam the Door When You Go, Atheneum, 1972.

All the Summer Voices (historical), illustrated by Robinson, Atheneum, 1973.

The Winds of Time, illustrated by Gail Owens, Atheneum, 1974, published as *The Watching Eyes*, Scholastic, 1975.

A Dance to Still Music, illustrated by Robinson, Atheneum, 1974.

The Clown, Atheneum, 1975, published as *I Wish You Love*, Scholastic, 1977.

Axe–Time, Sword–Time (historical), Atheneum, 1976.

Cabin in the Sky (historical), Atheneum, 1976.

The Faraway Island, Atheneum, 1977.

Make No Sound, Atheneum, 1977.

(With Angier) *Ask for Love and They Give You Rice Pudding*, Houghton, 1977.

Hey, That's My Soul You're Stomping On, Atheneum, 1978.

Me and You and a Dog Named Blue, Atheneum, 1979.

Rising Damp, Atheneum, 1980.

Making It, Little, Brown, 1980.

Child of the Morning, Atheneum, 1982.

Strike!, Atheneum, 1983.

The Woman in Your Life, Atheneum, 1984.

Face the Music, Atheneum, 1985.

A Horse Named Sky, Atheneum, 1986.

I Am the Universe, Atheneum, 1986.

You Put Up with Me, I'll Put Up with You, Atheneum, 1987.

The Hideaway, Atheneum, 1987.

The Sky Is Falling, Atheneum, 1988.

The Private War of Lillian Adams, Atheneum, 1989.

The Potato Kid, Atheneum, 1989.

Annie's Monster, Macmillan, 1990.

Stay Tuned, Atheneum, 1991.

Family Secrets, Atheneum, 1992.

Wolf at the Door, Atheneum, 1993.

Some of Corcoran's novels have been translated into German, Swedish, and Spanish.

JUVENILE MYSTERY NOVELS

Meet Me at Tamerlane's Tomb, illustrated by Charles Robinson, Atheneum, 1975.

The Person in the Potting Shed, Atheneum, 1980.

You're Allegro Dead, Atheneum, 1981.

A Watery Grave, Atheneum, 1982.

Which Witch Is Which?, Atheneum, 1983.

August, Die She Must, Atheneum, 1984.

Mystery on Ice, Atheneum, 1985.

The Shadowed Path (part of "Moonstone Mystery Romance" series), Archway, 1985.

When Darkness Falls (part of "Moonstone Mystery Romance" series), Archway, 1986.

JUVENILE NOVELS UNDER PSEUDONYM PAIGE DIXON

Lion on the Mountain, illustrated by J. H. Breslow, Atheneum, 1972.

Silver Wolf, illustrated by Ann Brewster, Atheneum, 1973.

The Young Grizzly, illustrated by Grambs Miller, Atheneum, 1974.

Promises to Keep, Atheneum, 1974.

May I Cross Your Golden River?, Atheneum, 1975, published as *A Time to Love, a Time to Mourn*, Scholastic, 1982.

The Search for Charlie, Atheneum, 1976.

Pimm's Cup for Everybody, Atheneum, 1976.

Summer of the White Goat, Atheneum, 1977.

The Loner: A Story of the Wolverine, illustrated by Miller, Atheneum, 1978.

Skipper (sequel to *May I Cross Your Golden River?*), Atheneum, 1979.

Walk My Way, Atheneum, 1980.

JUVENILE NOVELS UNDER PSEUDONYM GAIL HAMILTON

Titania's Lodestone, Atheneum, 1975.

A Candle to the Devil (mystery), illustrated by Joanne Scribner, Atheneum, 1975.

Love Comes to Eunice K. O'Herlihy, Atheneum, 1977.

HISTORICAL ROMANCE NOVELS

Abigail, Ballantine, 1981.

Abbie in Love (continuation of *Abigail*), Ballantine, 1981.

A Husband for Gail (conclusion of *Abigail*), Ballantine, 1981.

Beloved Enemy, Ballantine, 1981.
Call of the Heart, Ballantine, 1981.
Love Is Not Enough, Ballantine, 1981.
Song for Two Voices, Ballantine, 1981.
By the Silvery Moon, Ballantine, 1982.

OTHER

From the Drawn Sword (play), produced in Boston, MA, 1940.
Yankee Pine (play), produced at Bard College, Annandale–on–Hudson, NY, 1940.
The Mustang and Other Stories, Scholastic, 1978.

Contributor of radio scripts to *Dr. Christian* program; also contributor of short stories and other pieces to *Glamour, Charm, Woman's Day, Redbook, American Girl,* and *Good Housekeeping.*

■ Work in Progress

Other books for young people.

■ Sidelights

"Hallie pressed her cheek against the window of the plane. The jagged snow–covered peaks of the Rockies seemed almost close enough to touch. She looked down at the pockets of snow caught in the black rocks and shivered. She felt as if she had left the real world behind her and had ventured into some terror filled land of fantasy." So begins one of Barbara Corcoran's early novels, *Sasha, My Friend.* Leaving her life in California behind after her mother's death, Hallie grows and matures by the end of the novel, learning to enjoy her new life in Montana with her father. "She sat back in her chair," concludes Corcoran. "She was too tired to think much now, but it was nice to have the idea of a real school in the back of her mind. She looked over at her father. He had fallen asleep. His face had relaxed and he looked boyish, almost defenseless. She felt older than her father, almost as if the roles had been reversed and she was the parent. She leaned her head back and sighed. Growing up was strange."

Similar to many other Corcoran heroines and heroes, Hallie comes of age when confronted with new experiences that test her beliefs and endurance. It is through adventures and physical ordeals that Corcoran's characters are able to grow and reach a new level of maturity. And these growing experiences take place in mystery novels, historical novels, and contemporary novels. When not creating perceptive young adult characters, Corcoran also deals with the issue of animal welfare through wildlife books. Jean Fritz, writing in the *New York Times Book Review,* comments on one of the major messages of Corcoran's works: "'Trust life,' she says, 'Go into the world. There'll be good people out there as well as bad. There'll be help.' She handles her theme like a prism, holding it up to catch the light at different angles, turning it this way and that so that each book is a fresh experience and a variation of the pattern."

Historical Hamilton Provides Precocious Childhood

Corcoran herself varied from the pattern as early as the day of her birth. "According to my mother," she writes in *Contemporary Authors Autobiography Series (CAAS),* "my arrival, in Hamilton, Massachusetts, on April 12, 1911, was not first class. I broke her pelvis, and she never quite forgave me." This rough beginning behind her, Corcoran found herself growing up in an area that had been home to her mother's family for more than 250 years; both Corcoran's maternal grandparents spent their lives in Hamilton. Remembering her grandfather in *CAAS,* Corcoran relates, "He used to regale me with stories of the Civil War, which he got from books and newspapers. He was too young even to be a drummer boy. It was the great frustration of his life." And her grandmother, she writes, "was a sweetheart. My best friend and sharer of secrets and jokes. When she died I had my first real sorrow."

As a young child, Corcoran also shared her time and created memories with her father. Having worked his way through medical school, John Corcoran spent his days making house calls, often allowing his daughter to accompany him on weekends. And numerous other excursions were undertaken by father and daughter. In the author's memory, as she describes in *CAAS,* "he takes me to Bunker Hill Monument and the Peabody Museum and he lets me hitch my toboggan to the back of his car, and he lets me 'hook pungs' while my mother wrings her hands, expecting me to kill myself. He takes me out on the porch during thunderstorms and teaches me to like them."

Other outdoor activities with cousins and friends filled many of Corcoran's childhood winters. "In the years before I was twelve I spent a lot of time on skis and sleds and skates," she explains in *CAAS.* "I had the only toboggan on the hill, and my cousin Ernest brought me real racing skis from Canada. We built jumps on the side of the hill and collected bruises and sprained ankles." Racing down hills did nothing to hinder Corcoran's progress in other areas, such as school; she skipped the second grade and was planning to skip grade six as well until her father objected. Instead, Corcoran spent much of this year recovering from surgery for double mastoids, and later used this experience of temporary deafness in her novel *A Dance to Still Music.*

A change of schools the next year brought Corcoran encouragement to write and her first published pieces. "Since the first grade I had been writing `stories' on my father's prescription pads or whatever was handy," comments Corcoran in *CAAS.* "At twelve I wrote real stories on real paper for a real magazine, *The Turret.*" One of these stories, concerning a garter snake afraid of young girls, was inspired by the summers Corcoran spent at Camp Allegro in New Hamp-

In this successful 1974 work, a deaf runaway finds a new sense of belonging when she meets an understanding woman living in a houseboat.

shire, where it was most of her fellow campers who were the ones afraid of the snakes.

Another of Corcoran's favorite indoor activities was reading. "I was an avid reader, everything from the *Bobbsey Twins on a Houseboat* to *David Copperfield,*" recalls Corcoran in *CAAS.* "I startled my father when I was thirteen by asking for Darwin's *Origin of Species* for Christmas. I still have it." In addition to expanding reading tastes, Corcoran's thirteenth year brought one of her first traumas when her parents separated. "I was an only child, and my foundation was the three of us," she explains in *CAAS.* "Now there were two of us. My mother and I moved out of the house that I had thought of as the only conceivable place to live."

Adolescence found Corcoran attending Beverly High and racing around in her father's old Buick roadster, despite her lurking shyness. Dancing was another important activity, as Corcoran and her friends followed big band appearances all over the area, including Ella Fitzgerald and Benny Goodman. Scholarly success was not lost in the midst of all this activity, though. "I made the National Honor Society in spite of never understanding what algebra was all about," reveals Corcoran in *CAAS.* "And I was the class poet. My Camp Allegro friend, Frankie Jones, had introduced me to poetry, and I wallowed in Amy Lowell, Rupert Brooke, Edna Millay, Sara Teasdale, Keats, Shelley."

Facing the Realities of War

Breezing through her college boards—except for the chemistry section—Corcoran confidently began her freshman year at Wellesley in 1929. "Having always been the fair haired student in English, I expected to be exempted from freshman comp, and to make the news staff," writes Corcoran in *CAAS.* "I did neither. My ego was badly dented." And even though the professors and the campus were wonderful, it still took some time for Corcoran to adjust to her new surroundings. "There were highlights: like reading Wordsworth's *Prefaces* and being suddenly struck all of a heap by the wonder of abstract thought; like step singing; like Ella Keats Whiting (grandniece of John Keats) aglow over Chaucer; like Miss Manwaring reading poetry in her extraordinary voice; like sundaes at the Dainty Shoppe," describes Corcoran in *CAAS.*

After a shaky sophomore year filled with too many dances and not enough studying, Corcoran pulled her grades back up and graduated two years later in 1933. The "Real World" that Corcoran then entered was still suffering the effects of the Depression, so she lived at home while searching for a job and writing plays. The Works Progress Administration Writers Project provided Corcoran with her first job, where she wrote town histories for schools. It was her summer job as assistant stage manager and prop girl with the Oceanside Theatre that propelled Corcoran's writing forward, though.

Stage–struck by the whole experience, Corcoran had a new desire to attend Yale Drama School. Not willing to take on such an expense, her father did finance a couple of months in New York, where Corcoran engrossed herself in numerous Broadway productions. Speaking with others about her writing, Corcoran even sold a one–act play about the Spanish Revolution which was produced by several labor theatres. Leaving New York, Corcoran next travelled to North Carolina to visit a college friend for a couple of months before undertaking a series of jobs while she continued to write. "I was beginning to sell a few pieces to magazines. The first one was a humorous essay about summer theatre, sold to *Cue* for fifteen dollars," she remembers in *CAAS*. "They accepted it with a telegram, and I assumed that would be the first of many such happy telegrams, but I never got that kind of acceptance again."

Theatre work and play writing also remained an important part of Corcoran's summers, while her winters were occupied by jobs in New York. Aside from plays, Corcoran wrote short pieces for magazines and play and movie reviews for an Italian American newspaper. And the year 1940 saw two more of Corcoran's plays produced—the anti–Nazi play *From the Drawn Sword,* and *Yankee Pine,* a play relating the events of Shays' Rebellion. A play agent even tried to sell *Yankee Pine* on Broadway, but the real war that America was involved in made historical war plays less marketable.

The war years took Corcoran away from her writing and made her "useful." Forty–eight hour work weeks as a Navy inspector at a Sylvania factory proved to be an enlightening and stressful experience for Corcoran. "It was a new world for me," she reveals in *CAAS.* "I got to know women who had been working on the line all their lives. They

This 1980 mystery involves a murder on a New Orleans plantation.

were tough, funny, wary women, to whom I had to prove that I was okay in spite of being a college graduate. I made some good friends." An illness ended Corcoran's job at Sylvania, but she returned to Civil Service after working at an advertising job for a short time in Boston. Stationed in Arlington, Virginia, Corcoran decoded small sections of Japanese military telegrams. "We worked swing shift," explains Corcoran in *CAAS,* "and explored Washington by day. Compared to the Navy job, it was like a month in the country."

California Bound

Eventually returning home, Corcoran worked for a department store as an advertising manager before leaving the New England winter behind for sunny California with her mother, her cousin Helen, and one of the author's closest friends, Rosalie. "We headed south and southwest, shedding our winter underwear and heavy socks and sweaters as we went," describes Corcoran in

CAAS. "It took us a month to get to California. Provincial New Englanders that we were, we were fascinated by everything, from cotton fields to cactus. We encountered a flood in Mississippi, and Coolidge Dam, and an Indian reservation, desert, and Joshua trees. America in one long gulp."

A number of Corcoran's friends from the theatre were already living in California when she arrived, so she joined them as a prop girl for the Phoenix Theatre in Westwood. During this time, Corcoran and her family rented the third floor of Anne Lehr's house. Associated with the Hollywood Canteen, Lehr became a close friend, and Corcoran passed many happy years in her house. Eventually buying a house in the Valley, Corcoran began working at the west coast branch of Celebrity Service, where she stayed for eight years. In the meantime, she continued to sell pieces to magazines and took a course in television writing. "Mostly I learned what not to do," Corcoran relates in CAAS, "like not trying to hit a trend, because by the time a script was finished, the trend was over. I find that still to be true, even in children's books, which are on the whole far less trend influenced than adult books."

By 1953, Los Angeles was growing quickly, so after an enchanting trip to visit a friend in Missoula, Montana, Corcoran managed to get a job as a radio station copywriter and move there. Enrolling in a graduate program, Corcoran earned her M.A. and set forth for Mexico with a friend and $150. "Travelling without money is the way to have adventures," she asserts in CAAS. "It may be hell at the time, but it makes for good reminiscing long afterward." The fact that she had mono at the time made the trip even more of an adventure for Corcoran: "I have never remembered how long we stayed." Returning to Los Angeles, Corcoran went through another string of jobs, including teaching, a profession that she has maintained throughout most of her life.

Teaching eventually led Corcoran to Boulder, Colorado in 1960, and it was during her first year here that she sold a novel to Redbook. "The long Redbook story, which they called `The Runaways,' was rewritten after I started doing children's books," points out Corcoran in CAAS. "I went back to my original title, A Row of Tigers, and the only change I made was in viewpoint. I changed from the adult character's point of view to the child's." And as Corcoran's writing career began to take off in a new direction, her teaching enjoyment also con-

tinued to grow. It was shortly after her mother died that she moved back to California to teach at Palomar College.

Discovers New Audience

"During the summer I taught full time and I was also writing a novel called Sam," remembers Corcoran in CAAS. "It took me a long time to finish Sam because of the teaching schedule, but when it was finally done, I made an interesting discovery. My agent said I had written a good children's book. I told her that was not possible because I had no idea how to write children's books." Since this first children's book, Corcoran has written over seventy books for young people. "I talk to school children around the country quite a lot, and they always want to know where I `get my ideas,'" she relates in CAAS. "I try to explain that ideas are all over the place. The trick is simply in being always on the lookout for them. It's a habit, a way of looking at the world, that writers have. Even one's own most traumatic experiences are grist for the mill. Part of every writer, I think, stands aside watching himself react and taking mental notes."

Sam is the tale of a fifteen–year–old girl who has led an isolated existence on a small island in Montana with her antisocial father. When she enters school for the first time as a high school junior, she experiences a severe culture shock and is faced with many conflicts. "Corcoran portrays Sam's problems in making decisions and choices and creates an exciting story and an appealing main character," maintains Mary Lou White in an essay for the Dictionary of Literary Biography. Martha Gardner, writing in the Christian Science Monitor, concludes that Sam "is a mature, wise, and well developed story, as individual and appealing as Sam herself."

Corcoran based the story of Sam on the experiences of one of the students she taught at the University of Montana. "Her story fascinated me, and after I wrote the book, I returned several times to the theme of a young person abruptly encountering a place or a situation that is totally unfamiliar," Corcoran states in CAAS. Following the publication of this first children's book, Corcoran began to feel the toll of working too hard. After a trip to Denver, however, she returned to Palomar for four more years and began writing more children's books. It was 1969 by the time Corcoran decided to give up teaching and write full time. To do this, she returned to Missoula, where her friend Jeanne and two godchildren resided. "By this time I had an enchanting godson, Gigi's brother Jamie, who later grew up to be Jim," explains Corcoran in *CAAS*. "I had the delights of watching children develop, without having any of the problems. Both of them have provided me with much love and story material."

Among the stories resulting from this material and Corcoran's numerous other sources is her 1969 novel *Sasha, My Friend*. Similar to the story of *Sam*, this story follows the progress of fifteen year old Hallie after she moves from Los Angeles to live with her sick father on a tree farm in rural Montana. As she adapts to her new surroundings, Hallie adopts an orphaned wolf cub and eventually cultivates new friendships. "Themes of hard work, acceptance of people as they are, appreciation of nature, and family love and loyalty are well developed," notes White. And *Library Journal* contributor Cherie Zarookian asserts that *Sasha, My Friend* is written in an "unsentimental style that results

A young girl struggles to break free of her emotionally dependent mother in Corcoran's 1985 novel.

in an extremely moving and sensitive story."

Taking an approach similar to the one taken in *Sasha, My Friend*, Corcoran's *This Is a Recording* introduces another young heroine travelling from the city into nature. Marianne encounters a series of adventures when she is sent to stay with her grandmother in Montana while her parents consider divorce. In addition to experiencing a barn burning and an exciting hunting accident, Marianne also deals with her feelings about the impending split between her parents. "Though the story does not pretend to offer any great depth of insight into personalities and situations, the narrator's voice (Marianne's) has made the most of a brisk and lively surface," states Georgess McHargue in the *New York Times Book Review*. Zarookian, in her *School Library Journal* review, calls *This Is a Recording* a "superior, fast moving novel."

Just as she drew on the experience of her parents' divorce for *This Is a Recording*, Corcoran used her experience with temporary deafness while writing *A Dance to Still Music*. Published in 1974, this novel portrays fourteen–year–old Margaret's bitter struggle to accept her new deafness after a severe illness. At the same time, Margaret is dealing with a recent move to Florida, and eventually decides to hitchhike back to Maine. Along the way she encounters an injured fawn and an understanding woman who cares for her until she is ready to return home. White maintains: "Corcoran grasps the feelings of anger and frustration and skillfully develops the characters." And Fritz, writing in the *New York Times Book Review*, contends that *A Dance to Still Music* is "one of . . . Corcoran's most gripping stories." "I used my memory of the mastoid days to recreate what it feels like suddenly to be deaf," reveals Corcoran in *CAAS*. "It seemed to me that the deaf got a lot less sympathy than, for instance, the blind. People got tired of repeating, of having to raise their voices, of being misunderstood, and they were often impatient, or, worse, behaved as if the deaf person were not there. *A Dance to Still Music* remains my favorite of my own books."

Overseas Travels Bring Inspiration

Shortly after completing *A Dance to Still Music*, Corcoran fulfilled a life–long dream; she travelled to Europe with Jeanne and her godchildren. This lengthy trip took Corcoran and her fellow travellers to numerous cities and countries, including

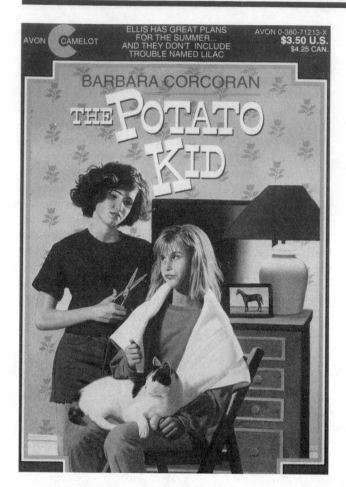

AVON CAMELOT
ELLIS HAS GREAT PLANS
FOR THE SUMMER...
AND THEY DON'T INCLUDE
TROUBLE NAMED LILAC
AVON 0-380-71213-X
$3.50 U.S.
$4.25 CAN.

BARBARA CORCORAN

THE POTATO KID

Initially resenting the difficult ten year old her family has taken in for the summer, fourteen-year-old Ellis slowly comes to understand Lilac's problems--and appreciate her friendship.

Finland, the Soviet Union, Samarkand (an ancient Arabic city), Budapest, and England. The time spent in Samarkand and Moscow eventually became the basis for two of Corcoran's books *Meet Me at Tamerlane's Tomb* and *The Clown.*

Meet Me at Tamerlane's Tomb is Corcoran's first mystery; it concerns Hardy, an overweight fourteen-year-old girl vacationing in Samarkand with her parents and younger brother. During the trip she is almost deceived into helping a drug smuggler as she comes to terms with her own insecurities. "The setting is exotic," relates White, "Hardy's character is fully developed, and the story is amusing, even though the plot is improbable. The book concludes with the two siblings' journal accounts of the adventure, which make an interesting contrast of children's writing styles." Also set in the Soviet Union, Corcoran's 1975 novel *The Clown* follows an orphaned girl who

travels to Moscow as a translator for her aunt and uncle. During the journey Lisa meets a young Russian clown and helps him escape to the free world by giving him her uncle's passport. *Bulletin of the Center for Children's Books* reviewer Zena Sutherland asserts that "the details of the planning and execution of the escape are intriguing," and concludes that *The Clown* is "a cracking good book."

Returning home to the United States, Corcoran finished a novel written under one of her pseudonyms—Paige Dixon. She had previously written under this name, and also writes under the name Gail Hamilton. The reasoning behind the use of pen names is directly tied to the marketing of her books. Once she became a full time writer, Corcoran began writing more than two books a year. Most publishers prefer that their authors aren't competing against themselves for sales, so Corcoran's publishers suggested she take another name. Because she was writing a book with a male protagonist at the time, *Lion on the Mountain,* Corcoran chose a male identity. "Later I used that name for all the wild animal books I have done, and for some others as well, whenever there was an overlap," she comments in *CAAS.*

One of the wild animal tales Corcoran wrote under the pseudonym Paige Dixon is *The Young Grizzly.* Describing the first few years of a young grizzly bear's life, Corcoran uses a bloodthirsty hunter and his hesitant son to emphasize the danger threatening the animals. A *Kirkus Reviews* contributor comments that Corcoran portrays the grizzlies "with unusual immediacy." And Patti Hagan, in the *New York Times Book Review,* states that *The Young Grizzly* "is a fine adventure story, giving a good accounting of mountain plants and animals."

With the animal tales of Paige Dixon, and her own novels, Corcoran sometimes writes even more than four books in a year, which requires yet another pseudonym. "Gail Hamilton was the pen name of a popular nineteenth century writer in my home town . . . who was a cousin of my grandfather's," explains Corcoran in *CAAS.* "She died before I was born, but I had always been intrigued by her books. The house she had lived in stood empty during my childhood; in fact, on Hallowe'en it was usually on our route because it qualified as a haunted house. By the time I was a teenager it had burned down, but I used to go and sit on the stones of the foundation, where some of the rose bushes she and her sister had planted still bloomed, and I would think about being a writer like Gail Hamilton."

Having already achieved this goal, Corcoran continued her productive schedule with the 1975 novel *May I Cross Your Golden River?*, which was written under the pseudonym Paige Dixon because of its male protagonist. In this more serious tale, eighteen–year–old Jordan must come to terms with a wasting disease of the muscles that will soon take his life. Corcoran examines both Jordan's progress toward acceptance and that of his family. Although McHargue, writing in the *New York Times Book Review*, finds *May I Cross Your Golden River?* to be rather predictable, she also maintains that "what makes the book worth reading is the warm and careful drawing of the Phillips family." A *Publishers Weekly* contributor, on the other hand, contends that the plot "is utterly convincing."

Productive Pace Continues

In the years following 1975, Corcoran won an NEA fellowship and continued to travel, eventually went back to part–time teaching, wrote a series of adult romance novels, and added numerous titles to her list of works for young adults. Among these titles are historical novels, modern problem novels, and mysteries. "Corcoran writes very quickly," White asserts, "not even pausing to make an outline. She spends two hours a day at the typewriter and also puts considerable time into revising. She is a compulsive writer, claiming that she is `restless when I'm not doing it.'"

One of the results of this restlessness is Corcoran's 1976 historical and critically acclaimed work, *Axe–Time, Sword–Time*. In this novel, set between the years 1941 and 1942, eighteen–year–old Elinor overcomes a learning disability and asserts her independence by taking a war factory job as her parents start divorce proceedings. "The homefront wartime era is re–created with accuracy, and autobiographical details from Corcoran's early years as a wartime factory worker add to the book's authenticity," asserts White. *Bulletin of the Center for Children's Books* reviewer Sutherland sees Elinor as facing common teen-age problems and concludes: "The writing is subdued but not sedate, the characters and relationships perceptively depicted."

Corcoran changed settings to one from her childhood in 1981 for a series of mysteries focusing on two young sleuths, Stella and Kim. Having attended Camp Allegro as a child, she uses the same location to set the action in her mystery *You're Allegro Dead*. Twelve year olds Stella and Kim are sent to a revival of Camp Allegro by their mothers, who attended the camp as children themselves. The visit becomes suspenseful when someone throws rocks at Stella and takes a shot at Kim. "Kim and Stella are believable characters and the clues are well placed," relates White. In their second adventure, *A Watery Grave*, Kim and Stella solve a murder mystery in their own New England town. "The story has suspense and smooth dialogue," states White. And the two friends find suspense and mystery at Camp Allegro once again in *Mystery on Ice*. Spending a winter holiday at the camp with their families and friends, Stella and Kim uncover the culprit behind a series of troubling incidents. "There's plenty of activity and a hale and hearty cast to keep the plot skating

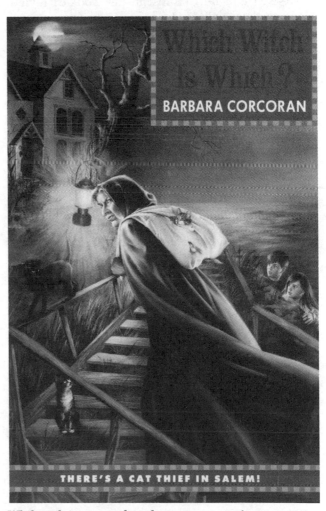

While solving a cat-burglar mystery, twins encounter a strange woman whom they believe to be a witch in this 1983 book.

smoothly along," comments Drew Stevenson in *School Library Journal.* And Denise M. Wilms, writing in *Booklist,* contends that readers will "keep on till the villain is unveiled in the final pages."

In addition to mysteries, modern–day teenage problems are the focus for many of Corcoran's realistic novels of the late 1980s and early 1990s. *You Put Up with Me, I'll Put Up with You,* published in 1987, begins when Kelly's widowed mother announces that they are moving back to her hometown with two of her friends to open a restaurant in an old school house. And on top of the move, Kelly also has to live in her grandmother's old house with these other women and their children. Determined to hate it from the start, she looks on disdainfully while everyone works on the restaurant and makes friends. As Kelly grows, though, the wall she's built begins to weaken and fall. Wilms, in her *Booklist* review, believes that Kelly's "change of heart seems to grow organically from story elements, and the supporting characters have enough dimension to make them real." *You Put Up with Me, I'll Put Up with You* is a "creative and highly readable story," concludes Judy Butler in *School Library Journal.*

Expands Family Focus

The melding of multiple families is also a major part of Corcoran's 1989 novel *The Potato Kid.* Fourteen–year–old Ellis is looking forward to a summer of horseback riding until her family decides to take on a needy child for the summer. Upon the arrival of ten–year–old Lilac, Ellis's grandfather suffers a mild heart attack, so Ellis is asked to watch out for Lilac. The two girls don't get along, and matters only get worse when Lilac's mother writes a letter telling her daughter she needs to get herself adopted because there is no longer any room for her at home. This letter, and a riding accident suffered by Ellis, eventually manage to spark the beginnings of a friendship between the two, and Ellis's grandparents decide to adopt Lilac. *The Potato Kid* "is populated with well developed, realistic characters," asserts Nancy P. Reeder in *School Library Journal.* And Jean Kaufmann, writing in *Voice of Youth Advocates,* states: "This is a smoothly written and heartwarming family story."

A family story of a different kind can be found in *Family Secrets.* Returning to the coastal town near Boston where her father grew up, Tracy learns that she was in fact adopted; her biological mother was one of her father's high school friends, Felicia Shaw. Shaw had Tracy's father and mother promise not to reveal the adoption until she died or until Tracy's eighteenth birthday; Felicia dies of cancer shortly before the family arrives, so Tracy is told. Desperate to learn everything she can about her mother, Tracy finds her answers through the delivery of a tape made by Felicia before her death. *Voice of Youth Advocates* contributor Judy Fink finds it strange that Tracy's family would move back to this town without first telling Tracy about her adoption, but also describes *Family Secrets* as "an involving and fast read, with elements of romance and suspense tied in with the theme of family being the people who care about you."

A lack of family is the problem that Corcoran's three young protagonists must overcome in her 1991 work *Stay Tuned.* Unhappy in the cheap, crime–ridden New York City hotel she's living in with her father, sixteen–year–old Stevie takes an interest in two children next door: thirteen–year old Eddie and his younger sister, Fawn. The recent death of their grandmother has left them alone. So, when Stevie takes it upon herself to leave her father to stay with relatives in New Hampshire, she takes Eddie and Fawn with her. Along the way they meet Alex, an eighteen–year–old who has also left his father because of a disagreement concerning Alex's future. The four end up at a campsite in Maine, where Alex teaches the others how to survive while allowing them to make their own decisions. Through the course of their journey, they all experience emotional growth and develop a greater understanding of others. "Corcoran's characters are likable, and readers who favor happy endings will overlook the book's implausibilities," relates Gerry Larson in *School Library Journal. Stay Tuned* is "a good read for reluctant patrons," writes Margaret Galloway in *Voice of Youth Advocates,* concluding: "There are few stories that are as engrossing as surviving on your own or with friends."

Teenage growth is one of the mainstays of Corcoran's writing, as is a love of animals, and an underlying sense of mystery and suspense. Over the course of her career, she has developed from a playwright into a prolific author of realistic fiction for children and young adults. "Corcoran's strengths in writing are that she can tell an engrossing story and that she can write on many themes," relates White. "Her main characters are usually well developed, and her animal tales are compassionate." Corcoran herself views her writing in a somewhat less important light. "I don't see myself as a great writer so I don't think either the world or I is being cheated of anything," she explains in the *Missoulian*. "I think I'm a competent writer. I know the tricks of the trade."

■ Works Cited

Butler, Judy, review of *You Put Up with Me, I'll Put Up with You, School Library Journal*, March, 1987, p. 169.

Corcoran, Barbara, *Sasha, My Friend*, Atheneum, 1969.

Corcoran, interview for the *Missoulian*, August 29, 1981.

Corcoran, essay in *Contemporary Authors Autobiography Series*, Volume 2, Gale, 1985.

Fink, Judy, review of *Family Secrets, Voice of Youth Advocates*, June, 1992, pp. 92 93.

Fritz, Jean, review of *A Dance to Still Music, New York Times Book Review*, November 17, 1974, p. 8.

Galloway, Margaret, review of *Stay Tuned, Voice of Youth Advocates*, June, 1991, p. 94.

Gardner, Martha, "The Facts about Teen–Age Fiction," *Christian Science Monitor*, November 2, 1967, p. B11.

Hagan, Patti, "Flukes, Feathers and Fur," *New York Times Book Review*, November 3, 1974, p. 46.

Kaufmann, Jean, review of *The Potato Kid, Voice of Youth Advocates*, February, 1990, p. 342.

Larson, Gerry, review of *Stay Tuned, School Library Journal*, April, 1991, p. 118.

Review of *May I Cross Your Golden River?, Publishers Weekly*, November 10, 1975, p. 55.

McHargue, Georgess, review of *This Is a Recording, New York Times Book Review*, October 3, 1971, p. 8.

McHargue, review of *May I Cross Your Golden River?, New York Times Book Review*, January 4, 1976, p. 8.

Reeder, Nancy P., review of *The Potato Kid, School Library Journal*, October, 1989, p. 116.

Stevenson, Drew, review of *Mystery on Ice, School Library Journal*, May, 1985, p. 109.

Sutherland, Zena, review of *The Clown, Bulletin of the Center for Children's Books*, January, 1976, p. 75.

Sutherland, review of *Axe–Time, Sword–Time, Bulletin of the Center for Children's Books*, September, 1976, p. 6.

White, Mary Lou, essay in *Dictionary of Literary Biography*, Volume 52, Gale, 1986.

Wilms, Denise M., review of *Mystery on Ice, Booklist*, April 15, 1985, p. 1190.

Wilms, review of *You Put Up with Me, I'll Put Up with You, Booklist*, March 15, 1987, pp. 1125 26.

Review of *The Young Grizzly, Kirkus Reviews*, March 15, 1974, p. 305.

Zarookian, Cherie, review of *Sasha, My Friend, Library Journal*, October 15, 1969, p. 3828.

Zarookian, review of *This Is a Recording, School Library Journal*, December, 1971, p. 63.

■ For More Information See

BOOKS

Contemporary Literary Criticism, Volume 17, Gale, 1981.

PERIODICALS

Library Journal, September 15, 1970, p. 3060.

New York Times Book Review, January 31, 1971, p. 26.

Publishers Weekly, August 28, 1987, p. 81.

School Library Journal, February, 1986, p. 94; October, 1986, pp. 171 72; November, 1987, p. 114; February, 1992, p. 85; September, 1993, pp. 228 29.

Voice of Youth Advocates, February, 1986, p. 391; December, 1986, p. 214.

—Sketch by Susan M. Reicha

Richie Tankersley Cusick

■ Personal

Born April 1, 1952, in New Orleans, LA; daughter of Dick (a petroleum engineer) and Louise (a homemaker; maiden name, Watts) Tankersley; married Rick Cusick (a book designer, calligrapher and graphic artist), October 4, 1980. *Education:* University of Southwestern Louisiana, B.A., 1975. *Hobbies and other interests:* Animals, reading, watching movies, listening to music (country, ethnic, pop, movie soundtracks), collecting, travel.

■ Addresses

Home and office—7501 Westgate, Lenexa, KS 66216. *Agent*—Mary Jack Wald Associates, Inc., Literary Representatives, 111 East 14th St., New York, NY 10003.

■ Career

Ochsner Foundation Hospital, New Orleans, LA, ward clerk, summers, 1970-72; Hallmark Cards, Inc., Kansas City MO, writer, 1975-84; free-lance writer. *Member:* Humane Society of the United States, National Wildlife Federation, and many other animal rights organizations, including Wolf Park, Wolf Haven, Defenders of Wildlife, and Save the Manatee.

■ Awards, Honors

Children's Choice Award, International Reading Association, 1989, for *The Lifeguard;* Book for the Teen Age citation, New York Public Library, 1990, for *Trick or Treat;* Edgar Award nomination, Mystery Writers of America, 1993, and Book for the Teen Age citation, New York Public Library, 1994, both for *Help Wanted.*

■ Writings

YOUNG ADULT

Evil on the Bayou, Dell, 1984.
The Lifeguard, Scholastic, 1988.
Trick or Treat, Scholastic, 1989.
April Fools, Scholastic, 1990.
Teacher's Pet, Scholastic, 1990.
Vampire, Archway, 1991.
Fatal Secrets, Archway, 1992.
Buffy the Vampire Slayer (novelization of screenplay by Joss Whedon), Pocket Books, 1992.
The Mall, Archway, 1992.
Silent Stalker, Archway, 1993.
Help Wanted, Archway, 1993.
The Locker, Archway, 1994.
The Drifter, Archway, 1994.
Someone at the Door, Archway, 1994.

Overdue, Archway, 1994.

ADULT

Scarecrow, Pocket Books, 1990.
Bloodroots, Pocket Books, 1992.

■ Sidelights

Richie Tankersley Cusick believes in ghosts. After all, she grew up with one, and another seems to have moved into the house she lives in now. She and her husband, Rick, think it may have come with the antique roll-top desk Rick gave Richie as a housewarming gift when they moved into their present home. Or maybe it was there all along. Wherever the ghost came from, Cusick isn't afraid of it, just as she wasn't afraid of the ghost who shared her home when she was younger. Her fascination with strange phenomena doesn't seem to allow room for fear to creep in. This, no doubt, is a trait that is extremely helpful in Cusick's line of work. She writes horror novels for teens and adults, and revels in exploring the dark side of human nature.

The ghost she grew up with was a friendly one, according to Cusick. "He was very mischievous," she told *Author and Artists for Young Adults (AAYA)* in an interview, "and he would cause havoc a lot of times. But I always felt like he was watching out for me. He used to knock on the wall above my bed. I'd talk to him, and he'd knock." Cusick has a particularly strong memory of the ghost looking out for her well-being when she was seriously ill during her junior year in college. "I had mono and hepatitis, and my mother had to leave because her mother was dying, and my father was working. The ghost came back that night—he hadn't been there in a long time. But he came back the night my mother left, when I was alone, and he knocked on the wall. And he knocked every night until I got well." Cusick and her parents always knew when the ghost was around, partly because they could sense his presence, and partly because things would disappear, only to turn up in strange places later on. (One of his favorite pranks was removing ornaments from the tree at Christmas when everyone was out of the house.) The ghost would make his presence known by making noise, too. "Once," Cusick remembered, "my parents were in the living room and heard loud banging and crashing noises coming from my room, but no one was in there. My father wasn't the type to believe in any of this, but even he

thought something really weird was going on."

A Southern Childhood with Midwestern Influences

Cusick and her parents moved into the house with the ghost when she was in junior high. Even before that, though, she had an upbringing that nurtured a fertile imagination and provided rich background material for some of the books she would write later in life. An only child, Cusick was born and raised in New Orleans. She spent her earliest years in Barataria, a tiny neighborhood literally situated on the bayou. Cusick's father worked for an oil company, and the family lived in a company camp. The men would often be

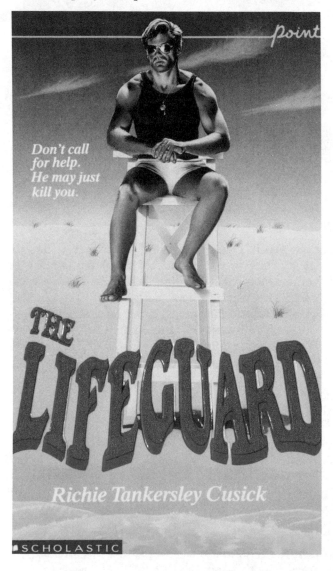

An apparent drowning accident may in fact have been a murder in Cusick's 1988 novel, which received a Children's Choice Award.

offshore for several days at a time, but some men were always left behind to help the women and children. "There was a chicken wire fence," Cusick related, "and mothers lived in constant fear of their kids falling into the bayou, and of the snakes. All the houses were up on concrete blocks (in case of flooding, because the land was below sea level).

"We were really out in the boonies. I remember there was a tavern where people hung out to visit. There was a country doctor who lived nearby. His big old house was at the end of a long driveway made of crushed oyster shells, because they didn't have gravel. I was very young—too young to start school—but I still remember the road into town that went over a drawbridge, and you could see the shrimp boats on the water. The trees had moss dripping down, and on the other side of the bridge there was a cemetery with all the graves built into tombs on top of the ground. On All Hallow's Eve, people would light candles and leave them burning at night, and shadows would flicker along the graves. Sometimes we'd take boat rides on the bayou, and we could see these old plantation homes back through the trees, just standing there empty and abandoned and wasting away.

"I also remember there was a big oak tree that overhung the road between Barataria and New Orleans. It was called Lafitte Oak, because according to legend, the ghost of the pirate Jean Lafitte would gallop his horse down this road every night at midnight. My mother used to drive like hell so we wouldn't be under that tree after dark."

Cusick drew heavily on vivid memories like these in writing one of her first books, *Evil on the Bayou,* and one of her adult novels, *Bloodroots,* both of which are set in the South. Her work is also strongly affected by her ties to the Midwest. Cusick now lives in Kansas near Kansas City, Missouri, and her parents were originally from the Midwest. As a child, Cusick spent summers and holidays with her grandparents and great-grandparents in Missouri, special times that helped to ignite her innate creativity. As she told *Something about the Author (SATA)*, "At Great-Grandma Watts's house I would make up stories out loud to myself and accompany them with my own 'soundtrack' which I would bang out on the piano (I couldn't play then and I still can't). At Great-Grandma McClure's house I would make up stories and recite them aloud, even though she

kept coming in and asking me who I was talking to. At Granny and Grandpa Watts' I would spend long summer days writing on the banks of the Gasconade River, fishing, exploring, and playing guitar and writing my own songs. At Grandma and Grandpa Tankersley's house I would write for hours in what I called my 'attic room'—which was really in the basement."

The times spent with her grandmother, Dereatha Tankersley, were particularly important to Cusick, who cites her grandmother as her biggest inspiration. "Grandma has always been there for me," she said in an interview with Barbara Kramer for *Mystery Scene* magazine. "When other people got annoyed with me because I'd start stories and never finish them, Grandma was the one who was never too busy to listen—she had a knack for drawing me out, making me think about where I could take the story and all its possibilities. She'd ask me questions about what I thought characters were like, or what I thought might happen." In addition to providing Cusick with creative stimuli, her grandmother also supplied love, friendship, and a sense of wonder. "She has a way of looking at the world with total wonder, and never takes anything for granted. . . ," Cusick told *SATA*. "She always has time for kindness and encouragement, and she has always believed in me. She has the most beautiful heart and spirit. I will always cherish her." Even at age ninety-four, Dereatha Tankersley continues to be a source of inspiration for Cusick and is, Cusick told Kramer, "my best friend."

Not too surprisingly, Cusick describes herself as having been a great reader as a child, and credits her parents with having encouraged her in this area. She was also the group storyteller in Brownies and Girl Scouts, entertaining the others with scary tales. Cusick, who loved frightening movies as a child (although her parents didn't want her to watch them), even wrote her first scary story when she was only eight or nine. It was called "Tommy Lizard's First Halloween," and featured the author's own drawing of Tommy vomiting a black jelly bean.

Writing as a Career

Although Cusick continued writing through high school and college, she told Jerome Maag of the *Journal Herald* of North Johnson County that she rarely finished her stories, perhaps because she always tried to write novels. "I was never very good at short stories," Cusick told Maag. "I always went for the long stuff. I just went with it, wherever it took me. I never knew how long it was going to be." While nothing came of these early attempts at creating fiction, Cusick's fascination with the written word did lead her to an early career as a different kind of writer. After college she joined the staff of Hallmark and turned out verse and prose that appeared on greeting cards, posters, the backs of puzzle packages, and in advertising—more or less everything that Hallmark produced. At the time, Hallmark had only eight staff writers, and they serviced the entire company. Cusick stayed in her position at Hallmark for nine years, finally leaving to become a freelance writer. "It was fun," Cusick said of her work at Hallmark, "but after nine years, coming up with one more way to say 'I love you' is a real challenge."

While she was working as a freelance writer, Cusick happened to read a book in the young adult "Twilight" series that was published by Dell's Cloverdale imprint. Prior to this time, Cusick told *AAYA,* "I hadn't really thought about getting into young adult novels, but I thought, 'this is something I'd really like to do.' So I wrote and asked them if they were accepting manuscripts, and they sent me back a tip sheet. I wrote the novel, and they took it. It was so easy." Cusick remarked, however, that she got paid very little for the book because she did not have a literary agent to represent her, and also signed a contract that was decidedly disadvantageous. "I think I owed them books until I died," Cusick said. As it turned out, Cusick found an agent who managed to get her out of the contract. Dell only published four more books in the series after Cusick's came out, and *Evil on the Bayou* was her first and last book for them. She wrote several more novels, but had no luck getting published again until a few years later, when she submitted a manuscript to Scholastic. They didn't purchase that novel, but liked her style enough to suggest she write a young adult novel for their summer promotion. The result was *The Lifeguard,* in which a teenage girl visits an exotic island and discovers that lifeguards can also be murderers. Cusick wrote four more books for Scholastic over the next four years, before moving to the Archway paperback imprint, where she has been producing novels at the rate of two or three every year.

Although Cusick's novels often make the young adult bestseller lists at Waldenbooks and B.

Cited as a Book for the Teen Age by the New York Public Library, this 1989 thriller revolves around a creepy old house where a murder took place.

Dalton's bookstores, she is aware that she has not yet achieved the status of some authors who enjoy instant name recognition among teens, and she worries that her books may be overlooked in the current glut in the young adult horror market. "You'd like to think that kids are discerning readers," she said in her interview, "but they're not always. The kids care if it's a good story more than about your writing skills." Nevertheless, Cusick pays as much attention to how her books as written as to the action. "I will agonize," she related. "I'll sit there for hours over a paragraph. If it doesn't sound right to me, I won't do it." The quality of her writing is important to her, and Cusick is appreciative when her readers recognize this. One of her favorite letters came from an eleven-year old named Geoff who, as Maag noted, "showed that he has a future as a publicist." Cusick told Maag that the reader "wrote that whenever he saw one of my books in the store, he thought, 'if it's a Cusick book, it's a quality book.'"

The critics, unfortunately, are not always as positive. "Basically, I always get crummy reviews," Cusick told *AAYA*. "You try to harden yourself, but sometimes it's difficult. I've had some reviews where the critics have commented on things that were never actually *in* the book. But you have to keep a good attitude. I try to tell myself, hey, even Anne Rice gets bad reviews sometimes!" Cusick's negative reviews have included Sybil Steinberg's description of *The Lifeguard* in *Publishers Weekly* as a "relentless procession of gruesome events and false alarms" that will leave most readers "more dazed than alarmed." (Nevertheless, *The Lifeguard* was selected as a Children's Choice book by the International Reading Association.) *Publishers Weekly* critic Diane Roback similarly faults *Vampire* as overly complicated, writing that "even die-hard fans of the genre will find little to relish in this tedious would-be horror tale." Still, Cusick's work has received a measure of praise from some critics. In *Voice of Youth Advocates*, Drue Wagner-Mees calls *Vampire* "an excellent mix of the macabre and contemporary campy, surreal characterizations" even as she criticizes *Silent Stalker* for dragging on "much too long." Stephanie Zvirin, in a *Booklist* review, calls *Trick or Treat* "a tried and true scenario, but one that is eerie enough to entertain," and Melinda D. Waugh, in *Kliatt,* writes that "*Bloodroots* is another winner from Cusick, sure to be a hit with the many lovers of the genre."

A Job That's Easy to Love

Reviews like these are gratifying, but regardless of what the critics have to say, Cusick always enjoys her job, although she commented that "writing is very hard work." Sometimes, though, the most difficult part is just convincing herself to get started. She told *SATA* that "the hardest part of writing is going up to my studio. Once I'm up there, I can lose myself in my research and writing and am very comfortable surrounded by all my clutter. But getting up there is the procrastination I'm best at—my husband refers to it as 'the long walk upstairs.'"

Once she's settled in, Cusick likes to set a mood for crafting horror by playing music—often movie soundtracks from horror movies—and sometimes by dimming the lights and writing by candlelight. She can get so wrapped up in her stories that, she said in her interview, "I lose all track of where I am and what hour of the day or night it is." As she told Maag, "I love that feeling of being in a story. It's magic." When a book goes well, Cusick told *AAYA,* there's nothing like that feeling. Sometimes the stories just take off, and "it's like you get in this car and hang on for the ride of your life." *Someone at the Door* was like that, and Cusick says she had the same experience, more or less, with *The Lifeguard* and *Trick or Treat.*

Cusick's method for crafting her stories may be somewhat unusual among writers of horror novels. "I never know who the bad guy is until about three-quarters of the way through," she told *AAYA*. "I don't outline. I hate outlines—they make me crazy." Instead of plotting out the action before starting to write, Cusick chooses her characters, using photographs from magazines or movie stills to provide her with visual images. Then she chooses a setting, and if a house or other dwelling (like the castle in *Silent Stalker*) figures prominently in the story, she'll find pictures or even house plans that are suitable. The pictures and plans go up on the bulletin board in her studio, so she can refer to them often as she writes. Then she starts writing. As she told Kramer, "a lot of times I don't know what [the characters] are going to be like, they'll just take off and do what they want."

This method of writing has its advantages and its drawbacks, Cusick said in her interview. "I think sometimes people don't figure out the endings too quickly because I haven't figured it out while I'm writing, so it's more spontaneous." This spontaneity "makes it more fun for me. I don't feel inhibited, and I don't have to stick to anything." On the other hand, Cusick also said that "sometimes I write myself into a corner. I did that with *The Drifter.* That book was horrible to write. In reading it you'd never know the agony I suffered." Cusick's most recently completed novel, ironically titled *Overdue* (which was its status at the publisher for months), was a similarly frustrating experience at times. Cusick said, "I told my editor, 'If I'd given you every four chapters I've started over, you'd have three books by now.' I'd get to chapter four and start over. I did that about seven times. I just couldn't go on until I got it right."

Another drawback to not knowing who her villain is until the end is that when Cusick finally identifies the bad guy, she has to go back and make sure everything fits together properly, and that there's nothing that happens that would rule out that person as the culprit. This process is eased along by Cusick's attitude, which is that nothing she has written is cast in stone. She learned to be professional and willing to make changes during her stint at Hallmark, where, she said, "you *couldn't* be married to your work. You had to go through committees, and six versions, and do backups." This experience helped her to learn that "sometimes what you write could be made better." Revisions have also been made easier by Cusick's trust in and good relationship with her editors and agent. "I've learned so much working with them. They bring out the best in me, and I feel like we make a great team."

Slaying Vampires with Buffy

One book that provided Cusick with an entirely different writing experience was the novelization of Joss Whedon's screenplay for *Buffy the Vampire Slayer*. Archway acquired the rights to the novelization, and then asked Cusick if she would be interested in writing it. In spite of a grueling schedule at the time—she was already under tight deadline pressure for two novels, one adult and one young adult—Cusick jumped at the chance. It was the right decision, in spite of the pressure. "The screenplay was absolutely wonderful," Cusick said. "Some of the one-liners were so funny—I was just roaring up there in my studio." The comic relief was a brief but welcome change from the straight horror Cusick usually writes.

Her role in writing the novelization consisted of fleshing out the screenplay by adding descriptions and atmosphere to the dialog. The process was challenging, partly because the movie was not yet made. At first Cusick didn't even know who was playing the major characters, making accurate descriptions difficult at best. Cusick also felt a certain amount of pressure not to tread on another writer's toes by changing his work. "With a screenplay," she said, "you can't really make it your own, and that's hard. I tried to be very careful not to mess around with the writing too much, to do word for word as much as possible."

Cusick's attempts to be true to the screenplay were somewhat thwarted by other forces, however. After the novelization was written, Archway sold it to a book club that planned to market the book to young children through elementary schools. To meet their standards, they wanted much of the language and the sexual innuendo edited out. It bothered Cusick to have to make some of the changes, because she felt they really altered the humor and flavor of the story, not to mention the personalities of the characters, but she respected and understood their concerns for their particular audience. When she received additional demands for changes that were irrelevant, however, Cusick and her editor at Archway refused. Although Cusick worried about toning down the novelization, in the end, she said, "I felt like the book followed the screenplay more closely than the movie," and the experience remained a positive one. "It was like a vacation for me," she told Steve Paul of the *Kansas City Star*. "I've never had so much fun."

A Fascination with the Dark Side

The mood in Cusick's own books tend to be much blacker than that of *Buffy the Vampire Slayer*. Cusick's fascination with the supernatural can be seen in many of her plots, with hints of ghosts, vampires and evil curses not uncommon. For example, in *Help Wanted*, Robin Bailey becomes entangled with a mysterious rich family when she takes a job cataloging books in their vast library. She befriends Claudia, the teenage stepdaughter in the family, and comes to believe Claudia's claim that she is being haunted by her dead mother. The reader, along with Robin, is led to think that some supernatural force may be at work, but in the end the villains are entirely human. This is also true of *The Drifter*, in which Carolyn Baxter and her mother move into a creepy old house on an island that is almost perpetually fog-shrouded. Carolyn becomes convinced she hears the voices of drowned sailors calling out to her, and that the house is haunted by a woman who was murdered there years before. Again, though, the supernatural events Carolyn thinks she has witnessed have actually been concocted by human beings with evil intentions. Cusick told *AAYA* that while she finds the occult interesting, it's the dark side of *human* nature that she ultimately prefers to address in her work. "We all have a dark side," she said. "I feel like if you acknowledge it, and sort of make friends with it, you can deal with it better." Cusick seems to enjoy exploring the reasons behind the cruelty human beings sometimes inflict on each other. Her villains are driven by greed, lust, jealousy, or a twisted desire for love—more or less the whole range of negative human emotions.

The author, who was born on April Fools Day, enjoys devising horrific pranks for her characters to play.

Her heroines, on the other hand, are always girls who are doing their best to be good people, but who suddenly find themselves caught up in horrendous and terrifying situations, through no fault of their own. As Cusick told Steve Paul, "sometimes we can be doing just what we're supposed to be doing, and these horrible things happen to us, and it's totally beyond our control. You don't know why it happened, and it fills you with such anguish." One real-life horror story that deeply affected Cusick was that of a local teenage girl who was abducted from the end of her own driveway while waiting for her schoolbus, and then killed. "She was doing exactly what she was supposed to be doing, being good," Cusick said in her interview, "and she ends up being murdered. Something like that is impossible to understand."

These "bad surprises," as Cusick calls them, are at the center of Cusick's novels, but unlike real life, her stories often end happily, with a hint of romance in the future for her heroines. Cusick thinks this is part of the appeal of her books and notes that her editor at Archway once pointed out that her female characters generally have three handsome and charming (if often enigmatic and potentially threatening) guys pursuing them. "What girl wouldn't like that idea?" Cusick asked, although she says the pattern is not one she follows intentionally.

Cusick also thinks that the scares her books provide may give teens a means of coping with some of the anxieties of growing up, although parents sometimes worry about the effects of horror novels on their children. "I just feel like it's a safe way to have fun," she told Steve Paul. "Kids have always liked to be scared. That's why we have roller coasters and ghost stories around the campfire. There are so many really scary stories out there all the time in real life. Kids today are faced with more responsibilities and legitimate fears than ever before. But if they get scared by a book, they can close it. . . . It's a fun way to be scared."

Cusick still enjoys a good scary book herself. She loves to read Elizabeth George, Stephen King and Mary Higgins Clark, and Anne Rice is her favorite contemporary author. Cusick's taste in literature is wide, however, and she cites books from Dickens, Hawthorne and the Bronte sisters to Sidney Sheldon and John Grisham as among her reading material. She also has a special fondness for young adult novels, especially those by Joan Aiken, Margaret Mahy, and Lois Duncan. She does not, however, read much young adult horror fiction while she's writing her own. "There's a reason for that," she says. "I don't want to be influenced by someone else's ideas."

Not that coming up with her own ideas presents a problem for Cusick. She keeps files on just about everything she finds interesting, including castles, teenagers, relationships, quotes, outdoor scenery, dogs, farms, Americana, and of course, the supernatural. Just about anything can spark her imagination, from books to movies to newspaper articles.

"There are millions of ideas everywhere," she said, "if you just look around."

Gargoyles and Ghosts

Perhaps some of her inspiration comes from the atmosphere Cusick has created in her own home. She is an avid collector, and while many of the objects she collects, like stuffed sheep and teddy bears, are chosen because they are peaceful or cute and cuddly, others are more sinister, like the collection of gargoyles that inhabits shelves in her studio. Another gargoyle guards the living room mantel, and visitors to her studio are greeted by a realistic skull that grins from the top of her computer. Every Halloween, Cusick's favorite holiday, she and her husband go all out to set the mood for terror: they lay out

In Cusick's 1992 suspense novel, Ryan's sister dies mysteriously, and Ryan may be the next target.

"poor, departed Elizabeth," a fake corpse, in the parlor, and set up "Death" beside her to keep vigil. Another "corpse" hangs from a noose in the downstairs hallway, and the front yard becomes a small graveyard, complete with sound effects. Even Hannah and Meg, Cusick's cocker spaniels (and the namesakes of the sisters in *Someone at the Door*), get into the act with scary costumes.

Then, of course, there's the ghost that Cusick is convinced shares their home, at least part of the time. The desk that may have brought the ghost to them was owned by the director of a funeral parlor back in the 1800s. When her husband purchased the desk, Cusick said, he commented to the previous owners that his wife would really like it if the desk were haunted. "They looked at each other and said something ambiguous, like 'oh, it's interesting, all right,'" Cusick related. Whether or not the ghost came with the desk, weird things happen in the Cusick household, and most of the time the activity seems to center on Richie's studio. A friend who was dog-sitting Hannah and Meg heard noises coming from the studio when no one else was in the house, and once had a particularly disturbing and vivid dream while staying at the Cusicks'. She dreamt she woke up and walked to the bedroom doorway, where she saw a young man going down the hall toward Cusick's studio. When she asked the young man a question, he turned and looked back over his shoulder at her, providing her with a visual image so real, Cusick said, that her friend could pick him out in a crowd today. Cusick's friend woke up to the sound of Hannah barking. The dog was standing in the hallway, looking at the spot where the apparition had appeared in the dream. Other strange occurrences have included a sliding glass door that closed itself when there was no wind, lights that turn themselves on, and even voices that Cusick and her husband have heard when no one else is in the house.

Cusick intends to keep herself perpetually open to the possibilities behind the strange happenings in her house and in life in general. No doubt this desire to explore the unexplainable will continue to be an influence in the fiction she writes, including the novels—for teens and for adults—she has in progress. "I believe in everything," she said. "Why not? There's so much we can't explain."

■ Works Cited

Cusick, Richie Tankersley, interview with Sarah Verney for *Authors and Artists for Young Adults,* 1994.

Kramer, Barbara, "Interview: Richie Tankersley Cusick," *Mystery Scene,* April, 1991, pp. 49-50.

Maag, Jerome, "Horror and Humdrum," *Journal Herald* (North Johnson County, KS), January 15, 1992.

Paul, Steve, "Vampire Slaying No Problem for Lenexa Woman," *Kansas City Star,* August 9, 1992.

Roback, Diane, review of *Vampire, Publishers Weekly,* June 7, 1991, p. 66.

Something about the Author, Volume 67, Gale, 1990.

Steinberg, Sybil, review of *The Lifeguard, Publishers Weekly,* July 8, 1988, p. 57.

Wagner-Mees, Drue, review of *Silent Stalker, Voice of Youth Advocates,* October, 1993, p. 224.

Waugh, Melinda D., review of *Blood Roots, Kliatt,* March, 1993, p. 4.

Zvirin, Stephanie, review of *Trick or Treat, Booklist,* February 1, 1990, p. 1078.

■ For More Information See

PERIODICALS

Children's Book Watch, November, 1992, p. 6.

School Library Journal, December, 1984, p. 101.

Voice of Youth Advocates, April, 1989, p. 26; October, 1990, pp. 215, 226; June, 1992, p. 93; April, 1993, pp. 24, 38.

—Sketch by Sarah Verney

Frank Deford

commentator, 1986-1989; ESPN, New York City, commentator, 1991—; *Vanity Fair,* New York City, feature writer, 1993—. Cystic Fibrosis Foundation, Washington, DC, trustee, 1973—, chairman, 1984—.

■ Awards, Honors

Eclipse Award, National Racing Association, 1975, 1984; award for excellence in sport journalism, Center for Study of Sport in Society, Northeastern University, 1985; award for distinguished service to journalism, University of Missouri, 1987; Emmy Award, 1988, for television writing and commentary; Sportswriter of the Year, National Association of Sportswriters and Sportscasters, 1982, 1983, 1984, 1985, 1986, 1987, 1988; National Magazine Writer of the Year, *Washington Journalism Review,* 1987, 1988; Nation's Best Sportswriter, *American Journalism Review,* 1993.

■ Personal

Born December 16, 1938, in Baltimore, Maryland; son of Benjamin F., Jr. (a businessman) and Louise (McAdams) Deford; married Carol Penner, August 28, 1965; children: Christian McAdams, Alexandra Miller (died 1980), Scarlet Faith. *Education:* Princeton University, A.B., 1962. *Politics:* Democrat. *Religion:* Episcopalian. *Hobbies and other interests:* Reading, history, traveling.

■ Addresses

Home and office—73 Clapboard Hill Rd., Westport, CT 06436. *Agent*—Sterling Lord, 1 Madison Avenue, New York, NY 10010.

■ Career

Author, sportswriter, television and radio commentator. *Sports Illustrated,* New York City, writer, 1962-1989; *The National Sports Daily,* New York City, editor-in-chief, 1989-1991; National Public Radio, Washington, DC, commentator, 1980—; Cable News Network, New York City, commentator, 1980-1986, 1991—; NBC Sports, New York City,

■ Writings

NONFICTION

There She Is: The Life and Times of Miss America, Viking, 1971.
Five Strides on the Banked Track: The Life and Times of the Roller Derby, Little, Brown, 1971.
Big Bill Tilden: The Triumphs and the Tragedy, Simon & Schuster, 1976.
(With Arthur Ashe) *Arthur Ashe: Portrait in Motion,* Houghton Mifflin, 1975.
(With Jack Kramer) *The Game: My 40 Years in Tennis,* Putnam, 1979.

(With Billie Jean King) *Billie Jean*, Viking, 1982, published in England as *The Autobiography of Billie Jean King*, Granada, 1982.

Alex: The Life of a Child (also see below), Viking, 1983.

Lite Reading, Penguin, 1984.

(Essays) *The World's Tallest Midget: The Best of Frank Deford*, Little, Brown, 1987.

(With Pam Shriver and Susan B. Adams) *Passing Shots: Pam Shriver on Tour*, McGraw-Hill, 1987.

Sports People (photographs by Walter Iooss, Jr.), H. N. Abrams, 1988.

FICTION

Cut 'n' Run, Viking, 1973.

The Owner, Viking, 1976.

Everybody's All-American, Viking, 1981.

The Spy in Deuce Court, G. P. Putnam's Sons, 1986.

Casey on the Loose, Viking, 1989.

Love and Infamy, Viking, 1993.

OTHER

(Editor) *Best American Sports Writing, 1993*, Houghton Mifflin, 1993.

Got to Do Some Coachin': Nolan's Play (four-act play), Rose Publishing, 1988.

(Author of script) *Arthur Ashe: Citizen of the World*, Home Box Office (HBO), 1994.

Contributor to *Champions: Their Glory and Beyond*, Little, Brown, 1993. Author of screenplay for *Trading Hearts*, 1988.

■ Adaptations

Everybody's All-American, Warner Brothers, 1988.

■ Work in Progress

Kathryn's Pool, a fictional account of a boy growing up in Baltimore in the early 1950s who befriends a young woman with polio.

■ Sidelights

"A guy stopped me in McDonald's the other day and asked me, 'Hey, aren't you famous?,'" novelist and sportswriter Frank Deford told *Authors and Artists for Young Adults (AAYA)* contributor Tom Pendergast. "I said, 'I'm fringe-famous.' That's what I am. I'll tell you the funniest thing that ever happened to me. I'm walking down 42nd St. in New York City, and I stopped at a corner and overheard these two guys who had passed me. One guy says to the other, 'There goes the best writer in the world.' The other guy says, 'Who?' The first one says, 'Well, Frank Deford.' And the second one says, 'Who's he?' And that was it. He hadn't the foggiest idea who I was. That's sort of the way people look at me. I get recognized just enough that its fun, and nobody says anything rotten to me."

Modesty aside, Deford is probably more than "fringe famous." Widely recognized as one of the greatest living sportswriters, Deford defined intelligent sportswriting during his twenty-seven years with the weekly *Sports Illustrated*. Deford offered *Sports Illustrated* readers probing features of athletes and coaches that went beyond mere scores and statistics to explore the motivations and emotions of people who dedicated their lives to competing. His "features" take more extended form in the many books he has written, profiling competitors from Miss America to tennis stars Billie Jean King and Arthur Ashe. And in the 1980s, Deford began to offer commentary on the world of sports for National Public Radio (NPR), Cable News Network (CNN), and ESPN radio.

In the 1990s, Deford shifted the attention of his features to "the movers and the shakers," and his prose portraits began to appear in *Newsweek* and *Vanity Fair*. Though he is best known for his connection with sports, Deford has always been more than a sportswriter, having published a number of novels that are set in the world of sports and, in 1993, penning his first historical novel, *Love and Infamy*, which earned Deford the kind of praise usually reserved for his sportswriting. Content now to pen a few magazine features a year, Deford concentrates on becoming what he has always wanted to be: a successful novelist.

A Terrible Childhood for a Writer

"For a writer, I had a terrible thing—a happy childhood," Deford remembered. "A writer should have a deprived and contentious childhood, but mine was especially peaceful and I had a mother and father who I adored." Born December 16, 1938, Deford grew up on the edge of Baltimore, Maryland, in an era when city could give way to country in the space of a block. "I grew up within the city limits," said Deford, "but down the street was what we called 'the mule pasture,' where a mule had been not long ago." His father, Benjamin, worked for a small company but was, ac-

Based on Deford's 1981 novel, the 1988 film *Everybody's All-American*, starring Dennis Quaid and Jessica Lange, concerns the star player in the 1957 Sugar Bowl, and his life in the South over the next twenty-five years.

cording to his son, "a frustrated farmer—if he had the money he would have just raised chickens." Louise, his mother, raised Frank and his two younger brothers, Mac and Gill, and kidded her husband by making up stationary for the Mossway Poultry Farm that listed her as president. "That house on Mossway was the only one I ever knew," recalled Deford, "and when I got married and had kids I still came back and slept in the same bedroom I had when I was a kid."

Deford was a writer before he was a jock, as he learned when he was 10 years old. "We would be assigned little compositions in class and I found out I loved to do it," he told Pendergast. Just as some kids learn that they can throw a ball better than others, Deford learned that he could write better and that it made others happy. "Teachers liked me because of it, and my friends liked me because of it," said Deford, who penned articles for the school newspaper, which he also edited. "I just loved to write and I did it well. Where I came from it was not considered sissy that I was a writer. It was something that made me more popular, more special."

Deford was also a jock from an early age, but insists that he wasn't very good at anything except basketball. "My problem was that I grew very late. I was so skinny. God, I was miserably skinny. Finally, I blossomed in my senior year and made all-city and everything else." Deford was good enough to make the Junior Varsity team at Princeton University, where he attended college beginning in 1957, but says that his career as a college athlete was summed up by his basketball coach, who told him, "Deford, you write basketball better than you play it." So Deford stuck to writing, running his college paper, the *Daily Princetonian,* writing two plays that were produced on campus, and submitting his short fiction for publication. For two summers, Deford worked as a copy boy for the Baltimore *Evening Sun,* gaining practical experience as a journalist while he gained a degree in history and sociology.

The World's Tallest Midget

"If anybody ever told me I would be a sportswriter when I got out of college, I would have said 'not that likely,'" Deford told Pendergast. Deford had paid no special attention to sportswriting in high school or college; it was just one of the many things he wrote about. When he graduated from Princeton in 1962, he wanted to go to New York City to write. *Sports Illustrated,* which began publication in 1954, fit the bill. Through much of the 1960s, Deford wrote sports coverage for the magazine, interviewing players and coaches and reporting on games. Deford looks on those days as the "good old days" of sportswriting: the players were not all millionaires and television coverage was not so universal or invasive, so athletes didn't mind spending time talking with sportswriters. In fact, they were often eager to "get some ink."

In the world of journalism, however, sportswriters were often looked down upon. They were not "real" writers, said those writers who thought they were, and sports departments in major newspapers were often called "toy shops." "Sportswriting is assumed to be second-rate," wrote Deford in *The World's Tallest Midget,* a collection of his best sportswriting published in 1987, "and, therefore, if any sportswriting is not second-rate, then, ergo, it must not be sportswriting." Being called a good sportswriter was thus a highly-qualified compliment, like being called the world's tallest midget. Deford suffered this snobbery along with other sportswriters and, though he insists he never felt embarrassed about being a sportswriter, admits that he sometimes asked himself, "Am I being frivolous doing this?"

"I can't imagine that any of us worth a dime doesn't go through a phase in which we question whether it is a fulfilled life in the toy shop," Deford continued. "I could visualize grandchildren coming up to me in my dotage and saying, 'Big Daddy, what did you do during Vietnam?' And I would reply that I had been at the NBA playoffs. Or, 'Poppy, where were you during the Civil Rights movement?' And I would explain that I missed that because of the Stanley Cup. But finally, I resolved the issue with myself: that I am a writer, and that incidentally I write mostly about sports, and what is important is to write well, the topic be damned."

By the end of the 1960s, Deford had embarked on a new kind of sportswriting, the feature, that helped him avoid the dilemma of being the world's tallest midget. Deford's features were personal profiles that explored the lives of interesting people who happened to be involved in sports, and he became known for his ability to offer insights into the inner workings of people's minds. Paul Loop, writing in the *Orange County Register,* described Deford's essays as "a mix of unlikely intellectualism, graceful, beautifully paced

Deford created the *National*—America's first all-sports daily—with publisher Peter Price, and was editor-in-chief from 1989 to 1991.

storytelling and a constant stretching for the essential detail that reveals character." For Deford, writing features was ideal: "I was extraordinarily happy doing features," he told Pendergast. "That's what I wanted to do and that's what I did best, and it didn't really make a hell of a lot of difference to me whether I was writing about sports guys or somebody else."

Among Deford's most notable features are those on University of Alabama football coach Bear Bryant, Indiana University basketball coach Bobby Knight, and East Mississippi Junior College football coach Bob "Bull" "Cyclone" Sullivan. The first two coaches were known for being tough, but Bull Cyclone, who no one outside of Scooba, Mississippi, had ever heard of, "was the toughest coach of them all," wrote Deford, "so tough he had to have two nicknames." People didn't have to be famous to be captured by Deford's pen, they just had to be interesting.

A High School Date

Deford described the process of interviewing for a feature as being "like a high school date. You are both trying to get something out of each other. You both want a good story, but your ideas of what makes a good story are two different things." One of the keys for Deford lies in being a sympathetic and nonconfrontational listener. "Part of it is a gift of getting people to talk, getting them to relax. I try to like people and find out what it is that they like, and to do that I have to be a bit of an actor. If I'm with someone who likes to stay up all night and party, for example, then I'll stay up all night and party. Then they think, 'Hey, this guy stays up all night and parties, he's my buddy.' But if someone wants to get up early and go to church, I'll go to church."

Sometimes just getting the story is the most difficult part, Deford told Pendergast. At one point Deford was asked to write a piece on Bobby Knight, who was hostile to *Sports Illustrated* because that magazine had often criticized him. "I wrote him a letter and we started a negotiation," remembered Deford, who joked that the North Korean nuclear arms negotiations could not have been any more elaborate than what he went through. "I remember early on I told him, 'Look, I've got no bone to pick with you, Bobby.' And the son-of-a-bitch had found a throwaway line about him I had put in a movie review two years before and read it back to me and said 'Oh,

yeah?' I was just dead in the water." But the negotiations went on, and finally Knight agreed. "Once he agreed to go out with me—to have the high school date with me—then he wanted me to take him to the prom," laughed Deford. "He was going to do everything he could to show me what was good and bright about him." The article, titled "The Rabbit Hunter," was so successful that *Sports Illustrated* ran it in a commemorative edition in 1994.

Deford knew that he was doing a good job when his colleagues said, "Man, you really got him," but says that the meaning of "getting someone" has changed over the years. "When I started out, 'getting someone' was the supreme compliment, because it meant that I had captured them. Now when you say you got someone, it means you exposed them. In that way I am sort of a dinosaur, because what I want to do is capture somebody and describe them and paint them. I love to place people in their context of time and place, where they came from, what they're connected to, what makes them tick. All those things I just adore doing, those are my favorite kinds of stories, not only writing about someone, but explaining them, where they came from, who they are."

Reaching the Top

Deford began to attract attention with his features in the 1970s, and it didn't hurt that he began to publish a number of popular books. In *There She Is: The Life and Times of Miss America*, Deford described the "incredibly arbitrary, imperfect, and inconsistent" system that crowns the most beautiful girl in America. *There She Is*, a look at the inner workings of an American cultural institution, received more publicity and more reviews than any of Deford's other works, and Audrey Cahill of *Library Journal* praised Deford for his "insight" and "keen understanding of human nature." Also during the 1970s, Deford published biographies of tennis greats Bill Tilden and Arthur Ashe, and two novels. His first novel, *Cut 'n' Run*, combined pro football, top-secret army operations, and financial speculation in what *Library Journal* contributor Charles R. Andrews called "a neat little comic come-on for the pro football fan." *The Owner*, Deford's second novel, again combined sports and humor in its portrait of a sleazy owner of a hockey team. Another of Deford's novels, *Everybody's All-American*, was made into a popular movie starring Dennis

Quaid and Jessica Lange.

In 1982, Deford was voted Sportswriter of the Year by the National Association of Sportswriters and Sportscasters, an award he owned for the next seven years. Critics have called him "the world's greatest sportswriter." The accolades confirmed what many had already been saying: Deford had arrived. But Deford refused to take this recognition too seriously: "I never set out to be the best sportswriter in the country," he recalled, "so being acclaimed as the best didn't mean that much to me. I don't mean I blew it off—I was delighted and proud of myself. But the award is kind of a fraud, because it's hard to know who is best when most sportswriters are writing for a local market. Plus, I always wanted to do something more or something else, and so I think that probably kept me in perspective."

Deford began to be known for more than his writing in the 1980s, as he began to offer radio and television commentary. "I was on CNN the first week it was on the air," he told Pendergast. "It was chaotic, but it was fun and it was like vaudeville: you could try stuff and fail and do wild things and have fun." Deford also began to do radio essays for NPR and ESPN radio. "I'm sort of a columnist of the air, which is great, because it's a lot of fun to come on and express an opinion." Though his radio and television commentaries are extremely popular—NPR audiences, who were thought to look down their noses at sports, have learned to treasure Deford's insights—Deford insists that these jobs are mere sidelines. *Publishers Weekly* interviewer Chris Goodrich asked Deford if he would quit doing commentary if he could support himself as a novelist. Deford's reply: "Would I? Watch my smoke!"

The Life and Death of a Child

In 1971, the year he published his first novel and just a few years after he began writing the kind of stories he loved to write, Deford and his wife Carol had their second child, a little girl they named Alexandra, Alex for short. In *Alex: The Life of a Child*, the memoir he wrote about his daughter in 1983, Deford recalls: "For a few months there, right after Alex was born, I thought I had just about everything a man could want . . . a job I loved, a career, a future, a house in the suburbs, and a VW bug and Ford Country Squire station wagon." But the dream didn't last long, for Alex couldn't keep her food down and was

pale and listless. The doctors at Children's Hospital in Boston diagnosed Alex with cystic fibrosis, a progressive disease that attacks the pancreas, the respiratory system, and the sweat glands. The bodies of cystic fibrosis victims produce too much mucus, and that mucus clogs the lungs and the pancreas, causing chronic respiratory infections and eventually death. There was and is no cure for cystic fibrosis, and her doctors expected Alex to die within days.

But Alex lived for eight years, fighting her disease with the help of her parents and her older brother, Christian, who she called "Chrish." For eight years the Defords battled the mucus that built up in Alex's lungs, giving her medicines that did no good, beating the mucus out of her chest only to have it return. "When every day I had to thump my little girl," wrote Deford, "pound away on her body, sometimes when she was pleading with me, crying out in pain to stop, something came over me, changed me." As much as the treatment changed Deford, so did Alex, for she showed more bravery than all those around her.

Deford captured that strength in the book he wrote about Alex. Just a year before her death in 1980, Alex Deford was preparing to endure another operation to inflate her collapsed lung. Her father writes: "So I started to lay her down where they would cut her open. And in that moment, I could not hold back any longer; one tear fell from all those welling in my eyes. And Alex saw it, saw my face as I bent to put her down. Softer, but urgently, she cried out, 'Wait!' We all thought she was only delaying the operation again, but instead, so gently, so dearly, she reached up, and with an angel's touch, swept the tear from my face. I will never know such sweetness again in all my life. 'Oh, my little Daddy, I'm so sorry,' is what she said. One nurse turned and bowed her head and began to sob. The other could not even stay in the room. She ran off to compose herself. It was some time before we could get going again."

"Alex is the single most significant and precious thing that ever happened to me in my life," Deford told Pendergast, "and her death was also so much more awful and so much more terrible than anything else that has ever happened to me, I can't even put it on the scale. But when you're given those cards you just play them the best you can." Deford joined the Cystic Fibrosis Foundation, and later became its chairman. He still gives

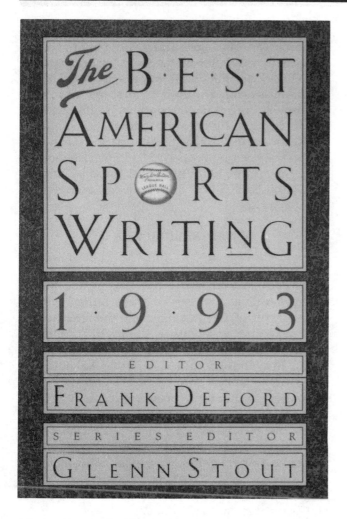

As one of the greatest living sportswriters, Deford was uniquely qualified to select the year's best in this genre.

called upon, though he says that as doctors have come closer to finding a cure he has had to devote less time to the cause. *Alex: The Life of a Child* helped the cause, for it gave the disease a human face. The book was made into a movie and sold more copies than anything else Deford has written. More importantly, said Deford, the publicity means that "Alex has a legacy, even though she died when she was eight years old."

"The only question is how well you deal with the trials in your life and how you deal with the successes in your life, your response to the good and the bad, to victory and defeat," Deford told *Hartford Courant* interviewer Jocelyn McClurg. "That's one thing athletes have to learn. I'm always very admiring of the ones who know how to lose. Anybody can win. That's easy."

The National

"It's tough being an old sportswriter," Deford told Pendergast. And in 1989, after 27 years with *Sports Illustrated*, Deford was beginning to feel like an old sportswriter. "Back in my twenties I enjoyed it, but the players were my contemporaries and they weren't making two million dollars a year and didn't mind hanging out with sportswriters." "You can stay in politics your whole life because you're always dealing with adults," he told Goodrich, "but now it's very hard for me to go into a locker room and talk to naked young men." After all those years, it was beginning to feel like he was writing the same story over and over again. And so it was time to try something new. He planned to travel to Europe and work on a novel he had begun, but Peter O. Price, an old friend who was then publisher of the *New York Post,* called and made him an offer. Price wanted him to be the editor of a new sports daily for the United States.

With the backing of Mexican millionaire Emilio Azcarraga, Deford and Price set out to create the *National,* the nation's first all-sports daily. All-sports daily papers were popular in countries all over the world, so they reasoned, why not the United States? "We started with the premise that we were going to provide the best: the best newspaper writing, the best pictures, and the best numbers," Deford told Pendergast. And, he told Melinda Beck of *Newsweek,* "This is the last challenge in daily journalism for the 20th century . . . . We'll give our readers the good parts of *USA Today*—but we'll go far beyond that. We're a paper for people who want to *read*." First on the agenda was luring the best sportswriters in the country, which Deford and Price did by offering big salaries and room to stretch.

For Deford, the *National* was both a pleasant change of pace and a chance to prove wrong those who sneered at sportswriting. "As a feature writer you are always a lone wolf," Deford said in his *AAYA* interview, "but doing the *National* was a collaborative effort. It was fun to work with other people for once." Among those Deford worked with were tennis writer John Feinstein and columnist Mike Lupica, formerly with the *New York Daily News*. Moreover, the *National* would reveal "the dirty little secret of American publishers," Deford intimated in *U.S. News & World Report*: "It is the sports page that sells papers."

The *National* was aimed at young, fairly well-off males, but Deford hoped that it could lure others into reading. "We knew that it was difficult to get young people to read, especially young men," Deford explained to Pendergast, "and one way to do it is to entice them with sports. We thought that if we could get young people reading us on a daily basis they might get trapped in the habit and start reading real newspapers." Others in the publishing industry were not so optimistic. Sports was too local, they said. People won't buy a national sports page, especially one that comes out every day.

Critics who predicted that the paper wouldn't succeed were right in the end, but for the wrong reasons. Readers liked the writing, and the staff was able to provide enough local coverage to build a

Published in 1993, Deford's first non-sports novel deals with two friends--one American and the other Japanese--facing the bombing of Pearl Harbor.

following. But the staff was never able to solve the problem of distributing the paper widely enough to reach its admittedly discriminating audience. "People want papers at six o'clock in the morning on their doorstep, and with us only selling 150,000 papers a day nationwide, it was just too difficult to make it work," recalled Deford. The paper launched its first issue on January 31, 1990; 18 months later, on June 13, 1991, the *National* closed its doors, and Deford looked for somewhere else to write.

A New Kind of Writing

It didn't take Deford long to find a new home. *Sports Illustrated* offered to hire him again, despite the hard feelings that existed when Deford left the magazine in 1989. (Management thought he left the magazine to create a competitor; Deford felt that the *National* had a different audience.) But Deford told the editor he couldn't come home again and signed a contract with *Newsweek* to provide occasional pieces. Still, he wanted to write longer pieces than that magazine published, and late in 1992 he signed a contract with *Vanity Fair* to write three profiles a year. Already he has written on Nike founder Phil Knight, Dallas Cowboys football team owner Jerry Jones, and the Bennett brothers, Bob and Bill, of Washington law and politics.

Free from a full-time magazine commitment, Deford was finally able to concentrate on writing the historical novel he had begun a few years earlier. "If there was any consolation when the *National* folded," Deford told *Connecticut Post* contributor Joe Meyers, "it was that I had something that I could immediately turn to, and I just threw myself into this book." *Love and Infamy*, published in 1993, tells the story of two best friends, a Japanese man educated in America and an American missionary raised in Japan, who confront the circumstances leading up to Japan's attack on Pearl Harbor in 1941. Compounding the difficulties of their conflicting national allegiances is the fact that the American has grown to love the Japanese man's wife.

"Writing [*Love and Infamy*] was fun, but it's also scary as hell since I don't know where this thing is going . . . and it's so different from anything else I've done," Deford told Meyers. Writing about Pearl Harbor was

Goodrich: "I've always been fascinated by Pearl Harbor, because there's no way in the world it should have happened—politically, because we should have straightened things out before it ever came to that, and militarily because 99 times out of 100 an attack like that wouldn't work." The book also gave him a chance again to develop characters on his own, instead of writing about real people. "I was intrigued by what became the confrontation between the two characters, the Japanese who didn't want to go to war and the American who did." "Your characters really do take on some kind of life on their own," he told Meyers. "It's fun to sit down at the typewriter and see where they're going to lead you today."

Deford was nervous as he awaited reviews of *Love and Infamy,* which was, after all, the first novel he had ventured to write outside the world of sports. But reviewers found in Deford's fiction the same lively pacing and vivid characters that had long characterized his sportswriting. "Deford's blend of history, irony, suspense, and romance is a skillful concoction," announced *Richmond Times-Dispatch* contributor Sharon Lloyd Stratton. "His novel is a remarkable piece of modern historical fiction." *Philadelphia Inquirer* reviewer Bill Kent praised Deford's even-handed treatment of the Japanese: "He has shown us a way to see Japan as a nation that is not so exotic as it is complicated, contradictory and compellingly fascinating, and well worth learning to love." And *Publishers Weekly* called *Love and Infamy* "a consistently captivating story of romance, politics and the clash of two cultures."

Next on Deford's agenda is a shorter novel about a boy growing up in Baltimore in the 1950s. The boy has moved to the city with his father, and befriends a girl with polio in the year before that disease was cured. But the book is not about disease, insists Deford, it is about childhood. Asked whether he was happy with the book, Deford replied: "I'm happy with everything I write, to some extent. I know how good my work is, whether its a B or an A or whatever, and I know that, with writing, you can go up a notch or down a notch, but it's awful hard to take it up two notches. You are really limited to what you are working with, and I know that and that's okay with me."

Such humility is characteristic of Deford,

whose vision of his own success seems not to rest upon what he has accomplished in the past but upon what he might accomplish in the future. Despite all the accolades, despite the fact that he is considered one of the better writers in America, despite his being "fringe famous," Deford can say: "I don't think I've ever taken myself all that seriously, because I have always had other goals that I have not achieved and that's probably very good that you never arrive where you set out to be. I always wanted to be a very successful novelist or playwright, and those things I have never achieved. That's been very good for me, it keeps me on my toes, let's me know you are not really that much of a hotshot, you're really not. So even though I am at the top of my profession, it isn't what I really want most of all, so I'm still struggling."

■ Works Cited

Andrews, Charles R., review of *Cut 'n' Run, Library Journal,* December 1, 1972, p. 3929.

Beck, Melinda, "Make Room in the Press Box," *Newsweek,* June 12, 1989, p. 53.

Cahill, Audrey, review of *There She Is: The Life and Times of Miss America, Library Journal,* October 15, 1971, p. 3337.

Deford, Frank, *There She Is: The Life and Times of Miss America,* Viking, 1971.

Deford, Frank, *Alex: The Life of a Child,* Viking, 1983.

Deford, Frank, *The World's Tallest Midget,* Viking, 1987.

Deford, Frank, in an interview with contributor Tom Pendergast for *Authors and Artists for Young Adults,* June 10, 1994.

Goodrich, Chris, "*PW* Interviews: Frank Deford," *Publishers Weekly,* December 6, 1993, pp. 52-53.

Kent, Bill, "Love and Intrigue in Prewar Japan," *Philadelphia Inquirer,* December 7, 1993.

Loop, Paul, "Deford Covers It All for *Sports Illustrated,*" *Orange County Register* (Santa Ana, California), August 23, 1987.

McClurg, Jocelyn, "A Good Sport," *Hartford Courant* (Connecticut), November 28, 1993.

Meyers, Joe, "Deford Shifts from Sports Writing to Historical Novel," *Connecticut Post* (Bridgeport), December 12, 1993.

Stratton, Sharon Lloyd, "Friends Clash in Deford Novel," *Richmond Times-Dispatch* (Virginia), January 2, 1994.

U.S. News & World Report, January 29, 1990, p.11.

■ For More Information See

PERIODICALS

Atlanta Journal, November 20, 1983.
Business Week, August 21, 1989, p. 30.
Charleston Gazette (West Virginia), November 21, 1984.
Des Moines Register (Iowa), May 31, 1987.
Durham Morning Herald (North Carolina), October 1, 1986.

Hour (Norwalk, Connecticut), August 9, 1988.
Inc., April, 1990, pp. 58-69.
Milwaukee Journal, June 25, 1987.
New Haven Register (Connecticut), October 23, 1983.
Newsweek, February 22, 1993.
New York Tribune, August 28, 1989.
Philadelphia Inquirer, January 9, 1994.
Time, January 16, 1984, p. 72; February 5, 1990, p. 66.
Virginian-Pilot (Norfolk), February 20, 1994.
Washington Post, January 28, 1990.

—Sketch by Tom Pendergast

Arthur Conan Doyle

United States, and Canada, 1917-25, South Africa, 1928, and Sweden, 1929. *Wartime service:* Served during the Boer War as chief surgeon of a field hospital in Bloemfontein, South Africa, 1900. *Member:* Athenaeum Club, Authors' Club.

■ Awards, Honors

Knighted, 1902; L.L.D., University of Edinburgh.

■ Writings

SHERLOCK HOLMES DETECTIVE FICTION

A Study in Scarlet (novel; first published in *Beeton's Christmas Annual,* November, 1887), illustrations by father, Charles Doyle, Ward, Lock, 1888, Lippincott, 1890.

The Sign of Four (novel; first published in *Lippincott's,* February, 1890), Blackett, 1890, Collier, 1891, reprinted with introduction by Graham Greene, Doubleday, 1977, published as *The Sign of the Four,* Lippincott, 1890, published as *The Sign of the Four; or, The Problem of the Sholtos,* introduction by P. G. Wodehouse, Ballantine, c. 1975.

The Adventures of Sherlock Holmes (short stories; originally published in *Strand* magazine, 1891-92), illustrations by Sidney Paget, Newnes, 1892, Harper, 1892.

The Memoirs of Sherlock Holmes (short stories; originally published in *Strand* magazine, 1892-93), illustrations by Paget, Newnes, 1893, illustrations by W. H. Hyde and Paget, Harper, 1894.

■ Personal

Born May 22, 1859, in Edinburgh, Scotland; died of a heart attack, July 7 (one source says July 6), 1930, in Crowborough, Sussex, England; buried at Windlesham, Crowborough, Sussex, England; son of Charles Altamont (a civil servant and artist) and Mary (Foley) Doyle; married Louise Hawkins, August 6, 1885 (died, 1906); married Jean Leckie, September 18, 1907; children (first marriage) Mary Louise, Kingsley; (second marriage) Denis, Adrian Malcolm, Lena Jean. *Education:* Edinburgh University, B.M., 1881, M.D., 1885. *Hobbies and other interests:* Golf, cricket, cycling.

■ Career

Writer. Assistant to physician in Birmingham, England, 1879; ship's surgeon on whaling voyage to Arctic, 1880; began writing as a way to supplement his physician's income, 1887; ship's surgeon on voyage to west coast of Africa, 1881-82; physician in Southsea, Portsmouth, England, 1882-90; ophthalmologist in London, England, 1891; appointed Deputy Lieutenant of Surrey, 1902. Lectured on spiritualism in Europe, Australia, the

The Hound of the Baskervilles (novel; serialized in *Strand* magazine, 1901-02), illustrations by Paget, Newnes, 1902, McClure, Phillips, 1902, reprinted with a foreword and afterword by John Fowles, Doubleday, 1977, published as *The Hound of the Baskervilles, Another Adventure of Sherlock Holmes with Biographical Illustrations and Pictures from Earlier Editions of the Novel*, introduction by James Nelson, Dodd, Mead, 1968.

The Return of Sherlock Holmes (short stories; originally published in *Strand* magazine, 1903-04), illustrations by Paget, Newnes, 1905, McClure, Phillips, 1905.

The Valley of Fear (novel; serialized in *Strand* magazine, 1914-15), Smith, Elder, 1915, published as *The Valley of Fear: A Sherlock Holmes Novel*, illustrations by Arthur I. Keller, Doran, 1915.

His Last Bow: Some Reminiscences of Sherlock Holmes (short stories; originally published in *Strand* magazine, 1893-1917), J. Murray, 1917, published as *His Last Bow: A Reminiscence of Sherlock Holmes*, Doran, 1917.

The Case-Book of Sherlock Holmes (short stories; separate stories originally published in *Strand*), J. Murray, 1927, Doran, 1927, reprinted with introduction by C. P. Snow, J. Murray, 1974.

The Annotated Sherlock Holmes: The Four Novels and the Fifty-six Short Stories Complete, edited with introduction, notes, and bibliography by William S. Baring-Gould, illustrations by Charles Doyle and others, C. N. Potter, 1967.

The Uncollected Sherlock Holmes, compiled by Richard Lancelyn Green, Penguin Books, 1983.

Many of the Sherlock Holmes short stories have been reprinted in different collections or published separately.

NOVELS

The Mystery of Cloomber, Ward & Downey, 1889, Munro, 1895.

The Firm of Girdlestone (semi-autobiographical), Chatto & Windus, 1890, Lovell, 1890.

The Doings of Raffles Haw (serialized in *Answers*, 1891-92), Lovell, 1891, Cassell, 1892.

Beyond the City: The Idyll of a Suburb, George Newnes, 1892.

The Parasite, Constable, 1894, published as *The Parasite: A Story*, illustrations by Howard Pyle, Harper, 1895.

The Stark Munro Letters: Being a Series of Sixteen Letters Written by J. Stark Munro, M.B., to his Friend and Former Fellow-Student, Herbert Swanborough, of Lowell, Massachusetts, During the Years 1881-1884 (autobiographical), Longmans, Green, 1895, Appleton, 1895.

Rodney Stone, illustrations by Paget, Smith, Elder, 1896, Appleton, 1896.

The Tragedy of the Korosko, illustrations by Paget, Smith, Elder, 1898, published as *A Desert Drama: Being the Tragedy of the Korosko*, Lippincott, 1898.

A Duet with an Occasional Chorus, Richards, 1899, Appleton, 1899.

The Lost World, Hodder & Stoughton, 1912, Doran, 1912.

The Poison Belt, illustrations by Harry Rountree, Hodder & Stoughton, 1913, Doran, 1913.

The Land of Mist, Hutchinson, 1925, Doran, 1926.

HISTORICAL NOVELS

Micah Clarke: His Statement as Made to His Three Grandchildren, Joseph, Gervas, and Reuben, During the Hard Winter of 1734, Longmans, Green, 1889, Harper, 1889.

The White Company (serialized in *Cornhill*, 1891), Smith, Elder, 1891, Lovell, 1891.

The Refugees: A Tale of Two Continents (serialized in *Harper's Monthly*, 1893), Longmans, Green, 1893, illustrations by T. De Thulstrup, Harper, 1893.

The Great Shadow (first published in *Arrowsmith's Christmas Annual*, 1892), Arrowsmith, 1893, Harper, 1893.

Uncle Bernac: A Memory of the Empire, illustrations by Robert Sauber, Smith, Elder, 1897, Appleton, 1897.

Sir Nigel (sequel to *The White Company*; serialized in *Strand* magazine, 1905-06), illustrations by Arthur Twidle, Smith, Elder, 1906, illustrations by the Kinneys, McClure, Phillips, 1906.

SHORT STORIES

Mysteries and Adventures, Scott, 1890, published as *The Gully of Bluemansdyke and Other Stories*, Scott, 1892, published as *My Friend the Murderer and Other Mysteries and Adventures*, Lovell, Coryell, 1893.

The Captain of the Polestar and Other Tales, Longmans, Green, 1890, Munro, 1894.

The Winning Shot (bound with *An Actor's Duel* by Campbell Rae Brown), Dicks, 1894.

Round the Red Lamp: Being Facts and Fancies of Medical Life (horror), Methuen, 1894, Appleton, 1894.

The Surgeon of Gaster Fell, Ivers, 1895.

The Exploits of Brigadier Gerard, illustrated by W. B. Wollen, Newnes, 1896, Appleton, 1896.

The Green Flag and Other Stories of War and Sport,
Smith, Elder, 1900, McClure, Phillips, 1900.
Adventures of Gerard, illustrations by Wollen,
Newnes, 1903, McClure, Phillips, 1903.
The Croxley Master: A Great Tale of the Prize Ring
(also see below), McClure, Phillips, 1907.
Round the Fire Stories, Smith, Elder, 1908, McClure,
1908.
One Crowded Hour, Paget, 1911.
The Last Galley: Impressions and Tales, illustrations
by N. C. Wyeth and Rountree, Smith, Elder,
1911, Doubleday, Page, 1911.
Danger! And Other Stories, J. Murray, 1918, Doran,
1919.
Tales of the Ring and Camp, J. Murray, 1922, published as *The Croxley Master and Other Tales of
the Ring and Camp,* Doran, 1925.
Tales of Terror and Mystery, J. Murray, 1922, pub-
lished as *The Black Doctor and other Tales of Ter-
ror and Mystery,* Doran, 1925.
Tales of Twilight and the Unseen, J. Murray, 1922,
published as *The Great Keinplatz Experiment and
Other Tales of Twilight and the Unseen,* Doran,
1925.
Tales of Adventure and Medical Life, J. Murray, 1922,
published as *The Man from Archangel and Other
Tales of Adventure,* Doran, 1925.
Tales of Long Ago, J. Murray, 1922, published as
*The Last of the Legions and Other Tales of Long
Ago,* Doran, 1925.
The Three of Them: A Reminiscence, J. Murray, 1923.
The Maracot Deep and Other Stories, J. Murray, 1929,
Doubleday, Doran, 1929.
The Complete Professor Challenger Stories, J. Murray,
1952.
Uncollected Stories: The Unknown Conan Doyle, com-
piled with an introduction by John Michael
Gibson and Richard Lancelyn Green, Secker &
Warburg, 1982.
Conan Doyle Stories, Hippocrene Books, 1985.

Many of Doyle's stories exist in separate collections or editions.

PLAYS

(With J. M. Barrie) *Jane Annie; or, The Good Con-
duct Prize* (comic opera; produced in London at
Savoy Theatre, 1893), Chappell, 1893.
Foreign Policy (one-act; based on his story "A
Question of Diplomacy"), produced in London,
1893.
Waterloo (one-act; based on his story "A Straggler
of '15"; produced as *A Story of Waterloo* in
Bristol, England, 1894), Samuel French, 1907.

Halves (prologue and three acts; based on story of
same title by James Payn), produced in Aber-
deen, Scotland, 1899.
(With William Gillette) *Sherlock Holmes* (four-act;
based on Doyle's story "The Strange Case of
Miss Faulkner"; produced in London and Off-
Broadway, 1899), Samuel French, 1922.
A Duet (A Duologue) (one-act comedy; based on
his novel *A Duet with an Occasional Chorus;* pro-
duced in London, 1902), Samuel French, 1903.
Brigadier Gerard (four-act comedy), produced in
London and New York City, 1906.
The Fires of Fate (four-act; based on his novel *The
Tragedy of the Korosko*), produced in Liverpool,
England, and New York City, 1909.
The House of Temperley, produced in London, 1909.
A Pot of Caviare (one-act; based on his story of
same title), produced in London, 1910.
The Speckled Band: An Adventure of Sherlock Holmes
(three-act; based on his story "The Adventure of
the Speckled Band"; produced in London and
Off-Broadway, 1910; produced on the West End,
1911), Samuel French, 1912.
The Crown Diamond (one-act; produced in Bristol,
England, 1921), privately printed, 1958.
It's Time Something Happened (one-act), Appleton,
1925.
Exile: A Drama of Christmas Eve (one-act), Appleton,
1925.

Also author of *Angels of Darkness* (three-act), *Sir
Charles Tregellis, Admiral Denver, The Stonor Case,
The Lift,* and *Mrs. Thompson* (based on the novel
of the same title by W. B. Maxwell).

WORKS ON SPIRITUALISM

The New Revelation, Hodder & Stoughton, 1918,
Doran, 1918.
The Vital Message, Hodder & Stoughton, 1919,
Doran, 1919.
Spiritualism and Rationalism, Hodder & Stoughton,
1920.
The Wanderings of a Spiritualist, Hodder &
Stoughton, 1921, Doran, 1921.
The Evidence for Fairies, Doran, 1921.
Fairies Photographed, Doran, 1921.
The Coming of the Fairies, Hodder & Stoughton,
1922, Doran, 1922.
(With others) *The Case for Spirit Photography,* pref-
ace by Fred Barlow, Hutchinson, 1922, Doran,
1923.
Our American Adventure, Hodder & Stoughton,
1923, Doran, 1923.
(Compiler) *The Spiritualists' Reader,* Two Worlds,

1924.

Our Second American Adventure, Hodder & Stoughton, 1924, Little, Brown, 1924.

(Contributor) James Marchant, editor, *Survival*, Putnam, 1924, Doyle's contribution published separately as *Psychic Experiences*, Putnam, 1925.

The History of Spiritualism, two volumes, Cassell, 1926, Doran, 1926.

Pheneas Speaks: Direct Spirit Communications in the Family Circle, Psychic Press, 1927, Doran, 1927.

Our African Winter, J. Murray, 1929.

The Roman Catholic Church: A Rejoinder, Psychic Press, 1929.

The Edge of the Unknown (essays), J. Murray, 1930, Putnam, 1930.

OTHER

Songs of Action (poetry; also see below), Smith, Elder, 1898, Doubleday & McClure, 1898.

The Great Boer War, Smith, Elder, 1900, McClure, Phillips, 1900.

(With Grant Allen) *Hilda Wade: A Woman with Tenacity of Purpose*, Richards, 1900, Putnam, 1900.

The Immortal Memory, Mitchell, 1901.

The War in South Africa: Its Cause and Conduct, Smith, Elder, 1902, McClure, Phillips, 1902.

The Fiscal Question: Treated in a Series of Three Speeches, Henderson, 1905.

An Incursion into Diplomacy, Smith, Elder, 1906.

The Story of Mr. George Edalji, privately printed, 1907, published as *The Case of Mr. George Edalji*, Blake, 1907.

Through the Magic Door (criticism), illustrations by W. Russell Flint, Smith, Elder, 1907, McClure, 1908, Doubleday, Page, 1925.

The Crime of the Congo, Hutchinson, 1909, Doubleday, Page, 1909.

Divorce Law Reform: An Essay, Divorce Law Reform Union, 1909.

Why He Is Now in Favour of Home Rule, Liberal Publication, 1911.

Songs of the Road (poetry), Smith, Elder, 1911, Doubleday, Page, 1911.

The Case of Oscar Slater, Hodder & Stoughton, 1912.

Great Britain and the Next War, Small, Maynard, 1914.

To Arms!, preface by F. E. Smith, Hodder & Stoughton, 1914.

The German War (essay), Hodder & Stoughton, 1914.

Western Wanderings, Doran, 1915.

A Visit to Three Fronts: June 1916, Hodder & Stoughton, 1916, published as *A Visit to Three Fronts: Glimpses of the British, Italian, and French Lines*, Doran, 1916.

The Origin and Outbreak of the War, Doran, 1916.

The British Campaign in France and Flanders, six volumes, Hodder & Stoughton, 1916-20, Doran, 1916-20, enlarged edition published as *The British Campaigns in Europe, 1914-1919*, Bles, 1928.

The Guards Came through and Other Poems, J. Murray, 1919, Doran, 1920.

The Poems of Arthur Conan Doyle: Collected Edition (contains *Songs of Action*, *Songs of the Road*, and *The Guards Came through and Other Poems*), J. Murray, 1922.

Memories and Adventures (autobiography), Hodder & Stoughton, 1924, Little, Brown, 1924, revised edition, Hodder & Stoughton, 1930.

(Translator from the French) Leon Denis, *The Mystery of Joan of Arc*, J. Murray, 1924, Dutton, 1925.

The Field Bazaar, Athenaeum (London), 1934, Pamphlet House, 1947.

Strange Studies from Life: Containing Three Hitherto Uncollected Tales Based on the Annals of True Crime, additional material by Philip Trevor, edited with an introduction by Peter Ruber, Candlelight Press, 1963.

Essays on Photography: The Unknown Conan Doyle, compiled with an introduction by J. M. Gibson and R. L. Green, Secker & Warburg, 1982.

Letters to the Press, edited by Gibson and Green, University of Iowa Press, 1986.

Contributor of works such as "The Truth About Sherlock Holmes" in a variety of genres to many magazines and newspapers, including *Strand*, *Chambers's Journal*, *Harper's*, *Blackwood's*, *Saturday Evening Post*, *McClure's*, *London Society*, *Cornhill*, *Lippincott's*, *Boston Herald*, *Philadelphia Inquirer*, *St. Louis Post-Dispatch*, and *New York Times*.

■ Adaptations

MOVIES

The Adventures of Sherlock Holmes, starring Maurice Costello, 1905; Essanany Film, 1916; Goldwyn Pictures, starring John Barrymore, 1922; Twentieth Century-Fox, starring Basil Rathbone and Nigel Bruce, 1939 (also known as *Sherlock Holmes*).

The Beryl Coronet, Society Francaise des Films & Cinematographes (S.F.F.C.), 1912; Alexander Film Corp., 1922.

The Copper Beeches, S.F.F.C., 1912.

The Mystery of Boscombe Vale, S.F.F.C., 1912.

The Reygate Squires, S.F.F.C., 1912.

Silver Blaze, S.F.F.C., 1912; as *Murder at the*

Baskervilles, Astor Pictures, 1941.

The Speckled Band, S.F.F.C., 1912; First Division Pictures, starring Raymond Massey, 1931; Realm Television Productions, 1949.

The Stolen Papers, S.F.F.C., 1912.

The House of Temperley (adaptation of *Rodney Stone*), London Film, 1913.

The Musgrave Ritual, S.F.F.C., 1913.

A Study in Scarlet, Samuelson Film, 1914; K.B.S. Productions, starring Reginald Owen, 1933.

The Firm of Girdlestone, London Film, 1915; Vitagraph Co., 1916.

The Hound of the Baskervilles, Vitascope Co, 1915; R-C Pictures, 1922; First Anglo Corp., 1932; Twentieth Century-Fox, starring Rathbone and Bruce, 1939; United Artists, starring Peter Cushing, 1959; Universal City Studios, starring Stewart Granger, 1972; Hemdale, starring Peter Cook and Dudley Moore, 1980; Mapleton, starring Ian Richardson, 1983.

Brigadier Gerard, John William Smith, 1915; Universal Film, 1916.

A Case of Identity, Alexander Film, 1922.

The Devil's Foot, Alexander Film, 1922.

The Dying Detective, Alexander Film, 1922.

The Man with the Twisted Lip, Alexander Film, 1922.

The Red Headed League, Alexander Film, 1922.

The Yellow Face, Alexander Film, 1922.

The Desert Sheik (adaptation of *The Tragedy of thc Korosko),* Truart Film, 1924; as *Fires of Fate,* 1923; British International Pictures, 1932.

The Lost World, First National Pictures, 1925; Encyclopaedia Britannica Films, 1948; Twentieth Century-Fox, starring Claude Rains, directed by Irwin Allen, 1960.

The Fighting Eagle (adaptation of *The Exploits of Brigadier Gerard),* Pathe Exchange, 1927.

The Return of Sherlock Holmes, Paramount, starring Clive Brook, 1929.

Sherlock Holmes' Fatal Hour (adaptation of "The Final Problem" and "The Empty House"), First Division Pictures, 1931.

Sherlock Holmes, Fox Film Corp., starring Clive Brook and Reginald Owen, 1932.

The Missing Rembrandt (adaptation of "The Adventure of Charles Augustus Milverton"), First Anglo Corp., starring Arthur Wontner, 1932.

The Sign of Four, World Wide Pictures, starring Wontner, 1932; Mapleton, starring Ian Richardson, 1983.

The Triumph of Sherlock Holmes (adaptation of *The Valley of Fear),* Gaumont British Limited, starring Wontner, 1935.

Sherlock Holmes and the Secret Weapon (adaptation of "The Dancing Men"), Universal Pictures, starring Rathbone and Bruce, 1942.

Sherlock Holmes and the Voice of Terror (adaptation of "His Last Bow"), Universal Pictures, starring Rathbone and Bruce, 1942.

Sherlock Holmes in Washington, Universal Pictures, starring Rathbone and Bruce, 1943.

Sherlock Holmes Faces Death, Universal Pictures, starring Rathbone and Bruce, 1943.

Sherlock Holmes and the Spider Woman (also known as *The Spider Woman),* Universal Pictures, starring Rathbone and Bruce, 1944.

The Pearl of Death (adaptation of "The Six Napoleons"), Universal Pictures, starring Rathbone and Bruce, 1944.

The Scarlet Claw (also known as *Sherlock Holmes and the Scarlet Claw),* Universal Pictures, starring Rathbone and Bruce, 1944.

The House of Fear (adaptation of "The Adventure of the Five Orange Pips"), Universal Pictures, starring Rathbone and Bruce, 1945.

The Woman in Green, Universal Pictures, starring Rathbone and Bruce, 1945.

Pursuit to Algiers, Universal Pictures, starring Rathbone and Bruce, 1945.

Terror by Night, Universal Pictures, starring Rathbone and Bruce, 1946.

Dressed to Kill (also known as *Sherlock Holmes and the Secret Code)* Universal Pictures, starring Rathbone and Bruce, 1946.

Sherlock Holmes and the Deadly Necklace (also known as *Valley of Fear),* Screen Gems, starring Christopher Lee, 1962.

A Study in Terror, Columbia Pictures, starring John Neville, 1965.

The Adventures of Gerard, United Artists, 1969.

The Private Life of Sherlock Holmes, Phalanx Productions, starring Stanley Holloway, 1970.

They Might Be Giants, Universal Pictures, starring Joanne Woodward and George C. Scott, 1971.

The Adventure of Sherlock Holmes' Smarter Brother, Twentieth Century-Fox, starring Gene Wilder and Madeline Kahn, 1975.

Murder by Decree, Ambassador Films, starring Christopher Plummer and James Mason, 1979.

Young Sherlock Holmes, Paramount, 1985.

Without a Clue, Orion, starring Ben Kingsley and Michael Caine, 1988.

PLAYS

John Michael Dinkow Hardwick and Mollie Greenhaigh, *Four Sherlock Holmes Plays,* J. Murray, 1964.

Marian Grudeff and Raymond Jessel, composers, *Baker Street: A Musical Adventure of Sherlock*

Holmes (libretto), Doubleday, 1966.

John M. D. and Mollie (Greenhaigh) Hardwick, *The Game's Afoot: Sherlock Holmes Plays,* J. Murray, 1969.

J. and M. Hardwick, *The Private Life of Sherlock Holmes,* Mayflower, 1970.

J. and M. Hardwick, *Four More Sherlock Holmes Plays,* J. Murray, 1973.

Dennis Rosa, *Sherlock Holmes and the Curse of the Sign of Four; or, "The Mark of the Timber Toe,"* Dramatists Play Service, 1975.

OTHER

The Sherlock Holmes Mysteries, starring Jeremy Brett, were produced by and aired on Britain's Granada Television, 1984-86, and were broadcast in the United States by the Arts & Entertainment cable network. Filmstrips have been made of *Silver Blaze, The Adventures of the Speckled Band, The Hound of the Baskervilles, A Scandal in Bohemia,* and *Final Problem,* Brunswick Productions, 1970-71. Several novels have been based on the Sherlock Holmes characters, including *The Crucifer of Blood,* by Paul Giovanni, *The Demon Device,* by Robert Saffron, and *The Seven Per-Cent Solution,* by Nicholas Meyer.

■ Sidelights

"I remarked to my mother with precocious wisdom that it was easy to get people into scrapes," Arthur Conan Doyle wrote in his autobiography, *Memories and Adventures,* "but not so easy to get them out again, which is surely the experience of every writer of adventures." Doyle found himself personally in this precarious situation with the most famous character of his creation—Sherlock Holmes. He had decided to kill off his famous detective because he felt that Holmes was overshadowing his writing career. That caused a huge uproar with the general public, and Doyle had to extricate himself from it by awkwardly resurrecting the sleuth a few years later.

Doyle was a prolific writer, producing work in many genres—from historical fiction to history to spiritualism. During his lifetime, however, Doyle was resentful that his Sherlock Holmes stories almost completely eclipsed his other work. While the public clamored for more Holmes stories, Doyle recoiled; he wanted to be known for his historical novels, and later, for his works on spiritualism. Unfortunately, what was true during his life is now true after his death—Doyle is remem-

bered almost solely for his Sherlock Holmes stories. Only a small amount of his other works are ever studied, mostly by Doyle scholars, while legions of people read journals on Holmes as well as attend conferences and workshops on the fictional detective.

Doyle was born May 22, 1859, in Edinburgh, Scotland. The family name was Doyle, but as he became older, he preferred to use surname Conan Doyle. His father, who was a civil servant by profession, had moved to Scotland from Ireland. "When my father was only nineteen a seat was offered him in the Government Office of Works in Edinburgh, whither he went. There he spent his working life, and thus it came about that I, an Irishman by extraction, was born in the Scottish capital," Doyle wrote in *Memories and Adventures.* His father's hobby was cartooning. Because of this, he became known in the literary and artistic communities of that day. Young Doyle was exposed to literary celebrities, including William Makepeace Thackeray, author of *Vanity Fair.* As a consequence, his imagination was encouraged, and literature became a constant companion.

Writes First Book

"During these first ten years I was a rapid reader, so rapid that some small library with which we dealt gave my mother notice that books would not be changed more than twice a day. My tastes were boylike enough . . . . I wrote a little book and illustrated it myself in early days. There was a man in it and there was a tiger who amalgamated shortly after they met," he wrote in his autobiography. Apparently, these early forays into writing left a mark in his brain, even though he was not to follow these stirrings for many years.

His family was solidly Roman Catholic, and as a boy Doyle was sent off to a Jesuit school in northern England. Later, he attended the Jesuit college Stonyhurst. He became known for his ability to spin a yarn, often keeping his classmates entertained for hours with mystery/adventure stories that were steeped in suspense. His instructors likewise marveled at his ability to write poetry. Doyle was also becoming quite adept at many different sports. Singlestick (similar to fencing, but played using a wooden sword-stick), boxing, cricket and soccer were among his favorite activities. In 1875 he went to Feldkirch College in Austria for a year to attend school. While there, the energetic Doyle ended up founding a newspaper, which had the motto "Fear not and put in print." The college was Jesuit-run, but while he attended classes there, he began to question his Catholic faith. He eventually withdrew from organized religion, but never became an atheist.

Meets Model for Holmes

The next year, Doyle studied medicine at Edinburgh University. It was here that he met the man who was to become the inspiration for his world-famous character Sherlock Holmes. Dr. Joseph Bell was the man's name, and he was physically and intellectually a match for the detective. "The most notable of the characters whom I met was one Joseph Bell, surgeon at the Edinburgh Infirmary," Doyle wrote in his autobiography. "Bell was a very remarkable man in body and mind. He was thin, wiry, dark, with a high-nosed acute face, penetrating grey eyes, angular shoulders, and a jerky way of walking. His voice was high and discordant. He was a very skilful surgeon, but his

strong point was diagnosis, not only of disease, but of occupation and character. For some reason which I have never understood he singled me out from the drove of students who frequented his wards and made me his out-patient clerk, which meant that I had to array his out-patients, make simple notes of their cases, and then show them in, one by one, to the large room in which Bell sat in state surrounded by his dressers and students." Doyle went on to explain how Bell, through a simple series of questions, found out that one patient was recently discharged from the army, a non-commissioned officer who had been stationed in Barbados. Bell was able to tell these facts by simple observations about the person.

"It is no wonder that after the study of such a character," Doyle continued, "I used and amplified his methods when in later life I tried to build up a scientific detective who solved cases on his own merits and not through the folly of the criminal." The two kept in touch for many years, and

Conan Doyle working in the study of his South Norwood, England, home in 1894.

Bell was, quite understandably, interested in the development of the Sherlock Holmes character. "Bell," wrote Doyle in his autobiography, "took a keen interest in these detective tales and even made suggestions which were not, I am bound to say, very practical."

Doyle often worked for physicians to earn money to pay his way through school. One of his boss's nephews was so impressed with the letters he received from Doyle that he encouraged him to write professionally. Apparently, Doyle just needed this little push to get him going, and he wrote almost constantly from that point on. In 1879, he had his first professional sale of a short story. Titled "The Mystery of Sasassa Valley," it was the story of South African adventurers who are on the trail of uncovering a native superstition and end up discovering a huge diamond instead, and was published in *Chambers's Journal*. Another work, "The American's Tale" was published in 1880 in London Society.

Heads for Real-Life Adventure

Craving for adventure that didn't happen on the written page, in 1880 Doyle signed on as the ship's surgeon for a seven-month Arctic whaling expedition. "It was in the *Hope,* under the command of the well-known whaler, John Gray, that I paid a visit to the Arctic Seas . . . ," he wrote in his autobiography. "I went in the capacity of surgeon, but as I was only twenty years of age when I started, and as my knowledge of medicine was that of an average third year's student, I have often thought that it was as well that there was no very serious call upon my services."

"I went on board the whaler a big, straggling youth, I came off it a powerful, well-grown man," the author continued. "I have no doubt that my physical health during my whole life has been affected by that splendid air, and the inexhaustible store of energy which I have enjoyed is to some extent drawn from the same source." He returned to Edinburgh University in 1881 to take his final examinations, which he passed with fair marks. He became a Bachelor of Medicine and a Master of Surgery, and was excited about the prospect of having a profession.

Once again, the young Doyle took a post on board a freighter bound for adventure. On the *Mayumba,* he headed for the African coast. He was quite avidly into his writing at this point, and was fill-

This photo, circa 1894, shows Conan Doyle (middle) with family and friends.

ing up notebook after notebook with observations and story ideas that sprung from his trip. Upon coming back to England, he was able to use his notes to write a story of the trip for the *British Journal of Photography*. He also submitted some short stories for publication in journals.

Now settled back in England, Doyle wanted to get down to the business of creating a medical practice. He joined Dr. George Budd, a former Edinburgh University student, in an office. The union turned out to be a short-lived one, partly because Dr. Budd was an outrageous man—somewhere between a fraud and a genius. With his mother encouraging him to leave his situation, eventually Doyle was discharged. He moved his practice to Southsea, England. His experience with Budd was to be summarized in the semi-autobiographical novel *The Stark Munro Letters,* published in 1895.

In those days, medicine wasn't the lucrative profession that it has become today. It was difficult to find enough patients to make a living. His Catholic relatives offered to write him letters of introduction to prospective Catholic patients in the area. He felt, however, that it would be hypocritical to accept this offer because he no longer practiced the faith. So Doyle became subject to rather a bleak kind of poverty, occasionally bolstered by the sale of one of his short stories to a local magazine.

In 1885 Doyle was awarded an M.D. from Edinburgh University. In that same year, he also decided to get married. Louise Hawkins, the sister of one of his few patients, became his bride. The addition of a wife didn't help Doyle's finances very much. However, his marriage seemed to help him develop more as a writer. Doyle wrote in his autobiography: "During the years before my marriage I had from time to time written short stories which were good enough to be marketable at very small prices . . . but not good enough to reproduce . . . . After my marriage, however, my brain seems to have quickened and both my imagination and my range of expression were greatly improved."

Doyle continued to publish in London's literary magazines. He began to enjoy larger fees for his work, although some of his stories appeared in journals which were anonymous. "It was about a year after my marriage that I realized that I could go on doing short stories for ever and never make headway. What is necessary is that your name should be on the back of a volume. Only so do you assert your individuality, and get the full credit or discredit of your achievement," he wrote in his autobiography. Doyle wrote a novel entitled *The Firm of Girdlestone* and attempted to get it accepted at several publishers around the town. But it was turned down by every one. Doyle, however, was not ready to give up. "I felt now that I was capable of something fresher and crisper and more workmanlike," he wrote in his autobiography. He had been fascinated by the works of Edgar Allen Poe, especially those which dealt with the masterful French detective, M. Dupin. Also, he was impressed with the writer Emile Gaboriau's detective Lecoq. These were among the few examples of detectives in literature in those days. This bit of information sparked Doyle's imagination. He wondered if he could bring into the world a new kind of detective.

The Birth of Sherlock Holmes

"I thought of my old teacher Joe Bell, of his eagle face, of his curious ways, of his eerie trick of spotting details. If he were a detective he would surely reduce this fascinating but unorganized business to something nearer to an exact science. I would try if I could get this effect. It was surely possible in real life, so why should I not make it plausible in fic-

tion?" he wrote in his autobiography. Doyle began jotting down plot ideas, character names and sketches for this potential detective. The character started out with the name of Sherringford Holmes, which was later altered to Sherlock Holmes. He settled on the less remarkable name Watson for Holmes's inimitable sidekick. And then he began to write the story that became *A Study in Scarlet.*

Doyle had to be as intelligent and probing as his character, Sherlock Holmes, to get the story right. As J. Randolph Cox wrote in *Concise Dictionary of Literary Biography:* "Today, a writer of detective literature can turn to many textbooks on police methods to keep the stories reasonably accurate. In 1886 there was no such textbook . . . . Doyle had to rely primarily on his imagination, his encyclopedic knowledge, his eye and memory for detail, his faculty for relating facts to causes, his ability to reconstruct the past from the present, plus some knowledge of human nature." In addition, his creation of the faithful friend and compassionate observer John Watson further distinguished this story from those that preceded it. Cox noted that "John Watson [was] a fully developed character in his own right." This technique, Cox continued, "added a dimension to the detective story which had been lacking in the works of his predecessors: the human element. But like most strokes of genius, this one was not fully grasped by the author at the time."

Doyle quickly sent the manuscript off to *Cornhill.* The editor, while admiring its style, rejected it because of its awkward length. It was too long for one issue, and too short to be serialized. The story was soon accepted by Ward, Lock for *Beeton's Christmas Annual,* to be published more than a year from its acceptance. He received only twenty-five pounds for all the rights to the story—and since Ward, Lock owned all the rights, they profited from subsequent reissues. When the story was finally published, it did not become an overnight success. However, the edition was a sell-out, and is now one of the rarest and most valuable periodicals in the world. The story was well-reviewed and Ward, Lock reprinted it as a novel in 1888. Doyle's father had supplied the illustrations for this edition. Sadly, he had been confined to an asylum for treatment of his alcoholism since 1879.

Completes First Historical Novel

While he was waiting for his first Sherlock Holmes mystery to be published, Doyle was busy researching the seventeenth century for his historical novel, *Micah Clarke*. Released in 1889, it became a critical and popular success. The book is an account of Micah Clarke's childhood, as he grows up hearing the stories of Oliver Cromwell and the Puritans, and his adventures as an adult during the Monmouth rebellion. Clarke joins up with the soldier Decimus Saxon (who supports the Duke of Monmouth against the King), is eventually defeated during the insurrection, and travels to Europe to continue his career as a soldier. John Dickson Carr wrote in *The Life of Sir Arthur Doyle* that "The power of *Micah Clarke,* aside from its best action scenes—the bloodhounds on Salisbury Plain, the brush with the King's Dragoons, the fight in Wells Cathedral, the blinding battlepiece at Sedgemoor—still lies in its characterization: that other imagination, the use of homely detail, by which each character grows into life before ever a shot is fired in war."

That same year Doyle's first child, Mary Louise, was born. He soon had a book of short stories published, entitled *The Mystery of Cloomber.* Gradually, the popularity of Sherlock Holmes was swelling in England. An editor of *Lippincott's* magazine asked Doyle to write another Sherlock Holmes story. In 1890 *The Sign of the Four* was published. This was an exotic story, featuring stolen treasure, murder by poison darts, an aboriginal dwarf, and a chase scene by water down the Thames River. In this story Holmes's attachment to his cocaine bottle is revealed. Critics basically ignored this novel, but the reading public liked it. In 1890, Doyle saw his previously rejected novel, *The Firm of Girdlestone*, get published. He had no idea at this point that Holmes would become anything more than a passing fancy, and was launching upon research that would lead to his historical novel *The White Company.*

This book, published in 1891, was to become Doyle's favorite work. Set in the fourteenth century, it is a tale of chivalry and adventure. When he was done with the manuscript, he is reported to have thrown his pen against the wall in elation, splashing it with ink. He became very fond of all the characters he had brought to life. The book was serialized in *Cornhill* before being published as a book, and later went through many editions. Some critics consider this book to be one of Doyle's finest historical novels.

While continuing to write, Doyle had also been busy studying eye surgery in Europe. In March

of 1891 he opened his practice, hopeful for a new source of income. Ironically, no patients ever came. After recovering from an illness, Doyle made the decision to give up medicine and become a full-time professional writer. It was to be a fortuitous and profitable venture for him.

The Power of the Periodical

In 1870, the Education Act had been passed, making provisions to teach many British citizens how to read. This increase in the reading public was coupled by an increase in and demand for reading materials. For the general public, serious, academic writing was not desirable. That's why many periodicals that published light fiction, as well as serialized stories, had become popular. It was exactly in these journals that Doyle was to earn much of his fame.

Doyle had an idea that what these periodicals needed to build reader allegiance was a series of stories with a continuing character. Using short stories instead of a serialized longer one was also one of his provisions—that way, readers wouldn't become discouraged if they missed an issue. Sherlock Holmes certainly seemed to fit the bill. "As far as anyone has been able to determine," wrote Cox, "Conan Doyle was the first person to hit upon this idea, and the *Strand* was the first magazine to put it into practice." The editor of the *Strand*, being a shrewd judge of English reading preferences, was thrilled with Doyle's idea. The author soon had a contract for six Sherlock Holmes stories. He received more for each of them—thirty-five pounds—than he had for his entire first novel. Doyle dashed off these stories in a remarkably quick period of time, at one time completing five within two months. Although he was finding these stories to be a quick source of cash, he had no intention of abandoning his more favored topic—historical fiction.

When the first Sherlock Holmes story was published in the *Strand* in 1891, the true audience appeal of the detective was known at once. The British public loved these tales almost immediately. One of the reasons was the clever illustrations, drawn by Sidney Paget. Paget was hired because the *Strand* editor mistakenly thought he was his more famous brother, Walter. The mistake was a fortuitous one, as Paget was responsible for the image most people have of the detective. Paget's Holmes appears to be more handsome than Doyle's description; the deerstalker cap and cape were also embellishments of the artist.

Doyle suddenly found himself famous all over the country. He moved from London to the suburbs, with many different writing projects in mind. *Strand* magazine wanted more Sherlock Holmes stories. Doyle didn't want to become known totally for these stories, so in order to discourage the magazine from it, he set what he thought was an outrageous sum for the work—fifty pounds per story. Doyle was taken aback when the price was immediately accepted. He quickly penned the six stories. In total it took him about three months to finish this order.

After completing the Holmes stories, he began work on another novel, this one set in Canada in the seventeenth century. *The Refugees* was supposed to be a sequel to *Micah Clarke,* but it became a full-fledged story in its own right. It was pub-

"HOLMES GAVE ME A SKETCH OF THE EVENTS."

Holmes and his faithful associate, Dr. Watson, discuss their latest case in the 1912 story "Silver Blaze."

lished in 1893 after being serialized. It received mixed reviews and is generally not considered one of his better works. However, Carr wrote that "the adventure-scenes in the great forests have never been surpassed for sheer vividness and power of action. They have diabolical reality, as though painted Indian-faces really did look through a suburban window." Doyle also dabbled briefly in the theater, when he adapted his short story "A Straggler of '15" into a play. He sent the script to Henry Irving, a theater manager and actor of the time. Irving altered the title to *A Story of Waterloo* and had it produced on tour in 1894 and at the Lyceum Theatre in London in 1896.

After the first twelve Holmes short stories were collected in *The Adventures of Sherlock Holmes* and published in book form, the editors of the were eager for more. Doyle, again wanting to be rid of the burden the detective had created for him, demanded what he considered an inappropriate amount for next twelve stories—one thousand pounds for the lot. His strategy backfired again, as the editors eagerly accepted his offer. As he was busy finishing the short stories, Doyle also completed a book on the Napoleonic wars entitled *The Great Shadow* and also helped his friend James Barrie produce a light opera, *Jane Annie; or, The Good Conduct Prize,* which upon performance was a resounding failure.

The Death of Holmes

In 1892, Doyle's son Kingsley was born. He and his wife later went on vacation to Switzerland where they had a chance to view the beautiful and dangerous Reichenbach falls. This experience stuck with the author, and because he felt plagued by the publisher's deadlines and the effort it took to keep coming up with Holmes plots, he decided to make a drastic move. The last Holmes story in this batch, "The Final Solution," was to end with Holmes and his arch rival Moriarity taking a deadly plunge into the Reichenbach Falls.

Even before the story was published, Doyle was receiving some backlash. When he wrote to his mother about his plans to kill off the famous detective, she wrote back, begging him to change his mind. Even though he and his mother were extremely close, he declined her request. Shortly before "The Final Solution" was to be published, Doyle's wife was diagnosed with tuberculosis. At the time, it was thought that the climate in Switzerland was good for tuberculosis patients, so the

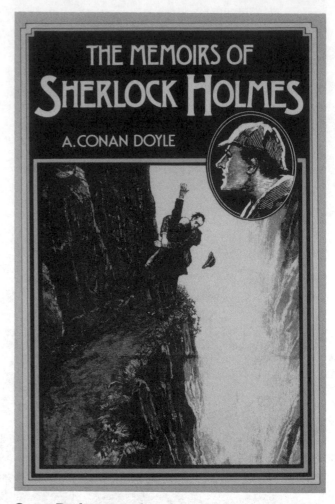

Conan Doyle outraged readers when he killed off his most famous creation, detective Sherlock Holmes, and Holmes's arch-rival, Professor Moriarty, in this 1893 collection of short stories.

couple moved and were there when the last Holmes story was published. The public outcry about the death of Holmes was more than anyone could have anticipated. Over twenty thousand readers canceled their subscriptions to the *Strand.* The author was besieged with nearly as much hate mail. In London, businessmen were seen wearing black crepe around their top hats as they walked to work. Nonplused, Doyle collected the second set of stories into *The Memoirs of Sherlock Holmes,* and launched upon a semi-autobiographical novel about his experiences with his former partner, Dr. Budd, entitled *The Stark Munro Letters.*

With his wife's health appearing to be better and the pressure of creating Sherlock Holmes stories out of the way, Doyle felt like he could relax. He is said to have introduced the Norwegian sport of skiing to Switzerland. Quite on target, he predicted that one day tourists would come to the country solely for taking part in the sport. He also had time to come to the United States for a reading tour, which popularized his work to this new audience.

Doyle was at work creating a new character that was to become nearly as popular as Holmes. Etienne Gerard, a soldier in Napoleon's army, was the subject of a series of stories he wrote for the *Strand*. The egotistical, comical and heroic Gerard was based on a real soldier, General Baron de Marbot. *The Exploits of Brigadier Gerard*, published in 1896, was the compilation of the first set of stories; the *Adventures of Gerard*, published in 1903, was the collection of the second series.

The Doyles moved back to England in 1895, heartened by news that the area of Surrey was good for tuberculosis patients. In the winter of that year, the couple went to Cairo, Egypt. They ended up taking a trip up the Nile, and witnessed a recent raid on a native village. Doyle's active imagination took this one step farther. In *The Tragedy of the Korosko*, he postulated the kidnapping of a British boating party in Egypt. In 1986, the Doyles returned to England, where they awaited the completion of their house Undershaw, in Hindhead, Surrey. In 1897, Doyle was to meet Jean Leckie, a beautiful twenty-four-year old woman. It is said that the two fell in love immediately, but kept their relationship platonic out of deference to Doyle's invalid wife.

Holmes Immortalized on Stage

That same year, 1897, Doyle wrote a play about his famous detective, Sherlock Holmes. After arguing with actor Beerbohm Tree about the implementation of the production, Doyle was discouraged. However, his agent had sent the play to New York actor William Gillette. Gillette was given permission to rewrite the play, even allowing the stone-cold and self-proclaimed woman-hating detective to fall in love. Although this was slightly out of character for the Holmes the public had come to know and love, the production became immensely popular in the United States. In fact, it became a trademark role for Gillette, undoubtedly cementing in the minds of the American audience the character of Holmes.

In 1899, fighting started between British colonists in South Africa, who were in charge of the government, and Dutch-descended settlers, commonly known as the Boers. Doyle was eager to sign up with the Army for the Boer War, but at age forty-one, even though in robust health, he was refused. He served instead as a physician in a private hospital near Bloemfontein. With his sharp eye, he noted that the British army was terribly outdated. He penned the essay "Some Military Lessons of the War," for *Cornhill*, in it suggesting that the army be fitted with rifles instead of swords, and spread out over the land instead of in strict formation. His suggestions were met with scorn and outrage from the military, but were later adopted. While there, he began to write *The Great Boer War*, a comprehensive history of the war and the conditions that caused it.

Returning to England, Doyle ran for a seat in Parliament representing his native Edinburgh. However, on election day, his former Catholic upbringing and schooling was announced prominently on signs and paraded around the polling place by his opponent. He lost the election, but only by a mere six hundred votes. The writer then returned to Surrey, and while on a golfing trip with a friend, was regaled by stories and legends of the Dartmoor area in Devonshire, England. The author became inspired by hearing these often bone-chilling tales, and began to make notes about a new story. In the beginning, he had no intention of making this story involve Holmes; after he started working on it, however, Holmes just naturally fit into the narrative. The resulting book, *The Hound of the Baskervilles*, became the most famous Holmes adventure of all time. Doyle got around Holmes's death by setting this adventure in 1886—five years prior to the detective's untimely end.

In the story, Holmes and Watson are charged with solving the death of Sir Charles Baskerville. The Baskerville clan are supposedly cursed, and their relatives pursued by a mysterious and ghostly demon hound. On the night of Sir Charles's death, the moans of an unearthly hound were said to be heard. Watson is sent to watch over the new heir to the Baskerville estate, and carry on an investigation while Holmes works in London. Through Watson's bumbling, Holmes is set up to become even more of a hero when he arrives to solve the case. When the story was being serialized in the *Strand*, the Sherlock Holmes play starring Gillette first appeared in London. Both story and play became a stirring success. The novel was later turned into the famous 1939 movie of the same name, starring Basil Rathbone as Holmes and Nigel

A supernatural hound threatens a family of English nobles in the 1939 film version of *The Hound of the Baskervilles* starring Basil Rathbone and Nigel Bruce.

Bruce as Watson.

Doyle Becomes a Sir

The Boer War was continuing to drag on even though the British appeared to be winning. The papers were filled with accusations of atrocities being committed by the British. Killing of Boer babies and the rape of Boer women were frequently reported. Doyle believed these charges to be untrue, and out of loyalty to his country, he decided to write an account of the war. *The War in South Africa: Its Cause and Conduct* was the result of Doyle collecting evidence from soldiers, civilians, and other observers of the war who disputed the reported atrocities. With his own money and private donations, Doyle had the book published, translated into every European language, and distributed all over the Western world. Because of these efforts, people felt that Britain was exonerated of the charges against it. So

grateful was King Edward VII for this action that he had Doyle knighted at his own coronation in 1902.

Shortly after this, Doyle was approached by an American publisher. The public was hungry for more Sherlock Holmes stories, and the publisher was willing to pay $5,000 per short story to resurrect the detective. The *Strand* offered over half that for the British rights to the stories. This was an offer too tempting for Doyle to refuse, so he began to concoct a reason why the detective had survived the tumble at Reichenbach Falls. Luckily, in Doyle's "The Final Solution," there had been no witnesses to see what had happened to Holmes. Thus, in "The Empty House" when Holmes returns, it is revealed that Moriarity had been the only one to go over the falls, and Holmes had used his apparent death to take a long hiatus and travel around the world as an explorer named

Sigerson.

The public bought this slightly unconvincing story, and it was reported that some lined up for blocks to purchase the journal. Eleven more stories were published in this series before being collected in the book *The Return of Sherlock Holmes* in 1905. Some critics have said that the Holmes stories before his death were the best efforts. However, Cox related that "many of the later stories repeat ideas and situations found in the early ones, but there are many which are the equal of anything in *The Adventures of Sherlock Holmes* or *The Memoirs of Sherlock Holmes,* just as there are weak efforts among the early gems."

The return of Sherlock Holmes in print was underscored by the stunning success of Gillette's stage play. In America, the illustrator Frederic Dorr Steele based his Holmes characterizations on the actor. All these efforts had the effect of making Holmes into a folk hero. Doyle was also successful with his play version of the Holmes story *The Speckled Band,* which premiered in 1910. The financial success which he had received primarily from the Holmes stories gave Doyle the chance to settle down, purchase cars and motorcycles, and return to the writing of historical fiction. In 1906 he published *Sir Nigel,* a story of the medieval knight Nigel Loring, which spanned the time before his earlier novel, *The White Company.* Doyle was hopeful that this book would be noticed for its genius, and would be considered his best work. Instead, critics mainly dismissed it as a fun adventure story. In the year of its publication, Doyle's wife Louise finally succumbed to the tuberculosis that had plagued her for years.

Although he had been in love with Jean Leckie for quite some time, Doyle held off marrying her for a while after his wife's death, complaining of depression and other illnesses. A year later, he married Leckie and the couple moved into the house Windlesham in Sussex. They had it remodeled and it became their home for the rest of the author's life. The couple had three children of their own. Doyle continued to write Sherlock Holmes short stories, completing twenty more before his death. In 1914, he finished the last Holmes novel, entitled *The Valley of Fear.* The tale concerns a murder in England that can be traced back to the murderous ways of a coal mining union in Pennsylvania. The story was set in the pre-Reichenbach falls days.

Moves into Other Genres

Doyle also dabbled in the theater at that time, dramatizing his novels *The Tragedy of Korosko* and *The House of Temperly,* both in 1909. He also moved on to writing novels of a science fictional nature. When his imagination was captivated by the discovery of fossilized dinosaur footprints near his home, he wrote *The Lost World,* featuring the larger than life adventurer Professor George Edward Challenger. This story is credited with spurring on many science fiction films, including three separate movie versions as well as the classic *King Kong.* Challenger reappeared in other stories, including *The Poison Belt,* in which the world is slated for destruction after its orbit collides with a stream of poison gas.

During World War I, Doyle once again attempted to volunteer for service, but was politely turned down. Instead, Doyle and his wife tried to assist in the war effort in any way they could. Doyle ended up writing several history books about the conflict, including one that spanned six volumes. During the war the Doyles lost many friends and relatives in the tragedy, including Jean's brother, Malcolm. Always interested in the subject of spiritualism, Doyle became a total convert when he claimed to have a visitation by the late Malcolm Leckie, who told him things that only the two of them knew. He began to write feverishly about the topic, completing *The New Revelation* in 1918 and the two-volume *The History of Spiritualism,* which was published in 1926. In the last years of his life, he frequently spoke out in defense of spiritualism, urging laws against mediums to be changed. He gave much of his own money to the cause, and unfortunately, was deluded by many fake spiritualists whom his friend Harry Houdini eventually exposed.

So fond was Doyle of his spiritual writings, that to do them he often turned down the enormous sum of ten shillings a word that would be paid to him to turn out more popular work. He put some of his beliefs into his fiction. In *The Land of Mist,* Professor Challenger comes around to believing that there is such a thing as communication with the dead. The crotchety Holmes, however, never makes that leap. Quite in character, Holmes flatly denies the existence of the supernatural in "The Adventure of the Sussex Vampire," published in

The 1985 film *Young Sherlock Holmes* featured Nicholas Rowe and Alan Cox as schoolboy versions of the famous detective duo who try to solve a bizarre murder spree in London.

1924.

Late in 1929, Doyle was stricken with a bad case of angina, but decided to continue speaking. He got somewhat better in early 1930, although he received oxygen frequently. On July 7, he died quietly, surrounded by his family. He was buried on the grounds of Windlesham under a headstone of simple British oak with an inscription reading "Steel True, Blade Straight." His memorial service was attended by over ten thousand family, friends, and fans.

Doyle's son Adrian became his famous father's literary executor. He joined John Dickson Carr in the 1950s to collaborate on a new series of Sherlock Holmes stories that appeared in *Collier's* magazine. Shortly after Doyle's death, a society called the Baker Street Irregulars formed to study the body of the Holmes works and to write spurious "scholarly" papers about the details of the stories. Various societies and journals of this sort have been in existence since the author's death, giving an immortality to Holmes and his creator. While Doyle pre-

ferred not to be distinguished solely by the creation of his famous detective, history had other ideas. It is apparent that Sherlock Holmes shall live on in perpetuity much longer than the other characters in the historical fiction Doyle loved best. To the millions of fans of Holmes all around the world, this is the biggest blessing.

■ Works Cited

Carr, John Dickson, *The Life of Sir Arthur Conan Doyle*, Coward McCann, 1946.

Cox, J. Randolph, "Sir Arthur Conan Doyle," *Concise Dictionary of British Literary Biography*, Vol. 5: *Late Victorian and Edwardian Writers, 1890-1914*, Gale, 1991, pp. 123-146.

Doyle, Sir Arthur Conan, *Memories and Adventures*, Little, Brown, 1924.

■ For More Information See

BOOKS

Baring-Gould, William S., *Sherlock Holmes of*

Baker Street: A Life of the World's First Consulting Detective, C. N. Potter, 1962.

Blackbeard, Bill, Sherlock Holmes in America, Abrams, 1981.

Brend, Gavin, My Dear Holmes: A Study in Sherlock, Allen & Unwin, 1951.

Brown, Ivor, Conan Doyle: A Biography of the Creator of Sherlock Holmes, Hamilton, 1972.

Butters, Roger, First Person Singular: A Review of the Life and Work of Sherlock Holmes, The World's First Consulting Detective, Vantage, 1984.

Cox, Dan R., Arthur Conan Doyle, Ungar, 1985.

Dakin, D. Martin, A Sherlock Holmes Commentary, Drake, 1972.

Dictionary of Literary Biography, Gale, Volume 18: Victorian Novelists after 1885, 1983, pp. 77-94, Volume 70: British Mystery Writers, 1869-1919, 1988, pp. 112-134.

Doyle, Adrian Conan, The True Conan Doyle, J. Murray, 1945.

Eyles, Allen, Sherlock Holmes: A Centenary Celebration, Harper, 1987.

Hailing, Peter, editor, The Sherlock Holmes Scrapbook, New English Library, 1973.

Hardwick, Michael, and Mollie Hardwick, The Sherlock Holmes Companion, Bramhall House, 1977.

Higham, Charles, The Adventures of Conan Doyle: The Life of the Creator of Sherlock Holmes, Norton, 1976.

Keating, H. D. F., Sherlock Holmes: The Man and His World, Thames & Hudson, 1979.

Lachtman, Howard, Sherlock Slept Here: A Brief History of the Singular Adventures of Sir Arthur Conan Doyle in America, with Some Observations upon the Exploits of Mr. Sherlock, Capra, 1985.

Pearsall, Ronald, Conan Doyle: A Biographical Solution, Wiedenfeld & Nicholson, 1977.

Pearson, Hesketh, Conan Doyle: His Life and Art, Methuen, 1943.

Rodin, A. E., and Jack D. Key, Medical Casebook of Doctor Arthur Conan Doyle: From Practitioner to Sherlock Holmes and Beyond, Krieger, 1984.

Symons, Julian, Portrait of an Artist: Conan Doyle, Deutsch, 1979.

Tracy, Jack, The Encyclopedia Sherlockiana, Doubleday, 1977.

Twentieth-Century Literary Criticism, Volume 7, Gale, 1982, pp. 214-242.

World Literature Criticism, Volume 2, Gale, 1992, pp. 1004-1021.

PERIODICALS

American Scholar, autumn, 1968.

Blue Book, July, 1912; May, 1953.

Bookman, December, 1892; February, 1901; July, 1901; May, 1902; August, 1903; November, 1912; July, 1914; July, 1922; October, 1927; August, 1929.

Collier's, August 15, 1908; December 29, 1923.

Harper's, May, 1948.

Hudson Review, winter, 1949.

Los Angeles Magazine, April, 1989, pp. 94–.

Los Angeles Times, January 14, 1987; January 18, 1987.

Maclean's, November 16, 1987, p. 60.

Newsweek, August 24, 1959; November 18, 1974.

New Yorker, February 17, 1945.

New York Review of Books, February 20, 1975, p. 15; August 17, 1978.

New York Times, March 9, 1952; January 17, 1987.

New York Times Book Review, April 2, 1944; January 21, 1968, p. 1; January 4, 1987, p. 1.

Science 83, September, 1983.

Scientific American, September, 1989, p. 188.

Smithsonian, December, 1986, pp. 60–.

Time, January 19, 1987, p. 47; August 17, 1987, p. 76.*

—Sketch by Nancy E. Rampson

Roddy Doyle

■ Personal

Born in 1958, in Dublin, Ireland; son of a printer and a homemaker; married; *children:* Two sons.

■ Addresses

Home—Dublin, Ireland. *Agent*—John Sutton, The Graphiconies, 22 South Great Georges Street, Dublin 2, Ireland.

■ Career

Playwright, screenplay writer and novelist, 1987—. School teacher for fourteen years at Greendale Community School in north Dublin.

■ Awards, Honors

Booker Prize shortlist, English Book Trust, 1991, for *The Van;* Booker Prize, English Book Trust, 1993, for *Paddy Clarke Ha Ha Ha.*

■ Writings

The Commitments (also see below), Random House, 1989.
The Snapper (also see below), Penguin, 1992.
The Van (also see below), Penguin, 1992.
Paddy Clarke Ha Ha Ha, Penguin, 1994.

PLAYS

Brownbread & War, Viking Penguin, 1994.

SCREENPLAYS

(With Dick Clement and Ian La Frenais) *The Commitments,* Twentieth Century-Fox, 1991.
The Snapper, Miramax, 1993.

Also author of screenplay for *The Van,* 1994.

■ Sidelights

Not many writers can lay claim to comparisons to James Joyce and Raymond Carver, but Roddy Doyle—armed with a lively literary style and comedic flair—has found himself in that happy position. His novels, which focus on working-class families in modern Ireland, rely heavily on dialogue. The books are peppered with the language of the author's native north Dublin: idiot becomes "eejit," Jesus becomes "Jaysis," and expletives abound. Rhoda Koenig of *New York* writes that "Doyle's novels are full of energy and have no time for sentiment." Although Doyle's background is more middle- than working-class, he treats his characters with great affection. Doyle is particularly sensitive to the telling details of their lives—such as the quiet thrill of receiving one's first letter or entering a library for the first time—that punctuate the drab and seemingly constricted lives of his protagonists.

Doyle initially made his living teaching school at Dublin's Greendale Community School, writing in his spare time. After working on an enormous, never-published political satire entitled "Your Granny's a Hunger Striker" throughout the early 1980s, the native Dubliner decided to take on a shorter subject. Doyle and a friend formed a company called King Farouk and published *The Commitments* privately in 1986. The book sold a mere one thousand copies until William Heinemann publishers expressed an interest in the text; as a result of this interest, Doyle's visibility increased substantially. The British publication led to a release in the United States, where Peggy Kaganoff of *Publishers Weekly* hailed *The Commitments* as a "cheeky first novel."

The Commitments also marked the beginning of

Doyle's first novel follows Jimmy Rabbitte's working-class Dublin soul band from its creation to a possible record contract.

Doyle's earthy, rough-and-tumble "Barrytown" trilogy, which focused on blue-collar life in contemporary Ireland. Barrytown—whose name the author once claimed to have borrrowed from a Steely Dan song—is a fictional setting that bears a striking resemblance to Doyle's neighborhood in the suburbs of north Dublin. *The Commitments* tells the story of Jimmy Rabbitte who, smitten with the Motown sound, decides to form a soul band in Dublin. Reasoning that the Irish are the African-Americans of Europe, Rabbitte is hardly surprised when he's swamped with responses to his ad for band members. He winnows the applicants down to a manageable group headed by Joey "The Lips" Fagan, a trumpet player in his 50s, who not only knows what soul is, but appears to be drenched in it (he even claims to have jammed with James Brown).

Appointing himself manager, Rabbitte assembles the "world's hardest working band," and installs Joey as the "ambassador at large of soul." Taking advantage of a called-off bingo game at the local community center, fledgling group books its first big gig—and gets the chance to play before a whopping thirty-seven-person audience. The group moves on to larger venues and are soon faced with the question of whether or not they'll get a record deal (and whether they'll be able to remain together until they do).

Examining the book in the *New York Times Book Review,* Kinky Friedman noted that Doyle offered a "veritable Berlitz course in the city's colorful, sexual street slang." Friedman observed that Joey Rabbitte's definitions of soul include sex, revolution, dignity, fun, "the rhythm o' the people," Guinness Stout and God. "*The Commitments* combines at least a wee bit of all these, along with a number of other more funky, far-flung ingredients," Friedman concluded, ingredients which provide the reader with "a pungent, steaming crock full of inimitably Irish imagination."

Doyle's next effort was collaborative. Working with Dick Clement and Ian La Frenais, the author co-wrote the script for Alan Parker's film version of *The Commitments.* The film brought the musical element of the book alive using a cast of almost entirely first-time actors. *People*'s Ralph Novak gave the film high marks for its performances and for Parker's direction; the critic summed up his review by noting that "the cathartic power of music has never been more graphically demonstrated." In the *New Republic,* Stanley Kauffmann

Doyle co-wrote the script for the well-received 1991 screen adaptation of his *The Commitments.*

found the film "amusingly bitter and vice versa" and stated that it is "the being and atmosphere of dirty Dublin that give the film its pull."

From Soul Music To Soul Searching

"A hilarious glimpse of everyday life in Barrytown" was how Stephen Leslie described *The Snapper* in the *Times Literary Supplement* when the novel appeared in Britain in 1990. The second installment of the "Barrytown" trilogy has the same gritty, working-class setting as *The Commitments.* The Rabbittes are again at the center of the story, but this time the narrative is focused on Jimmy's sister Sharon. When Sharon finds herself pregnant, she refuses to name "the snapper's" father, claiming that a visiting Spanish sailor is the culprit. The plot has less to do with such surprising revelations than with uncovering more about the Rabbittes and their life, especially Dessie, a blustering, sentimental paterfamilias who has to get his mind around the fact that his daughter cannot be controlled.

Although there is no conflict about whether or not Sharon will carry the child to term, there is a lot of family discussion concerning how the new ad-

dition will affect the existing Rabbitte brood. Over time, these often loud exchanges help bring father and daughter—and the entire family— closer together. Bruce Allen wrote in the *New York Times Book Review* that "the story slogs along good-naturedly, buoyed by an abundance of conversational exchanges (`What's perception?' asks Sharon. `Sweat,' replies her father), robust metaphors and hilariously foul-mouthed dialogue." Allen took the novel to task, however, for its predictability, complaining that it seemed "overlong." *Booklist*'s Gilbert Taylor echoed many of Allen's criticisms, but managed to include a left-handed compliment for Doyle as well: "Doyle achieves his entertaining effects exclusively through dialogues set in the home or the pubs."

Other critics were more sympathetic to Doyle's work. While agreeing that the novel

In the second installment in the "Barrytown Trilogy," published in 1992, Jimmy Rabbitte's sister Sharon becomes pregnant, causing conflicts with their father, Jimmy Sr.

Doyle's 1993 film version of *The Snapper*, directed by Stephen Frears, starred Tina Kellegher and Colm Meaney.

lacked a bit in the plot department, a reviewer for the *Los Angeles Times Book Review* declared that the author's "writing is so good the reader cares not a whit." The reviewer also praised Doyle for his "enormous wit and good humor," especially in terms of presenting parent-child relationships and writing sensitively about pregnancy. In the same vein, *Publishers Weekly* contributor Kaganoff concluded that the "endearing characters and a number of hysterical lines" made *The Snapper* an enjoyable read.

The last volume in the Barrytown trilogy was *The Van*. Unlike its predecessors, this novel is darker and more ambitious, especially in it's attempt to examine Jimmy Senior's midlife crisis more closely. Doyle worked from material that on the surface seems to hold little promise—the depression of the unemployed Jimmy Rabbitte and the fast-food truck that helps him back to self-respect. Over the course of the novel, Doyle puts the reader squarely back in the center of the family (all of whom have things to keep them busy *except* Jimmy). Then, when things are really starting to look bleak for Jimmy, his friend Bimbo buys a decrepit fish and chips van. Doyle describes the run-down vehicle in less-than-glowing terms, noting that "it was like something out of a zoo gone stiff, the same color and all." Bimbo and Jimmy devise a plan to make money by following the Irish soccer team to World Cup victory and sell-

ing fish and chips to the hungry spectators. Jimmy, who can hardly find his way around a kitchen sink, suddenly finds himself scouring and getting batter together for the cod fillets. The partnership eventually sours after Jimmy Senior and Bimbo's wife tangle.

Reviewing *The Van* in the *Times Literary Supplement*, Anne-Marie Conway lauded the "ghastly authenticity about every scene in the novel" as well as Doyle's ability to write comically but "never once patronizingly about these characters." She concluded that *The Van* "could have been depressing; that it is warm and funny (if somewhat over-long) is a tribute to an interesting new writer on the Irish scene." In a like vein, *Booklist*'s Peter Robertson complimented the author on his "gift of gab, and a nose for the low-key aside." And Tim Appelo wrote glowingly of *The Van* in the Los Angeles Times Book Review, remarking on Doyle's ability to "dazzle without warming."

Some reviewers, however, were less enchanted. In the *New York Times Book Review*, Bruce Allen complained of the fairly "tedious" first hundred pages and the "wobbly narrative mechanics" but noted that Doyle's "versatility and brio agreeably overshadow the sentimental excesses . . . that afflict his fiction." Allen concluded that "Doyle's a little like the beloved brat" who "may shock the neighbors, yet you know you can't take you eyes off him."

A Ten-Year-Old Boy's View Of The World

Doyle's next novel was *Paddy Clarke Ha Ha Ha*. The story is set in 1968 and features a ten-year-old narrator/protagonist who lives in the same neck of the woods as the Rabbittes. Young Paddy Clarke's thoughts range from the strange to the truly bizarre. Numbers—and number-related items—delight him. Paddy knows the life expectancy of a mouse (eighteen months) and that there are thirty-five million corpuscles in a person's blood; he is also fascinated by bad smells, scabs, bodily emissions, and "the kind of laughing that only forbidden things could make." Advertising and video games have no place in Paddy's world because his adventures spring from his own mind and body and the schemes his peers dream up. For all its joviality, *Paddy Clarke Ha Ha Ha* also reveals itself to be about the dissolution of Paddy's parents' marriage (which in turn changes Paddy from a rowdy, joyful boy into a hardened and protective pre-adolescent).

"Earthy and exuberant...with brash energy, cheerful irreverence, and a street idiom that reads like poetry" —*San Francisco Chronicle*

the van

Author of The Commitments and The Snapper

Roddy Doyle

Shortlisted for the prestigious Booker Prize, this 1992 work concerns the unemployed Jimmy Rabbitte Sr., who begins helping his friend sell fish and chips from a van and winds up having an affair with the man's wife.

In an interview with Lynn Karpen of the *New York Times Book Review,* Doyle allowed that he based the book "to some extent" on his own past. "The breakup of Paddy's parents luckily didn't happen in my family," he said, "but aside from that the geography, the incidental detail was very much from memory." The book's success led to another change in Doyle's life: he resigned from teaching at the end of the spring semester in 1993—"June 4, 1993, half twelve" to be exact—in order to devote all his time to writing.

Critical response to *Paddy Clarke* was generally favorable, though Peter Kemp of the *Times Literary Supplement* found some of Paddy's observation "novelist-like." He concluded that *Paddy Clarke Ha Ha Ha* made "an impressive and likeable addition to a line of Irish writing that got memorably un-

derway with the opening scenes of Joyce's *A Portrait of the Artist as a Young Man.*" Gail Caldwell of the *Boston Globe* said of Doyle: "In his dash-punctuated dialogue and proletarian poetics, he captures a working-class Ireland,with a near-boisterous affection for language—as apparent in schoolyard jeers as it is in the implicit laments that warring parents never utter." Paul Gray expressed his disappointment in *Time,* where he noted that the novel "while intermittently funny, fresh and affecting, is ultimately frustrating." In Britain, a reviewer for *The Spectator'* deemed *Paddy Clarke Ha Ha Ha* "truthful, hilarious, painfully sad and frequently all three . . . Doyle has written one of best novels I have read about what it is to be a precocious ten-year old, caught between self-absorption and a wild, sponge-like curiosity." Mary Flanagan's review in the *New York Times* found that the novel's premise "is not to tell a story but to enter a world. And this world is "brilliantly realized" with "luminous writing."

In large part because he presents life as it is *really* lived in contemporary Ireland, Doyle has been criticized by some of his countrymen for his often less-than-glowing depictions. To this, the author has replied that his job is to present things and people as they are—no matter how tough or bleak. As *Los Angeles Times Book Review* contributor Tim Appelo noted: "Doyle is no sloppy green-tongued laddie belching malodorous Hibernic sentimentality. Every act, every syllable has a plausible consequence, and he stays extraordinarily close to ordinary life. Often Doyle reminds me of what I imagine Raymond Carver would be writing had he lived and quit indulging in that drab verse: propulsive stories of everyday events charged with hilarity and knowing sorrow. Like Carver, Doyle has an immensely good heart, but he's too good a writer to give in to it."

■ Works Cited

Allen, Bruce, review of *The Snapper* and *The Van, New York Times Book Review,* October 11, 1992, p. 15.

Ansen, David, review of *The Snapper, Newsweek,* December 27, 1993, p. 48.

Apelo, Tim, review of *The Van, Los Angeles Times Book Review,* September 20, 1992, pp. 3, 15.

Buck, Joan Juliet, review of *The Snapper, Vogue,* October, 1993, p. 215.

Caldwell, Gail, review of *Paddy Clarke Ha Ha Ha, Boston Globe,* December 19, 1993.

Conway, Anne-Marie, review of *The Van, Times*

Literary Supplement, August 16, 1991, pp. 21-22.

Doyle, Roddy, *The Van,* Penguin, 1992.

Doyle, Roddy, *Paddy Clarke Ha Ha Ha,* Penguin, 1994.

Flanagan, Mary, review of *Paddy Clarke Ha Ha Ha, New York Times Book Review,* January 2, 1994, pp. 1, 21.

Friedman, Kinky, review of *The Commitments, New York Times Book Review,* July 23, 1989, p. 11.

Gray, Paul, review of *Paddy Clarke Ha Ha Ha, Time,* December 6, 1993, p. 82.

Kaganoff, Peggy, review of *The Commitments, Publishers Weekly,* June 2, 1989, p. 77.

Kaganoff, Peggy, review of *The Snapper, Publishers Weekly,* June 22, 1992, p. 55.

June 22, 1992.

Karpen, Lynn, *New York Times Book Review,* January 2, 1994.

Kauffmann, Stanley, review of *The Commitments, New Republic,* September 16 & 23, 1991, pp. 30-31.

Kemp, Peter, review of *Paddy Clarke Ha Ha Ha, Times Literary Supplement,* June 11, 1993, pp. 21-22.

Koenig, Rhoda, review of *The Snapper* and *The Van, New York,* August 3, 1992, p. 56.

Leslie, Stephen, review of *The Snapper, Times Literary Supplement,* December 21, 1990.

Novak, Ralph, review of *The Commitments, People,* August 26, 1991, pp. 13-14.

Robertson, Peter, review of *The Van, Booklist,* June 15, 1992, p. 1806.

Rockwell, John, "Is It Autobiography or Fiction? But Then, Does It Really Matter?," *New York Times,* December 20, 1993, p. C11.

Review of *The Snapper, Los Angeles Times Book Review,* July 19, 1992.

Taylor, Gilbert, review of *The Snapper, Booklist,* June 15, 1992, p. 1806.

Review of *Paddy Clarke Ha Ha Ha, The Spectator,* June 12, 1993, p.

Turbide, Diane, "Dublin Soul," *Maclean's,* August 30, 1993, p. 50.

■ **For More Information See**

BOOKS

Dictionary of Literary Biography Yearbook: 1993, Gale, 1994, p. 11.

PERIODICALS

Los Angeles Times Book Review, July 19, 1992, p. 6.

Publishers Weekly, November 1, 1993, p. 9; July 12, 1993, p. 76.

—Sketch by Megan Ratner

Danny Elfman

■ Personal

Born May 29, 1953, in Amarillo, TX; son of Milton (a teacher) and Blossom (a teacher and writer; maiden name, Bernstein) Elfman; separated; children: Lola, Mali (daughter).

■ Addresses

Home—Santa Monica, CA. *Agent*—The Kraft Agency, Inc., 6525 West Sunset Blvd., Ste. 402, Los Angeles, CA 90028-7212; or MCA, 70 Universal City Plaza, Universal City, CA 91608-1002. *Management*—LA Personal Development, 1201 Larrabee, Penthouse 302, West Hollywood, CA 90069.

■ Career

Composer and musician. Member of the Mystic Knights of the Oingo Boingo theatre ensemble, 1971-79; singer, songwriter, guitarist, and percussionist for the group Oingo Boingo, 1979—. Recorded albums with Oingo Boingo, including *Oingo Boingo* (EP), IRS, 1980, *Only a Lad*, A&M, 1981, *Nothing to Fear*, A&M, 1982, *Good for Your Soul*, A&M, 1984, *Dead Man's Party*, MCA, 1986, *BOI-NGO*, MCA, 1987, *Boingo Alive*, MCA, 1988, *Skeletons in the Closet* (compilation), A&M, 1988, *Dark at the End of the Tunnel* (compilation), MCA, 1990, and *Best O'Boingo*, MCA, 1991. Also recorded solo albums, including *So-lo*, MCA, 1985, and *Music for a Darkened Theatre: Film and Television Music* (compilation of his film and television music), MCA, 1990. Appeared in films, including *Hot Tomorrows*, American Film Institute, 1978, and *Back to School*, Orion, 1986.

■ Awards, Honors

Grammy Award, best instrumental composition, 1989, for "The Batman Theme" from the movie *Batman;* Grammy Award nomination, best score, 1989, for *Batman;* Emmy Award nomination, outstanding achievement in main title theme music, 1990, for *The Simpsons;* Grammy Award nomination, best score, 1991, for *Dick Tracy.*

■ Writings

FILM SCORES

Forbidden Zone, Borack, 1980.
Pee-wee's Big Adventure, Warner Bros., 1985.
Back to School, Orion, 1986.
Wisdom (including songs "Tears Run Down" and "Rock Me Baby"), Twentieth Century-Fox, 1986.
Summer School, Paramount, 1987.
Beetlejuice, Warner Bros., 1988.
Big Top Pee-wee, Paramount, 1988.
Hot to Trot, Warner Bros., 1988.

Midnight Run, Universal, 1988.
Scrooged, Paramount, 1988.
Batman, Warner Bros., 1989.
Darkman, Universal, 1990.
Dick Tracy, Touchstone-Buena Vista, 1990.
Edward Scissorhands, Twentieth Century-Fox, 1990.
Nightbreed (including song "Skin"), Twentieth Century-Fox, 1990.
Batman Returns, Warner Bros., 1992.
Sommersby, Warner Bros., 1993.
Tim Burton's Nightmare before Christmas, Disney, 1993.
Black Beauty, Warner Bros., 1994.
Ed Wood, Touchstone, 1994.

Also composer of score for *Article 99,* 1992, and of "March of the Dead Theme," *Army of Darkness,* 1993.

FILM SONGS

"Little Girls," *Tempest,* Columbia, 1982.
"Goodbye, Goodbye," *Fast Times at Ridgemont High,* Universal, 1982.
"Who Do You Want to Be Today," "Something Isn't Right," and "Bachelor Party Theme," *Bachelor Party,* Twentieth Century-Fox, 1983.
"Weird Science," *Weird Science,* Universal, 1985.
"Not My Slave," *Something Wild,* Orion, 1986.
"Same Man I Was Before," *My Best Friend Is a Vampire* (also known as *I Was a Teenage Vampire*), Kings Road Entertainment, 1988.
"Flesh 'n Blood," *Ghostbusters II,* Columbia, 1989.
"Winning Side," *She's out of Control,* Columbia, 1989.
Main title theme and song, *Pure Luck,* Universal, 1991.

Also contributor to the soundtrack of *Buffy the Vampire Slayer,* Twentieth-Century Fox, 1992.

TELEVISION SERIES THEMES

"Fast Times," *Fast Times,* CBS, 1986.
Sledge Hammer!, ABC, 1986.
Beetlejuice (animated), ABC, Fox, 1989.
The Flash, CBS, 1990.
The Simpsons, Fox, 1990.
Batman: The Animated Series, Fox, 1993.

OTHER TELEVISION MUSIC

Pee-wee's Playhouse, CBS, 1986.
A Special Evening of Pee-wee's Playhouse, CBS, 1987.
Theme song, *Simpsons Roasting on an Open Fire* (also known as *The Simpsons Christmas Special*), Fox, 1989.
Theme music, *Tales from the Crypt,* HBO, 1990-91.

Also wrote music for *Amazing Stories* and *Alfred Hitchcock Presents.*

■ Work in Progress

Little Demons, a musical based on an original story by Elfman, being developed by Disney.

■ Sidelights

"Watching the rough cut of a film he is scoring, Danny Elfman hunches in his seat, singing notes into a pocket tape recorder," describes Rosina Rubin in *Premiere.* "These abbreviated melodies capture his first instincts about the movie, harmonizing on its ideas and emotions. `One of the great challenges,' he says, `is to get inside the director's head and view the film through his perspective.'" This is just what Elfman does, especially in his dark, extravagantly dramatic, and funnily ironic collaborations with director Tim Burton. Beginning his musical career with the band Oingo Boingo, of which he is still a member, Elfman is a self-taught musician who stumbled into composing film scores. And since his first taste of the freedom allowed in movie music, Elfman has gone on to score numerous films, including *Beetlejuice, Batman, Dick Tracy, Edward Scissorhands,* and *Tim Burton's Nightmare before Christmas.* "I'm not a genius," states Elfman in an interview with Richard Zoglin for *Time.* "If I have a talent, it's being a good observer and being very tenacious."

Tenaciousness has been necessary for Elfman to survive in the world of composing, especially with his lack of experience and schooling. Despite the absence of genuine training, though, Elfman had really been preparing for the job since his childhood, when he was first exposed to some of film's greatest composers. "As a kid I would see movies five, six, seven times if I liked them, and I learned early on that a lot of my favorite '50s and '60s fantasy films had wonderful music by Bernard Herrmann," recalls Elfman in an interview for *Egg.* This early awareness of the intrinsic relationship between a film's score and its characters and moods made writing soundtracks all that more important to Elfman. In an interview with Stephen Rebello for *Movieline,* Elfman similarly remembers: "As a kid watching movies, I suddenly became aware that music was elevating the picture, doing something *else* to the movie. In every classic film I've seen, the music stood out as a character to make a bold statement."

Self-Taught Musical Beginnings

These early insights into music did not begin to manifest themselves until many years later. It was only after returning home in 1971 from a year-long trip through the continent of Africa that Elfman first began to uncover his musical talents. His brother, Richard, asked Elfman to join the Mystic Knights of the Oingo Boingo, a theatre ensemble that performed a multi-media revue in the streets, and eventually indoors on stage. Eight years later, Richard left the group to focus on his career in independent filmmaking, leaving Elfman and the remaining members to form the rock band Oingo Boingo.

During this time, Elfman taught himself to play practically every instrument in the band, and learned composition by transcribing the music of jazz great Duke Ellington. A few years and several LPs later, the band hit the Top 40 in 1985 for the first time with the theme song from the movie *Weird Science*. And even though Elfman's career as a composer of film scores took off around the same time, he continues to write songs and play guitar and percussions for Oingo Boingo. In an *American Film* interview, Elfman explains that the songs he does reach people "on a much more personal, direct level" than the film scores he writes.

The next step of Elfman's musical career was once again initiated by his brother, who asked him to compose the score for his 1980 cult film *Forbidden Zone*. It was after seeing this film that actor Paul Reubens (known as the character Pee-wee Herman) became interested in having an innovative and unconventional composer for his film *Pee-wee's Big Adventure*. A fan of Oingo Boingo, Tim Burton, the film's director, was also interested in having Elfman compose the score. "Though I never took it seriously as a potential job," relates Elfman in his interview with Zoglin, "I thought it would be hip to do a meeting." This meeting, states Zoglin, "led to Elfman's first great score—playful, lyrical, full-bodied—and launched his movie career."

Although he took on the job of scoring *Pee-wee's Big Adventure*, Elfman did so with some trepidation and uneasiness; his experience writing for the band was entirely different from the task he had

Elfman's Gershwin-inspired score for the 1990 film *Dick Tracy* received a Grammy Award nomination.

just undertaken. "Soon he fell in love with the freedom to change tempos, rhythms, and keys at will," relates Rubin, and used his imagination to create music that would have appealed to the young filmgoer of his childhood. Released in 1985, *Pee-wee's Big Adventure* was Elfman's first full orchestral score and marked his first collaboration with film director Tim Burton. In an interview for *Keyboard*, Elfman reveals that he "really learned to write [music] on *Pee-wee's [Big] Adventure*. My scores aren't what you would call legit, but they communicate my ideas effectively, and ultimately that's what composition is all about."

This first score, and many others, were influenced by such composers as Herrmann (*Psycho* and *Citizen Kane*) and Nino Rota (*8½* and *The Godfather*), who continue to provide inspiration to Elfman. In *Pee-wee's Big Adventure*, for example, Elfman explains in a *Fanfare* interview that he "was looking for a type of music that was very innocent and light. Bringing in the Nino Rota element felt right for me. . . . I wanted to find something that immediately put [Pee-wee] over as something from another world living here."

Elfman and Burton Revive Darkness

Following *Pee-wee's Big Adventure*, the strong partnership between Elfman and Burton continued to grow. Elfman relates in *Fanfare*: "Tim puts me into areas that are very challenging and fun to work with, and yet he allows me the creativity of figuring out how to make it come alive musically." Burton, in his interview with Rebello, gives his take on the successful collaboration with Elfman: "Danny kind of stumbled into film music a little like I stumbled into film. He grew up liking movies. I grew up liking movies. Film music had an impact on both of us. That's *all* the expertise we had going into this. We're just trying to bumble our way through it, without a lot of preconceived ideas. He totally understands the tone I like, which is usually an even mix of funny, tragic, overly dramatic, all at the same time. He understands that it doesn't matter if it's a comedy, a horror movie, whatever. He understands the complexities of things. In my case, he helps us to understand what the hell the movie's all about."

The pair's second film together was 1988's *Beetlejuice*, which is often referred to as one of Elfman's best works. The score combines satirical, riotously entertaining, and horror themes in a conflicting musical blend that adeptly complements the comic elements of the film. "A funnier, more boldly innovative or more manic score would be virtually impossible to imagine. . . . Elfman's work is as joyous and rollicking as the film itself," maintains Frederic Silber in *Fanfare*.

The next film Elfman and Burton collaborated on continued the dark themes of *Beetlejuice*, in addition to being a huge commercial success. Burton's shadowy and grim interpretation of Gotham City and the superhero himself in *Batman*, released in 1989, provides the perfect backdrop for Elfman's dark and otherworldly style. It was the score for this film that won Elfman his first Grammy nomination, for best score, and a Grammy Award for best instrumental. The visual imagery provided by Burton proved inspirational for Elfman as he wrote his score, which is filled with hard percussion, dreamy organs, and blasting horns. Robert L. Doerschuk, writing in *Keyboard*, asserts that the *Batman* score could change movie soundtracks forever: "By writing a soundtrack that stands on its own as an album release *and* could challenge the *Star Wars* theme in pops concert programs, Elfman demonstrates that with sufficient talent and dedication . . . [he] can transcend the idiom formerly defined by the technology of his studio and write effectively for orchestra."

Edward Scissorhands, released in 1990, once again has Burton and Elfman creating a fairy tale that is pure and sweet and dark and eerie at the same time. Elfman's score, which utilizes a melancholic choral backdrop, manages to effectively reflect and enhance the title character's feelings and expressions as he is first brought into a bright new world and then cast out.

Comedy, Horror, and Comic Strips

In addition to his numerous ventures with Burton, Elfman has also worked with a variety of directors on several films that fit into assorted genres. In 1988 alone, Elfman contributed scores to *Wisdom*, a box-office failure written, directed by, and starring Emilio Estevez, *Hot to Trot*, a comedy, and *Big Top Pee-wee*, the sequel to Pee-wee's first adventure. Of Elfman's contribution to *Wisdom*, Silber writes in *Fanfare:* "Suspenseful, hypnotic, pulsating, dream-like, the score succeeds so admirably in every thematic aspect where the film failed so miserably." The film which Elfman views as the turning point in his composing career was also released in 1988—the comedic hit *Midnight Run*. Elfman explains in *Fanfare*, "Finally, after all those years, I was asked to do a `contemporary' score." His last film of 1988, however was not such a pleasant experience. By the time the comedy *Scrooged* was finished, most of Elfman's music had been edited out or was buried in the film.

1989 saw Elfman returning to the genre he loves most—horror. Both *Nightbreed* and *Darkman* feature shadowy scores that combine striking overtures with a sort of tribal chanting. Elfman did not obtain these jobs in the normal fashion, however. Instead of reviewing scripts and picking films he wished to work on, Elfman sought out the directors themselves—Clive Barker and Sam Raimi. "I wanted very much to work with them, since I love horror," relates Elfman in *American Film*. "So I've returned to the genre that inspired me in the first place." Raimi, in his interview with Rubin, praises the imagery of Elfman's work, stating: "He has a very great, old-fashioned sense of drama that he creates through his music." And a reviewer in the *1991 Motion Picture Guide Annual* commends Elfman's score for Raimi's film, asserting: "*Darkman* has the right look, even the right sound, owing to another thundering, mock-operatic score by *Batman* composer Danny Elfman."

Another comic strip hero brought to the big screen pulled Elfman away from the horror genre again in 1990. *Dick Tracy*, directed by and starring Warren Beatty, provides the 1930s era setting in which Elfman sets his Gershwinesque score. The film earned Elfman his next Grammy Award nomination for best score. The experience of working on *Dick Tracy* was not an entirely enjoyable one for Elfman, though, mostly because of numerous rewrites. "Warren was insane," he recalls in *Movieline.* "But, see, what overshadows all the craziness involved in working with Warren is that I wanted to write a big, romantic Gershwinesque melody and that's what I got to write."

By 1992, however, Elfman was off in a different direction again with the score for *Article 99,* the story of a Vietnam veteran's hospital. For this film, Elfman took a more conventional approach, unlike the one when he worked with Burton on the 1992 sequel to *Batman. Batman Returns* is even darker than Burton's first tale of the superhero, and the movie, along with Elfman's score, were less favorably received. Ty Burr, in *Entertainment Weekly,* contends that Elfman has run out of ideas: "Here are the same windswept demon choirs, tin-

kling music boxes, Fellini carny music, and chic Wagnerian pooting that sounded so great in *Edward Scissorhands,* Elfman's peak. But like *Batman Returns* itself, this new score is neurotically hyperactive. It's as if Elfman, stumped for new material, simply opted to throw the old stuff at us faster and louder. That's fine if you're a punching bag. If not, not."

Halloween and Christmas Collide

Elfman's next collaboration with Burton was received much more favorably by critics and audiences alike. *Tim Burton's Nightmare before Christmas* was a giant undertaking; a ground-breaking stop-action animation film, it took over three years to make. And Elfman was involved from the beginning, helping to mold the actual narrative as he wrote the score. The movie began with an outline of a story written by Burton, but the first attempts to write an actual script fell flat and deadlines

The 1992 sequel *Batman Returns,* directed by Tim Burton and starring Michelle Pfeiffer and Michael Keaton, featured another dark yet playful score by Elfman.

were missed. So, Elfman began writing songs to tell the story instead. "It became a clean, pure process of my beginning writing from the first song and working chronologically," explains Elfman in *Movieline.* "I'd call Tim every three or four days, he'd come and we'd talk about where the story went next, he'd leave and I'd already be hearing the beginning of the next song in my head. I started demoing them all up, singing them, until, eventually, we were really excited to be telling the whole story and fleshing out the characters in music."

Partway through the composition of *Nightmare,* Elfman realized that he was writing from the viewpoint of his own character. So, he went to Burton and suggested that he would be the best person to sing the part of Jack Skellington, and Burton agreed. The ten songs that fill the score of *Nightmare* tell the tale of Jack, the King of Halloweentown. Tired of fright, Jack mistakenly finds his way to Christmastown and is enchanted with its joy, brightness, and high spirits. Deciding to bring Christmas to Halloweentown, Jack kidnaps Santa and takes his place, delivering frightening gifts from his coffin-shaped sleigh. The results are disastrous, and Jack learns what it means to be misunderstood.

"*Tim Burton's Nightmare before Christmas* restores originality and daring to the Halloween genre," contends Peter Travers in *Rolling Stone.* "This dazzling mix of fun and fright also explodes the notion that animation is kid stuff." "In *Nightmare before Christmas,*" maintains Zoglin, "Elfman's witty, melodically intricate songs drive the action forward as surely as does the animation." Rebello also praises the music of *Nightmare* in *Movieline:* "Elfman's score, like the screenplay and style of animation, is so rich in unexpected mood shifts, clever lyrics and musical genre-bending, it seems far simpler, yet more sophisticated, than Disney's recent animated smashes."

The one thing *Nightmare* is not is a typical animated Disney movie; and that's just the way Elfman prefers it. "I can't work as a composer for hire anymore," he explains in *Movieline.* "I have a pretty clear idea of what kind of music I do and don't want to write and, at this point, I'd rather die than to try and force a contemporary ballad on a timeless or old-fashioned musical. By the same token, *Nightmare* could never work by trying to squeeze it into that *Beauty and the Beast* framework—you know, a six-song contemporary

In collaboration with Burton, Elfman wrote the songs, helped create the story, and also sang the role of Jack Skellington in the groundbreaking 1993 film, *Tim Burton's Nightmare Before Christmas.*

Broadway-ish Disney musical. That would be like trying to graft the head of a tiger onto the body of a gorilla. You understand, I'm not saying what I do is better, it's just more to my taste."

Critical Nonacceptance

The actual scoring of the films that Elfman does decide to take on can often be a very stressful experience, especially when the reasonable schedule that is in place at the start of the project begins to dwindle because of early delays. Elfman helps alleviate some of this stress by working with the same people for most of his films, including fellow Oingo Boingo member Steve Bartek, who orchestrates his work, music editor Bob Badami, and conductor Shirley Walker. And despite the fact that he could begin to cash in on his growing reputation, Elfman remains adamant about only working on projects that interest him creatively. "All I can hope is that I have the ability to keep expanding musically, because when I tire of a certain style, I can't keep doing it," reveals Elfman in his interview with Rubin. "I'm not the type of professional who can just go, `What the hell, it's a job.'"

This desire to grow and expand has not always brought Elfman critical acclaim or recognition from his peers. "You have to remember that . . . I'm totally self-taught and instinctive," he points out in his interview with Rebello. "I have so many friends who are directors, writers, cinematographers and editors, but the single most snobbish and elitist group of all in movies are film composers. They're the only ones that will punish you for your lack of schooling and who won't accept you because you're self-taught. They just insist that you don't exist. And, although I taught myself to write notation on paper, I'll always be perceived by some as a `hummer'—someone who hums the melodies and turns them over to teams of orchestras who do my work. . . . It's amazing, but, once something like that starts, there's no reason to worry about it because there's nothing you can do about it."

Such rumors have not stopped Elfman from expanding his career. On top of all his film composing, Elfman has also written several extremely successful television themes for such shows as the popular animated series *The Simpsons* and the highly acclaimed *Tales from the Crypt*. And these, along with numerous other television and soundtrack themes, were released together on Elfman's 1990 compilation *Music for a Darkened Theatre: Film and Television Music.*

"The thing is, of course, Elfman doesn't just make movie music,"explains Rebello. "His unapologetically pushy, evocative, moody scores for such movies as *Sommersby* and *Midnight Run* are stuff I find myself humming. His compositions for Burton's movies are stuff that seem to navigate the Burton mindscape the way Nino Rota's do Federico Fellini's and Bernard Herrmann's do Alfred Hitchcock." Whether composing songs for Oingo Boingo, film scores, or television themes, Elfman is always ready to expand artistically. "Will new challenges bring satisfaction to Elfman's restless spirit?," asks Rebello. "He nods his head in the affirmative, then drawls, in pure Elfmanese, `Maybe, but no doubt I'll find a whole new level of critical nonacceptance.'"

■ Works Cited

Burr, Ty, review of *Batman Returns, Entertainment Weekly,* July 24, 1992, p. 56.

Review of *Darkman, 1991 Motion Picture Guide Annual,* Cinebooks, 1991.

Doerschuk, Robert L., review of *Batman, Keyboard,* October, 1989.

Elfman, Danny, in an interview for *American Film,* February, 1991, p. 42.

Elfman, Danny, in an interview for *Egg,* December/January, 1991.

Elfman, Danny, in an interview for *Fanfare,* November/December, 1989.

Elfman, Danny, in an interview for *Keyboard,* September, 1987.

Rebello, Stephen, "Danny Elfman's Nightmare," *Movieline,* November, 1993, pp. 54-58, 86-87.

Rubin, Rosina, "Cameos: Composer Danny Elfman," *Premiere,* January, 1991, p. 42.

Silber, Frederic, review of *Beetlejuice, Fanfare,* September/October, 1988.

Silber, Frederic, review of *Wisdom, Fanfare,* May/June, 1989.

Travers, Peter, review of *Tim Burton's Nightmare before Christmas, Rolling Stone,* November 11, 1993, pp. 80-81.

Zoglin, Richard, "Music from the Darkside," *Time,* October 11, 1983, pp. 80-81.

■ For More Information See

PERIODICALS

Entertainment Weekly, October 22, 1993, p. 82.
New Republic, July 9, 1990, p. 32.
Newsweek, November 1, 1993, p. 72.
New York Times, December 9, 1990.
Seventeen, August, 1987, p. 158; November, 1990, p. 86.*

—*Sketch by Susan M. Reicha*

Frank Frazetta

■ Personal

Has published illustrations under name Fritz; born February 9, 1928, in Brooklyn, NY; son of Alfred Frank and Mary (Prinz) Frazetta; married Eleanor Doris Kelly (manager of Frazetta Prints, Inc.), November 17, 1956; children: Frank, Bill, Holly, Heidi. *Education:* Attended Brooklyn Academy of Fine Art. *Hobbies and other interests:* Baseball.

■ Addresses

Office—Frazetta Prints, P.O. Box 919, Marshalls CK, PA 18335; Frank Frazetta Museum, 383 Park Ave., Boca Grande, FL.

■ Career

Artist. Illustrator of comic strips during 1950s, including "Johnny Comet" (title changed to "Ace McCoy"), 1952-53, "Flash Gordon," 1953, and "L'il Abner." Also illustrator of numerous covers of books, periodicals, and albums, and of men's magazines, including *Gent, Cavalcade,* and *Playboy.* Formerly associated with comic-book publishers, including Baily, Pines, Fawcett, and National.

Founded Frazetta Prints, Inc. Co-producer of *Fire and Ice* (animated film), 1983. *Member:* National Cartoonists Association.

■ Awards, Honors

Two Hugo awards, one in 1966; four awards from Warren Publishers; and awards from other organizations and periodicals, including *Playboy.*

■ Writings

ILLUSTRATOR

The Fantastic Art of Frank Frazetta, Rufus Publications, 1975.
Frank Frazetta: Book Two, Bantam, 1977.
Frank Frazetta: Book Three, Bantam, 1978.
Frank Frazetta: Book Four, Bantam, 1980.
Frank Frazetta: The Living Legend, Sun Litho-Print/ Frazetta Prints, 1980.
Frank Frazetta: Book Five, Bantam, 1985.
Small Wonders: The Funny Animal Art of Frank Frazetta, Kitchen Sink Press, 1991.
Frazetta Pillow Book, Kitchen Sink Press, 1993.

■ Sidelights

If you had to choose your future career today and you could only be a baseball player or an artist, which would you choose? Would it be the ballpark or the studio? The roar of the crowds or the gentle scratching of the brush on the canvas? What if you excelled in both and wanted more than anything to do both? This is the decision that faced Frank Frazetta as a young man. Frazetta put off choosing between his two boyhood passions as long as possible. At first, working as an artist seemed an ideal career because he could work only a few hours each week and still have plenty of time for baseball. But, eventually, the artistry of a well-hit ball was rejected—at least for professional purposes—in favor of the artistry of a well-executed illustration. His decision made, Frazetta went on to become one of the acknowledged masters of comic book and illustrative art.

Talents Noted Early

Frazetta's love of baseball seems quite natural considering his upbringing. He was born and raised in Sheepshead Bay, a tough, gang-dominated section of Brooklyn, New York. Relief from roaming street fighters—and the best entertainment in town—could be found in the bleacher seats at Ebbets Field, then home of the beloved Brooklyn Dodger baseball team (later relocated to Los Angeles). Besides being a big Dodger fan, Frazetta was a great ballplayer and from a very young age enjoyed playing just as much as watching the great American pastime. As evidence of his athletic ability, while still in high school the youth was offered a contract by the New York Giants (also later relocated to California). More professional offers followed when, as a member of the Parade Grounds League that played in Ebbets

Frazetta developed the "Snowman" character while still in elementary school, and first published the cartoon in 1944.

Field, Frazetta had a whopping .487 batting average and led the league in hits and runs scored. He was also voted the league's Most Valuable Player.

Recognition of his artistic ability also came early for Frazetta. At the age of eight, he already demonstrated such talent that his parents enrolled him in the Brooklyn Academy of Fine Arts. There he studied under an Italian artist, Michael Falanga, whose instructive technique was to let his young charges concentrate on whatever type of drawing or other artistic endeavor they liked best. The hours of practice, along with their own enthusiasm for their work, would improve their skills. When his mentor died, Frazetta was just thirteen; although eager to make it on his own, he continued his studies three more years. At sixteen, he accepted a job as an assistant to John Giunta, a popular science-fiction cartoonist of the forties and fifties. While doing fill-in work for Giunta, the fledgling cartoonist—who signed most of his work with his childhood nickname, "Fritz"—produced a comic of his own featuring "Snowman," a character he had first developed while still in elementary school. The comic appeared in the now-classic December, 1944, issue of Baily Comics' *Tally-Ho.*

Professional recognition of Frazetta's work came from an unexpected source when he was offered a position by Walt Disney. At that time, the Walt Disney Studios in California were flourishing, buoyed by the success of their early ground-breaking, full-length animated motion pictures such as *Snow White and the Seven Dwarfs,* which had appeared in 1938, and *Fantasia,* which followed two years later. While another artist might have jumped at the chance to work at such a prestigious firm, Frazetta turned down the Disney position. He found, however, in the invitation itself a kind of professional validation of his artistic pursuits. Disney's interest seemed to give him the encouragement he needed to continue his artistic efforts with renewed enthusiasm. The baseball/art conflict was finally settled, but surprisingly, it was Frazetta's love of baseball that kept him from agreeing to the offer to go west. "I think if the Dodgers had moved to Los Angeles before then," Frazetta commented in *American Artist,* "I might have gone. But in those days, California was too far removed from Major League baseball for my liking." He also figured that as a professional ballplayer, "You're too old while you're still young! In art, you're as old as your imagination."

Early Comic Book Work

While still a teenager, Frazetta was able to make a living contributing drawing to comics produced by many of the major comic book houses thriving during comics' so-called "golden age." In 1946, he was given the go-ahead for his first solo story published in Prize's *Treasure Comics.* Later, he worked on humorous animal illustrations featuring such characters as Hucky Duck and Barney Rooster. In 1949, his work took on a more serious tone as he received his first major assignment, drawing National's "Shining Knight" series in *Adventure Comics.* Later, while working at Magazine Enterprises, he contributed to such popular series as "Dan Brand" and "Ghost Rider" and collaborated with another artist, Al Williamson, on science-fiction pieces. It was in these latter tales especially that one can catch a first glimpse of the mature artist who would become a leading figure in the science fiction and fantasy world.

The imaginative landscapes, scantily clad females, and massive beasts that would come to be expected from Frazetta's fans as an essential part of his art can be found in early works produced during his twenties. By this time he had thrown off the influence of his mentors, Falanga and Giunta, and developed the style that would be uniquely his. If any influence could be sensed, it was from the youth's study of several original *Tarzan* pages drawn by the legendary Hal Foster lent to him by an art editor at Standard. The strong lines and sensual curves of the jungle setting were perfect subjects for Frazetta to tackle. "For it is . . . characteristic of [Frazetta]," noted Betty Ballantine in her introductory essay to *Frank Frazetta: Book Two,* "whatever the subject, to make it bigger, curvier, stronger, more venomous, more heroic, more alive, more dead. In a word—more. A good part of what strikes the eye in a Frazetta is his ability to believably exaggerate in order to emphasize the essential quality of whatever his subject may be." As an example of just how much power is felt coming from a Frazetta painting, one of his most famous figures, a warrior from the painting entitled "The Death Dealer," has been painted on U.S. Army airplanes and Boeing helicopters as a quiet but forceful inspiration to pilots.

The year 1952 marked another important landmark in the career of the young artist. That year, Maga-

Burroughs's "Tarzan" adventure stories were a powerful influence on the artist, and Frazetta eventually used this inspiration to illustrate the covers of numerous Burroughs works.

zine Enterprises published *Thun'da: King of the Congo,* the only comic book Frazetta ever completely illustrated. This first issue included four tales written by Gardner Fox, one of the major comic book authors of the time, and featured a Foster-like hero. When Thun'da's plane crashes, he finds himself in a lost land of prehistoric jungles, dinosaurs, and primitive humans. The excellence of the drawings and the uniqueness of the product was recognized immediately. Two decades after its original publication Frazetta fans were again able to enjoy the comic when it was produced in an expensive limited edition version. The influence of the Tarzan adventures of Edgar Rice Burroughs was evident in *Thun'da* and an important source of inspiration for nearly all of Frazetta's work. "I was really into Tarzan," the artist recalled in *Frank Frazetta: Book Five.* "I'd read all the Burroughs books—had a lot of fun with them. In fact, that was one of my aspirations as a kid. To be an artist and possibly do a Tarzan strip—Oh *boy!* I think it was my dream. And it seems the Burroughs people were never particularly interested. Somehow they never wanted me even though the Frazetta fans were out there plugging away."

When to his disappointment Frazetta was not asked to work on the Tarzan comic strip, he in-

stead started his own. The same year *Thun'da* was published, Frazetta was hired by the McNaught Syndicate to produce "Johnny Comet" (later titled "Ace McCoy"). It focused on the exploits of the somewhat Tarzan-like race car driver of the title. The strip was short-lived, however, and soon Frazetta was back drawing for comic books, including *Personal Love.* He also produced several impressive Buck Rogers covers featuring the science-fiction adventure hero for *Famous Funnies.* A syndicated strip, however, was assurance of a steady income, so soon Frazetta was back ghosting Dan Barry's "Flash Gordon" strip—also science fiction. In 1954, he left the science-fiction world behind and went to work as Al Capp's assistant on his "Li'l Abner" comic strip, a humorous look at country living. This working relationship was to last nearly a decade.

Lucrative Career Move

Another advantage of working on a comic strip—Frazetta estimated he needed a day and a half to complete his weekly assignments, while collecting full-time pay—was the ample free time it provided for the artist to pursue his baseball hobby and other interests. But the relationship between Capp and Frazetta eventually soured, and Frazetta found himself looking for work once again. He described his subsequent job search to Donald Newlove in *Esquire:* "So I . . . was taking these great covers around to the publishers—and they were too good!. . . . I told them, Hey, I'm the guy whose covers always used to boost your circulation before I left to do *Li'l Abner!* Didn't get through. I was 'old-fashioned.' So I get a job to do a little head of Ringo Starr. And that got me a phone call to do the movie poster of Woody Allen's *What's New, Pussycat?* My God, suddenly I had a check for five thousand dollars, a whole year's pay, earned in one afternoon!"

When he left "Li'l Abner" Frazetta began his career as a free-lance illustrator. He began to do more and more cover and poster art and less cartooning. His wife, Eleanor (more commonly known as Ellie), whom he had married in 1956, became head of his poster-print production team and saw to it that the artist retained reproduction rights for all his art. No longer would he stand by helpless after selling his work for a couple hundred dollars and watch as subsequent sellers got even more for it. During this time period he worked on covers for *Eerie, Creepy,* and *Vampirella*—a line of black-and-white graphic story magazines—and so impressed their creator, James Warren, that he named a corporate award in the artist's honor. Of course, several were bestowed on Frazetta. Also, during the mid-sixties Frazetta finally got his chance to draw Tarzan when he was hired to do the paperback cover paintings for a series of Tarzan novels being reprinted by Ace. Other Edgar Rice Burroughs novels also received the Frazetta treatment, including the Burroughs science-fiction adventures featuring John Carter, Prince of Mars, and David Innes, explorer of the world beneath the surface of the Earth.

With his covers, Frazetta could create an impression impossible in the small context of a comic strip. Newlove described the impact of these works: "Those covers gripped the fancy not just with their eroticism but often with their compelling sense of composition, of a picture that delivered fantasy with a looming hammerblow." Ballantine also commented on the Tarzan paintings, noting: "Frazetta's Tarzan is far and away the most believable of all the Tarzans conceived. He is of course beautifully well-developed, lean, hard, tall and ropily muscled. It is entirely credible that this man could travel for miles by swinging through the trees hour-by-hour, or even grapple with a lion." Frazetta was later hired by Lancer to do a series of covers for paperback reprints of Robert E. Howard's novels about the adventures of Conan the Barbarian. These books led to a rediscovery of the long-overlooked author and sold more than ten million copies, many purchased for the covers alone. In 1966, Frazetta entered the realm of the elite of the science fiction world when he was presented with that genre's symbol of excellence, the Hugo award.

The cover art seemed to bring out the best in Frazetta and he found making the paintings to his liking. In *Frank Frazetta: Book Five,* Ballantine included Frazetta's explanation for enjoying cover art more than the strips he had been doing: "Covers at a certain stage were easier. After all, you sat there and devoted all your energies to creating *one* picture, *a* painting. Whereas a strip is an awful lot of work with a certain sacrifice of quality because you just don't have the time. But it's fun too. A lot of fun. I love telling stories and moving figures from panel to panel, but again, it didn't pay very well then. You could starve to death. But with a cover, suddenly you're noticed overnight, it's such an easy way for an artist to go."

Because of the three-dimensional effect of Frazetta's style, his paintings were particularly suited for covers; they were the kind of art that had the ability to not only illustrate the work but also convince the browser to buy the book because of their excellence and the dramatic situations they captured. Commenting on this aspect of the artist's work in *Frank Frazetta: Book Three,* Ballantine wrote: "Frazetta is . . . famous for the furious activity of his paintings, the violent movement, the muscular tension which create the illusion that his subjects are about to leap out of their two-dimensional frame." Discussing "Frazetta's ability to grab the viewer," Ballantine praised "his marvelous use of sinew, curve and muscle to convey a strongly sensual quality. This feeling runs all through his work, whether his subject is human, or the feline and reptilian forms he uses so much, or even his roots and trees and water."

In 1971, Frazetta moved to the eastern Pennsylvanian town of East Stroudsburg, where he concentrated on painting covers and poster art. His artwork was used to advertise many well-known feature films, including Neil Simon's *After the Fox,* Roman Polanski's *The Fearless Vampire Killers,* and Clint Eastwood's *The Gauntlet.* He also produced some promotional material for the ABC television series *Battlestar Galactica.* His work remained focused on the realm of the fantastic, the powerful, and the brooding. "I love the Old Masters for their unquestionable abilities in composition and draftsmanship," Frazetta told Nick Miglin in *American Artist,* "but they were reserved, restrained by their time. . . . Today there's *no* restraint, and I'd be a fool to restrict myself in any way to please fans, critics, or peers. I'm an artist of my time; that's the only thing I can be. I find barns boring, so why paint barns? Barns already exist. They don't need me to create them. What I do create *doesn't* exist, and to me that's . . . more exciting."

Another Artistic Opportunity

Always looking for another vehicle for his art, Frazetta decided to enter the world of movie making, not knowing for sure how such a project would come together. "I was sitting around, resting on my laurels and doing the same thing over and over," Frazetta recalled in a *Cinefantastique* interview with Kyle Counts. "I needed a challenge. That's when I made up my mind that I was going to Hollywood to make a movie, although I didn't know how, when or with whom." During the late 1970s, the artist had been approached by several moviemakers to collaborate on a film in one capacity or another, but it was not until Ralph Bakshi, a former animator with the "Terrytoons" cartoon series, asked him to coproduce an animated film that Frazetta went ahead with his filmmaking plans.

Frazetta and Bakshi, who made a name for himself as director of two previously released full-length animated features, *Fritz the Cat* and *Lord of the Rings,* began their collaborative effort, tentatively titled "Sword and the Sorcery," during the summer of 1980. Along with his duties as co-producer, Bakshi also directed, while the script was provided by two prominent comic book writers, Roy Thomas and Gerry Conway. In *Comics Scene* Frazetta described his part in the making of the film to James Van Hise: "I did a minimum of drawing, but I did a lot of teaching. I taught the animators how to draw like Frazetta, from the background artists right on down to the figure artists and the colorists. I also worked with the actors and the stuntsmen and told them how I wanted them to move and look. I designed the costumes, put on makeup and directed in part with Ralph, and he's a real strong director." Even though the project was an animated film, costumes and makeup were necessary because of the innovative technique used to make the movements of the animated figures more life-like. Actors were filmed going through the scenes then rotoscoped by the animators who converted the action into animation by tracing the outlines of the figures on the film.

The film was released in 1983 by Twentieth-Century Fox as *Fire and Ice.* The story follows the plight of Teegra, a beautiful princess, who is kidnapped and then saved after a bitter battle featuring the Subhumans, the evil Ice Lord and his Dragonhawks, and Darkwolf, the muscular hero. Apparently pleased with the way the film turned out, Frazetta told Counts: "It is an adult film, not a kiddie film. Certainly, it's visually beautiful and kids should love it to death, and it has enough fast power that everybody should have a good time. It's not a hokey little animated film; it's quite a dazzling film." *HBO's Guide to Movies* found the plot "predictable" but claimed that the movie "stretch[ed] the confines of animation."

The posters in his *Fantastic World of Frank Frazetta* books showcase the artist's ability to create a strongly realized world through exaggerated forms and gestures.

A Distinctive Style

The bulk of Frazetta's books are collections of his paintings for covers and other illustrative projects. In her *Voice of Youth Advocates* review of one of these collections, *Frank Frazetta: Book Five,* Mary K. Chelton referred to the "evocative grandeur" of Frazetta's work and noted that the collection would be "of immense interest to kids interested in SF art." *Booklist* contributor Stephanie Zvirin felt that the audience for Frazetta's *Small Wonders: The Funny Animal Art of Frank Frazetta* would be "budding cartoonists" who would be eager to see the roots of Frazetta's artistic development. *Small Wonders,* unlike the other Frazetta collections, ignores his science fiction/fantasy work and features a collection of comic strips done by Frazetta when he began his career as an illustrator. While Frazetta is best known for his later work, according to reviewer Gordon Flagg in *Booklist,* the illustrator's "ornate and distinctive style was already largely developed" when these early comics were produced. Flagg found that even in these humorous strips "Frazetta's masterly technique" is evident in his drawings of "moody forests, lush jungles, and some decidedly *unfunny animals*" that are found alongside comically-drawn barnyard animals.

In *Frank Frazetta: Book Three,* Ballantine explained Frazetta's technique in more detail. "Frazetta works largely in oils," she noted, "preferring this medium to acrylic which he finds too flat. He uses wood, masonite or canvas for his paintings but much of his most interesting work is done in black ink or pencil, sometimes with a color wash, in the extensive 'doodlebooks' which he has built up over the course of time." *Frank Frazetta: Book Three* is filled with reproductions of pages from one of Frazetta's doodlebooks from around 1953. According to Ballantine, the doodlebooks are like sketch pads used for both planning a larger piece of artwork or as a surface on which the artist can limber up before the actual painting of a piece begins. Among the most reoccurring subjects in the doodlebook are wild animals and female nudes, some again showing Frazetta's humorous side.

Ballantine observes that success has paid off for the artist, who now lives in a comfortably large house with a private lake surrounded by enough land to give him the privacy he had always craved. Income from his print and poster business is enough to make daily work unnecessary, and so Frazetta tends to be very selective of any project proposal that comes his way. His long and varied career has given us a variety of images of the man—as the master of comic book art, the gifted painter, the creator of incredible SF worlds, and even the baseball player. Yet for all one may know about the artist, the source of his talent, of his imagination, remains a mystery. "Probably one of the more fruitless discussions one can get into," declared Ballantine in *Frank Frazetta: Book Two,* "is to ask an artist how he does it; and trying to analyse Frazetta, supposing that one could, would take many more pages than are available here. Better by far to sit back, marvel, and enjoy the product of his talent."

■ Works Cited

Ballantine, Betty, in introduction to *Frank Frazetta: Book Two,* Bantam, 1977.

Ballantine, Betty, in introduction to *Frank Frazetta: Book Three,* Bantam, 1978.

Ballantine, Betty, in introduction to *Frank Frazetta: Book Five,* Bantam, 1985.

Chelton, Mary K., review of *Frank Frazetta: Book Five, Voice of Youth Advocates,* June, 1986, p. 93.

Counts, Kyle, "Fire and Ice," *Cinefantastique,* December, 1981.

Eagan, Daniel, editor, *HBO's Guide to the Movies,* Harper, 1991.

Flagg, Gordon, review of *Small Wonders: The Funny Animal Art of Frank Frazetta, Booklist,* February 1, 1992, p. 1001.

Miglin, Nick, "Frank Frazetta at Bat," *American Artist,* May, 1976.

Newlove, Donald, "The Incredible Paintings of Frank Frazetta," *Esquire,* June, 1977.

Van Hise, James, "Frank Frazetta," *Comics Scene,* May, 1963.

Zvirin, Stephanie, review of *Small Wonders: The Funny Animal Art of Frank Frazetta, Booklist,* February 1, 1992, p. 1015.

■ For More Information See

BOOKS

Nardelli, Fred, *Frank Frazetta Index,* Nardelli, 1975.

—Sketch by Marian C. Gonsior

John Grisham

The Pelican Brief, Doubleday, 1992.
The Client, Doubleday, 1993.
The Chamber, Doubleday, 1994.

■ Adaptations

The Firm was adapted as a film directed by Sydney Pollack and starring Tom Cruise, Gene Hackman, and Jeanne Tripplehorn, Paramount Pictures, 1993; *The Pelican Brief* was adapted as a film directed by Alan J. Pakula and starring Julia Roberts and Denzel Washington, 1994; *The Client* was adapted as a film directed by Joel Schumacher and starring Susan Sarandon and Tommy Lee Jones, 1994; Ron Howard has been selected to direct the movie version of *The Chamber.*

■ Work in Progress

Three more novels to complete a four–book Doubleday contract that began with *The Chamber.*

■ Sidelights

In a Victorian–style house at the top of a hill on a sixty–seven acre farm, a former lawyer and state representative named John Grisham overlooks all that he has gained in a few short years and wonders how he came to be a famous, best–selling author. "We think of ourselves as regular people, I swear we do," Grisham says in an *Entertainment Weekly* article by Kelli Pryor. "But then someone will drive 200 miles and show up on my front porch with books for me to sign. Or an old friend

■ Personal

Born in 1955 in Arkansas; son of a migrant construction worker and a homemaker; married Renee Jones; children: Ty, Shea. *Education:* Mississippi State University, B.S.; University of Mississippi, J.D.

■ Addresses

Home—Oxford, MS. *Agent*—Jay Garon–Brooke Associates, Inc., 101 West 55th St., Suite 5K, New York, NY 10019.

■ Career

Writer. Called to the bar in Mississippi, 1981; lawyer in private practice in Southaven, MS, 1981–90; served in Mississippi House of Representatives, 1983–90.

■ Writings

NOVELS

A Time to Kill, Wynwood, 1989.
The Firm, Doubleday, 1991.

After viewing a rape victim testify against her attacker in court, Grisham produced this 1989 work, his debut novel.

will stop by and want to drink coffee for an hour. It drives me crazy. It happened yesterday. It will happen today."

Skyrocketing to the top of his profession in only a couple of years, it's understandable that Grisham should have a difficult time adjusting to his new lifestyle. *A Time to Kill, The Firm, The Pelican Brief,* and *The Client* have sold tens of millions of copies; movie versions of his books have been blockbusters at the ticket office, making their author a household name and giving Grisham a case of the celebrity bends. "I find myself taking long walks on my farm with my wife, Renee, wondering what in the world happened," the author admits in a *People* article by Kim Hubbard and David Hutchings.

Poor Boy Makes Good

Grisham's early years growing up in the South were humble ones. His father travelled all over the country to find jobs as a construction worker, taking his wife and five children wherever he went. It was a difficult life, but as Grisham notes in *People,* "We didn't have a lot of money, but we didn't know it. . . . We were well fed and loved and scrubbed." Each time the family moved to a new town, one of the first things that Grisham would do was go to the library and get a library card. Although he wasn't a great student, Grisham liked to read, and not earning straight A's didn't affect his self–confidence. "I've always been really confident, even in sports, where I had nothing to be confident about," he tells Hubbard and Hutchings.

When in 1967 his family moved to a more permanent home in Southaven, Mississippi, near Memphis, Grisham began to enjoy a more stable lifestyle. Sports—especially baseball—were of greater interest to him as a high school student than literature, although Grisham did enjoy reading John Steinbeck's novels. After high school he decided to study to become a tax lawyer, attending Mississippi State, where he earned his bachelor's degree (despite the D he received in English composition) before continuing on to the University of Mississippi, where he graduated with a law degree. Despite his original interest in taxes, while attending law school he developed a keen interest in criminal law.

After graduating, Grisham set up a private practice in criminal law in Southaven. He won his first case, defending a man who had fatally shot his lover six times after she had fired a gun at him. Though such cases proved he was adept at his new line of work, Grisham was dissatisfied and decided to try his hand at the more lucrative field of civil law. Again, Grisham won his cases, only to find that he still wasn't content working as a lawyer. He needed to try something new, something personally satisfying.

The idea came to him one day that he might be able to make a difference in the world by working as a politician to reform his state's educational system. Running as a Democrat in 1983, Grisham was elected to the Mississippi state legislature to begin a four–year term that was lengthened to a second term when he won the next election. Life as a politician, it turned out, was not all it was cracked up to be. While still running his private law practice, Grisham found himself working sixty-, seventy-, and even eighty-hour weeks so that he could serve in the legislature; yet after seven years of effort, he found that he just couldn't get around all the bureaucracy that was designed to maintain the status quo. Nothing he did significantly altered the education system in the way he had envisioned, so he resigned his office.

By this time, Grisham had already been exploring a new option—writing books—though he wasn't yet serious about making a career of it. His first novel, *A Time to Kill,* was inspired by a court case in which a young girl had been raped. Grisham had witnessed the girl testifying against her assailant in court, and he was so moved by the real-life drama that he became obsessed with the case. Pryor quotes Grisham's reaction to the trial: "'I felt everything in those moments. . . . Revulsion, total love for that child, hate for that defendant. Everyone in that courtroom wanted a gun to shoot him.'" Pryor continues, "Grisham could not shake that feeling. He knew if it had been his daughter, the defendant would be a dead man. He became so obsessed that he started getting up at 5 a.m. and writing a novel about a black father who machine-guns the crackers who raped his little girl."

Writing his first novel, let alone publishing it, was no easy task for Grisham. "Because I have this problem of starting projects and not completing them," he reveals to *Publishers Weekly* interviewer Michelle Bearden, "my goal for this book was simply to finish it. Then I started thinking that it would be nice to have a novel sitting on my desk, something I could point to and say, 'Yeah, I wrote that.' But it didn't consume me. I had way too much going on to make it a top priority. If it happened, it happened." Finishing the manuscript in 1987, Grisham mailed copies out to agents in the hope of finding someone to represent him. Several disappointing responses later, he received a reply from Jay Garon, who was eager to help out the lawyer-turned-writer.

Finding the Right Formula

Garon had as hard a time finding a publisher as Grisham had had finding an agent. In 1988 the book was finally purchased by Wynwood Press, and five thousand copies were printed the follow-

ing year. Grisham got a check for $15,000 for the deal. No one at the time had ever heard of a novelist named Grisham, of course, so the book was far from a blockbuster. The author himself wound up buying a thousand copies, which he peddled at garden-club meetings, libraries, and to friends; he gave away a lot of copies as gifts. Ironically, as Pryor reports, "Those first editions are now worth $3,900 each. And the novel Grisham . . . couldn't give away has 8.6 million copies in print and has spent 80 weeks on the best-seller lists."

Grisham didn't allow the initially poor sales of his first book to discourage him, however. Instead, he learned from the experience; he learned, too, what it was that readers would buy. With the help of

In this 1991 thriller, a young lawyer lands a dream job with an affluent law firm—until two partners end up murdered and an FBI investigation ensues.

a *Writer's Digest* article that outlined the basic rules authors should follow when plotting suspense novels, Grisham began writing his next book, *The Firm*. *The Firm* is a thriller about Mitchell McDeere, a young man fresh out of Harvard law school who is offered an $80,000–a–year job at the firm of Bendini, Lambert & Locke. McDeere thinks he's lucky beyond his wildest dreams, until one day two of the firm's partners are mysteriously murdered and the FBI begins to investigate. McDeere soon discovers that his firm is a front for laundering Mafia money, and he becomes entangled in a high–stakes game of death and deceit from which there seems to be no escape.

Although the story didn't excite him as much as *A Time to Kill,* Grisham was encouraged by his wife Renee to finish what he had started. He then prepared himself to repeat the arduous task of searching for a publisher and acting as his own book salesman, until his wife stunned him with some shocking news. The bad news was that someone had gotten hold of a bootlegged copy of his manuscript; the good news was that this person wanted to give Grisham $600,000 to turn the script into a movie. "The following day," Bearden reports, "news of the deal lit up phone lines on both coasts. Within two weeks, Grisham had a contract with Doubleday—one of the many houses that had passed on *A Time to Kill* two years earlier."

When the book was published, a number of critics quickly recognized that Grisham hadn't attained a high art form with *The Firm,* but they nevertheless praised his writing skills. *Los Angeles Times Book Review* critic Charles Champlin, for example, writes that the "character penetration is not deep, but the accelerating tempo of paranoia–driven events is wonderful." In a more glowing review, Susan Toepfer says in *People* that "*The Firm* is a thriller of the first order, powered to pulse-racing perfection by the realism of its malevolent barristers."

The Firm was more successful than Grisham had ever hoped it would be. In addition to becoming a movie, the book was on the *New York Times* best–seller list for almost an entire year. By the time the film came out, with Tom Cruise in the lead role, there were more than seven million paperback and hardcover copies in print. The success of *The Firm* gave Grisham the means he needed to quit his private law practice and the legislature, as well as have his dream house built

just outside Oxford, Mississippi.

A Second Blockbuster

Now that he had found his niche, the author plunged ahead into his next suspense book, *The Pelican Brief,* which he wrote in a mere one hundred days. Some critics complained, however, that Grisham followed the plot and premise of his previous book a little too closely. Comments John Skow in *Time,* "*The Pelican Brief* . . . is as close to its predecessor as you can get without running *The Firm* through the office copier." A corrupt law firm is again up to no good in *The Pelican Brief,* but rather than mere lawyers, it is two Supreme Court judges who are murdered. A law student named Darby Shaw suspects that the judges were assassinated so that more conservative justices can be appointed by the president. Shaw reasons that the person responsible for the murders, whoever he or she is, is facing trial before the Supreme Court and is trying to influence the case's outcome. When she discovers some evidence—though nothing definitive—for her hypothesis, Shaw writes the information down in the "pelican brief." Just telling people about the brief has lethal consequences, and soon Shaw is running for her life. Searching for help, she finds a reporter named Gray Grantham, and the two of them begin digging for answers.

Critical reaction to *The Pelican Brief* was similar to that of its predecessor. Frank J. Prial, writing in the *New York Times Book Review,* observes that while the story has flaws, "Grisham has written a genuine page–turner. He has an ear for dialogue and is a skillful craftsman." And Aric Press comments in *Newsweek,* "The setup is swell, and the chase is daring, but there's no brain food here." Grisham feels that the reviews of his second blockbuster were harsher than they were for *The Firm.* "As a rookie," the author reflects in Bearden's article, "people were really pulling for me with *The Firm,* but the second time around, those same people were secretly wishing I would fail so they could rip me to shreds."

Grisham admits that his books, beginning with *The Firm,* follow a formula that he describes in *Entertainment Weekly* this way: "You throw an innocent person in there and get 'em caught up in a conspiracy and you get 'em out." He also admits to rushing through the writing of *The Pelican Brief* and *The Client,* resulting in "some damage" to the books' quality. Yet he says in Pryor's article that

Denzel Washington and Julia Roberts starred in the film adaptation of the 1992 novel *The Pelican Brief*, in which a law student and a reporter search for the killer of two Supreme Court justices.

he feels persecuted by the critical community. "I've sold too many books to get good reviews any-more," he comments. "There's a lot of jealousy, because [reviewers] think they can write a good novel or a best–seller and get frustrated when they can't. As a group, I've learned to despise them."

Grisham has been criticized, too, for writing books that seem ready made for film adaptation. Both *The Firm* and *The Pelican Brief* have been made into movies, but some reviewers feel that with *The Client* Grisham was thinking movie deal even before he began typing. In a *New York Newsday* article, Adam Begley comments that "Mark [the book's young protagonist] is a character in a novel who knows that he's really a hammy child actor spending time in textual purgatory before he's translated back into celluloid heaven." *The Client* is about an eleven–year–old boy named Mark Sway whose life is placed in peril when he learns a terrible secret from a lawyer just before the man commits suicide. It seems that the lawyer was a Mafia attorney, and Mark has learned the location of the buried body of a U.S. senator—an important clue in an impending trial. As a result, a

mobster named Barry "the Blade" Muldanno is after the boy. Mark is also put in danger by the police and the FBI, who are, in turn, the pawns of a villainous district attorney who doesn't care whether or not Mark is in danger as long as the D.A. gets a lot of publicity by bust-ing the mobsters. Luckily for Mark, he finds help from a sympathetic lawyer named Reggie Love, who specializes in cases involving children's rights. Reggie's bold determination and Mark's re-markably useful knowledge of television po-lice shows work together to help them foil the bad guys.

Despite criticism like Begley's that *The Client* is a ready–made movie script, a number of reviewers thoroughly enjoyed the book. One *Time* con-tributor, for example, remarks that while *The Firm* and *The Pelican Brief* were "a bit overwhooped and underthrilling," *The Client* "works a lot better." And Ray Olson writes in a *Booklist* review that Reggie and Mark "make a sterling team, although, really, this is Mark's book and one helluva good read." Toepfer, writing in

A lawyer must protect a young boy who has learned a Mafia secret in *The Client,* a film starring Susan Sarandon and Tommy Lee Jones based on Grisham's 1993 story.

People, observes that though *The Client* is not as gripping, "it more than compensates with a newfound Grisham humor and slapstick energy."

The Client marks a slight departure for Grisham in that it portrays a much more flattering view of lawyers—through the character of Reggie—than the book's two predecessors did. Bearden also notes that the author "concentrated mainly on character development" in *The Client.* This is even more true with Grisham's 1994 book, *The Chamber,* which the author has described as a return to the more detailed and atmospheric writing that he did for *A Time to Kill. The Chamber,* says Grisham in Pryor's article, is "much more about the people. It will appeal to different kinds of readers." According to Pryor, the author feels that this book, the result of nine months of writing, "is his best work ever."

A New Direction

At almost five hundred pages, *The Chamber* takes its time telling its story, which is set in slow-paced Mississippi, just like *A Time to Kill.* It's the tale of

Klansman Sam Cayhall, who is on death row for the murder of the twin sons of a Jewish civil rights attorney. After years in prison, his grandson, a young lawyer named Adam Hall, shows up to defend him. The first thirty pages of the novel, as *Entertainment Weekly* critic Mark Harris observes, are written "with the unadorned swiftness of a writer who can't wait to get past his setup and into the good stuff." Over a quarter of a century's worth of events occur in the opening pages, documenting the crime, in which three conspirators plot the bombing of the Jewish attorney's office, and a succession of trials that ends when one of the guilty men turns in his partner–in–crime, Sam. Cayhall is sent to prison, where he waits for ten years as his lawyers make several appeals. Finally, after running out of options, Cayhall has only one month before his execution date.

At this point, Sam's grandson Adam, whose bar exams are not far behind him, comes to "face the family demon," as Harris puts it. What follows is a careful study of one family's history, the relationship between a lawyer and his client, and descriptions of what life is like for death row inmates, all seasoned with a relaxed Southern atmosphere. "That's a curiously rich milieu for a Grisham novel," comments Harris, "and it allows the author to do some of his best writing since his first novel, *A Time to Kill.*" Harris does complain, though, that *The Chamber* lacks the suspense and plot twists of his more typical works, but nevertheless feels that in "many ways, [Grisham's] measured approach pays off."

Grisham's stellar success—*The Chamber* enjoyed a record hardback first printing of two–and–a–half–million copies—has helped engender the rise of the legal thriller subgenre. Besides Grisham, two other novelists stand out in this category: Scott Turow, who led the way with *Presumed Innocent,* and Steve Martini, the author of *Compelling Evidence.* Although some have charged that Grisham was one of those to follow in Turow's footsteps, Grisham's *A Time to Kill* had already been written—though not published—when *Presumed Innocent* appeared in bookstores.

While these writers have produced some quality books, Grisham observes in an article he wrote for the *New York Times Book Review* that there are a lot of would–be–author lawyers who produce inferior work in the hopes of signing big book contracts. "For the moment, the genre is hot," Grisham says in this 1992 article, "and the bandwagon will keep rolling as publishers search for the next Scott Turow or George Higgins. After Tom Clancy introduced the techno–thriller, the market was flooded with dozens of imitators. Some of these books sold well, but the frenzy eventually abated. Still, the good techno–thriller writers were left standing. The same thing will happen with legal suspense." Within two years of Grisham's prediction, the genre began to lose speed. "An old–fashioned legal thriller is not what it once was," remarks one agent in an *Entertainment Weekly* article by Nisid Hajari, "because too many people started to write them."

Even if legal suspense books fall into complete disfavor with the reading public, however, it wouldn't be the worst thing to happen to Grisham, who told television interviewer Katie Couric on *Now* that if he could no longer write he would "coach baseball." Grisham coaches little league, and his son Ty is on the Little League all–star team. His daughter, Shea, also likes athletics and plays soccer. The career and life decisions that Grisham and his wife have made are for the benefit of their two children, and whether this goal is achieved by selling books or working as a country lawyer is of no great consequence to Grisham. Having accomplished in a few years more than most writers ever do, Grisham realizes that there might come a time to quit. Comparing novelists to athletes in Bearden's article, the author says, "There's nothing sadder than a sports figure who continues to play past his prime."

Works Cited

Bearden, Michelle, "PW Interviews: John Grisham," *Publishers Weekly*, February 22, 1992, pp. 70–71.

Begley, Adam, review of *The Client, New York Newsday*, March 7, 1993.

Champlin, Charles, "Criminal Pursuits," *Los Angeles Times Book Review*, March 10, 1991, p. 7.

Review of *The Client, Time*, March 8, 1993, p. 73.

Grisham, John, "The Rise of the Legal Thriller: Why Lawyers Are Throwing the Books at Us," *New York Times Book Review*, October 18, 1992, p. 33.

Grisham, John, interview with Katie Couric, *Now*, NBC–TV, June 1, 1994.

Hajari, Nisid, "Thrillered to Death," *Entertainment Weekly*, April 1, 1994, p. 19.

Harris, Mark, "Southern Discomfort," *Entertainment Weekly*, June 3, 1994, p. 48.

Hubbard, Kim, and David Hutchings, "Tales Out of Court," *People*, March 16, 1992, pp. 43–44.

Olson, Ray, review of *The Client, Booklist*, February 1, 1993, p. 954.

Press, Aric, "A Breach of Contract," *Newsweek*, March 16, 1992.

Prial, Frank J., "Too Liberal to Live," *New York Times Book Review*, March 15, 1992, p. 9.

Pryor, Kelli, "Over 60 Million Sold," *Entertainment Weekly*, April 1, 1994, pp. 15–20.

Skow, John, "Legal Eagle," *Time*, March 9, 1992, p. 70.

Toepfer, Susan, review of *The Firm, People*, April 8, 1991, pp. 36–37.

Toepfer, Susan, review of *The Client, People*, March 15, 1993, pp. 27–28.

For More Information See

PERIODICALS

Library Journal, June 15, 1989.
New Republic, August 2, 1993, p. 32.
Newsweek, December 20, 1993, p. 121.
New York Times Book Review, March 24, 1991, p. 37; March 7, 1993, p. 18.*

—Sketch by Janet L. Hile

James Haskins

■ Personal

Also writes as Jim Haskins; born September 19, 1941, in Demopolis, AL; son of Henry and Julia (Brown) Haskins. *Education:* Georgetown University, B.A. (psychology), 1960; Alabama State University, B.S. (history), 1962; University of New Mexico, M.A. (social psychology), 1963; graduate study at New School for Social Research, 1965–67, and Queens College of the City University of New York, 1968–70.

■ Addresses

Home—325 West End Ave., Apt. 7D, New York, NY 10013. *Office*—Department of English, University of Florida, Gainesville, FL 32611.

■ Career

Smith Barney & Co., New York City, stock trader, 1963–65; New York City Board of Education, New York City, teacher, 1966–68; New School for Social Research, New York City, visiting lecturer, 1970–72; Staten Island Community College of the City University of New York, Staten Island, NY, asso-

ciate professor, 1970–77; University of Florida, Gainesville, professor of English, 1977—. New York *Daily News,* reporter, 1963–64. Visiting lecturer or professor at Elisabeth Irwin High School, 1971–73, Indiana University/Purdue University—Indianapolis, 1973–76, and College of New Rochelle, 1977. Director, Union Mutual Life, Health and Accident Insurance, 1970–73; member of board of advisors or directors, Psi Systems, 1971–72, and Speedwell Services for Children, 1974–76. Member of Manhattan Community Board No. 9, 1972–73, academic council for the State University of New York, 1972–74, New York Urban League Manhattan Advisory Board, 1973–75, and National Education Advisory Committee and vice–director of Southeast Region of Statue of Liberty—Ellis Island Foundation, 1985–86. Consultant, Education Development Center, 1975—, Department of Health, Education and Welfare, 1977–79, Ford Foundation, 1977–78, National Research Council, 1979–80, and Grolier, Inc., 1979–82. Member of National Education Advisory Committee, Commission on the Bicentennial of the Constitution, 1987–92. *Member:* National Book Critics Circle, Authors League of America, Authors Guild, 100 Black Men, Civitas, Phi Beta Kappa, Kappa Alpha Psi.

■ Awards, Honors

Notable children's book in the field of social studies citations from *Social Education,* 1971, for *Revolutionaries: Agents of Change,* from *Social Studies,* 1972, for *Resistance: Profiles in Nonviolence* and *Profiles in Black Power,* and 1973, for *A Piece of the*

Power: Four Black Mayors, from National Council for the Social Studies—Children's Book Council book review committee, 1975, for *Fighting Shirley Chisholm,* and 1976, for *The Creoles of Color of New Orleans* and *The Picture Life of Malcolm X,* and from Children's Book Council, 1978, for *The Life and Death of Martin Luther King;* World Book Year Book literature for children citation, 1973, for *From Lew Alcindor to Kareem Abdul Jabbar;* Books of the Year citations, Child Study Association of America, 1974, for *Adam Clayton Powell: Portrait of a Marching Black* and *Street Gangs: Yesterday and Today;* Books for Brotherhood bibliography citation, National Council of Christians and Jews book review committee, 1975, for *Adam Clayton Powell;* Spur Award finalist, Western Writers of America, 1975, for *The Creoles of Color of New Orleans;* Coretta Scott King Award, and children's choice citation, Children's Book Council, both 1977, both for *The Story of Stevie Wonder;* Carter G. Woodson Outstanding Merit Award, National Council for the Social Studies, 1980, for *James Van DerZee: The Picture Takin' Man;* Deems Taylor Award, American Society of Composers, Authors and Publishers, 1980, for *Scott Joplin: The Man Who Made Ragtime;* Ambassador of Honor Book, English–Speaking Union Books–Across–the–Sea, 1983, for *Bricktop;* Coretta Scott King honorable mention, 1984, for *Lena Horne;* American Library Association (ALA) best book for young adults citation, 1987, for *Black Music in America: A History through Its People;* Alabama Library Association best juvenile work citation, 1987, for "Count Your Way" series; "Bicentennial Reading, Viewing, Listening for Young Americans" selections, ALA and National Endowment for the Humanities, for *Street Gangs, Ralph Bunche: A Most Reluctant Hero,* and *A Piece of the Power;* certificate of appreciation, Joseph P. Kennedy Foundation, for work with Special Olympics.

■ Writings

JUVENILE

Resistance: Profiles in Nonviolence, Doubleday, 1970.
Revolutionaries: Agents of Change, Lippincott, 1971.
The War and the Protest: Vietnam, Doubleday, 1971.
Religions, Lippincott, 1971, revised edition as *Religions of the World,* Hippocrene Books, 1991.
Witchcraft, Mysticism and Magic in the Black World, Doubleday, 1974.
Street Gangs: Yesterday and Today, Hastings House, 1974.
Jobs in Business and Office, Lothrop, 1974.

The Creoles of Color of New Orleans, Crowell, 1975.
The Consumer Movement, F. Watts, 1975.
Who Are the Handicapped?, Doubleday, 1978.
(With J. M. Stifle) *The Quiet Revolution: The Struggle for the Rights of Disabled Americans,* Crowell, 1979.
The New Americans: Vietnamese Boat People, Enslow, 1980.
Black Theatre in America, Crowell, 1982.
The New Americans: Cuban Boat People, Enslow, 1982.
The Guardian Angels, Enslow, 1983.
(With David A. Walker) *Double Dutch,* Enslow, 1986.
Black Music in America: A History through Its People, Crowell, 1987.
(With Kathleen Benson) *The Sixties Reader,* Viking, 1988.
India under Indira and Rajiv Gandhi, Enslow, 1989.
Black Dance in America: A History through Its People, Crowell, 1990.
(With Rosa Parks) *The Autobiography of Rosa Parks,* Dial, 1990.
The Methodists, Hippocrene Books, 1992.
The March on Washington, introduction by James Farmer, HarperCollins, 1993.
(Reteller) *The Headless Haunt and Other African–American Ghost Stories,* illustrated by Ben Otera, HarperCollins, 1994.

JUVENILE BIOGRAPHIES

From Lew Alcindor to Kareem Abdul Jabbar, Lothrop, 1972.
A Piece of the Power: Four Black Mayors, Dial, 1972.
Profiles in Black Power, Doubleday, 1972.
Deep Like the Rivers: A Biography of Langston Hughes, 1902–1967, Holt, 1973.
Adam Clayton Powell: Portrait of a Marching Black, Dial, 1974.
Babe Ruth and Hank Aaron: The Home Run Kings, Lothrop, 1974.
Fighting Shirley Chisholm, Dial, 1975.
The Picture Life of Malcolm X, F. Watts, 1975.
Dr. J: A Biography of Julius Irving, Doubleday, 1975.
Pele: A Biography, Doubleday, 1976.
The Story of Stevie Wonder, Doubleday, 1976.
Always Movin' On: The Life of Langston Hughes, F. Watts, 1976.
Barbara Jordan, Dial, 1977.
The Life and Death of Martin Luther King, Jr., Lothrop, 1977.
George McGinnis: Basketball Superstar, Hasting, 1978.
Bob McAdoo: Superstar, Lothrop, 1978.
Andrew Young: Man with a Mission, Lothrop, 1979.
I'm Gonna Make You Love Me: The Story of Diana

Ross, Dial, 1980.
"Magic": A Biography of Earvin Johnson, Enslow, 1981.
Katherine Dunham, Coward–McCann, 1982.
Sugar Ray Leonard, Lothrop, 1982.
Donna Summer, Atlantic Monthly Press, 1983.
About Michael Jackson, Enslow, 1985.
Diana Ross: Star Supreme, Viking, 1985.
Leaders of the Middle East, Enslow, 1985.
Corazon Aquino: Leader of the Philippines, Enslow, 1988.
The Magic Johnson Story, Enslow, 1988.
Shirley Temple Black: From Actress to Ambassador, illustrated by Donna Ruff, Puffin Books, 1988.
Sports Great Magic Johnson, Enslow, 1989, revised and expanded edition, 1992.
Thurgood Marshall: A Life for Justice, Henry Holt, 1992.
Colin Powell: A Biography, Scholastic, 1992.
I am Somebody! A Biography of Jesse Jackson, Enslow, 1992.
The Scottsboro Boys, Henry Holt, 1994.

JUVENILE; UNDER NAME JIM HASKINS

Jokes from Blacks Folks, Doubleday, 1973.
Ralph Bunche: A Most Reluctant Hero, Hawthorne, 1974.
Your Rights, Past and Present: A Guide for Young People, Hawthorne, 1975.
Teen–Age Alcoholism, Hawthorne, 1976.
The Long Struggle: The Story of American Labor, Westminster, 1976.
Real Estate Careers, F. Watts, 1978.
Gambling—Who Really Wins, F. Watts, 1978.
James Van DerZee: The Picture Takin' Man, illustrated by James Van DerZee, Dodd, Mead, 1979.
(With Pat Connolly) The Child Abuse Help Book, Addison Wesley, 1981.
Werewolves, Lothrop, 1982.
(Editor) The Filipino Nation, three volumes, Grolier International, 1982.
(With Stifle) Donna Summer: An Unauthorized Biography, Little, Brown, 1983.
(With Benson) Space Challenger: The Story of Guion Bluford, an Authorized Biography, Carolrhoda Books, 1984.
Break Dancing, Lerner, 1985.
The Statue of Liberty: America's Proud Lady, Lerner, 1986.
Bill Cosby: America's Most Famous Father, Walker, 1988.
(With Helen Crothers) Scatman: An Authorized Biography of Scatman Crothers, Morrow, 1991.
Christopher Columbus: Admiral of the Ocean Sea,

Scholastic, 1991.
Outward Dreams: Black Inventors and Their Inventions, Walker, 1991.
I Have a Dream: The Life and Words of Martin Luther King, Millbrook Press, 1992.
The Day Martin Luther King, Jr. Was Shot: A Photo History of the Civil Rights Movement, Scholastic, 1992.
Amazing Grace: The Story Behind the Song, Millbrook Press, 1992.
Against All Opposition: Black Explorers in America, Walker, 1992.
One More River to Cross: The Story of Twelve Black Americans, Scholastic, 1992.
Get On Board: The Story of the Underground Railroad, Scholastic, 1993.

"COUNT YOUR WAY" SERIES; UNDER NAME JIM HASKINS

Count Your Way through China, illustrated by Martin Skoro, Carolrhoda Books, 1987.
Count Your Way through Japan, Carolrhoda Books, 1987.
Count Your Way through Russia, Carolrhoda Books, 1987.
Count Your Way through the Arab World, illustrated by Skoro, Carolrhoda Books, 1987.
Count Your Way through Mexico, illustrations by Helen Byers, Carolrhoda Books, 1989.
Count Your Way through Canada, illustrations by Steve Michaels, Carolrhoda Books, 1989.
Count Your Way through Africa, illustrations by Barbara Knutson, Carolrhoda Books, 1989.
Count Your Way through Korea, illustrations by Dennis Hockerman, Carolrhoda Books, 1989.
Count Your Way through Israel, illustrations by Rick Hanson, Carolrhoda Books, 1990.
Count Your Way through India, illustrations by Liz Brenner Dodson, Carolrhoda Books, 1990.
Count Your Way through Italy, illustrations by Beth Wright, Carolrhoda Books, 1990.
Count Your Way through Germany, illustrations by Byers, Carolrhoda Books, 1990.

ADULT NONFICTION; UNDER NAME JIM HASKINS

Diary of a Harlem School Teacher, Grove, 1969, 2nd edition, Stein & Day, 1979.
(Editor) Black Manifesto for Education, Morrow, 1973.
(With Hugh F. Butts) The Psychology of Black Language, Barnes & Noble, 1973, enlarged edition, Hippocrene Books, 1993.
Snow Sculpture and Ice Carving, Macmillan, 1974.
The Cotton Club, Random House, 1977, 2nd edi-

tion, New American Library, 1984, revised edition, Hippocrene Books, 1994.

(With Benson and Ellen Inkelis) *The Great American Crazies,* Condor, 1977.

Voodoo and Hoodoo: Their Tradition and Craft as Revealed by Actual Practitioners, Stein & Day, 1978.

(With Benson) *The Stevie Wonder Scrapbook,* Grosset & Dunlap, 1978.

Richard Pryor, a Man and His Madness: A Biography, Beaufort Books, 1984.

Queen of the Blues: A Biography of Dinah Washington, Morrow, 1987.

ADULT NONFICTION; UNDER NAME JAMES HASKINS

Pinckney Benton Stewart Pitchback: A Biography, Macmillan, 1973.

A New Kind of Joy: The Story of the Special Olympics, Doubleday, 1976.

(With Benson) *Scott Joplin: The Man Who Made Ragtime,* Doubleday, 1978.

(With Benson) *Lena: A Personal and Professional Biography of Lena Horne,* Stein & Day, 1983.

(With Bricktop) *Bricktop,* Atheneum, 1983.

(With Benson) *Nat King Cole,* Stein & Day, 1984, updated and revised edition, Scarborough House, 1990.

Mabel Mercer: A Life, Atheneum, 1988.

Winnie Mandela: Life of Struggle, Putnam, 1988.

Mr. Bojangles: The Biography of Bill Robinson, Morrow, 1988.

(With Lionel Hampton) *Hamp: An Autobiography* (with discography), Warner, 1989, revised edition, Amistad Press, 1993.

(With Benson) *Nat King Cole: A Personal and Professional Biography,* Scarborough House, 1990.

(With Joann Biondi) *Hippocrene U.S.A. Guide to Historic Black South: Historical Sites, Cultural Centers, and Musical Happenings of the African–American South,* Hippocrene Books, 1993.

(With Biondi) *Hippocrene U.S.A. Guide to Black New York,* Hippocrene Books, 1994.

OTHER

Editor of Hippocrene's "Great Religions of the World" series. Contributor to texts, including *Children and Books,* 4th edition, 1976; Emily Mumford, *Understanding Human Behavior in Health and Illness,* 1977; *New York Kid's Catalog,* 1979; *Notable American Women Supplement,* 1979; Jerry Brown, *Clearings in the Thicket: An Alabama Humanities Reader,* 1985; and *Author in the Kitchen.*

Contributor of articles and reviews to periodicals, including *American Visions, Now, Arizona English Bulletin, Rolling Stone, Children's Book Review Service, Western Journal of Black Studies, Elementary English, Amsterdam News, New York Times Book Review, Afro–Hawaii News,* and *Gainesville Sun.*

■ Adaptations

Diary of a Harlem Schoolteacher has been recorded by Recordings for the Blind; *The Cotton Club* inspired Francis Ford Coppola's film of the same name, produced by Orion, 1984.

■ Sidelights

Born in the rural South at a time when African Americans did not enjoy the full rights of American citizenship, James Haskins absorbed the hard realities of life around him, translated them into a fascination with fact, and, as an adult, became the author of over one hundred works of nonfiction. "It has always seemed to me that truth is not just `stranger than fiction,' but also more interesting," Haskins explained in an essay for *Something about the Author Autobiography Series (SAAS).* Haskins also cites the desire to provide information as another reason for writing only nonfiction, and further explains his commitment to facts by writing: "I was born into a society in which blacks were in deep trouble if they forgot about the real world. For if they daydreamed and were caught off–guard, they could pay dearly."

Demopolis, Alabama in 1941, the year of Haskins's birth, was a segregated community. Because there were no adequate medical facilities for African–Americans, Haskins was born at home, where, appropriately, he locates the literary lessons of his early childhood. Haskins recalled for *SAAS* that a strong tradition of storytelling existed in his family and among his relatives. "My Aunt Cindy was the greatest storyteller who ever lived," he declared, describing her mixed–up versions of traditional folktales as ones in which Hansel and Gretel meet the Three Little Pigs. Haskins credits these stories with stimulating an interest in the unseen, complex "goings on under the surface of the real world." Among these interests was Voodoo, which the Haskins family regarded with skepticism, but which was a real part of everyday life for many people in the black community. Like other interests he developed as child, Haskins continued to think about the belief and practice of such mysticism, and later wrote a book about the subject.

Once he began reading, however, Haskins encountered obstacles to the pursuit of his interests. "There was not a lot of money for books, and the Demopolis Public Library was off limits to blacks," Haskins remembered in *SAAS*. His mother managed to get him an encyclopedia, one volume at a time, from a local supermarket. This constituted the majority of his reading, until a white woman for whom his mother worked learned of his interest in books. With access to the library, the woman checked out books for Haskins once a week, which she passed along through his mother. In this way, Haskins was able to read a wide assortment of fiction. "I enjoyed these stories," Haskins noted in *SAAS*, "but since my first major reading was the encyclopedia, this is probably another reason why I prefer nonfiction."

Haskins attended a segregated elementary school. The district did not have the most recent textbooks or best sports equipment, but, Haskins points out, there was an atmosphere of respect between teachers and students that transcended the limits of the environment. Because teaching was the highest profession African Americans had entry to at the time, they were greatly respected in black community. They "earned that respect," Haskins reasoned in *SAAS*, "by caring about their students as if it were their mission in life to educate us." In particular, Haskins's teachers departed from standard lessons and emphasized African–American contributions to American history. "In fact, if my teachers had followed the official curriculum, I would have grown up thinking that blacks had never done anything in the history of the world except be slaves," he wrote. "But they taught us that there had been many important black heroes in history."

As a teenager, Haskins and his mother moved to Boston, where he was admitted to the prestigious Boston Latin School. While attending school with a majority of white students was a new experience for Haskins, he quickly made the adjustment, and did well academically. After graduating from high school, Haskins decided to return to Alabama to attend Alabama State University in Montgomery. Haskins admitted in his autobiographical essay to being somewhat lonely in Boston, and he wanted once again to be surrounded by people like himself. He drew additional incentive to return to Alabama from the recent activities of the

This 1977 biography profiles the famed black leader who spearheaded the Civil Rights movement of the 1960s.

civil rights movement, which had its roots in that state.

College and the Civil Rights Movement

As Haskins explained, the protests began over the segregation of Montgomery city buses, and gained such momentum that leaders of the cause formed the Montgomery Improvement Association to unite African Americans on issues of common concern. A young Martin Luther King, Jr. was chosen to head the association, and his charismatic leadership attracted Haskins and others to Montgomery to take part in the struggle for equal rights for all. Haskins contacted King shortly after his enrollment at Alabama State. The young student was soon "putting leaflets under doors in the dormitories at Alabama State and stuffing envelopes and doing other fairly innocent tasks," he recalled in *SAAS*. Even this level of activism, however, was met with opposition by the university administration, and when Haskins was arrested for marching on downtown Montgomery, he was expelled from Alabama State.

Haskins then went to Georgetown University in Washington, D.C., where he graduated with a bachelor's degree in psychology in 1960. In the years since his expulsion from Alabama State, public sentiment toward the civil rights movement had improved, and Haskins returned to Montgomery to pick up the work he had left behind. Haskins also returned to Alabama State, where he earned a second bachelor's degree, this time in history. Haskins continued his education at the University of New Mexico, earning a graduate degree in social psychology.

Begins Teaching Career in New York City

Haskins worked for a time in New York City at the brokerage house of Smith Barney & Co. as a stock trader, but found that he wasn't quite satisfied with his career. "And then, gradually, it dawned on me that what I wanted to be was like the people who had made the strongest impression on me," Haskins commented in his *SAAS* essay, "and those people were teachers." Haskins took a job teaching special education at Public School 92 in Harlem. His students were challenged by a variety of handicaps, he noted, but most simply lacked the kind of supportive environment necessary to develop as individuals. Haskins undertook a variety of alternative teaching methods, including bringing newspapers to class for his students to read in place of outdated textbooks, and taking his students on learning excursions outside school.

"While I could not do much about their home lives, I worried about my students constantly and wondered what kind of future awaited them," Haskins confessed in his *SAAS* essay. He shared his concerns with friends and associates, and one, a social worker named Fran Morill, suggested that he keep a record of his feelings. She gave him a diary, and Haskins kept a daily journal of his experiences at P.S. 92. The result was Haskins's first publication, *Diary of a Harlem School Teacher.* Ronald Gross of the *New York Times Book Review* characterized the work as "plain, concrete, unemotional, and unliterary. . . . By its truthfulness alone does it command our concern. The book is like a weapon—cold, blunt, painful."

Following the publication of *Diary of a Harlem School Teacher,* Haskins was approached by publishers who wondered if he might be interested in writing books for children. "I knew exactly the kind of books I wanted to do—books about current events and books about important black people so that students could understand the larger world around them through books written at a level they could understand," Haskins told *SAAS.*

Begins Writing for Young Readers

Published in 1971, *Resistance: Profiles in Nonviolence* was Haskins' first book for children. With this work Haskins tried to place nonviolence in a historical context culminating in, but not exclusive to, Martin Luther King, Jr. Shortly after *Resistance,* Haskins published *A Piece of the Power: Four Black Mayors,* which chronicles the political successes of Carl Stokes, Richard Hatcher, Charles Evers, and Kenneth Gibson. In addition to telling how these men began their careers and ultimately came to hold power, "James Haskins tells us something about what happens next and it is interesting and useful information," asserted Fred and Lucille Clifton in the *New York Times Book Review.* A *Kirkus Reviews* writer took issue, however, with the fact that the book provides little guidance to the complex issues surrounding the men profiled, calling the work "competent but totally non–interpretive."

In 1975 Haskins published another work with an historical emphasis, *The Creoles of Color of New Orleans.* In this book Haskins examines the culture of Louisiana's Creoles, a mixed population of African–American descent which was exempt from slavery. In the absence of any definitive political freedom, the Creoles embraced the values of slave–owning whites, and set themselves up in differentiation and opposition to black slaves. In an *Interracial Books for Children Bulletin,* Patricia Spence credited Haskins for dealing openly with the prejudices of the Creoles, but faulted him for failing to locate Creoles in the larger context of a racially segregated society: "Such a framework is necessary to foster understanding of the Creole's value system as the product of a racist environment." *The Creoles of Color of New Orleans* attracted the attention of other readers and critics, and was selected as a Spur Award finalist by the Western Writers of America.

In *Street Gangs: Yesterday and Today* Haskins studies the history of organized violence among adolescents and teenagers to explain the gang culture which absorbs so many young Americans. Haskins concludes that gang membership brings a sense of inclusion and a feeling of worth that is otherwise lacking in the gang member's life. This has been true, he claims, throughout American history. "The strength of Haskins' book is in its historical material," wrote Colman McCarthy in a *Washington Post Book World* review. McCarthy notes, in particular, the descriptions of street gangs that formed in the new states following the revolutionary war, and the notorious Bowery Boys of nineteenth-century New York City. In a *Bulletin of the Center for Children's Books* review, Zena Sutherland praised the "strong direct prose" of *Street Gangs,* and credited the book with linking the problems of contemporary youth to the past. For the insight it provided into a disturbing aspect of American urban life, *Street Gangs* received a Books of the Year citation from the Child Study Association of America.

In this 1987 work, Haskins chronicles the struggles and triumphs of black musicians from the 1800s to the present.

Haskins has, since 1970, taught writing and lectured on literature for young readers at several colleges and universities. Haskins began teaching at this level at the New School for Social Research, in New York City. He then taught at Staten Island Community College of the City University of New York, Indiana University—Purdue University in Indianapolis, and the State University of New York at New Paltz. In 1977, Haskins assumed his current post as a professor of English at the University of Florida in Gainesville. Commenting on the development of his career in his *SAAS* essay, Haskins observed that he really has two careers. Teaching is Haskins' primary career, while writing remains a fascinating sideline that allows him to simultaneously pursue his own interests, and share them with others.

Cotton Club Inspires Movie

In 1977 Haskins published an adult book, *The Cotton Club,* an in-depth account of a night club in Harlem that showcased African-American entertainers for a white audience during the 1920s. Among the luminaries that performed in this segregated setting were Cab Calloway, Lena Horne, and Duke Ellington. In the *New York Times Book Review,* Jervis Anderson concluded that the *Cotton Club* "memorializes that Harlem nightspot—one of the classiest joints in the history of New York late-night entertainment. It is a detailed, instructive and entertaining work." *The Cotton Club* inspired a 1984 movie of the same name. Although the melodramatic film departed greatly from Haskins's book, he was invited to visit the movie set, and also met the actors and actresses who starred in the film. "I even got a director's chair with my name on it," he recalled fondly in *SAAS,* "though I had nothing really to do with the movie."

Among Haskins's more recent historical works for young readers is *The Sixties Reader,* which he co-wrote with Kathleen Benson. The reader is an attempt to present some of the major social movements of the 1960s through documentary evidence, with little interpretation. In a *Voice of Youth Advocates* review of the book, Patrick Jones compared it to other works which deal with the same period for young readers, pointing out that the strength of *The Sixties Reader* is a reliance on fact and a desire to present information rather than anecdotes. "The book is a starting point," Jones wrote. "Each of the chapters focuses on a movement, then important documents, statements, lyrics, or interviews are presented." This allows readers to appreciate not only the events of the period, but how those events were shaped in the minds of those present, concluded Jones.

As a writer, Haskins has a professed interest in biography. "It seemed to me that young people ought to have some living black heroes to read about," he noted in *SAAS*, "and because of the gains made by black people there were more black heroes to write about." Haskins was reluctant at first to write about African–American sports stars, however, because he felt that children needed role models other than athletes. But when professional baseball player Hank Aaron was on the verge of breaking Babe Ruth's career mark for home runs, Haskins noticed a debate emerging over who was the better athlete and the better person. Inspired by the need for fairness in this dialogue, Haskins wrote his first sports biography, *Babe Ruth and Hank Aaron: The Home Run Kings*. Several other sports biographies followed, and they have been among Haskins's more popular works, a fact the writer has come to accept. "I realized that it doesn't matter so much *what* kids read as it does *that* they read," he proclaimed.

Among Haskins's later sports biographies is *Sports Great Magic Johnson*. From high school championships in Lansing, Michigan, to professional championships with the Los Angeles Lakers, basketball superstar Earvin "Magic" Johnson has a remarkable record of winning. Well before the emergence of Michael Jordan as the dominant player in the National Basketball Association (NBA), critics and fans hailed Magic Johnson as the greatest player ever to play the game. In a *School Library Journal* review, Tom S. Hurlbut characterized Haskins's work as straightforward, and noted that Johnson's personal and family life are covered, "keeping the biography focused on the person rather than just the athlete." In 1992 Haskins updated the volume to reflect the emergence of Johnson, who is infected with HIV, as an activist in the fight against AIDS.

Haskins has also written biographies of entertainment celebrities as well. To research *The Story of Stevie Wonder*, Haskins traveled to Los Angeles to spend a couple of days with the musician. "He made music all the time and everywhere," Haskins recalled of

Ragtime musician Scott Joplin is the subject of this 1978 work which received the American Society of Composer, Authors and Publishers-Deems Taylor Award.

Wonder in *SAAS*, "beating on the table with a fork or making rhythms with his feet on the steps." Haskins has also written a biography of pop superstar Michael Jackson. In *About Michael Jackson*, Haskins provides a glimpse of the childhood and personal life of the intensely private and reclusive star. In a *Voice of Youth Advocates* review, Jerry Grim wrote that although he found the writing "trite" in places, "the artist comes out looking like a human being and not a two–dimensional poster." Hurlbut's *School Library Journal* review of the book faulted Haskins, however, for skirting the more controversial issues of Jackson's life, including his plastic surgery and family difficulties, saying they are "only dealt with in passing."

Haskins's biography of Bill Cosby, *Bill Cosby: America's Most Famous Father*, attempts to reveal the early influences that gave direction to comedian's life. "Young people will relate to the impatience with school that brought on bad grades and dropping out of high school," commented Luvada Kuhn in a *Voice of Youth Advocates* review. They will also respect the struggle Cosby faced to pass his GED (General Equivalency Diploma) test and go on to college, Kuhn concluded. In a *School Library Journal* review Todd Morning noted that Cosby's career is surveyed in detail, and credits Haskins for presenting the charge that "there is a certain amount of anger and arrogance beneath the affable surface" of the actor.

Real–Life Black Heroes Star in Books

Haskins's recent profiles of blacks in positions of leadership include books about Jesse Jackson, Winnie Mandela, Colin Powell, and Thurgood Marshall. *I Am Somebody! A Biography of Jesse Jackson* tells of Jackson's childhood in rural Greenville, South Carolina, of the determination that led Jackson to succeed in sports and academics and win a college scholarship, of his rise to the forefront of the civil rights movement, and his eventual prominence among black political figures. Jeanette Lambert, in a *School Library Journal* review, called the book "incisive," and credited Haskins with providing a fair portrait of Jackson, in which both strengths and flaws of character are discussed "in a balanced manner." In a *Voice of Youth Advocates* review of *I Am Somebody*, Alice M. Johns appreciated Haskins's depiction of Jackson as a leader who increased his power and influence by helping "people to participate in full citizenship."

Winnie Mandela: Life of Struggle is similar to the Jackson biography in that its subject has been intimately involved in a civil rights struggle, this time in South Africa. Born in remote village, Winnie Mandela became the first black medical social worker in South African history. In the process of her educational she was introduced to the ideology of African nationalism, which she soon advocated. This advocacy became the determining factor in her life after her marriage to the leader of the outlawed African National Congress, Nelson Mandela. After his imprisonment, Winnie continued to oppose apartheid and to keep the vision of a democratic South Africa alive. To promote her cause, Winnie has "endured police harassment, numerous arrests, physical mistreatment, solitary confinement, and banishment to a community with a language different from her own," pointed out Virginia B. Moore in a *Voice of Youth Advocates* review, making for an

"easy–to–read, fast–paced and gripping profile." In a *School Library Journal* review Nancy J. Schmidt praised Haskins's facility for connecting "Mandela's personal story with that of milestones in the black South African struggle." In the "moving" portrayal that results, Schmidt remarked, Mandela is both a person and the leader of a globally significant social movement.

Colin Powell takes a look at the life of the first African American to head the Joint Chiefs of Staff of the United States. Hazel Moore, in a *Voice of Youth Advocates* review, found the description of Powell's struggle to succeed academically sufficiently inspiring to recommend the book. "The person, more than the military leader, emerges from the portrait Haskins paints," she added. *Thurgood Marshall: A Life for Justice* follows a similar format, emphasizing Marshall's beginnings in the Civil Rights movement, then following him through his years as attorney to the National Association for the Advancement of Colored People (NAACP), and finally, to the bench of the United States Supreme Court. In a *School Library Journal* review, Mary Mueller particularly appreciated the "discussion of the difference between Marshall's constitutional tactics and those used by the Direct Actions Civil Rights Movement, led by Martin Luther King, Jr."

Haskins returned to the subject of overall black contributions to history with *Against All Opposition: Black Explorers in America*. From the seafaring adventurers of the African nation of Mali in the 1300s, to the Arctic travels of Matthew Henson, and the experiences of astronauts Ronald McNair and Guion Stewart Bluford, Jr., Haskins sheds light on accomplishments which racism has suppressed. In *Voice of Youth Advocates*, Diane Yankelevitz found the work informative, but asserted that the specificity that makes the work valuable as a reference prevents it from being "very interesting as general reading." A similar work, *Get on Board: The Story of the Underground Railroad*, recounts the history of the network of abolitionists and free African–American men and women who helped escaped slaves flee north. In addition to describing the organization and structure of the railroad, the roles played by the "conductors," who provided safe passage, and the "stationmasters," who provided shelter, Haskins includes accounts from men and women who "rode" the railroad to freedom. "Although the firsthand stories are interesting on their own, the book is not successful" because of its organization, wrote Elizabeth M.

Will Hobbs

■ Personal

Full name, William Carl Hobbs; born August 22, 1947, in Pittsburgh, PA; son of Gregory J. and Mary (Rhodes) Hobbs; married Jean Loftus (a teacher and realtor), December 20, 1972. *Education:* Stanford University, B.A., 1969, M.A., 1971. *Hobbies and other interests:* Hiking in the mountains and canyons, white water rafting, archeology and natural history.

■ Addresses

Office—c/o Atheneum Books for Young Readers, 866 Third Ave., New York, NY 10022.

■ Career

Pagosa Springs, CO, and Durango, CO, public schools, taught junior high and senior high reading and English, 1973-89; writer, 1990—. *Member:* Authors Guild, Society of Children's Book Writers, Phi Beta Kappa.

■ Awards, Honors

Notable Book, Children's Book Council, 1989, Best Book for Young Adults, American Library Association, 1989, Teachers' Choice Award, International Reading Association, 1990, Regional Book Award, Mountains and Plains Booksellers Association, 1990, Spur Award, Western Writers of America, and Colorado Book Award, all for *Bearstone;* Colorado Blue Spruce Young Adult Book Award, 1992, and second prize, Friends of the Earth Children's Book Award, both for *Changes in Latitudes;* Best Book for Young Adults and Best Book for Reluctant Young Adult Readers, American Library Association, 1992, and Pick of the List citation, American Booksellers Association, all for *Downriver;* Best Book for Young Adults, American Library Association, 1993, for *The Big Wander;* Pick of the List citation, American Booksellers Association, 1993, and Best Book for Young Adults, American Library Association, both for *Beardance.* State Award nominations include California, Colorado, Florida, Indiana, Kansas, Kentucky, Maryland, Nebraska, Oklahoma, South Carolina, Texas, Utah, Vermont, Virginia, and Washington.

■ Writings

Changes in Latitudes, Atheneum, 1988.
Bearstone, Atheneum, 1989.
Downriver, Atheneum, 1991.
The Big Wander, Atheneum, 1992.
Beardance, Atheneum, 1993.

Contributor to *Writers in the Classroom,* Christopher-Gordon, 1990; *Bearstone* was reprinted in its entirety in a seventh grade literature anthology,

Prentice-Hall, 1993. Contributor of articles to periodicals, including "Living and Writing *Bearstone*," *Colorado Communicator,* spring, 1992, and *California Reader,* winter, 1992; and "Teaching a Will Hobbs Novel?," *Colorado Reading Council Journal,* spring, 1993. Hobbs's works have been published in Sweden, Denmark, the United Kingdom, and The Netherlands.

■ Sidelights

He winds up a toy pterodactyl, watches it cross his desk. By the time it gets to the other side, he must start writing. That's the deal. Thus begins the writing day of Will Hobbs. For about six hours a day he commits himself to the task of putting something on paper, and, he told *AAYA,* "I owe at least three books, especially *Beardance,* to that little guy. I might have given up if it hadn't been for my deal with the pterodactyl." Since 1988 he has published five books, and they have all been well received by his young adult audience. He knows this audience very well because he taught reading and English for seventeen years, mostly in Durango, Colorado.

Hobbs's father was an engineer in the Air Force, so the family moved often. Born in Pittsburgh, Pennsylvania, the author was only six months old when the family moved to the Panama Canal Zone. After that, his moves included Virginia, Alaska, California, and Texas. Being close to his three brothers and one sister made the moves easier. They were all involved in scouting, and Hobbs developed a love for nature and the outdoors at an early age. Hobbs explained to *AAYA* that his mother "contributed the gusto to my makeup. She feels that life is best lived as an adventure. At the age of seventy-three she rafted the Grand Canyon." His father introduced him to rivers in Alaska. Hobbs recounted, "Years later he joined me for three trips up the Pine River, where *Bearstone* takes place. It's my idea of heaven on earth, and I'll always be able to find him up there."

Although Hobbs has hiked and backpacked in many regions, it was the Southwest that captured his imagination. He spent two summers during high school and two during college in New Mexico as a guide and camp director at Philmont Scout Ranch. In 1973, with his wife, Jean, he moved to southwestern Colorado. There he enjoys the beauty of the San Juan Mountains and the Weminuche Wilderness, the largest wilderness area

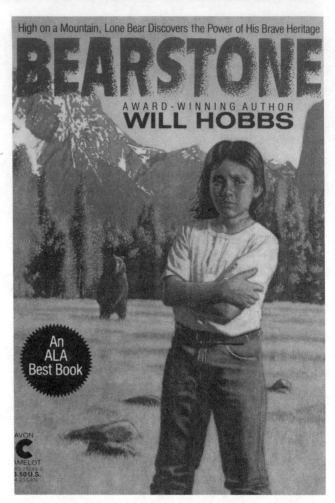

High on a Mountain, Lone Bear Discovers the Power of His Brave Heritage

BEARSTONE

AWARD-WINNING AUTHOR
WILL HOBBS

An ALA Best Book

AVON
CAMELET

This award-winning 1989 novel focuses on a Native American boy, Cloyd Atcitty, who witnesses the illegal slaughter of a grizzly bear.

in Colorado. In 1979 he began building a home eighteen miles northeast of Durango, and completed it in 1989. Nieces and nephews come for backpacking trips, river trips, and other explorations of the Southwest. Hobbs and his wife have no pets at present, but he told *AAYA* that from their home they have seen black bears, coyotes, badgers, and bald and golden eagles, and "in late winter, a herd of elk comes out of the forest in the late afternoons and browses in the meadow, digging up the grass under the snow."

Hobbs was thirty-three before he started writing novels. It was the summer of 1980. The story was *Bearstone,* and it took six different manuscripts and eight years before it was published. In the *California Reader,* Hobbs noted that the writing of *Bearstone* "fulfilled my dream of setting a story for others to enjoy in the upper Pine River country of the Weminuche Wilderness, one of three favorite places in the geography of my heart." It is in wilderness settings such as this that many of his characters are tested—to push themselves and to learn their limits. Their journeys are often difficult.

The Hurt You Get Over Makes You Stronger

School Library Journal contributor George Gleason described *Bearstone* as "far above other coming-of-age stories." *Bearstone* tells the story of a Ute Indian boy from Utah, Cloyd Atcitty, who has been sent by his tribe to a group home in Colorado. When that doesn't work out, he is sent to spend the summer with an old rancher. Angry and hostile, Cloyd distrusts the old man's affection. While exploring the mountains nearby, Cloyd discovers an Indian burial site and a small bearstone. Thus he begins his self-discovery as he renames himself "Lone Bear" and learns how to "live in a good way," as his grandmother has taught him.

Cloyd and the old man, Walter Landis, have dreams. Walter wants to reopen his old gold mine, and Cloyd wants to explore the mountains his ancestors knew. Together they ride up to the high country and grow closer. A bear hunter who is an old friend of Walter's visits their camp, and Cloyd tells the man about a large bear he saw near the Continental Divide. It turns out that the bear is a grizzly, and it is illegal to kill them. However, the hunter does kill the bear as Cloyd tries in vain to shout a warning. Later the hunter lies to the game warden about the circumstances. Cloyd faces the dilemma of whether to tell and get revenge, or keep silent.

Cloyd is the focus of the story, and his character is based on a student from a Durango group home whom Jean Hobbs had taught. The old rancher who teaches Cloyd so much about life and forgiveness is also based on someone Hobbs knows. The author had helped this rancher bring in hay, gaining a feel for the ranching life and listening to his stories about the mine that he was going to reopen someday. After *Bearstone* came out, Hobbs was invited to visit Native American students from the home in Durango, who identified with Cloyd. Hobbs wrote in the *California*

An avid outdoorsman, Hobbs sits in front of "The Window" on Colorado's Continental Divide, a site which plays a prominent role in the author's works *Bearstone* and *Beardance*.

This 1991 work concerns a group of troubled teenagers who embark on a treacherous rafting trip down the Colorado River.

Reader that it was "a big honor, especially to see how attached they were to [the story]."

Bearstone was the novel Hobbs struggled with the most. *Changes in Latitudes* came more quickly. The author told *AAYA* that he starts his stories "usually with a single image that I have a strong feeling about." The image in this case came from a photo in *National Geographic* of a sea turtle swimming underwater. Letting his imagination take over, the author wondered what it would be like to swim with the turtles, and he began to find a story in which he could encourage his readers to care about endangered species. What he ended up with is a novel about two kinds of endangered species: the turtles and a family that is on the verge of breaking up. The novel's

title is drawn from Jimmy Buffett's song, "Changes in Latitudes, Changes in Attitudes."

"The character I knew right from the first line, better than any I've created before or since, was Travis, the narrator in *Changes in Latitudes*," Hobbs told *AAYA*. Travis, the oldest of three kids, is cynical and self-absorbed. At sixteen he attempts to hide himself from his problems by withdrawing into his own "cool" world. On vacation in Mexico with his mother, who has taken the trip without their father, Travis is only close to his little brother, Teddy. It is through Teddy that Travis becomes interested in the plight of the sea turtles. Nancy Vasilakis, writing in *Horn Book*, applauded Hobbs's talents as he "neatly balances the perilous situation of these ancient lumbering sea creatures against the breakdown of his family." She also commended the author for his "sensitive ear for the language of the young." When Teddy dies trying to rescue some of the turtles, Travis discovers that he can't run away from problems and relationships, and that hurt will, indeed, make you stronger.

Living on the Edge

"'October in the mountains,' Al said with a grin. 'You live a whole lot closer to the edge.'" The leader of a group of young people participating in an outdoor program, Al offers his prophetic wisdom at the beginning of Hobbs's third novel, *Downriver*. The idea for this story—which is set in another of the author's favorite places, the Grand Canyon—came from Hobbs's desire to have readers experience one of the great American adventures. Having rowed his raft through the rapids of the Grand Canyon eight times himself, Hobbs knows intimately the dangers and the beauty of the journey. Narrated by Jessie, a fifteen-year-old girl who's been sent away from home, this adventure story takes seven teens down the Grand Canyon where they are tested over and over again. Jessie begins the journey feeling that she has no future: "I could see nothing but the frightening dark tunnel that was my future. I saw no images there, no hopes, only blackness." She and the rest of the group, known as "The Hoods in the Woods," leave their leader behind and take off on their own. Now they're making their own decisions, some good and some bad, and living with the consequences. It is the journey down the river that helps Jessie to find a new life and her way back home as well.

Although *Downriver* takes place in a setting that Hobbs knows well, it was not an easy book to write. It took three drafts, using different narrators each time, before he settled on Jessie. He told *AAYA,* "The first two didn't end up in the story. I guess I was auditioning them as narrators, and when their voices didn't prove to be the one to tell the story, I didn't have other roles for them to play." Although his characters are often based on someone he knows, Hobbs describes them as "coming into their own in their interactions with events and other characters in ways I could never have predicted. Sometimes I'm amazed by the depth they insist on." For example, he had created a two-dimensional character sketch of Star, the homeless girl in *Downriver,* before he started writing. When he placed her as Jessie's cabin-mate in the story, he found out more about her, and "she kept fascinating and surprising me throughout the story."

Hobbs was fourteen years old in 1962, the same age as Clay Lancaster in *The Big Wander.* "I recognize a kindred spirit in Clay Lancaster. We both have an adventuring outlook, we're both romantics, and goofy things tend to happen to both of us," Hobbs explained to *AAYA.* He placed Clay in Glen Canyon in the summer of 1962, the last summer before it was flooded by Lake Powell. To write the story, Hobbs kept an image in his mind of a boy, a burro, and a dog adventuring in a "blank spot on the map," the magnificent canyon country of Utah. Clay and his brother head for the Southwest to look for a missing uncle, but the brother returns home. On his own, with no one to tell him what to do, Clay takes off on a big wander—a journey that leads him to a Navajo family, through remote canyons, and eventually to his uncle. In the process he has adventures escaping the dangers of quicksand, flash floods, and bad guys, and finds time for a little romance.

When Hobbs writes a story, first he reads and reads. He does research about the settings, backgrounds, and historical events that will provide the foundation for his stories. For *The Big Wander* he hiked into his settings, then studied maps, photos, and writings about the canyons and the places "no one knew." In addition to reading, he watched old westerns in the evenings. He knew that he wanted the uncle to be a former rodeo star, which would qualify him as a hero akin to Clay's big-screen heroes from the westerns. However, it was an anti-western, *The Misfits,* that gave him the idea of including the wild horses that Clay's uncle was trying to save.

While Hobbs was doing research for *The Big Wander* he developed ten plot outlines. He knew his character, but he wasn't sure about the problem he wanted him to solve. Each of Hobbs's protagonists has to learn to survive alone, but ultimately is able to achieve personal goals by establishing a strong relationship with someone else. When Hobbs decided that Clay's missing uncle would be involved in saving the wild horses, the author had found the problem he needed. When he added Sarah, who had grown up on a ranch, Hobbs had the necessary members of a team.

According to Hobbs, the novel turned out very differently than he had anticipated. He called it "a song of innocence, with such a whimsical tone and so many comic incidents." Humor is a key ingredient, and the lighthearted tone is set from the first page when Clay and his brother are riding in the noisy old pick-up. Hobbs had two former students in mind as an audience as he created the novel. Both were reluctant readers, but Hobbs knew they liked stories that had adventure and humor. Describing his second draft, the author said, "I'd be dreaming about the story as I slept, and wake up reaching for a scratch-pad. I'd find myself writing intuitively, racing, just trying to keep up with my fingers . . . . When I wrote that last chapter, I was Clay Lancaster, and I was galloping down the Escalante on that spotted pony."

Denning with Bears

Imagine Cloyd digging deep into the ground to make a den for two orphaned bears who need to hibernate for the winter in order to survive. Imagine that he has to den with them for some of that winter. In *Beardance,* the sequel to *Bearstone,* Cloyd and Walter return to the mountains to search for a lost Spanish gold mine. Because Cloyd is a Ute, and the Utes believe that bears are kin, he feels a strong urge to know if any other grizzlies survive in the Colorado mountains; there has been a sighting of a mother and three cubs. His grandmother has told him that in the old times one could become an animal and an animal could become a person. He feels a strong connection to bears, and

Hobbs--here backpacking with his niece, Sarah, in Utah's canyon country--chose this location as the setting for his 1992 novel, *The Big Wander*.

carries with him the painful memories of his tragic experience with the grizzly in *Bearstone.*

Cloyd meets a woman named Ursa who is an expert on grizzlies. Together they locate the mother grizzly and cubs, and Ursa teaches him a great deal about these animals. The high country is dangerous for humans and animals, and the mother and one cub die in an accident. Cloyd almost loses his life when he is buried in an avalanche in one of the most suspenseful and terrifying episodes in the book. The two remaining cubs are now orphans, and Cloyd devises an extraordinary plan to help them survive. He locates the body of the mother bear, skins her, and uses the fur as a means for attracting the young bears and building their trust. Naming them Brownie and Cocoa, Cloyd becomes a kind of surrogate mother, and eventually designs a den for them to hibernate in. Unfortunately, at first the cubs don't understand what the den is about, and Cloyd feels compelled to

stay with them as winter sets in. He sleeps there with the cubs, slipping in and out of a dream-like state as he faces starvation. At times his soul drifts above the scene, shifting between images of boy and bear as Cloyd connects to his ancient heritage and the lore of the Utes. At last the cubs sleep, and he returns to civilization, changed forever by his weeks of endurance, and anxious to see Walter once again.

Hobbs told *AAYA* that *Beardance* started with the image of the boy denning with bears, but "I began too early in the action. It was only when I threw away my first eight chapters and began with the boy and the old man riding into the mountains, that the story began to click. After that I had to hang onto my hat—the story took off at a gallop."

Hobbs advises young writers, "Put the readers in your characters' shoes. Let them smell, hear, see, taste, and touch through your characters' senses."

Thus, the fortunate reader who has "seen" the rugged wilderness, "touched" the fur of the cubs, "tasted" the snow as it tumbled down during the avalanche, "heard" the rushing waters in the Grand Canyon, and "smelled" the campfires of Walter and Cloyd, have lived in these worlds. In his article "Teaching a Will Hobbs Novel?" for the *Colorado Reading Council Journal,* Hobbs stated, "I believe that if kids come to care about and identify with the characters in stories, they will also learn more about and ultimately care more about preserving the treasures of our natural world."

■ Works Cited

Gleason, George, review of *Bearstone, School Library Journal,* September, 1989, p. 272.

Hobbs, Will, *Bearstone,* Atheneum, 1989.

Hobbs, Will, *Downriver,* Atheneum, 1991.

Hobbs, Will, "Living and Writing *Bearstone,*" *California Reader,* winter, 1992, pp. 15-16.

Hobbs, Will, "Teaching a Will Hobbs Novel?," *Colorado Reading Council Journal,* spring, 1993, pp. 7-9.

Hobbs, Will, interview with Caroline S. McKinney for *Authors and Artists for Young Adults,* November, 1993.

Vasilakis, Nancy, review of *Changes in Latitudes, Horn Book,* May-June, 1988, p. 358.

■ For More Information See

BOOKS

Something about the Author, Volume 72, Gale, 1993.

PERIODICALS

Booklist, November 1, 1989, p. 540.

Bulletin of the Center for Children's Books, April, 1988.

Daily Camera (Boulder, CO), March 10, 1993.

Horn Book, January-February, 1993, p. 91.

Publishers Weekly, February 12, 1988, p. 88; February 1, 1991, pp. 80-81; November 2, 1992, p. 72.

School Library Journal, March, 1988, p. 212, 214; March, 1991, p. 212; November, 1992, p. 92; December, 1993, p. 134.

Voice of Youth Advocates, December, 1993, p. 292.

—Sketch by Caroline S. McKinney

Dorothea Lange

■ Personal

Born in 1895 in Hoboken, NJ; died October 11, 1965, in San Francisco, CA; married Maynard Dixon (an artist and illustrator), 1920 (divorced October, 1935); married Paul Schuster Taylor (an economist), December, 1935; children: John and Daniel Dixon. *Education:* Seminar with Clarence White at Columbia University, 1917.

■ Career

Photographer and author. Photographer's assistant at various portrait studios (including that of Arnold Genthe) in New York City, until 1918; Marsh's, San Francisco, CA, photo finishing department, 1918-19; managed own portrait studio in San Francisco, 1920-35; Farm Security Administration/California Rural Rehabilitation Administration, photographer, 1934-39; War Relocation Authority, photographer, 1941-43; Office of War Information, photographer, 1943-45. San Francisco Art Institute, instructor. Contributor of photographs to *Life* magazine in the 1950s. *Exhibitions:* Brockhurst Gallery, Oakland, CA, 1934; "La Donna Rurale Americana" (The American Country Woman), Biblioteca Communale, Milan, Italy, 1961; "The Bitter Years, 1935-1941," Museum of Modern Art, 1962; "Women and Women's Work," W.A.A.M., 1974; "An American Exodus," SITES, 1965; "Celebrating A Collection: The Work of Dorothea Lange," Oakland Museum, Oakland, 1978, and traveling exhibit after 1981. Permanent collections of Lange's work are housed in the Library of Congress, the National Archives, and the Oakland Museum.

■ Awards, Honors

John Simon Guggenheim Memorial Fellowship, 1941.

■ Writings

PHOTOGRAPHER AND AUTHOR

Dorothea Lange Looks at the American Country Woman: A Photographic Essay, with a commentary by Beaumont Newhall, Amon Carter Museum, 1967.

(With Suzanne Riess) *The Making of a Documentary Photographer* (interview), University of California, Bancroft Library/Berkeley, 1968.

(With Paul Schuster Taylor) *An American Exodus: A Record of Human Erosion in the Thirties,* originally published in 1939, revised edition, Yale University Press, 1969, reprint of original edition, Arno Press, 1975.

(With Margaretta K. Mitchell) *To a Cabin,* Grossman, 1973.

PHOTOGRAPHER

Dorothea Lange, Museum of Modern Art/ Doubleday, 1966.

(With others) Maisie and Richard Conrat, *Executive Order 9066: the Internment of 110,000 Japanese Americans,* introduction by Edison Uno, epilogue by Tom C. Clark, California Historical Society/MIT Press, 1972.

Therese Thau Heyman, *Celebrating a Collection: The Work of Dorothea Lange,* with contributions by Daniel Dixon, Joyce Minick, and Paul Schuster Taylor, Oakland Museum, 1978.

John Krich, *Bump City: Winners & Losers in Oakland,* City Miner Books, 1979.

Howard M. Levin and Katherine Northrup, editors, *Dorothea Lange, Farm Security Administration Photographs, 1935-1939, from the Library of Congress,* introduction by Robert J. Doherty, with writings by Paul S. Taylor, TextFiche Press, 1980.

Dorothea Lange (Aperture History of Photography series), Aperture, 1981.

Photographs of a Lifetime, with an essay by Robert Coles and an afterword by Therese Heyman, Aperture, 1982.

Jan Arrow, *Dorothea Lange,* Macdonald, 1985.

Milton Meltzer, *Dorothea Lange: Life through the Camera,* illustrations by Donna Diamond, Viking Kestrel, 1985, Puffin, 1986.

John Steinbeck, *The Harvest Gypsies: On the Road to the Grapes of Wrath,* introduction by Charles Wollenberg, Heydey Books, 1988.

Brian Q. Cannon, *Life & Land: Farm Security Administration Photographers in Utah, from 1936 to 1941,* Utah State University Press, 1988.

OTHER

Also author of essays for *Life* magazine, including "Utah: Three Mormon Towns" (with Ansel Adams) and "Irish Country People" (with Daniel Dixon).

■ Sidelights

Dorothea Lange used to say that she decided to become a photographer in an effort to "maintain myself on the planet," according to Christopher Cox in the introduction to Aperture's *Dorothea Lange.* Whether she meant that she thought photography would earn her a living or satisfy her intellect or both, it is clear that Lange's work has done much to physically and spiritually sustain countless Americans. Her photographs influenced the United States government in its decision to aid those most affected by the Great Depression. The view through the lens of her camera alerted Americans to the plight of the Dust Bowl migrants during the same time. It was Lange's work that sensitively recorded the inhumanity of the relocation of Japanese-Americans during World War II. Lange is remembered today for the fact that, as she documented history, she helped determine the future.

Lange was born in Hoboken, New Jersey, to a family that, in the words of Lange's son Daniel Dixon in *Celebrating A Collection,* "was shattered" by the later desertion of her father. According to Dixon, the "wound" caused by this trauma "never healed." Nevertheless, Lange's mother Joan was hard-working and capable. Soon after her husband abandoned the family, she saw Lange through the bout of polio that left the young girl with a permanently lame leg. Lange's mother also worked two jobs to support the family. In retrospect, it appears that Joan's efforts to care for her family were effective in the long run as well as the short. In the opinion of Joyce Minick writing in *Celebrating a Collection,* Joan's careers as a librarian and social worker "must have represented on some level a certain mobility and conscious choice to the younger Lange. Certainly her mother's career brought Lange into contact with a world different from her own." Another woman in Lange's family influenced her later work. Dixon relates that a dressmaking aunt with whom Lange lived for a time exposed the young woman to "the pride of craftsmanship."

A Bold Decision

After Lange had completed high school and was studying to become a teacher, she made what seemed to be an abrupt decision to become a photographer. Despite the fact that she had never taken a photograph and didn't own a camera, she sought work at the best studio portrait salons in New York City and found it. The first time Lange met Arnold Genthe, a promoter of the "candid" portrait and the most famous of her employers, he insulted her: "Take those cheap red beads off, they're no good." Lange complied, as Minick writes, "out of deference to a world which she was then only a guest." Lange took advantage of her position at Genthe's studio and began to learn the skills that would change transform her status as "guest" into "permanent member." She learned about photography, developing film, and running a studio.

During the time she worked for Genthe, Lange became educated about the work and theories of other prominent photographers. She attended a Clarence White seminar at Columbia University. White, according to Cox, was one of those "struggling to overturn" the Romantic photography that Genthe epitomized. Lange was inspired by White's work and philosophy. After taking his seminar, she was ready to begin her own work as a pho-

tographer. She bought a camera and equipment and began to experiment by taking photos of friends and relatives.

At the age of 22, Lange decided to leave New York and travel around the world with a friend. Their journey ended in San Francisco, when a pickpocket stole the young women's money. Lange immediately found a job at a dry-goods store with a photo-finishing department on Market Street. Cox notes that "Lange lived instinctively, but . . . always found herself in the right place at the right time." Similarly, Minick observes that finding that job in San Francisco was "per-

Lange's Depression era photos documented the plight of the American farmer.

haps one of the first instances in her career when time and events were clearly in her favor."

A Studio of Her Own

Lange's job in San Francisco allowed the charismatic young woman to make friends with bohemian photographers, path-breaking woman photographers, and the fashionable set which patronized them all. Lange soon met Jack Boumphrey, who financed the opening of Lange's own portrait studio just one year after she had arrived in the city. Lounging around her studio at tea-time each day, Lange was a striking character—her place of business became a trendy social spot. Minick relates, "While Lange's darkroom was located in the basement of the building, her studio 'parlor' faced a sunny courtyard, had its own fireplace, and its central feature was a big, black velvet couch that, Lange says, played host to many a proposal of marriage."

Cox writes that Lange "became the favored photographer of a circle of wealthy families

Perhaps Lange's most memorable photograph, "Migrant Mother," taken at Nipomo, California, in 1936, vividly captures the despair and hardships of the Dust Bowl migrants.

who had settled in the Bay Area during the Gold Rush and become leaders of the city's civic and cultural life." Those viewing Lange's portraits from this stage in the photographer's career will not find the work she is known for now. Lange's efforts then were focused on providing quality, commissioned portraiture that flattered her fashionable clients in a meaningful way. She would either stage the portraits she took in her studio or follow her subjects around their homes or at parties with her cumbersome cameras. According to Beaumont Newhall in *Dorothea Lange Looks at the American Country Woman,* Lange once told her son Daniel, "In those days I used to try to talk people into having their pictures taken in their old, simple clothes."

Less than a year after Lange met Maynard Dixon, a famous artist and illustrator of Western scenes, they were married. Lange was just twenty-four years old; Dixon, who was forty-five, had a daughter. The couple had two children together, John and Daniel. Until the beginning of the Great Depression, the marriage seemed solid. Lange appreciated Dixon's work as an artist and especially enjoyed taking trips with him to the southwest, where he did much of his work.

Out of the Studio and into the Street

When the stock market crashed in 1929, Lange's life was transformed. Her business survived, but she and Dixon moved into their separate studios and the boys were sent to boarding school to save money. In spite of the problems in her personal life, and because of the troubles caused by the Depression, the inspiration for and character of Lange's work dramatically changed at this time. Newhall quotes Lange's recollection of one particular event at that time: "One morning, as I was making a solio proof at the south window, I watched an unemployed young workman coming up the street. He came to the corner, stopped, and stood there a little while. Behind him were the waterfront and the wholesale districts; to his left was the financial district; ahead was Chinatown and the Hill of Justice; to his right were the flophouses and Barbary Coast. What was he to do? Which way was he to go?" The man's plight and his indecision captivated Lange. She took her large camera out into the street and began photographing the people she saw there.

Like her decision to stop studying to be a teacher and learn the art of photography, Lange's decision to take her camera out of the studio and into the street was a critical one. This latter decision, however, would change American history as well as how we view that history today. As Therese Thau Heyman exclaims in *Celebrating a Collection,* "When Dorothea Lange left behind her the control of the studio, traditional milieu of the artist, and moved to the aggressive action of the reporter, the world beyond her studio, the street, she became what we recognize today—the selector of the thirties. Her images of the time form a prime resource for our views of the period."

Yet once Lange had taken her first street photographs, she did not know what to do with them. Work of this kind was rare, and her customers were unlikely to appreciate it or support it financially. Nevertheless, Lange knew that there was something special about these photographs. Roger Sturtevant, who was once Lange's assistant and became a renowned architectural photographer, was among those who encouraged Lange in this belief. It was Sturtevant who rescued the image that would be titled "White Angel Breadline" from equipment that Lange borrowed from him. Willard Van Dyke, a photographer who founded Group f/64 with Ansel Adams, offered to exhibit Lange's street photographs at his studio at 683 Brockhurst in Oakland.

These first photographs taken by Lange in San Francisco during the Depression years are consistently thought-provoking, and often haunting. In "White Angel Breadline" (1933), a man in the center of the photograph supports himself on a the bar of a wooden rail fence as if he is waiting for an order at a lunch counter. Yet his face, with his eyes hidden by a hat, is grim, and his empty metal cup captures the eye's attention. The remainder of the picture is filled with hatted men, their backs to the photographer—they are also waiting in the line to receive food from the "White Angel." "Man beside Wheelbarrow" (1934) features a man sitting against a concrete-brick wall, his hatted head is down, and an upturned wheelbarrow beside him betrays his predicament. "Mended Stockings" is a shot of a woman's crossed legs; a line of mending runs from her worn shoes to her skirt.

Lange's Photographs Make a Difference

Images like these, displayed in Willard Van Dyke's Oakland gallery, won the immediate attention of Paul Taylor. Taylor was a professor of economics

Throughout her life, Lange enjoyed taking photographs of family members, as in this 1931 image of her son entitled "John".

who had used photographs to illustrate the social and economic problems he had been studying. Taylor was attempting to gain funds for the refugees streaming into California. He requested that Lange work on his team, which was conducting a study for the California affiliate of the Federal Emergency Relief Administration. The work Lange conducted with Taylor was effective. As Heyman notes, "Because of it, government budgets were approved; substantial sums for food and camps were voted; articles in the 1935-36 San Francisco *News* brought action immediately."

Heyman observes that, given this success, it is not surprising that Lange wrote to Maynard Dixon telling him that she wanted to end their marriage. "I want to marry Paul, he needs me." Lange, however, also needed Taylor. According to Newhall, "Paul Taylor helped Dorothea to grasp the economic and sociological background of agricultural workers, and this knowledge she brought to her photography." He quotes Taylor as stating, "I suppose I did do some explaining . . . what it now seems that I did most importantly was to enable Dorothea to confront the situation herself, firsthand."

After their marriage in Albuquerque in 1935, Lange and Taylor continued to work together. They toured the country during the summers from 1935 to 1939 with the hope that, in the words of Heyman, "social conditions would change for the better, in part because of their reporting." During this time, Lange took the photograph that would remain in the American consciousness for years, "Migrant Mother." It happened when Lange made a quick decision to stop at a camp in Nipomo, which she had already passed on her way home to Berkeley. As Heyman relates, this picture was published in the *San Francisco News* and aid was sent to the camp soon after. The photo, as Cox writes, is an "icon" of the 1930s.

At home in Berkeley, Lange and Taylor worked to put together the book which emerged in 1939 as *An American Exodus: A Record of Human Erosion in the Thirties.* According to Heyman, the finest photographs in this work "are of people who appear totally indomitable, unvanquished by their reverses . . . . Her people have an emotional complexity, an ambiguity which breaks stereotype and makes us look again." In part because the attention of the public was focused on the war in Europe, *An American Exodus* was not very successful. As Heyman relates, "Few copies sold; the rest were remaindered."

Reviewing this work over thirty years after it was first published, John Szarkowski of the *New York Times Book Review* asserts that the book "remains one of the best and truest documents we have of the breakdown of America's earlier agrarian ideal." Szarkowski notes that unlike most photographic

In her most powerful compositions, Lange unveiled the sorrow and pain in her subjects' lives.

Lange's decision to take her photography out of the portrait studio and into the streets dramatically altered the course of her work.

books of the time, the photographs in this book "were no longer illustrations, and the text no longer captions, but each maintained its own integrity."

Lange's Last Years

As Daniel Dixon wrote in *Celebrating a Collection,* with "World War II came the end of my mother's work for the Farm Security Administration and the beginning of her long and finally fatal illness." Lange occupied herself with domestic people and problems during the war years. In 1941, she won a Guggenheim grant for a proposed study of Hutterites, Amana, and Shakers in the United States. While she was too ill to complete the project, some of the photos she took for the project have been published. Also, according to Heyman, Lange and her husband "were among the first to speak out and insist on fair play in the relocation of the Japanese Americans in California in 1942." While many of her photographs of the internment

were not released to the public during those years, Maisie and Richard Conrat (who worked for Lange during this period) collected some of them and, along with other photographs and contributions, published the work as *Executive Order 9066: The Internment of 110,000 Japanese Americans.*

Among the moving photographs in *Executive Order 9066* made by Dorothea Lange are many images of parents and grandparents with small children. One taken on May 8, 1942, in Hayward, California, displays an upright and prosperous-looking grandfather, waiting somberly yet proudly for an evacuation bus with his grandchildren. Long white tags dangling from their coats betray their destination. In another photograph of two children taken on the same day, the same white tags jump from the image and highlight the expressions on their faces. Lange also made some thought-provoking photographs of signs concerning the evacuations and relocations or bearing overtly racist statements. One of the most striking of these was taken in April, 1942, in Oakland, California. A large white "SOLD" sign looms above the Wanto Grocery, but pasted across the windows of the market is an even more prominent sign which states "I AM AN AMERICAN." A note with the picture explains that the owner of the store placed the sign on the store the day after the attack on Pearl Harbor in December, 1941, and that he was later forced to close his store and evacuate.

After the war, Lange photographed the original meetings of the United Nations. Heyman relates that the stressful experience of working among fast-paced, often indifferent and unscrupulous press photographers contributed to stomach ulcers and Lange's physical collapse. It was eight years before she would work again, and when she did, it was on occasional assignment for *Life* magazine.

In her last years, Lange began to spend more time photographing subjects close to home. She was especially enthusiastic about making photos of the beautiful oak trees at her Berkeley home and of family members enjoying themselves at their cabin. These latter photos were collected and arranged with poems by Margaretta K. Mitchell in the volume *To a Cabin* after Lange's death. Christina Bostick of *Library Journal* remarks that the pictures of the children in this book are "evocative," although Sanford Schwartz of *New York Times Book Review* feels that these photographs do not represent Lange's best work.

Lange was also very enthusiastic about photographing her son John's young family. "I believe that my mother had given herself an assignment," wrote Daniel Dixon in *Celebrating a Collection*. "Between bouts of illness, she was recording the growth and development of a young American family that just happened to be her own. The story is fragmentary. But the purpose seems clear. The documentary photographer was still at work."

When Lange was told that she had terminal cancer in 1964, she faced her impending death with courage and worked as hard as she could to finish various projects, including a retrospective exhibit of her work for the museum of Modern Art in New York and *The American Country Woman*. *The American Country Woman*, a photographic essay, features fifteen women and their homes, communities, or environments. "These are women of the American soil," wrote Lange in the text that accompanies her photos. "They are a hardy stock. They are of the roots of our country. They inhabit our plains, our prairies, our deserts, our mountains, our valleys, and our country town. They are not our well-advertised women of beauty and fashion, nor are they a part of the well-advertised American style of living . . . . They are *of themselves* a very great American style. They live with courage and purpose, a part of our tradition."

Lange, who like the women she praised lived with courage and purpose, died in Berkeley in 1965. She remains, in the words of Sanford Schwartz, a critic for the *New York Times Book Review*, "a special and beloved figure in the history of photography."

■ Works Cited

Bostick, Christina, review of *To a Cabin, Library Journal*, March 1, 1974, p. 649.

Conrat, Maisie, and Richard Conrat, *Executive Order 9066: The Internment of 110,000 Japanese Americans*, photographs by Dorothea Lange and others, California Historical Society, 1972.

Cox, Christopher, introduction to *Dorothea Lange*, Aperture, 1981.

Heyman, Therese Thau, *Celebrating a Collection: The Work of Dorothea Lange*, with contributions by Daniel Dixon, Joyce Minick, and Paul Schuster Taylor, Oakland Museum, 1978.

Lange, Dorothea, *Dorothea Lange Looks at the American Country Woman*, with a commentary by Beaumont Newhall, Amon Carter Museum, 1967.

Schwartz, Sanford, review of *To a Cabin, New York Times Book Review*, December 2, 1973, p. 95.

Szarkowski, John, review of *An American Exodus, New York Times Book Review*, March 8, 1970, p.6.

■ For More Information See

BOOKS

The Britannica Encyclopedia of American Art, Encyclopaedia Britannica Educational Corporation, 1973.

Dictionary of American Art, Harper, 1979.

Women Artists: An Historical, Contemporary, and Feminist Bibliography, Scarecrow, 1978.

PERIODICALS

Booklist, February 15, 1983, p. 758.

Book World, November 28, 1982, p. 16; May 22, 1983, p. 11.

Library Journal, June 1, 1966; December 1, 1982, p. 2251.

Los Angeles Times Book Review, December 5, 1982, p. 16.

New York Times Book Review, June 10, 1984, p. 36.

Publishers Weekly, November 12, 1982, p. 60; April 27, 1984, p. 85.

Society, July-August, 1993, pp. 64-8.

OBITUARIES

Newsweek, October 25, 1965.

Time, October 22, 1965.*

—Sketch by R. Garcia-Johnson

H. P. Lovecraft

Providence, RI, 1914–1918; publisher, *The Conservative*, 1915–1919 and 1923; regular contributor to *Weird Tales* (and other "pulp" magazines) after 1923. *Member:* United Amateur Press Association (president, 1917–1918, 1923).

■ Writings

FICTION

The Shunned House (stories), Recluse Press, 1928.
The Battle That Ended the Century, Barlow, 1934.
The Cats of Ulthar, Dragonfly Press, 1935.
The Shadow over Innsmouth, illustrated by Frank A. Utpatel, Visionary Publishing, 1936.
The Outsider and Others, collected by August Derleth and Donald Wandrei, Arkham, 1939.
Beyond the Wall of Sleep (includes *The Dream Quest of Unknown Kadath* and *The Case of Charles Dexter Ward*), collected by Derleth and Wandrei, Arkham, 1943.
The Weird Shadow over Innsmouth and Other Stories of the Supernatural, Bartholomew House, 1944.
The Dunwich Horror, Bartholomew House, 1945.
(With Derleth) *The Lurker at the Threshold*, Arkham, 1945.
Best Supernatural Stories of H. P. Lovecraft, edited with introduction by Derleth, World Publishing, 1945.
The Lurking Fear and Other Stories, Avon, 1948, published as *Cry Horror!*, 1958, new editions under original title, Panther, 1964, Beagle, 1971.
The Curse of Yig, Arkham, 1953.
The Dream Quest of Unknown Kadath, introduction

■ Personal

Full name, Howard Phillips Lovecraft; also wrote under the pseudonyms Lawrence Appleton, Houdini, John J. Jones, Humphrey Littlewit, Gent., Henry Paget–Lowe, Ward Phillips, Richard Raleigh, Ames Dorrance Rowley, Edgar Softly, Edward Softly, Augustus T. Swift, Lewis Theobald, Jr., Albert Frederick Willie, and Zoilus; born August 20, 1890, in Providence, RI; died of cancer and Bright's disease, March 15, 1937, in Providence, RI; son of Winfield Scott (a traveling salesman) and Sarah (Phillips) Lovecraft; married Sonia H. Greene (a businesswoman), 1924 (divorced, 1929). *Education:* Self–educated. *Hobbies and other interests:* Avid correspondent; astronomy; the language, literary forms and lifestyles of the 18th century; the physical sciences.

■ Career

Writer of supernatural and horror fiction, producing a voluminous number of short stories, novels, poetry and essays; also worked throughout his career as a ghostwriter, revisionist, and amateur journalist. Astrology columnist, *Evening News,* by George T. Wetzel, Shroud, 1955, new edition with introduction by Lin Carter, Ballantine, 1970.

(With Derleth) *The Survivor and Others*, Arkham, 1957.

The Shuttered Room and Other Pieces, collected by Derleth, Arkham, 1959.

Dreams and Fancies, Arkham, 1962.

(With Derleth) *The Shadow out of Space*, introduction by Sam Moskowitz, [New York], 1962.

The Dunwich Horror and Others: The Best Supernatural Stories of H. P. Lovecraft, collected with introduction by Derleth, Arkham, 1963, revised edition, edited by S. T. Joshi, 1985.

At the Mountains of Madness and Other Novels, collected with an introduction by Derleth, Arkham, 1964, revised edition, edited by Joshi, introduction by James Turner, 1985.

Dagon and Other Macabre Tales, collected with introduction by Derleth, Arkham, 1965, revised edition, edited by Joshi, 1987.

The Case of Charles Dexter Ward, complete edition, Belmont Books, 1965.

The Dark Brotherhood and Other Pieces, Arkham, 1966.

Three Tales of Horror, illustrated by Lee Brown Coye, Arkham, 1967.

The Colour out of Space and Others, Lancer Books, 1967.

(With Derleth) *The Shadow out of Time and Other Tales of Horror*, Gollancz, 1968, abridged edition as *The Shuttered Room and Other Tales of Horror*, Panther, 1970.

At the Mountains of Madness and Other Tales of Terror, Panther, 1968, Beagle Books, 1971.

The Haunter of the Dark and Other Tales of Horror, edited with an introduction by Derleth, Gollancz, 1969.

(With others) *Tales of the Cthulhu Mythos*, collected by Derleth, Arkham, 1969, reprinted with illustrations by Jeffrey K. Potter and with an introduction by James Turner, 1990.

The Tomb and Other Tales, collected by Derleth, Panther, 1969, Ballantine, 1970.

Ex Oblivione, Squires, 1969.

Nyarlathotep, Squires, 1970.

What the Moon Brings, Squires, 1970.

Memory, Squires, 1970.

(With others) *The Horror in the Museum and Other Revisions*, Arkham, 1970, 3rd revised and enlarged edition, edited by Joshi, 1989.

The Doom That Came to Sarnath, edited with introduction by Lin Carter, Ballantine, 1971.

Nine Stories from "The Horror in the Museum and Other Revisions," Beagle Books, 1971.

(With others) *The Spawn of Cthulhu*, edited with introduction by Lin Carter, Ballantine, 1971.

(With Derleth) *The Watchers out of Time and Others*, foreword by April Derleth, Arkham, 1974.

(With others) *The Horror in the Burying Ground and Other Tales*, Panther, 1975.

Herbert West: Reanimator, edited by Marc A. Michaud, Necronomicon, 1977.

Writings in the Tryout, edited by Michaud, foreword by Joshi, Necronomicon, 1977.

(With others) *New Tales of the Cthulhu Mythos*, Arkham, 1980.

The Best of H. P. Lovecraft: Bloodcurdling Tales of Horror and the Macabre, introduction by Robert Bloch, Ballantine, 1982.

Herbert West: Terminator, Necronomicon, 1985.

The Night Ocean, Necronomicon, 1986.

Re-Animator: Tales of Herbert West, edited by Steven Jones, illustrated by Mikael Oskarsson, Malibu Graphics Publishing Group, 1991.

Author of about sixty stories, many of which were first published, beginning in 1923, in pulp magazines such as *Weird Tales, Amazing Stories,* and *Astounding Stories.* These include "The White Ship," "The Silver Key," "The Rats in the Walls," "The Statement of Randolph Carter," "The Horror at Red Hook," "The Music of Erich Zann," "The Moon Bog," "The Cats of Ulthar," "Through the Gates of the Silver Key," "Celephais," "The Unnameable," "The Picture in the House," "The Festival," "From Beyond," "The Dreams in the Witch-House," "The Thing on the Doorstep," "Pickman's Model," "The Shunned House," "The Nameless City," "The Call of the Cthulhu," and "The Whisperer in the Darkness." These and other stories have been collected in a number of multi-work volumes, including *Eleven Great Horror Stories,* 1969, *Ghosts,* 1971, *Summoned from the Tomb,* 1973, *Cries of Terror,* 1976, and *Feast of Fear,* 1977. Also ghostwriter and revisionist under multiple pseudonyms.

POETRY

The Crime of Crimes, Harris, 1915.

Fungi from Yuggoth, Evans, 1941.

Collected Poems, illustrated by Frank Utpatel, Arkham, 1963, published as *Fungi from Yuggoth and Other Poems*, Ballantine, 1971.

The Prose Poems of H. P. Lovecraft, four volumes, Roy Squires, 1969–70.

Four Prose Poems, Necronomicon, 1987.

The Fantastic Poetry, edited by Joshi, illustrations by Jason Eckhardt, Necronomicon, 1990.

Also author of privately printed poems; contributor of poetry to amateur publications.

OTHER

Looking Backward, C. W. Smith, c. 1920.
Further Criticism of Poetry, Fetter, 1932.
Some Current Motives and Practices, Barlow, c. 1936.
A History of the Necronomicon, Rebel Press, 1938, Necronomicon, 1984.
The Notes and Commonplace Book, Futile Press, 1938, as *Commonplace Book,* Necronomicon, 1987.
Marginalia, collected by Derleth and Wandrei, Arkham, 1944.
Supernatural Horror in Literature (essay), introduction by Derleth, Abramson, 1945, reprinted with new introduction by E. F. Bleiler, Dover, 1973.
Something about Cats and Other Pieces, collected by Derleth, Arkham, 1949.
Autobiography: Some Notes on a Nonentity, annotated by Derleth, Arkham, 1963.
Selected Letters, Arkham, Volume 1: *1911–1924,* Volume 2: *1925–29,* Volume 3: *1929–31,* edited by Derleth and Wandrei, Volume 4: *1932–34,* Volume 5: *1934–37,* edited by Derleth and J. Turner, 1965–76.
Hail, Klarkash-Ton!, Squires, 1971.
Medusa: A Portrait, Oliphant Press, 1975.
(With Willis Conover) *Lovecraft at Last,* foreword by Harold Taylor, Carrollton, Clark, 1975.
The Conservative: Complete, 1915–1923, edited by Michaud, foreword by Frank Belknap Long, Necronomicon, 1976.
To Quebec and the Stars, edited by L. Sprague de Camp, D. M. Grant, 1976.
Writings in The United Amateur 1915–1925, edited by Michaud, Necronomicon, 1976.
First Writings: Pawtuxet Valley Gleaner, 1906 (essays), edited by Michaud, foreword by Ramsey Campbell, Necronomicon, 1976.
A Winter Wish (essays and poetry), edited by Tom Collins, Whispers Press, 1977.
(With R. H. Barlow) *Collapsing Cosmoses,* Necronomicon, 1977.
Writings in The Tryout, edited by Michaud, Necronomicon, 1977.
The Californian 1934–1938, Necronomicon, 1977.
Memoirs of an Inconsequential Scribbler, Necronomicon, 1977.
Uncollected Prose and Poetry, edited by Joshi and Michaud, Necronomicon, 1978.
(With J. F. Hartmann) *Science Versus Charlatanry: Essays on Astrology,* edited with introduction and notes by Joshi and Scott Connors, The Strange Company, 1979.
H. P. Lovecraft in "The Eyrie," edited by Joshi and Michaud, Necronomicon, 1979.
Juvenalia, 1897–1905, introduction by Joshi, Necronomicon, 1984.
The H. P. Lovecraft Christmas Book, edited by Susan Michaud, illustrated by Jason C. Eckhardt, Necronomicon, 1984.
H. P. Lovecraft: Uncollected Letters, Necronomicon, 1986.
H. P. Lovecraft: The Conservative (essays), edited by Joshi, Necronomicon, 1986.
H. P. Lovecraft: Commonplace Book, edited by David E. Schultz, Necronomicon, 1987.
(With Sonia H. Greene) *European Glimpses,* Necronomicon, 1988.
The Vivisector (essays), Necronomicon, 1990.

Contributor of nonfiction to amateur publications. Editor of works by other writers, including Jonathan E. Hoag, John Ravenor Bullen, and Eugene B. Kuntz.

■ Adaptations

The Case of Charles Dexter Ward inspired the film *The Haunted Palace,* directed by Roger Corman, 1963; "The Colour out of Space" was adapted as the film *Die, Monster, Die!,* directed by Daniel Haller, 1965; "The Shuttered Room" was adapted for a film directed by David Greene, 1968; "The Dunwich Horror" was adapted for a film directed by Haller, 1970; *Herbert West: Reanimator* was adapted as the film *Re-Animator,* directed by Stuart Gordon, 1985; "From Beyond" was adapted for a film directed by Gordon, 1986; "The Unnameable" was adapted for a film directed by Jean-Paul Ouellette, 1988. Two stories, "Pickman's Model" and "Cool Air," have been adapted for television.

■ Sidelights

"Nothing," H. P. Lovecraft once wrote, "has ever seemed to fascinate me so much as the thought of some curious interruption in the prosaic laws of nature, or some monstrous intrusions on our familiar world by unknown things from the limitless outside." An apt sentiment, considering that Lovecraft was arguably the twentieth century's master of the genre of fiction known as supernatural horror. Through numerous stories, Lovecraft created worlds where men become powerless witnesses to unspeakable forces they can barely comprehend. Since his death in 1937, Lovecraft has become exceptionally popular, and the stories of his "Cthulhu Mythos" have served as inspiration for many modern writers of horror and science fiction.

Howard Phillips Lovecraft was born in 1890 in Providence, Rhode Island, in the home of his maternal grandfather, Wipple V. Phillips. The descendant of a once–prosperous New England family, Lovecraft was born and raised in the Victorian mansion that belonged to his grandfather, a prosperous industrialist whose extensive library of eighteenth– and nineteenth–century books became the backbone of the young writer's education. His father, a traveling salesman who suffered from syphilis, died in 1898 following five years of institutionalization for general paresis, a type of paralysis. His grandfather, who was the dominant intellectual influence on his life, died in 1904. There followed poor financial management of the family's holdings, with the result that Lovecraft and his mother, Sarah Phillips Lovecraft, were forced to abandon the Phillips family mansion for more meager accommodations in a nearby duplex. The house left a mark on him, however: "Here I spent the best years of my childhood," he would later write. "The house was a beautiful and spacious edifice, with stable and grounds, the latter approaching a park in the beauty of the walk and trees." Critics and commentators on his work in later years would site that environment as a prominent and powerful element of and influence on the author's work.

Lovecraft was a sickly child, possibly because of a nervous, overprotective mother who doted on her only son. Whatever the reason for his illness, the result was that Lovecraft attended school only sporadically. In 1908, although it was his intention to attend Brown University to prepare for a career as a university professor, he suffered a nervous breakdown which prevented him from attaining enough credits to graduate from high school and thus qualify for college. Though lacking a solid formal education, Lovecraft had the benefit of his grandfather's voluminous library, which launched him on a lifetime of self–education that focused on eighteenth–century history, Gothic horror stories, astronomy, Greek and Roman antiquities, and the physical sciences. His early life was the life of a reclusive, semi–invalid lost in a world of books and history. Isolated as he was, it is not surprising that he came to see himself, with his

mother's encouragement, as someone who was unlike anyone else. Yet, despite that mental and physical isolation, it was during this period of illness and changing family fortunes that Lovecraft began to write, work that would ultimately reconnect him to the world at large. More practically speaking, he also at this time began obtaining work as a ghostwriter and revisionist—developing skills that would provide him with financial stability throughout his life.

An Enthusiastic Correspondent

In 1914 Lovecraft joined the United Amateur Press Association, a non–professional group for writers interested in creating a variety of publications and in the exchange of letters, the latter which was a lifelong avocation of Lovecraft's, an avid correspondent whose selected letters were posthumously collected in five volumes. His association with the UAPA prompted him to publish, from 1915 through 1919 and again in 1923, a magazine called *The Conservative,* but it was his correspondence that proved the more compelling outlet for his personal and artistic expression. Indeed, from 1911, and particularly from 1914, until his death, Lovecraft poured an encyclopedic range and depth of knowledge into these essay–like letters, devoting ample space in particular to such life–long obsessions as the splendors of the past, the ills of the modern world, cultural racism (as was quite often common among American white men of his age and background at that time, he was averse to non–Anglo–Nordic races and cultures), and the mysteries and wonders of scientific truth.

During these early years of his amateur career, he also began contributing poems and essays to various amateur journals. As can often be the case with a writer as well–read as Lovecraft, much of this early work bears the mark of those writers who influenced him most—in this case the writing of, primarily, eighteenth–century writers. Hence his poetry resembled that of Alexander Pope and James Thomson, his essays were influenced by Joseph Addison and Samuel Johnson, and his earliest attempts at fiction, horror stories written sometime after 1898 and later destroyed, were heavily influenced by the works of Edgar Allan Poe. He wrote no fiction between 1908 and 1917.

Amidst of all of this social and intellectual activity, Lovecraft, who became president of the UAPA in 1917–1918, in 1918 resumed writing short fiction at the behest of editor W. Paul Cook, and began submitting his work to pulp magazines such as *Weird Tales,* which, along with similar publications such as *Amazing Stories,* began publishing his work regularly from 1923 onward. This time around, his stories were heavily influenced by the work of Lord Dunsany, a well–known Irish fantasist. Among the better–known stories Lovecraft wrote during this period are "Dagon," "The White Ship," "The Silver Key," "The Doom That Came to Samath" and "The Cats of Ulthar." This early cycle of stories (the first of three "cycles" or groups of writings that marked Lovecraft's body of work) shared a dreamlike quality and imagery, a fairy tale style that "culminated in the extraordinary short novel Lovecraft called *The Dream Quest of Unknown Kadath,*" according to Lin Carter in an introduction to the Ballantine edition of the book. Lovecraft's novella is a fantastic tale in which the hero, Randolph Carter, sets off in search of a magnificent city he knows only from visions. Entering the world of his dreams, Randolph encounters such marvelous places and things that, according to Carter, "Few more magical novels of dream–fantasy exist than this phantasmagoric adventure."

Meanwhile, Lovecraft at this time also began socializing with other amateur journalists, and in 1921 he met Sonia H. Greene, a Jewish businesswoman of Russian descent from New York City. They were subsequently married in 1924, and he moved from Providence, where he had lived all of his life, to join his wife in New York City. Unfortunately, due to financial difficulties (according to Lovecraft), the couple was separated 10 months later and the author returned to Providence in 1926. Lovecraft, who had disliked New York City both for its architectural modernity and its urban hodgepodge of races and cultures, was to remain in Providence for the rest of his life. Though he did travel extensively, later documenting his journeys in letters and such as "Vermont:

The Providence, Rhode Island mansion in which Lovecraft grew up is present in many of his stories, including "The Rats in the Walls" and "The Shunned House."

A First Impression," "Charleston," and *A Description and Guide to the City of Quebec,* he was content to support himself with ghostwriting and revision work, all the while continuing his voluminous correspondence from his New England home base, and writing and publishing his essays, poetry and fiction mainly in amateur journals and magazines.

Extending the Horror Tradition

H. P. Lovecraft is best remembered and recognized, however, for his chilling tales of the supernatural, and for his views and writings on the art of the supernatural tale in particular—his essay on the subject, "Supernatural Horror in Literature," is considered a classic critical study and history of the genre. Indeed, even upon his death from Bright's disease (a kidney ailment) and intestinal cancer in March 1937 at the age of 46, his by then widely published stories of the macabre had already begun to acquire a cult following.

After his death, that cult following was nurtured by such colleagues and collaborators as August Derleth, Donald Wandrei, Clark Ashton Smith, Robert E. Howard, Robert Bloch, Frank Belknap Long, and Henry Kuttner, to name a few. In his *H. P. L.: A Memoir,* Derleth claimed that there was "no basis for comparison of Lovecraft's work to that of any other contemporary writer; among writers in the field of the macabre, apart from occasional work by men and women who were better known in other fields—like Edith Wharton, Wilbur Daniel Steele, Gertrude Atherton, Gouverneur Morris, Irvin S. Cobb, Dubose Heyward, Conrad Aiken, etc.—there were only Clark Ashton Smith and the late Reverend Henry S. Whitehead whose work was consistently good enough to command attention, and yet was not on the Lovecraft plane." In short, Derleth concluded, "Lovecraft was an original in the Gothic tradition; he was a skilled writer of supernatural fiction, a master of the macabre who had no peer in the America of his time."

But Lovecraft, ironically, did not enjoy much fame while he was alive. Save the small cult following that he had, his work was largely overlooked by more mainstream, professional publications and did not win any major genre awards (at best receiving honorable mentions once or twice). Even posthumously his writing continues to draw both ardent fans and disdainful critics. Edmund Wilson, writing about Lovecraft's work in an essay

H. P. LOVECRAFT

HERBERT WEST REANIMATOR

Originally published in 1977, this work was the basis for the film *Re-Animator.*

originally published in the *New Yorker,* remarked: "The only real horror in most of these fictions is the horror of bad taste and bad art. Lovecraft was not a good writer. The fact that his verbose and undistinguished style has been compared to Poe's is only one of the many bad signs that almost nobody any more pays any real attention to writing." Larry McMurtry, writing in the *Washington Post,* described Lovecraft as "a totally untalented and unreadable writer" whose "prose is terrible, a third–rate imitation of Poe; and, as to context, he really has none. Even his fabled letters, about which one has heard so much, are the letters of a sad, silly, juvenile, self–deluded introvert." Author and critic Ursula LeGuin added her two cents in the *Times Literary Supplement,* writing that Lovecraft, "the object of a small but tenacious cult . . . , dangles like a rabbit from the jaws of his unconscious. Seldom in his life and never in his writing did he try to fight back, to summon up a shred of coherent reasoning, a scrap of authentic prose, as a bulwark against the terrors and compulsions that tyrannized his mind." And Colin Wilson, in an essay entitled "The Assault on Rationality: H. P. Lovecraft," called him "a somewhat hysterical and neurotic combatant." Lovecraft himself would have made no defense to these attacks, since he harbored no high opinion of himself, writing in "The Defense Reopens!": "No one is more acutely conscious than I of the inadequacy of my work. Nothing exasperates me more than the failure of my written products to duplicate the visions and nightmares that lie behind them. I am a self–confessed amateur and bungler, and have not much hope of improvement—but the visions clamour for expression and preservation, so what is one to do?"

Forging a New Type of Supernatural Tale

But admirers of Lovecraft's particular brand of horror believe that he changed the shape of the supernatural tale. Fritz Leiber, for example, a well–respected American science fiction writer, wrote in a 1949 essay that Lovecraft was "the Copernicus of the horror story. He shifted the focus of supernatural dread from man and his little world and his gods, to the stars and the black and unplumbed gulfs of intergalactic space . . . . He created a new kind of horror story and new methods for telling it." Likewise, Barton Levi St. Armand, in *The Roots of Horror in the Fiction of H. P. Lovecraft*, observed that Lovecraft achieved "nothing less than a mating of Gothic horror and cosmic terror, an unholy marriage of inside and outside."

In "Heritage of Horror," an introduction by Robert Bloch to *The Best of H. P. Lovecraft*, Bloch contends that Lovecraft's personality, predilections, fears, neuroses, beliefs and attitudes, shaped by the personal circumstances of his life and by the nature of the times in which he lives, can be plainly seen to permeate his work. For example, noted Bloch, Lovecraft's "lifelong aversion to cold is apparent in stories such as 'Cool Air' and his short novel, 'At the Mountains of Madness.' An allergy to seafood is embodied in 'The Shadow over Innsmouth,' and a tone–deaf distaste for music as dissonance echoes in 'The Music of Erich Zann.' A love of cats is obvious in many tales; so is a fondness for colonial architecture and outrage over its gradual destruction." Architecture, in general, can play an important role in the Lovecraft cosmos, whether it is the power and mystery of colonial New England houses or the secrets of

ancient edifices. "Age and aging . . . is omnipresent in his work," Bloch observed, and "old houses and old tombs are abundantly in evidence." This is particularly true of such tales as "The Rats in the Walls," "The Lurking Fear," "The Shadow over Innsmouth," "The Shadow out of Time" and "The Shunned House," to name a few.

Theses physical settings for Lovecraft's stories distinguished his tales of terror. Angela Carter, in "Lovecraft and Landscape," observed: "Lovecraft's is an expressionistic landscape of imminent dread; his very world is inimical to man. But these landscapes, although man is never at home in them, can sicken and die, as a man does. Worse, they can go mad. Even the stars above them are rendered in human terms." In the fictional New England town he called Arkham, where many of his stories take place, Lovecraft evokes "menace, anguish, perturbation, dread," the critic continued. "The cities themselves, whether those of old New England or those that lie beyond the gates of dream, present the dreadful enigma of a maze, always labyrinthine and always, the Minotaur at the heart of this labyrinth, lies the unspeakable in some form or else in some especially vile state of formlessness—the unspeakable, a nameless and unnameable fear."

But the revelation of the "unspeakable" is not the primary component of Lovecraftian terror, according to Donald R. Burleson. As the critic observed in *H. P. Lovecraft: A Critical Study*: "The horror, ultimately, in a Lovecraft tale is not some gelatinous lurker in dark places, but the realisation, by the characters involved, of their helplessness and their insignificance in the scheme of things—their terribly ironic predicament of being sufficiently well–developed organisms to perceive and feel the poignancy of their own motelike unimportance in a blind and chaotic universe which neither loves them nor even finds them worthy of notice, let alone hatred or hostility." Burleson later added that rather than being derivative of Poe or Dunsany or Nathaniel Hawthorne, Lovecraft's work "*assimilated* such influences, transmuting and developing them for artistic purposes that are highly individual."

Lovecraft, explained Derleth in "H. P. Lovecraft and His Work," "believed that nothing was so essentially terrifying to the human spirit as a dislocation in space and time." Even Lovecraft's ex–wife had an opinion on his work, Derleth relayed, saying once that "his love of the weird and mys-

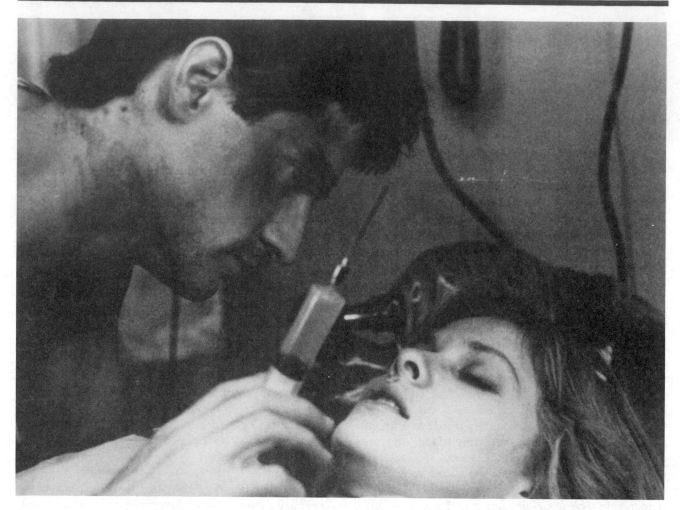

Bruce Abbott starred as Dan Cain in the 1985 film *Re-Animator*.

terious, I believe, was born of sheer loneliness." Maurice Levy, a French critic and scholar, observed in "Lovecraft: A Study in the Fantastic," that Lovecraft was "a man without hope. Unstable, sick, unhappy, obstinately rejecting what he considered the delusions of faith, fed on nihilistic philosophies, he had frequently thought of suicide." Lovecraft himself wrote in "The Call of Cthulhu," a story written in 1926 that was one of the first of a series of stories devoted to a wide–ranging and wholly original mythos: "The most merciful thing in the world, I think, is the inability of the human mind to correlate all its contents. We live on a placid island of ignorance in the midst of black seas of infinity, and it was not meant that we should voyage far."

The Lovecraft Mythos

Lovecraft's fiction is generally divided into three main groups. The first is the group of fantastic tales that were influenced by Dunsany and that culminated in *The Dream Quest of Unknown Kadath*. These dreamlike romances are in sharp contrast to the second group of stories, a diverse assortment of horror tales set in and around New England—as rooted in the real as the Dunsanian tales are afloat in the fantastic. The third group, "The Cthulhu Mythos" (a phrase never used by Lovecraft but apt nonetheless) is a series of interconnected narratives that share a common cosmic or mythic world populated by a pantheon of Gods invented by Lovecraft and his collaborators.

The Dunsanian stories begin with "Polaris," a story the author wrote a year before he ever read the writing of Lord Dunsany, and culminate in *The Dream Quest of Unknown Kadath*. They are typified by dream settings and phantasmagoric people, creatures and events, set in imaginary places with names like Sarnath, Olathoe, Leng, Ib, Kadath and Lomar, and inhabited by gugs, ghasts, zoogs, Inutos, Gnoph–kehs, and moon–beasts. They are myths modeled on the classics of Greek and Roman mythology. The New England tales, by contrast, have a more realistic setting, capturing the architecture, landscape, and traditions of Lovecraft's native Providence and environs. Into these tales he poured his adoration of New England, its "roofs and gables and chimneys, and accessory details of verdure and background, which in the magic of late afternoon assume a mystic majesty and exotic significance beyond the power of words to describe," the author wrote in a 1927 letter. "All that I live for is to capture some fragment of this hidden and unreachable beauty; this beauty which is all of dream, yet which I feel I have known closely and reveled in through long aeons before my birth or the birth of this or any other world."

While the Dunsanian stories may embody the sense of wonder Lovecraft experienced in his native surroundings, the New England tales capture the dark side of that region's lore and locales.

Written by Lovecraft and others, the stories in this 1966 collection portray a mythic world inhabited by the god Cthulhu.

Typical New England tales include "The Picture in the House," "The Unnameable," "The Festival," "Pickman's Model" and "The Shunned House," which was inspired by a home Lovecraft actually lived in in Providence. The New England tales, which are also sometimes called the Arkham cycle (a name Lovecraft sometimes used in referring to these stories), feature haunted Massachusetts settings (a la Poe and Hawthorne) in a fictional place called Arkham that Lovecraft based on Salem. The culmination of these tales is *The Case of Charles Dexter Ward,* which tells the story of an eighteenth century wizard's evil aspirations as reimagined for the twentieth century.

The Cthulhu Mythos, which was begun by Lovecraft and expanded and developed by his colleagues and collaborators, marked Lovecraft's biggest departure and his greatest addition to the supernatural lexicon. According to Levy, "It is in the Cthulhu Mythos that Lovecraft's tales gain their profound unity. Except for some details, all develop the same central theme; all make reference to the same deities; all put on stage the same characters devoted to the same occult practices. Above all, the same images recur under the author's pen with an obsessive insistence, to form a tight web around the mythic contents of the work, ensuring its cohesion and giving it its consistency." Stories generally included in this grouping include—in addition to the first Cthulhu tale, "The Nameless City"—"The Whisperer in Darkness," "The Mound," "The Haunter of the Dark," "The Shadow out of Time" and *At the Mountains of Madness* (one of his last tales).

These stories, as created by Lovecraft, revolve around a pantheon of extra–dimensional beings named Cthulhu, Yog–Sothoth, Shub–Niggurath, Azathoth and Nyarlathotep. As Leiber points out, these are powerful deities, "quite enough in themselves to awaken all our supernatural dread, without any medieval trappings whatsoever. White magic and the sign of the cross are powerless against them and only the accidents of space and time—in short, sheer chance—save humanity." Also prominently featured in the Mythos, according to Glen St. John Barclay, is "a mad Arab, Abdul Azred, the author of a terrifying work called the *Necronomicon,* all about 'nameless aeons and inconceivable dimensions to worlds of elder outer entity.'" So pervasive is the power of the *Necronomicon* in the mythos—by Lovecraft and authors after him—that librarians today still receive requests for the imaginary "book of the dead."

"Cool Air," "The Shadow Over Innsmouth," and "The Music of Erich Zann" are among the stories in this 1982 collection.

Weird Tales

In a 1927 letter to Farnsworth Wright, a year after he wrote "The Call of the Cthulhu," Lovecraft set forth a central statement of his literary philosophy. "Now all my tales are based on the fundamental premise that common human laws and interests and emotions have no validity or significance in the vast cosmos–at–large . . . ," he wrote, as cited by Burleson. "To achieve the essence of real externality, whether of time or space or dimension, one must forget that such things as organic life, good and evil, love and hate, and all such attributes of a negligible and temporary race called mankind, have any existence at all." Indeed, Levy observed that Lovecraft's universe is a place of "bizarre dimensions . . . , where time and space stretch or contract in incomprehensible ways." This is the threatening, unknown universe of the Cthulhu Mythos, the emotional terrain of stories

such as "The Call of Cthulhu," "The Dunwich Horror," "The Whisperer in the Darkness" and "The Shadow over Innsmouth." It is this third group of stories, possibly more than the other two, that most uniquely defines Lovecraft's contribution to the genre of supernatural fiction. Neither tales of horror nor strictly of Gothic dimensions, the Cthulhu Mythos more than any other qualifies as what Lovecraft himself termed a tale of the "weird." In a 1926 letter he explained: "As to what is meant by 'weird'—and of course weirdness is by no means confined to horror—I should say that the real criterion is *a strong impression of the suspension of natural laws or the presence of unseen worlds or forces close at hand.*"

Leiber broke down three elements to Lovecraft's writing style "which he was able to use effectively in both his earlier poetic period and later, more objective style." The first of these is a device of "confirmation rather than revelation," in which the end of a story does not surprise the reader so much as confirm what has long been anticipated. "The reader knows, and is supposed to know, what is coming." The second element, closely related to the first, involves his use of a "terminal climax," which is to say a story in which the highest dramatic point and the end of the tale come together. "Use of the terminal climax," according to Leiber, "made it necessary for Lovecraft to develop a special type of storytelling, in which the explanatory and return–to–equilibrium material is all deftly inserted before the finish and while the tension is still mounting." The third element of his style is his use of "orchestrated prose—sentences that are repeated with a constant addition of more potent adjectives, adverbs, and phrases."

Peter Penzoldt, in an essay entitled "The Pure Tale of Horror," examines the author's oeuvre and concludes that "the most dominant motif in Lovecraft's work is the nameless, ancestral horror lurking beneath the earth, or ready to invade us from the stars; the dethroned but still potent gods of old." Levy remarks upon the recurrence of images of the sea, the land, and the home (especially structures native to New England), concluding that his "tales unequivocally bring to light the connection between the fantastic and the oneiric [relating to dreams]." As Derleth reported in *H. P. L.*, Lovecraft himself stated that all of his stories, "unconnected as they may be, are based on the fundamental lore or legend that this world was inhabited at one time by another race who, in practising black magic, lost their foothold and were expelled, yet live on outside ever ready to take possession of this earth again."

Creating a Comprehensive World View

"Throughout the Lovecraft opus are scattered references to his philosophical *Weltanschauung* [or detailed conception of the world]," Dirk W. Mosig observed in his essay "The Prophet from Providence," "as well as impressive glimpses of his vivid vision of the intellectual crisis of the future, felt today more than ever before. His works, like those of Franz Kafka, are full of allegories, analogies, parables, and symbols, resulting not from a hollow didacticism, but from the deep undercurrents of philosophical thought which permeate his writings and make them extremely relevant today." Indeed, Levy adds that reading Lovecraft's stories as "a journal of a treatment," one finds that "here again is an important aspect of mythic behavior, this notion of decadence from high times, from times signifying the beginning, an

The story "Dagon" has a dreamlike quality influenced by the Irish fantasist Lord Dunsany.

aspect that, as we have seen, occupies an important place in the author's *Weltanschauung*. There would doubtless be much to say about the rapports that existed in him between racism and mythic thought, and his 'fascism' could in part be explained by this return to the 'myth of origins.'"

"It is my privilege only to admire from the abyss of mediocrity," Lovecraft wrote in a 1921 essay entitled "The Defense Reopens!," "and to copy in my feeble way. But what I have said of imaginative literature may help to explain what it is that I am feebly and unsuccessfully *trying to do.* It may explain why I do not tag my tales with copy–book morals or try to confine the events to cheerful, every–day happenings of unimpeachable probability." H. P. Lovecraft was a lonely and complicated man, a product of a strange combination of circumstance that conspired to isolate him in a cold New England land where his own eccentricities turned in on himself, producing, from time to time, dreams of the horrible and the supernatural. That he was able to turn his own fear and dread into art may be his final moment of victory over his critics and the general lack of recognition and financial struggle he experienced in his own lifetime. Perhaps, as some believed, he was simply mad—certainly his politics were spiky and, quite often, difficult to stomach—but there is no doubt that H. P. Lovecraft's name belongs in the annals of twentieth–century science fiction. "The imaginative writer," he wrote in "The Defense Reopens!," "devotes himself to art in its most essential sense. It is not his business to fashion a pretty trifle to please the children, to point a useful moral, to concoct superficial 'uplift' stuff for the mid–Victorian holdover, or to rehash insolvable human problems didactically. He is the painter of moods and mind–pictures—a capturer and amplifier of elusive dreams and fancies—a voyager into those unheard–of lands which are glimpsed through the veil of actuality but rarely, and only by the most sensitive. He is the one who not only sees objects, but follows up all the bizarre trails of associated ideas which encompass and lead away from them."

■ Works Cited

Barclay, Glen St. John, "The Myth That Never Was: Howard P. Lovecraft," in *Anatomy of Horror: The Masters of Occult Fiction*, Weidenfeld & Nicholson, 1978, pp. 81–96.

Bloch, Robert, "Heritage of Horror," an introduction to *The Best of H. P. Lovecraft,* Del Rey, 1982, pp. 1–14.

Burleson, Donald R., *H. P. Lovecraft: A Critical Study,* Greenwood Press, 1983.

Carter, Angela, "Lovecraft and Landscape," in *The Necronomicon,* edited by George Hay, Neville Spearman, 1978, pp. 173–181.

Carter, Lin, introduction to *The Dream Quest of Unknown Kadath,* Ballantine, 1970.

Derleth, August, "H. P. Lovecraft and His Work," in *The Dunwich Horror and Others,* Arkham House, 1963, pp. xiii–xvii.

Derleth, August, *H. P. L.: A Memoir,* Abramson, 1945.

LeGuin, Ursula, "New England Gothic," *Times Literary Supplement,* March 26, 1976, p. 335.

Leiber, Fritz, "A Literary Copernicus," in *Discovering H. P. Lovecraft,* edited by Darrell Schweitzer, Starmont House, 1987, pp. 4–17.

Levy, Maurice, *Lovecraft: A Study in the Fantastic,* translated by S. T. Joshi, Wayne State University Press, 1988.

Lovecraft, H. P., "The Defense Reopens!," in *In Defense of Dagon,* edited by S. T. Joshi, Necronomicon, 1985, pp. 11–21.

Lovecraft, H. P., *The Dunwich Horror and Others,* Arkham, 1985.

Lovecraft, H. P., *Selected Letters,* 5 volumes, Arkham, 1965–76.

McMurtry, Larry, "Master of the Turgid," *Washington Post,* February 17, 1975, p. D4.

Mosig, Dirk W., "The Prophet of Paradise," *Crypt of Cthulhu,* Volume 4, No. 8, August 1, 1985.

Penzoldt, Peter, "The Pure Tale of Horror," in *The Supernatural in Fiction,* P. Nevill, 1952, pp. 165–171.

Price, Robert M., "H. P. Lovecraft and the Cthulhu Mythos," *Crypt of Cthulhu,* Vol. 5, No. 1, November 1, 1985.

St. Armand, Barton Levi, *The Roots of Horror in the Fiction of H. P. Lovecraft,* Dragon Press, 1977.

Wilson, Colin, "The Assault on Rationality: H. P. Lovecraft," in *The Strength to Dream: Literature and Imagination,* Houghton, 1962, pp. 1–10.

Wilson, Edmund, "Tales of the Marvellous and the Ridiculous," in *Classics and Commercials: A Literary Chronicle of the Forties,* Farrar, Straus, 1950, pp. 286–290.

■ For More Information See

BOOKS

Cannon, Peter, *H. P. Lovecraft,* Twayne, 1989.

Carter, Lin, *Lovecraft: A Look behind the "Cthulhu Mythos,"* Ballantine, 1972.

Davis, Sonia H., *The Private Life of H. P. Lovecraft,* Necronomicon, 1985.

De Camp, L. Sprague, *Lovecraft: A Biography,* Doubleday, 1975.

Faig, Kenneth W., Jr., *H. P. Lovecraft: His Life, His Work,* Necronomicon, 1979.

Joshi, S. T., *H. P. Lovecraft,* Starmont House, 1982.

Long, Frank Belknap, *Howard Phillips Lovecraft: Dreamer on the Nightside,* Arkham, 1975.

St. Armand, Barton Levi, *H. P. Lovecraft: New England Decadent,* Silver Scarab Press, 1979.

Schultz, David E. and S. T. Joshi, editors, *An Epicure in the Terrible: A Centennial Anthology of Essays in Honor of H. P. Lovecraft,* Fairleigh Dickinson University Press, 1991.

Schweitzer, Darrell, *The Dream Quest of H. P. Lovecraft,* Borgo Press, 1978.

Short Story Criticism, Volume 3, Gale, 1989.

Twentieth-Century Literary Criticism, Gale, Volume 4, 1981, Volume 22, 1987.

Twentieth-Century Science Fiction Writers, 2nd edition, St. James Press, 1991, pp. 502–505.

PERIODICALS

New York Times Book Review, January 16, 1944, p. 19.

Village Voice, March 19, 1985, p. 45.*

—*Sketch by Mindi Dickstein*

Patricia A. McKillip

■ Personal

Full name, Patricia Anne McKillip; born February 29, 1948, in Salem, OR; daughter of Wayne T. and Helen (Roth) McKillip. *Education:* California State University, San Jose (now San Jose State University), B.A., 1971, M.A., 1973.

■ Addresses

Home—Roxbury, New York. *Agent*—Howard Morhaim Literary Agency, 174 Fifth Ave., Room 709, New York, NY 10010.

■ Career

Writer.

■ Awards, Honors

World Fantasy Award for best novel, 1975, for *The Forgotten Beasts of Eld;* Hugo Award nomination, World Science Fiction Convention, 1979, for *Harpist in the Wind.*

■ Writings

FANTASY

The House on Parchment Street, illustrated by Charles Robinson, Atheneum, 1973.
The Throme of the Erril of Sherrill, illustrated by Julie Noonan, Atheneum, 1973.
The Forgotten Beasts of Eld, Atheneum, 1974.
The Night Gift, Atheneum, 1976.
The Riddle-Master of Hed (first book in trilogy), Atheneum, 1976.
Heir of Sea and Fire (second book in trilogy), Atheneum, 1977.
Harpist in the Wind (third book in trilogy), Atheneum, 1979.
Riddle of Stars (trilogy; contains *The Riddle-Master of Hed, Heir of Sea and Fire,* and *Harpist in the Wind*), Doubleday, 1979 (published in England as *Chronicles of Morgan, Prince of Hed,* Future Publications, 1979.
The Changeling Sea, Atheneum, 1988.
The Sorceress and the Cygnet, Ace, 1991.
The Cygnet and the Firebird, Ace, 1993.

SCIENCE FICTION

Moon-Flash, Atheneum, 1984.
The Moon and the Face, Atheneum, 1985.
Fool's Run, Warner, 1987.

FOR ADULTS

Stepping from the Shadows, Atheneum, 1982.

■ Sidelights

Patricia McKillip began her storytelling career out of sheer pragmatism. As the second oldest in a family of six children, she often was saddled with babysitting duties and found that she could keep the crew content by spinning a yarn or two. Her interest in storytelling prompted her to begin recording her tales, and she amassed a number of manuscripts by the time she was in her teens. McKillip kept writing while in college (partly because she was convinced that she would not survive at a "normal," full-time job) and was able to get her first book published before she needed to hit the pavement to look for work. Since that time, she has published many novels, mastering several different genres and earning popular acclaim.

McKillip's first critics, her siblings, turned out to be a fine audience for her. McKillip admitted to Charles L. Wentworth in an interview for *Contemporary Authors (CA)* that her siblings "were a captive audience, but I don't remember them rebelling or throwing things." Her sister, Kathy, was intrigued by the original version of what would become *The Riddle-Master of Hed*—enough so that she eventually drew the map for the *Riddle of Stars* trilogy. McKillip dedicated *The Riddle-Master of Hed* to her older sister, Carol, who closely followed the development of her early stories.

As a teenager, McKillip also liked playing music. But writing soon took over most of her free time. She was a shy and awkward teen, not fond of socializing or parties. When she was fourteen, she began writing a fairy tale that eventually totaled thirty pages. After that, she was hooked, and continued to write in many formats—plays, poetry, novels. She read extensively and with enthusiasm.

Discovers the Magic of Tolkien

McKillip cited two authors that were to influence her at an early age. The first was J. R. R. Tolkien, writer of the fantasy trilogy *The Lord of the Rings*. "I read him when I was about seventeen, which is a pretty crucial age for reading Tolkien," McKillip told *CA*. "It's an age when your mental doors are open to fantasy, I think—maybe more so than they would be now. I was bowled over that anybody could conceive of such a world as

Living near a graveyard in England as a child inspired the author's first novel.

his." At a time when few authors attempted fantasy, Tolkien brought the genre into the mainstream, an accomplishment that proved inspirational to McKillip.

Gore Vidal's work was a revelation to the high school-aged McKillip in quite another way. She came upon his novel *The City and the Pillar*, a work about homosexual love. "I'd never read anything like it," she said in her *CA* interview. "It certainly didn't have the effect on my writing that Tolkien had, but I was intrigued by both the mysterious habits of the adult world as well as by the kind of experience modern adult writers were allowed, and felt compelled, to put in their novels. I don't remember it as a blatant or cynical novel but something at once very personal and very modern," quite unlike the standard high school fare McKillip was used to reading.

McKillip recalls her teen writing attempts as being tolerated, if not wholly embraced, by the adult members of her family. "Certainly no one discouraged me, and I rarely made writing as a career a subject for discussion. I knew the kinds of things I'd hear, so I just kept quiet about it and wrote. My parents never chased me outside when I wanted to write—which was most of the time. They let me grow at my own speed, which strikes me now as an extraordinary way for modern parents to behave," she explained to Wentworth. The support for her career has grown as she has gotten older, with family members offering feedback on the works they have read.

First Novel Published

McKillip went to college to study music with the dream of becoming a concert pianist. She realized that her dream was a little lofty, and decided to round out her knowledge of history, literature, and folklore. She used her college years to educate herself in a variety of topics while she was writing and polishing her own literary efforts. After getting a bachelor's degree, she continued on for a master's degree, while working to get published. "Since I didn't think I was capable of holding down a full time job," McKillip told *Something About the Author (SATA)*. "I thought I'd better get published before I left college, so I could support myself." She achieved this goal at the age of twenty-five when her ghost story *The House on Parchment Street* was published.

Much of the inspiration for this book was taken from a childhood experience when her family resided in England. She lived in a big, old house facing a graveyard in an isolated and rural area. "The countryside was very peaceful, and evocative of all kinds of tales," she told *SATA*. The book won praise from reviewers, despite the usual curse of the first novel. A *Library Journal* reviewer termed it "an entirely plausible contemporary ghost story peopled with three-dimensional characters."

The House on Parchment Street launched her in the world of children's fiction. Although she had long wished to be a writer, she had never thought too much about her categorization. "I never deliberately decided to write for children," she once told *CA*. "I just found them particularly satisfying to write about, and *The House on Parchment Street* happened to be the first thing I sold."

While *The House on Parchment Street* had a contemporary flavor that relied on a supernatural storyline, many of McKillip's later books delved more deeply into fantasy and science fiction. *The Forgotten Beasts of Eld* contains the trappings of a classic fantasy novel—talking animals, dragons, wizards, and warriors. The story revolves around Sybel, a female wizard, and the warrior Coren. Georgess McHargue, a reviewer for the *New York Times Book Review* liked the level of humanity in the fantastical characters, declaring that the book "works best on the strictly human level. Trust, loneliness, love's responsibilities and the toxicity of fate are the themes that underlie" the story. "When [Sybel and Coren] manage to save their love in the end it is through a growth of courage and understanding far more meaningful than surviving any number of exotic eternal perils. That is why, finally *The Forgotten Beasts of Eld* is a very good book." However, McHargue found the often dense and flowery language and images in the book to be distracting.

When questioned about the richness of her prose,

McKillip received a 1975 World Fantasy Novel Award for her story of a female wizard's love for a warrior.

Patricia A. McKillip

The third in a trilogy, this 1979 novel was nominated for a Hugo Award.

McKillip told *CA* that "I think it's a little rich sometimes myself. I'd like to get to a point where words mean themselves and you don't have to dance around them and talk about them and *make* them be themselves; they would just, as Ezra Pound said, not *mean* but *be*. I'm still trying to learn about writing. I'm certainly my own harshest critic—or at least I try to be."

Publishes Famous Trilogy of Her Own

In 1976, McKillip published the first book in what was to become the *Riddle of Stars* trilogy. *The Riddle-Master of Hed* was the first book to appear. The plot follows the fortunes of Morgan from his beginnings as ruler of Hed, a peaceful and sleepy kingdom, to his ultimate destiny as a trained "riddle-master." Several reviewers noted that, as in *The Forgotten Beasts of Eld*, the trilogy's great-

est appeal comes from McKillip's strong, believable characters. Even after surviving many trials and a final "mythical and archetypal purification," Morgan "manages to maintain his humanity, . . . a humanity that endears him to the reader," wrote Roger C. Schlobin in *Science Fiction and Fantasy Book Review*. Another reader pointed out McKillip's keen grasp of the morality faced by most people in their lives. Glenn Shea, writing in the *New York Times Book Review*, remarked that McKillip "understands that we spend much of our time choosing, not between good and evil, but the lesser of two ills."

After publishing this trilogy, McKillip was recognized as a top notch fantasy writer. Schlobin wrote that "the canon of excellent women fantasists must now be expanded to include another superb effort." Oddly enough, her next book after completing this trilogy was entirely out of the genre. *Stepping from the Shadows* is about a young girl named Frances who wants to be a fantasy writer. Frances, who is painfully shy, has an imaginary sister with whom she shares all of her hopes, joys, and pains. Charles Champlin of the *Los Angeles Times* praised the book both for its realism and its ability to talk about the inner life of a child. "McKillip has put an imaginary playmate on paper and the more sophisticated truth that we all have an outside view of ourselves as well as the inside view; we perceive ourselves as strangers. . . . McKillip's memory of the coming of age of an author is rich, particular and extremely appealing."

After this book, McKillip once again started writing in a different genre, this time science fiction. *Moon-Flash, The Moon and the Face,* and *Fool's Run* were all science fiction—the first two titles for a young adult audience. She explained her views on the two genres in her *CA* interview: "For my own purposes, I try to keep the two separate. If I'm writing fantasy I use elements of epic, fantasy, myth, legend; and if I put magic in it, it's magic out of the imagination and out of the heart. When I write science fiction, . . . I try to turn my back on traditional fantasy elements and extrapolate a plot from history, or daily life, or whatever science happens to stick in my head."

McKillip returned to fantasy again, publishing *The Changeling Sea* in 1988. In this book, a young girl named Periwinkle meets a dragon and gets mixed up with magic, hexes, and a changeling prince. Ann A. Flowers, writing in *Horn Book*, called the work "a beautiful, dreamy, magical story, perfectly reflected in the author's cool, delicate style." The publication of *The Sorceress and the Cygnet* and *The Cygnet and the Firebird* soon followed. Both novels center on the character Corleu, a peasant who is different from his people, and a great sorceress, Nyx Ro. A *Publishers Weekly* review found that the "inspired imagery" and "perfectly paced plot" of *The Sorceress and the Cygnet* made for "one of the year's best" fantasies.

The Real Life of a Fantasist

McKillip tends to be a private person who spends a lot of her time researching and writing her novels. Regarding personal appearances and attending conventions, she told Wentworth: "If I keep things down to a bare minimum, I can enjoy them, like doing an occasional convention. . . . We exist so much in our own heads and houses that I could see myself writing books and then flinging them out like I was flinging them over a cliff and never getting responses to them, so it does help to get out a little in the public and let people respond to your books."

Regarding her 1982 book, *Stepping from the Shadows*, which explored the private feelings and remembrances of a young fantasist who one imagines might not be too far from McKillip's experience, she told Wentworth: "I don't think I could write that book now and publish it." McKillip further related that she "really didn't expect people from the science fiction and fantasy world to read it or to like it as much as they seemed to. . . . It was a scary book both to write and to realize that I was going to have to live up to afterwards, but I don't know—there doesn't seem to be any choice in the matter sometimes."

McKillip seems to follow her own internal muse when writing fiction—switching from fantasy to science fiction to suit the story she is trying to tell. It appears that she is always able to achieve a level of believability with her characters that is notable; her ability to make up fantastical settings is also remarkable. As for the future, McKillip told *CA* that she would "like to do some more contemporary things, and—I don't know—I'd like to do more of everything. I like all these different worlds. But I really would like to be better at contemporary novels, maybe because there

are so many backgrounds and people I'd like to write about—not in any personal way, but just people I know who suggest stories that might be nice to write."

■ Works Cited

Champlin, Charles, review of *Stepping from the Shadows, Los Angeles Times*, March 26, 1982.

Flowers, Ann A., review of *The Changeling Sea, Horn Book*, November-December, 1988, p. 790.

Review of *The House on Parchment Street, Library Journal*, May 15, 1973.

McHargue, Georgess, review of *The Forgotten Beasts of Eld, New York Times Book Review*, October 13, 1974, p. 8.

McKillip, Patricia A., interview with Charles L. Wentworth in *Contemporary Authors, New Revision Series*, Volume 18, Gale, 1986, pp. 316-320.

Schlobin, Roger C., review of the *Riddle of Stars* trilogy, *Science Fiction and Fantasy Book Review*, May, 1979, pp. 37-38.

Shea, Glenn, review of *The Riddle-Master of Hed, New York Times Book Review*, March 6, 1977, p. 29.

Something about the Author, Volume 30, Gale, 1986.

Review of *The Sorceress and the Cygnet, Publishers Weekly*, March 29, 1991.

■ For More Information See

PERIODICALS

Analog, January, 1980.

Bulletin of the Center for Children's Books, January 1975, p. 82; July, 1979, p. 196; September, 1984, p. 10.

Christian Science Monitor, November 2, 1977, p. B2.

Fantasy Review, November, 1985.

Library Journal, April 15, 1987, p. 102.

Locus, January, 1990, p. 52.

Publishers Weekly, March 13, 1987, pp. 75, 81; July 26, 1993, p. 61.

School Library Journal, June/July, 1987, p. 117; October, 1991, p. 160.

Science Fiction Chronicle, July, 1991, p. 30.

Voice of Youth Advocates, October, 1982, p. 32; June, 1991, p. 112.

Washington Post Book World, January 9, 1986.

—Sketch by Nancy E. Rampson

Andre Norton

Library of Congress, 1941; novelist, 1947—; editor, Gnome Press, 1950-58. *Member:* American Penwomen, Science Fiction Writers of America, American League of Writers, Swordsmen and Sorcerers Association.

■ Awards, Honors

Award from Dutch government, 1946, for *The Sword is Drawn;* Ohioana Juvenile Award honor book, 1950, for *Sword in Sheath;* Boys' Clubs of America Medal, 1951, for *Bullard of the Space Patrol;* Hugo Award nominations, World Science Fiction Convention, 1962, for novel *Star Hunter,* 1964, for novel *Witch World,* and 1968, for story "Wizard's World"; Headliner Award, Theta Sigma Phi, 1963; Invisible Little Man Award, Westercon XVI, 1963, for sustained excellence in science fiction; Boys' Clubs of America Certificate of Merit, 1965, for *Night of Masks;* Phoenix Award, 1976, for overall achievement in science fiction; Gandalf Master of Fantasy Award, World Science Fiction Convention, 1977, for lifetime achievement; Andre Norton Award, Women Writers of Science Fiction, 1978; Balrog Fantasy Award, 1979; Ohioana Award, 1980, for body of work; named to Ohio Women's Hall of Fame, 1981; Fritz Leiber Award, 1983, for work in the field of fantasy; Nebula Grand Master Award, Science Fiction Writers of America, 1984, for lifetime achievement; Jules Verne Award, 1984, for work in the field of science fiction; Second Stage Lensman Award, 1987, for lifetime achievement; Science Fiction Book Club Reader's Award, First Place, 1991, for *The Elvenbane.* Sev-

■ Personal

Given name Alice Mary Norton; name legally changed, 1934; has written as Andrew North and under joint pseudonym Allen Weston; born February 17, 1912, in Cleveland, OH; daughter of Adalbert Freely and Bertha (Stemm) Norton. *Education:* Attended Western Reserve University (now Case Western Reserve University), 1930-1932. *Politics:* Republican. *Religion:* Presbyterian. *Hobbies and other interests:* Collecting fantasy and cat figurines and paper dolls, needlework.

■ Addresses

Home—1600 Spruce Ave., Winter Park, FL 32789. *Agent*—Russell Galen, 381 Park Ave. S., Suite 1020, New York, NY 10016.

■ Career

Cleveland Public Library, Cleveland, OH, children's librarian, 1930-41, 1942-1951; Mystery House (book store and lending library), Mount Ranier, MD, owner and manager, 1941; special librarian for a citizenship project in Washington, DC, and at the

eral of Norton's books have been named Junior Literary Guild and Science Fiction Book Club selections.

■ Writings

SCIENCE FICTION

Star Man's Son, 2250 A.D., Harcourt, 1952, published as *Daybreak, 2250 A.D.* (bound with *Beyond Earth's Gates* by C. M. Kuttner), Ace Books, 1954.

Star Rangers ("Central Control" series), Harcourt, 1953, published as *The Last Planet,* Ace Books, 1955.

The Stars Are Ours! ("Astra" series), World Publishing, 1954.

Star Guard ("Central Control" series), Harcourt, 1955.

The Crossroads of Time ("Time Travel" series), Ace Books, 1956.

Star Born ("Astra" series), World Publishing, 1957.

Sea Siege, Harcourt, 1957.

Star Gate, Harcourt, 1958.

Secret of the Lost Race, Ace Books, 1959, (published in England as *Wolfshead,* Hale, 1977.)

The Beast Master ("Beast Master" series), Harcourt, 1959.

The Sioux Spaceman, Ace Books, 1960.

Storm over Warlock ("Planet Warlock" series), World Publishing, 1960.

Star Hunter, Ace Books, 1961.

Catseye, Harcourt, 1961.

Lord of Thunder ("Beast Master" series), Harcourt, 1962.

Eye of the Monster, Ace Books, 1962.

Judgment on Janus ("Janus" series), Harcourt, 1963.

Ordeal in Otherwhere ("Planet Warlock" series), Harcourt, 1964.

Night of Masks, Harcourt, 1964.

Quest Crosstime ("Time Travel" series), Viking, 1965 (published in England as *Crosstime Agent,* Gollancz, 1975).

The X Factor, Harcourt, 1965.

Victory on Janus ("Janus series"), Harcourt, 1966.

Operation Time Search, Harcourt, 1967.

Dark Piper, Harcourt, 1968.

The Zero Stone ("Zero Stone" series), Viking, 1968.

Uncharted Stars ("Zero Stone" series), Viking, 1969.

Ice Crown, Viking, 1970.

Android at Arms, Harcourt, 1971.

Breed to Come, Viking, 1972.

Here Abide Monsters, Atheneum, 1973.

Forerunner Foray, Viking, 1973.

Iron Cage, Viking, 1974.

The Many Worlds of Andre Norton (short stories), edited by Roger Elwood, Chilton, 1974, published as *The Book of Andre Norton,* DAW Books, 1975.

Outside, Walker & Co., 1975.

(With Michael Gilbert) *The Day of the Ness,* Walker & Co., 1975.

Knave of Dreams, Viking, 1975.

No Night without Stars, Atheneum, 1975.

Perilous Dreams (short stories), DAW Books, 1976.

Voor Loper, Ace Books, 1980.

Forerunner ("Forerunner" series), Tor Books, 1981.

Moon Called, Simon & Schuster, 1982.

Voodoo Planet [and] *Star Hunter,* Ace Books, 1983.

Forerunner: The Second Venture ("Forerunner" series), Tor Books, 1985.

Brother to Shadows, Morrow, 1993.

(With P. M. Griffin) *Fire Hand,* Tor Books, 1994.

"SOLAR QUEEN" SCIENCE FICTION SERIES

(Under pseudonym Andrew North) *Sargasso of Space,* Gnome Press, 1955, published under name Andre Norton, Gollancz, 1970.

(Under pseudonym Andrew North) *Plague Ship,* Gnome Press, 1956, published under name Andre Norton, Gollancz, 1971.

(Under pseudonym Andrew North) *Voodoo Planet,* Ace Books, 1959.

Postmarked the Stars, Harcourt, 1969.

(With Griffin) *Redline the Stars,* Tor Books, 1993.

"TIME WAR" SCIENCE FICTION SERIES

The Time Traders, World Publishing, 1958.

Galactic Derelict, World Publishing, 1958.

The Defiant Agents, World Publishing, 1962.

Key out of Time, World Publishing, 1963.

"MOON MAGIC" SCIENCE FICTION SERIES

Moon of Three Rings, Viking, 1966.

Exiles of the Stars, Viking, 1971.

Flight in Yiktor, Tor Books, 1986.

Dare to Go A-Hunting, Tor Books, 1990.

"STAR KA'AT" SCIENCE FICTION SERIES; WITH DOROTHY MADLEE

Star Ka'at, Walker & Co., 1976.
Star Ka'at World, Walker & Co., 1978.
Star Ka'ats and the Plant People, Walker & Co., 1979.
Star Ka'ats and the Winged Warriors, Walker & Co., 1981.

EDITOR; SCIENCE FICTION

Malcolm Jameson, *Bullard of the Space Patrol,* World Publishing, 1951.
Space Service, World Publishing, 1953.
Space Pioneers, World Publishing, 1954.
Space Police, World Publishing, 1956.
(With Ernestine Donaldy) *Gates to Tomorrow: An Introduction to Science Fiction,* Atheneum, 1973.
Grand Masters' Choice, Tor Books, 1991.

FANTASY

Rogue Reynard (juvenile), Houghton, 1947.
Huon of the Horn (juvenile), Harcourt, 1951.
Steel Magic, World Publishing, 1965, published as *Gray Magic,* Scholastic Book Service, 1967.
Octagon Magic, World Publishing, 1967.
Fur Magic, World Publishing, 1968.
Dread Companion, Harcourt, 1970.
High Sorcery (short stories), Ace Books, 1970.
Dragon Magic, Crowell, 1972.
Garan the Eternal (short stories), Fantasy Publishing, 1973.
Lavender-Green Magic, Crowell, 1974.
Merlin's Mirror, DAW Books, 1975.
Wraiths of Time, Atheneum, 1976.
Red Hart Magic, Crowell, 1976.
Yurth Burden, DAW Books, 1978.
Quag Keep, Atheneum, 1978.
Iron Butterflies, Fawcett, 1980.
Wheel of Stars, Simon & Schuster, 1983.
Were-Wrath, Cheap Street, 1984.
The Magic Books, Signet, 1988.
Moon Mirror, Tor Books, 1989.
Wizards' Worlds, Tor Books, 1990.
(With Susan M. Shwartz) *Imperial Lady,* Tor Books, 1990.
(With Marion Zimmer Bradley and Julian May) *Black Trillium,* Doubleday, 1990.
(With Mercedes Lackey) *The Elvenbane,* Tor Books, 1991.
Mark of the Cat, Ace Books, 1992.
Golden Trillium, Bantam Books, 1993.
(With Shwartz) *Empire of the Eagle,* Tor Books, 1993.
The Hands of Lyr, Morrow, 1994.

"WITCH WORLD" FANTASY SERIES

Witch World, Ace Books, 1964.
Web of the Witch World, Ace Books, 1964.
Three against the Witch World, Ace Books, 1965.
Year of the Unicorn, Ace Books, 1965.
Warlock of the Witch World, Ace Books, 1967.
Sorceress of the Witch World, Ace Books, 1968.
Spell of the Witch World (short stories), DAW Books, 1972.
The Crystal Gryphon (first volume in "Gryphon" trilogy), Atheneum, 1972.
The Jargoon Pard, Atheneum, 1974.
Trey of Swords (short stories), Ace Books, 1977.
Zarthor's Bane, Ace Books, 1978.
Lore of the Witch World (short stories), DAW Books, 1980.
Gryphon in Glory (second volume in "Gryphon" trilogy), Atheneum, 1981.
Horn Crown, DAW Books, 1981.
'Ware Hawk, Atheneum, 1983.
(With A. C. Crispin) *Gryphon's Eyrie* (third volume in "Gryphon" trilogy), Tor Books, 1984.
The Gate of the Cat, Ace Books, 1987.
(Editor) *Tales of the Witch World,* Tor Books, 1987.
Four from the Witch World, Tor Books, 1989.
(With Griffin) *Storms of Victory,* (first volume in "The Turning"), Tor Books, 1991.
(With Griffin and Mary H. Schaub) *Flight of Vengeance* (second volume in "The Turning"), Tor Books, 1992.
(With Crispin) *Songsmith,* Tor Books, 1992.
(With Patricia Matthews and Sasha Miller) *On Wings of Magic* (third volume in "The Turning"), Tor Books, 1994.

EDITOR; FANTASY

(With Robert Adams) *Magic in Ithkar,* Tor Books, 1985.
(With Adams) *Magic in Ithkar II,* Tor Books, 1985.
(With Adams) *Magic in Ithkar III,* Tor Books, 1986.

(With Adams) *Magic in Ithkar IV,* Tor Books, 1987.

(With Martin H. Greenberg) *Catfantastic,* DAW Books, 1989.

(With Greenberg) *Catfantastic II,* DAW Books, 1992.

(With Greenberg) *Catfantastic III,* DAW Books, 1994.

HISTORICAL NOVELS

The Prince Commands, Appleton, 1934.
Ralestone Luck, Appleton, 1938.
Follow the Drum, Penn, 1942.
The Sword is Drawn, (first volume of "Swords" trilogy), Houghton, 1944.
Scarface, Harcourt, 1948.
Sword in Sheath, (second volume of "Swords" trilogy), Harcourt, 1949 (published in England as *Island of the Lost,* Staples Press, 1954).
At Sword's Points (third volume of "Swords" trilogy), Harcourt, 1954.
Yankee Privateer, World Publishing, 1955.
Stand to Horse, Harcourt, 1956.
Shadow Hawk, Harcourt, 1960.
Ride Proud, Rebel!, World Publishing, 1961.
Rebel Spurs, World Publishing, 1962.

OTHER

(With Grace Hogarth, under joint pseudonym Allen Weston) *Murder for Sale* (mystery), Hammond, 1954, reprinted under names Norton and Hogarth as *Sneeze on Sunday,* Tor Books, 1992.
(With mother, Bertha Stemm Norton) *Bertie and May,* (biography), World Publishing, 1969.
(Editor) *Small Shadows Creep: Ghost Children,* Dutton, 1974.
The White Jade Fox (gothic), Dutton, 1975.
(Editor) *Baleful Beasts and Eerie Creatures,* Rand McNally, 1976.
Velvet Shadows (gothic), Fawcett, 1977.
The Opal-Eyed Fan (gothic), Dutton, 1977.
Snow Shadow (mystery), Fawcett, 1979.
(With Phyllis Miller) *Seven Spells to Sunday* (juvenile), McElderry, 1979.
Ten Mile Treasure (juvenile mystery), Pocket Books, 1981.
(With Enid Cushing) *Caroline,* Pinnacle, 1982.
(With Miller) *House of Shadows* (mystery), Atheneum, 1984.
Stand and Deliver, Tor Books, 1984.
(With Miller) *Ride the Green Dragon* (mystery), Atheneum, 1985.

(With Robert Bloch) *The Jekyll Legacy* (horror), Tor Books, 1991.

Contributor to numerous periodicals and anthologies. Many of Norton's early novels have been reprinted by Del Rey, Ace Books, Fawcett, and other publishers. Her works have been translated into eighteen languages.

■ **Sidelights**

"Andre Norton, like all special writers, is more than just an author. She is a guide who leads us, the real human beings, to worlds and situations that we might expect to live, were we given extraordinary longevity . . . . Is it any wonder that millions upon millions of readers . . . have chosen to go with her in her travels?" So states Roger Schlobin in his 1982 essay "Andre Norton: Humanity amid the Hardware" in *The Feminine Eye,* and over a decade later, his comments still ring true. Author of more than 150 books published over a sixty-year span, Norton has developed a large following that spans several generations and remains impressively loyal. The immutability of her appeal is evident in the list of Norton's books that are currently in print, which range from recent novels to reprints of her earliest works.

Norton is best known as a writer of science fiction and fantasy novels, and most of her work falls into these two categories. Fans of her novels in these genres may be surprised to find that she has also written several gothic novels, mysteries, action-adventure novels, and even a biography of her mother. In fact, Norton's writing career began not with science fiction, but with children's historical adventure stories, a genre for which her background would seem to have prepared her particularly well.

Born February 17, 1912, Alice Mary Norton was the daughter of Bertha Stemm and Adalbert Norton, both descendants of pioneers. Seventeen years younger than her sister, Alice tended to develop relationships with adults rather than her contemporaries, and undoubtedly benefited from the greater sophistication of ideas and verbal skills these relationships afforded her. Books and reading were important elements of the Norton family life, with weekly family trips to the library a regular routine. Norton's mother had a keen interest in American history in particular, and nurtured Norton's own fascination with, as Norton described it in her essay "On Writing Fantasy" (in

This 1985 sequel to *Forerunner Foray* again investigates the lives of the Forerunners, an ancient race visited by mind-exploring telepaths from the future.

The Many Worlds of Andre Norton), "the kind of history which deals with daily life, the beliefs and aspirations of people long since dust." In later years, Norton's mother was to prove a valuable sounding board for ideas and half-written manuscripts.

A rich family history also sparked Norton's interest in the subject. On her mother's side, her family roots can be traced back to the settlers who helped found Fort Zane, the first white settlement in Ohio, and on her father's, to ancestors who arrived in this country in 1634. One of Norton's maternal great-grandmothers was Wyandot Indian, her great-grandfather having been the first white person to legally marry an Indian in what later was to become the state of Ohio. Among the ancestors on her father's side, Norton counts one of the witnesses at the Salem witchcraft trials, a courageous soul who

dared to speak up in favor of Rachel Nourse, the first "witch" accused.

Starting Young as a Novelist

During her teens Norton became interested in writing, and joined the staff of her high school newspaper. She wrote her first novel as a high-school senior. (She later reworked this story, and it became her second published book, *Ralestone Luck*.) Intending to pursue a career as a history teacher, Norton entered Western Reserve University. However, the Depression hit during her freshman year, and Norton was forced to leave school in order to find a job. She took a position as a librarian at the Cleveland Public Library, and, realizing she would not be able to continue her formal education, took various writing courses at night while continuing to write in her spare time.

As a librarian, Norton was assigned to the children's book section. One of her responsibilities was to find suitable material for the children's hour, leading Norton to become well-versed in both popular and classic children's literature. At this time she was already interested in writing science fiction, but the only market for the genre was magazines, and Norton found it difficult to write short stories. Instead she turned to children's historical fiction. During this time she wrote *The Prince Commands,* which was to become her first published novel—a sale that was made when Norton was just twenty years old. This was followed by several more juvenile adventure novels, including three spy novels about the Dutch underground in World War II (the "Sword" series) that earned Norton an award from the Netherlands government. Norton continued to work in this genre throughout the 1930s and 1940s, firmly establishing herself as a writer who could be counted on to provide older children with fast-paced and historically accurate entertainment.

For these early novels Norton—whose legal name was still Alice Mary Norton—adopted the pseudonym Andre Norton. The use of a male-sounding pseudonym was deemed necessary by her publishers, who feared that her given name would turn off her potential readers, expected to be almost exclusively boys. Norton was apparently pleased with the pseudonym, since she later took it as her legal name. The name change also served Norton well when she turned to writing science fiction in the fifties, very much a male-dominated field at that time.

Norton continued her career as a librarian at the Cleveland Public Library until 1950, when she chose to resign because of health problems. Upon leaving her position as a librarian, Norton became an editor at Gnome Press, a job that allowed to pursue her own writing and also to serve as the editor of a science fiction anthology published by World Publishing. By then science fiction was enjoying a tremendous growth in readership and respectability, boosted in part by technological advances that suddenly made space travel an impending reality rather than just an incredible dream. As the public interest grew, the genre moved beyond the short stories found in pulp magazines and into the realm of "legitimate" hard cover publishing and novel-length works. Norton's position as the editor of World Publishing's anthology provided her with an entree into the field, and her first science fiction novel, *Star Man's Son, 2250 A.D.*, was published in 1952 by Harcourt Brace. Like her earlier adventure novels, it was originally marketed as a book for older children and enjoyed considerable popular success as such. However, Donald Wollheim, then the editor of Ace Books, recognized that the book also had a potentially high appeal for adult readers. He acquired the paperback rights and published the novel with a new title, *Daybreak—2250 A.D.* omitting from the cover all reference to the book as a story for young readers. As Wollheim wrote in his introduction to *The Many Worlds of Andre Norton:* "I presented it simply as a good novel for anyone who reads science fiction. It was so accepted and it has been selling steadily ever since."

Nevertheless, Norton continued to be known primarily as an author of science fiction for young adults, even though each of her novels, when published in paperback by Ace as adult science fiction, sold in the hundreds of thousands. Unfortunately, her obvious popularity with science fiction fans did not serve to gain her critical recognition. In this respect, the initial marketing of her novels as juveniles may have caused the critics, fairly or not, to relegate her to an inferior status as an author. Lin Carter, a well-known fantasy writer and editor, wrote in 1966 that he had been discouraged from seeking information on Norton because she was "a writer of minor or peripheral interest at best."

Ironically, those in children's literature also failed for many years to acknowledge Norton as a writer of significance. In a *Dictionary of Literary Biography* essay, Francis J. Molson speculates that specialists in children's literature may have disregarded Norton's contributions to the field because she wrote science fiction. Molson explains that the critics "still think of [science fiction] . . . as escapist reading in the manner of the Tom Swift books, consisting of quick-moving, incident-packed, poorly written stories which contain pasteboard, stereotypic characters and featuring implausible futuristic technology and gadgetry." The critic goes on to note that "there is little chance of Norton's ever being universally acclaimed an important author of children's fiction as long as there are those who cling to a bias against science fiction."

Awards and Overdue Recognition

By the mid-sixties and into the seventies, however, Norton finally began to receive well-deserved recognition within the science fiction and

Norton has proven herself a master at both science fiction and fantasy.

fantasy world. She was nominated three times for the Hugo Award, for the novels *Star Hunter* in 1962 and *Witch World* in 1964, and for a short story, "Wizard's World," in 1968. Hugo Awards, which are given annually at the World Science Fiction Convention, are presented to the authors of the best works published during the previous year, as determined by fans. In 1977 Norton was presented with the Gandalf, a special Hugo for overall excellence in science fiction and fantasy. She has also received the Life Achievement Award from the World Fantasy Convention. In addition, over the past two decades, Norton's contribution to the field has been recognized by her fellow authors. She was the first woman elected to Lin Carter's Swordsmen and Sorcerers Guild, a select company of writers of fantasy, and is the only woman ever to have received the Nebula Grand Master Award for lifetime achievement from the Science Fiction Writers of America. In all, Norton has received a total of twenty-three awards for her work over the years.

From the fifties on Norton's novels can be roughly divided into two categories: straight science fiction novels mostly written prior to 1965, and her more recent fantasy novels, such as the books in the "Witch World" sequence, including *Gate of the Cat,* among others. Whichever milieu Norton works in, however, there are common themes that can be traced throughout her novels, as well as traits her protagonists nearly always share. In her introduction to the Gregg Press edition of *Sargasso of Space,* Sandra Miesel sums up the Norton formula in this manner: "The typical Norton hero is a misfit seeking his rightful place. He is usually poor, young, powerless, and frequently a victim, orphan, cripple or outcast. His character-building struggle against his enemies is commonly plotted as chase-capture-escape-confrontation. The hero grows in wisdom, knowledge, and virtue under stress . . . . Finally, the victorious hero saves others besides himself."

A look at Norton's formula makes it easy to see why her books have always appealed to teenage readers, even though "much of her work is fully as adult in theme and telling as almost all general SF," according to John Clute in *The Encyclopedia of Science Fiction.* The "character-building struggle" Miesel refers to has been frequently noted by other commentators on Norton's work. As Molson writes, "one

theme, above all others, is pervasive in Norton's science fiction and fantasy: the centrality of passage or initiation." Molson goes on to describe this rite of passage as being presented "in ways that youth finds especially relevant, appealing, and if it so wishes, supportive." In his essay "The Formulaic and Rites of Transformation in Andre Norton's Magic Series," Roger Schlobin also notes that "Much of Norton's juvenile fiction . . . concentrate[s] on the dynamics of coming-of-age, self-realization, and rites of transformation as her young people discover themselves and their strengths."

This central concern is evident as early as *Star Man's Son, 2250 A.D.* When Fors, a mutant, is refused entry into the Star Men brotherhood of seekers, he realizes that his unusual parentage and physical appearance will always force him into the role of an outsider in his own land. He secretly leaves, accompanied by a big cat, Lura, with whom he can communicate telepathically, to search for a lost city that is rumored to be free of radiation. Fors's journey leads him through a land ravaged by a long-ago nuclear war, into violent encounters with the Beast Things (the savage offspring of human beings exposed to radiation), and to friendship with the prince of a previously unknown tribe. Throughout his adventures he is constantly tested, not only in terms of physical strength and mental agility, but most important, ethically. Fors, of course, passes his tests, although not without great effort (as do all of Norton's protagonists) and emerges stronger and more mature, having discovered his own self-worth.

The setting is different and the central character is female, but a similar process occurs in the 1970 novel *Ice Crown.* Roane, an orphan who has been raised by an uncle who shows her no love, undergoes her own rite of passage as she attempts to aid the aristocracy of a small kingdom on the planet Clio. Roane and her uncle have come to Clio, a closed planet whose inhabitants are still under the influence of a long-defunct mind-control experiment, on a mission to find archeological treasure. Roane is strictly forbidden to interfere with the destinies of the planet's inhabitants, but cannot resist coming to the aid of the princess Ludorica, whom she stumbles upon while on a scouting trip. Roane is soon drawn into Ludorica's search for the "Ice Crown"—the source of Ludorica's family's power to rule—and, in the process, begins to turn away from much that she has been taught by her own people. In the end, Roane's heroic actions help free Clio's people from the mind-control that has gripped them, and she, in turn, discovers a new life and identity among those she has chosen to befriend.

This pattern is repeated throughout Norton's novels, be they science fiction or fantasy, with seemingly endless variations. In *Here Abide Monsters,* Nick Shaw, a young man who has lost his mother and become alienated from his father, travels to a parallel world where he uses his developing mental powers to bring about the fall of a group that employs advanced technology to threaten the world's other inhabitants. In *Mark of the Cat* Hynkkel, a young nobleman in disgrace with his family, embarks on a quest that leads to friendship with a race of intelligent sandcats, and, finally, to an emperor's throne. In *Dread Companion* a young governess follows her two charges to a nightmarish parallel world and must rely on her own courage and endurance—and the help of more than a little magic—to bring the children back to safety.

Beyond the Formula

While it is easy enough to discern the formula behind all of Norton's adventure stories, there is much more to her work than a look at the basic plots might indicate. As the critics have often noted, Norton's achievement as a storyteller is remarkable. Her swiftly-moving plots, engaging protagonists and vividly described exotic settings have earned Norton a reputation as an author who consistently provides high-quality entertainment.

Perhaps the most noteworthy of Norton's accomplishments is the depth of her imaginative vision. Critic Marcus Crouch has proclaimed that "Andre Norton's strength lies in atmosphere. She gives a tangible quality to the most improbable invention by clothing it in vividly imagined detail, and her highly charged style . . . evokes with equal success the terrors of darkness and the blinding glare of light. Hers is an astonishingly complete vision." In a *Horn Book* review of *The X Factor,* Jane Manthorne comments on Norton's ability to vividly describe new worlds and sensations, observing that Norton is able "to construct a fantastic never-never land of new color, new sound, new motion. Readers feel truly like off-worlders with off-world eyes." Charlotte Spivack, author of *Merlin's Daughters: Contemporary Women Writers of Fantasy,* concurs. "Not only does she succeed in holding her reader," Spivack writes, "but her cosmos lingers in the mind, with its unforgettable images of alien species, jewels and talismans resonant with psychic powers, and magical transcendence of time and space."

Against this backdrop of strange and often mystical new worlds, Norton develops a variety of serious themes. According to critic John Rowe Townsend, "the sheer size of her world, which is infinitely extended in time and space, and in which nothing is outside the bounds of possibility, is matched by the size of the themes she tackles." Chief among these, of course, is the concept of self-realization or coming-of-age that is central to nearly all her novels. Closely linked, and as important, is Norton's celebration of the individual, or as Schlobin describes this theme in "Humanity amid the Hardware," her "reverence for the self, especially as it seeks to realize its potentials." "Effective plotting is her predominant skill," Schlobin states, "and her complete devotion to the individual and the powers of the individual is the primary characteristic of her content."

Norton's belief in what Miesel describes as "the inviolable dignity of the individual" is expressed in many ways throughout her work. Among the more prevalent is the casting of large organizations, such as the trading cartels in the "Solar Queen" novels, or the ruling forces of a society, such as the apathetic Earth government in *Eye of the Monster,* as villains. This "distrust of the megaestablishments of humanity comes not from a stress on the groups themselves," Schlobin notes; "rather, it originates in the value placed on the individual and the dangers that threaten the individual." As Miesel states, "repressive groups threaten the freedom and most especially the integrity of living beings. Norton has a visceral horror of external control or compulsion of any sort. Persons should be free in body, inviolate in spirit."

Miesel also points out that further evidence of Norton's respect for the individual can be seen in her staunchly anti-racist stance. Long before the practice was commonplace, Norton's casts of characters were multi-racial. This is true in works as early as *Star Man's Son: 2250 A.D.,* which features a post-atomic war culture established by black Air Force veterans, and *The Beast Master,* whose protagonist is a young Native American. In the "Solar Queen" series, Dane Thorson's best friend is black, and a black, an Asian, an American Indian and a caucasian all work together as equals in *The Sioux Spaceman*. Miesel notes that for the most part, Norton "lets the situations speak for themselves," in these early novels, with the exception of a couple of rare, pointed comments. The author deals more directly with prejudice in later novels such as *Lavender-Green Magic* and *Wraiths of Time*.

Interestingly, in Norton's early novels this egalitarian approach did not also apply to women. It is not that their worth is downgraded in these books, but rather that female characters are simply not included. The conspicuous absence of women was not a statement of Norton's personal belief regarding the worth of women, however. Before the publication of *Witch World* in 1963, Norton's editors had insisted that she omit female characters, since science fiction was considered to have a strictly masculine appeal. With the "Witch World" books female characters became increasingly more important in Norton's work, and she has written about active, intelligent heroines in many of her other novels as well. *Year of the Unicorn, Moon of Three Rings, Dread Companion,* and *Forerunner Foray* all describe the maturation of young women, making it clear that Norton's concern for the individual extends to both sexes as well as to all races.

An Anti-Science SF Writer

Another means by which Norton communicates her regard for the individual is her obvious distrust of science and machines. "In the battle between technology and nature, Miss Norton took a stand long before the great majority of us had any doubts," Rick Brooks proclaims in "Andre Norton: Loss of Faith," his introduction to *The Many Worlds of Andre Norton*. He later adds that "Norton consistently views the future as one where the complexity of science and technology have reduced the value of the individual." Miesel notes that this anti-science bent is evident in the "Solar Queen" series, where "the wages of technology is death. Machine-dominated civilizations turn into radioactive slag heaps . . . . High technology run amok may soon send humanity tumbling after the Forerunners into oblivion." This can also be seen in the "Witch World" series, where the super science of Kolder is the ultimate evil. Brooks quotes Norton herself as saying: "Yes, I am anti-machine. The more research I do, the more I am convinced that when western civilization turned to machines so heartily with the Industrial Revolution in the

The Acclaimed Author of *THE GATE OF THE CAT*

ANDRE NORTON

WITCH WORLD

This 1964 Hugo Award-nominated work debuted Norton's successful "Witch World" fantasy series, in which a group of telepathic witches battles the Kolder, invaders from a mechanistic, parallel universe.

early nineteenth century, they threw away some parts of life which are now missing and which the lack of leads to much of our present frustration. When a man had pride in the work of his own hands, when he could see the complete product he had made before him, he had a satisfaction which no joys of easier machine existence could or can give."

Norton's antipathy towards technology is sometimes voiced by her characters, such as when Aunt Margaret of *Octagon Magic* says, "in the name of progress more than one crime is committed nowadays. I wonder just who will rejoice when the last blade of grass is buried by concrete, when the last tree is brought down by a bulldozer, when the last wild thing is shot, or poisoned, or trapped." Similarly, a character in *Star Born* muses on the price of a technologically advanced society: "To

Norton coedited this 1989 book, the first of three collections focusing on the furry, cuddly creatures.

Raf, the straight highways suggested something else. Master engineering, certainly. But a ruthlessness too, as if the builders, who refused to accept any modifications of their original plans from nature, might be as arrogant in other ways."

If Norton distrusts machines in general, her "special wrath is reserved for computers," as Miesel observes, noting that "in *Star Hunter* Lansor's inability to adapt to the 'mechanical life of a computer tender' is supposed to demonstrate his depth of sensitivity and intelligence." Computers programmed to do evil or that have somehow run amok are the villains in more than a few of her novels, among them, *Judgment on Janus, Victory on Janus, Ice Crown,* and *No Night without Stars.* As Brooks quotes Norton herself, she feels that "the more computers are brought in to rule our lives— with their horrible mistakes and no one to appeal to to correct them—then the more alienated man will become. So I make my machines the villains—

because I believe . . . that man was happier . . . when he used his own personal skills and did not depend upon a machine. And I fear what is going to happen if more computers take over ruling us."

This anti-science stance may seem odd for one of the major science fiction authors of the twentieth century. However, as Townsend has noted, Norton "is not much interested in science-for-science's sake." The critic explains that "Miss Norton handles her gadgetry with great aplomb. She never draws special attention to it; it is simply there." Brooks concurs, stating that "Miss Norton has little knowledge of technology and rarely tries to explain the scientific wonders in her stories . . . . Technology is a necessary evil to get there for the adventure and to get some of the story to work. And the adventure is as much to mold her universe to her views as to entertain." It is in shaping and describing this universe that Norton's interest lies. As Schlobin explains in "Andre Norton: Humanity amid the Hardware," "the major thrusts of Norton's science fiction must be grouped with those of other such luminaries as Frank Herbert, Ursula K. LeGuin, and Gene Wolfe. They all write what could be variously labeled as 'social,' 'humanistic,' or 'soft' science fiction. While all their works contain the extrapolated factual material characteristic of science fiction, they really focus on the future of humanity and its possible traits and societies."

On the flip side of Norton's aversion for technology and science is her deep love of nature and animals, and a belief in humanity's need for a spiritual connection with the two. As Townsend maintains, "The value of the old ways of life, of the simple and natural against the sophisticated, artificial and ever-changing, is a frequent issue in Miss Norton's work . . . . There is a part of her . . . which is deeply aware of instinctual life, is conscious of the rooting of myth in the cycle of life and death, the turning of the seasons." Norton's belief in the benefits of renewing and maintaining humanity's ties to the natural world can be seen in her extensive use of magic in the Witch World series and fantasies like *Moon Called, Dread Companion,* and one of her newest novels, *The Hands of Lyr.* Jewels, talismans and touchstones figure prominently in these stories, with psychic and other powers often conveyed through the use of these artifacts. As a *Times Literary Supplement* critic notes, in Norton's work, "power is generated by the obedience to the nature of things, by stones that have lain in earth or other talismanic objects." In the "Witch World" series in particular, female characters are often portrayed as possessing magical abilities that stem from their strong connections to the land, to being somehow plugged into a collective unconscious, and from their awareness of an intrinsic order of the cosmos.

Telepathy, Animals, and the Natural Order

Norton's desire for closer ties between humanity and the natural world can also be seen in the significant role animals play in many of her novels. Her protagonists are often telepathically linked with animals, such as Travis Fox and the mutant coyotes in *The Defiant Angels*, Maelen of *Moon of Three Rings* and the animals in her traveling show, Karara Trehern and the dolphins in *Key out of Time*, and, of course, Fors and Lura of *Star Man's Son, 2250 A.D.* Animals are also often portrayed as the intellectual equals of humans, and not infrequently, as ethically and morally superior to humans, largely because of their stronger links to nature. For example, in both *Breed to Come* and *Iron Cage*, the planets inhabited by intelligent animals must be defended against possible colonization by humans. In *Breed to Come*, Earth, devastated and then deserted by people, is the home of cats, dogs and cattle that have evolved to human levels of sophistication. These animals band together to head off possible re-colonization of Earth by humans, who would undoubtedly destroy the planet's resources once again. Similarly, in *Iron Cage*, intelligent bears must resist an attempt by humans to dominate animals by caging them and using them for experiments. As Margery Fisher notes in a *Growing Point* review of *The Jargoon Pard*, Norton seems concerned that "man is distancing himself from the animal kingdom in which so much of his ancestry and aptitude rests."

Schlobin nicely sums ups Norton's feeling regarding the natural world in his essay on the Magic series: "Wisdom is unequivocally linked to nature and natural processes. Turning away from nature and tradition and depending upon technology . . . is a crime against humanity's essential bonds, and no good comes of it . . . . The combination of knowledge, experience, and understanding of the past and nature yields wisdom and harmony." Through magic, through mystical quests and through strange worlds and creatures, Norton celebrates the bonds that connect man to nature and the cosmic order. As Brooks states, "the chief value of Andre Norton's fiction may lie not in entertainment or social commentary, but in her 're-enchanting' us with her creations that renew our linkages to all life." Wollheim agrees, writing that "Andre Norton is at home telling wonder stories. She is telling us that people are marvelously complex and marvelously fascinating. She is telling us that life is good and that the universe is vast and meant to enhance our life to infinity. She is weaving an endless tapestry of a cosmos no man will ever fully understand, but among whose threads we are meant to wander forever to our personal fulfillment . . . . Basically this is what science fiction has always been about."

Now in her sixth decade as an author, Norton continues not only to weave her own tapestry, but to also help others develop their visions. She has collaborated with several up-and-coming fantasy authors, and has introduced others through her editing of the "Catfantastic" anthologies. In addition, Norton recently purchased seventy acres on a plateau in the center of Cherokee sacred land, where she will establish a retreat for genre writers. At her home in semi-rural Florida, Norton currently has two novels in the works. These will undoubtedly join the already staggering volume of Norton's work in ensuring her an unrivaled place in the history of the science fiction genre.

■ Works Cited

Brooks, Rick, "Andre Norton: Loss of Faith," *The Many Worlds of Andre Norton*, edited by Roger Elwood, Chilton, 1974, pp. 178-200.

Carter, Lin, "Andre Norton: A Profile," introduction to *The Sioux Spaceman* by Andre Norton, Ace Books, 1966.

Clute, John, "Andre Norton," *The Encyclopedia of Science Fiction*, edited by Peter Nicholls, Granada, 1979.

Crouch, Marcus, *The Nesbit Tradition: The Children's Novel in England, 1945-1970*, Ernest Benn, 1972.

Fisher, Margery, review of *The Jargoon Pard*, *Growing Point*, October, 1975.

Manthorne, Jane, review of *Quest Crosstime* and *The X Factor*, *Horn Book*, December, 1965, pp. 636-637.

Miesel, Sandra, introduction to *Sargasso of Space* by Andre Norton, Gregg Press, 1978.

Molson, Francis J., "Andre Norton," *Dictionary of Literary Biography*, Volume 52: *American Writers for Children since 1960: Fiction*, Gale, 1986, pp. 267-278.

Norton, Andre, *Octagon Magic*, World Publishing, 1967.

Norton, Andre, *Star Born*, World Publishing, 1957.

Norton, Andre, "On Writing Fantasy," *The Many Worlds of Andre Norton*, Chilton, 1974.

Schlobin, Roger C., "Andre Norton: Humanity amid the Hardware," *The Feminine Eye*, edited by Tom Staicar, Ungar, 1982.

Schlobin, Roger C., "The Formulaic and Rites of Transformation in Andre Norton's Magic Series," *Science Fiction for Young Readers*, edited by C. W. Sullivan III, Greenwood Press, 1993, pp. 37-45.

"Sorcery for Initiates," *Times Literary Supplement*, September 28, 1973, p. 1114.

Spivack, Charlotte, *Merlin's Daughters: Contemporary Women Writers of Fantasy*, Greenwood Press, 1987.

Townsend, John Rowe, "Andre Norton," *A Sense of Story: Essays on Contemporary Writers for Children*, Lippincott, 1971, pp. 143-149.

Wollheim, Donald, introduction to *The Many Worlds of Andre Norton*, Chilton, 1974.

■ For More Information See

BOOKS

Contemporary Literary Criticism, Volume 12, Gale, 1980, pp. 455-472.

Dictionary of Literary Biography, Volume 8: *Twentieth-Century American Science Fiction Writers*, Part 2, Gale, 1981, pp. 53-56.

Platt, Charles, *Dream Makers Volume II: The Uncommon Men and Women Who Write Science Fiction*, Berkley, 1983.

Schlobin, Roger C., *Andre Norton*, Gregg Press, 1979.

Schlobin, Roger C., *Andre Norton: A Primary and Secondary Bibliography*, G. K. Hall, 1980.

Shwartz, Susan, editor, *Moonsinger's Friends: An Anthology in Honor of Andre Norton*, Bluejay Books, 1985.

PERIODICALS

Christian Science Monitor, November 7, 1968, p. B7; May 1, 1969, p. B5; November 12, 1970, p. B4; November 3, 1976, p. 20.

Extrapolation, fall, 1985.

Fantasy Review, September, 1985.

Los Angeles Times, December 27, 1984.

New York Times Book Review, August 31, 1952, p. 12; December 14, 1958, p. 18; December 3, 1967, p. 103; September 20, 1970, p. 47; February 24, 1974, p. 8; January 25, 1976, p. 12;

Riverside Quarterly, January, 1970, pp. 128-131.

School Library Journal, September, 1977, p. 153.

Times Literary Supplement, March 2, 1967, p. 172; June 6, 1968, p. 584; October 16, 1969, p. 1202; July 2, 1971, p. 767; April 28, 1972, p. 480; April 6, 1973, p. 382; September 19, 1975, p. 1052; July 16, 1976, p. 878.

Voice of Youth Advocates, August, 1986, p. 164; June, 1990, p. 118; August, 1992, p. 178; October, 1993, p. 232.

—Sketch by Sarah Verney

Joan Phipson

■ Personal

Real name, Joan Margaret Fitzhardinge; writes under the name Joan Phipson; born November 16, 1912, in Warrawee, New South Wales, Australia; daughter of Harry (a merchant) and Margaret Phipson; married Colin Hardinge Fitzhardinge (a rancher); children: Anna, Guy. *Education:* Frensham School, Mittagong, New South Wales, Australia.

■ Addresses

Home—Wongalong, Mandurama, New South Wales 2792, Australia. *Agent*—A. P. Watt & Son, 20 John St., London WC1N 2DL, England.

■ Career

Author of children's books. *Wartime service:* Women's Auxiliary Australian Air Force, World War II. *Member:* Australian Society of Authors.

■ Awards, Honors

Children's Book Council of Australia Book of the Year Awards, 1953, for *Good Luck to the Rider*, and 1963, for *The Family Conspiracy;* Boys' Clubs of America Junior Book Award, 1963, for *The Boundary Riders; New York Herald Tribune* Children's Spring Book Festival Award, 1964, for *The Family Conspiracy; Elizabethan* Silver Medal for *Peter and Butch;* Writers Award, 1975, for *Helping Horse;* Honour Book Award, International Board on Books for Young People, 1985, for *The Watcher in Garden;* Australia's Dromkeen Award, for entire body of work.

■ Writings

FICTION

Good Luck to the Rider, illustrated by Margaret Horder, Angus & Robertson, 1952, Harcourt, 1968.

Six and Silver, illustrated by Horder, Angus & Robertson, 1954, Harcourt, 1971.

It Happened One Summer, illustrated by Horder, Angus & Robertson, 1957.

The Boundary Riders, illustrated by Horder, Angus & Robertson, 1962, Harcourt, 1963, published with *The Family Conspiracy,* John Ferguson, 1981.

The Family Conspiracy, illustrated by Horder, Angus & Robertson, 1962, Harcourt, 1965, published with *The Boundary Riders,* John Ferguson, 1981.

Threat to the Barkers, illustrated by Horder, Angus & Robertson, 1963, Harcourt, 1965.

Birkin, illustrated by Horder, Lothian/Constable Young, 1965, Harcourt, 1966.

A Lamb in the Family, illustrated by Lynette Hemmant, Hamish Hamilton, 1966.

The Crew of the "Merlin" (young adult), illustrated by Janet Duchesne, Angus & Robertson, 1966, published as *Cross Currents*, Harcourt, 1967.

Peter and Butch, Longman, 1969, Harcourt, 1970.

The Haunted Night, Macmillan (Australia)/ Harcourt, 1970.

Bass and Billy Martin, illustrated by Ron Brooks, Macmillan, 1972.

The Way Home (young adult), Macmillan/Atheneum, 1973.

Polly's Tiger (for children), illustrated by Gavin Rowe, Hamish Hamilton, 1973, illustrated by Eric Blegvad, Dutton, 1974.

Helping Horse (young adult), Macmillan, 1974, published as *Horse with Eight Hands*, Atheneum, 1974.

The Cats (young adult), Macmillan, 1976, Atheneum, 1977.

Hide till Daytime, illustrated by Mary Dinsdale, Hamish Hamilton, 1977, Penguin, 1979.

Fly into Danger (young adult), Atheneum, 1978, published as *The Bird Smugglers*, Methuen, 1979.

Keep Calm, (young adult), Macmillan, 1978, published as *When the City Stopped*, Atheneum, 1978.

Fly Free (young adult), Atheneum, 1979, published as *No Escape*, Macmillan, 1979.

Mr. Pringle and the Prince, illustrated by Michael Charlton, Hamish Hamilton, 1979.

A Tide Flowing (young adult), Methuen/Atheneum, 1981.

The Watcher in the Garden (young adult), Methuen/Atheneum, 1982.

Beryl the Rainmaker, illustrated by Laszlo Acs, Hamish Hamilton, 1984.

The Grannie Season, illustrated by Sally Holmes, Hamish Hamilton, 1985.

Dinko, Methuen, 1985.

Hit and Run (young adult), Methuen/Atheneum, 1986.

Bianca (young adult), Atheneum/Viking Kestrel, 1988.

The Shadow, Nelson, 1989.

OTHER

Christmas in the Sun, illustrated by Horder, Angus & Robertson, 1951.

A Lamb in the Family, Hamish Hamilton, 1966.

Bennelong, illustrated by Walter Stackpool, Collins, 1975.

Most of Fitzhardinge's books appear in Braille

editions, and have been published in foreign editions in seven different languages.

■ Adaptations

The Boundary Riders, Fly into Danger, A Tide Flowing, Watcher in the Garden, Dinko, and *Hit and Run* have been recorded on audio cassette.

■ Sidelights

Although she had always loved reading and words, Australian children's novelist Joan Phipson didn't start writing until she was caring for her first child on a sheep and cattle ranch after World War II. "Our property was not very far from neighbours . . . but because of the petrol rationing we were fairly isolated," Phipson wrote in *Something about the Author Autobiography Series* (*SAAS*). While she liked to write short stories and verse, she never dreamed of writing for children. But after her first child was born, Phipson said: "I sat down one hot summer afternoon, pulled the typewriter towards me and . . . [wrote] what I thought I would have liked to read when I was about nine years old." The book was purchased by Angus & Robertson, a Sydney publisher. They requested a novel for older children; Phipson sent it chapter by chapter. "They wanted it in a hurry," she explained in *SAAS*. "With only one draft, without any revision to speak of" she mailed out *Good Luck to the Rider,* the story of the Trevors and Barkers, a ranch family who would appear in her later books. That year, *Good Luck to the Rider* won the Australian Children's Book Award.

Phipson didn't grow up in the Australian bush; on the contrary, she practically grew up on shipboard. Her parents had moved from Birmingham, England, to Sydney, Australia, almost on a whim. Phipson's father had read a novel about Australia, and liked it so much that he decided to move. But her mother missed her home and required many trips back to England, and so Joan traveled a great deal. Joan's father worked as "a merchant . . . not as a Company Director, or a Business Executive," Phipson recalled in *SAAS*. He enjoyed reading, and his talents included "writing, and particularly writing witty verse, drawing and painting." These talents would sometimes annoy his wife, for one of his habits was to illustrate his conversation by sketching on restaurant tablecloths. He also loved the English language, and taught his daughter how to tell good writing from bad.

Phipson's children, Anna and Guy, riding at their ranch in Australia in the 1950s.

A Childhood in India

When her father joined the Australian army in World War I, "Everyone knew that the troops were destined for France. This meant that my mother was about to be deserted on what she still regarded as very foreign soil," Phipson said in *SAAS*. So Joan and her mother went to visit her father's family in India for eighteen months. Her uncle was a doctor for the Indian Medical Service, stationed in Bombay. At that time, her mother was reading *The Jungle Books* to her daughter. After moving to Kasauli, "I was able to relate to *The Jungle Books* particularly because of the jackals that came nightly to scavenge our dog's bones, the leopard, always waiting during the hours of darkness to make a meal of the dog himself, and of the black panther my mother once saw lying on a rock in a clearing in the jungle," Phipson related in *SAAS*. Joan and her mother lived in several houses in India; from one, they could see where a valley road ran through the jungle. "'That's the Grand Trunk Road,' said my mother in thrilling tones. 'That's where Kim and his guru walked.'" Joan didn't read Rudyard Kipling's *Kim*

until later, but when she did, the scene came back to her.

Joan's Indian homes included Bombay, Kasauli, at the foot of the Himalayas, and Simla, where they "inhabited a cottage in the hotel grounds," said Phipson in *SAAS*. "It was a noisy cottage because monkeys liked to jump off the branches of nearby trees and slide down the roof." One night when Joan was in bed, her mother "burst into the bedroom and said. . . . 'The Armistice has been signed and I'm going to put on a white dress.'" Phipson's mother went down to the hotel ballroom and danced all night to celebrate the end of the war.

Phipson said in *SAAS* that she was "a much pampered and spoilt only child." Some of her relatives agreed. When celebrating with two of her ninety–plus–year–old aunts, they assured her that she had been extremely difficult. "'Oh, your mother spoiled you dreadfully,' said [one aunt]. . . . 'Actually, you were quite nasty,' said the [other]. . . . 'In fact you were downright horrible.'" For instance, Phipson recalled tormenting her

While flying from Australia to London, Margaret suspects that the elderly couple sitting with her are smuggling parrots.

house, where we children rode stick horses when real ponies were not available. . . . This boarding house became a kind of heaven to me, and, indeed, if ever I get to heaven I know I shall find myself there again."

One of Phipson's first jobs was as a junior typist for Reuters news service. The Spanish Civil War was going on, and she finally felt in contact with real life. After a three to four–year visit to England, Phipson returned to Australia, just before the Second World War broke out. "Women's Lib had not arrived in those days, and the reason that after a few years I got my job as a copywriter in a radio station was because a good many of the male staff had joined the army . . . ," Phipson recalled in *SAAS*. "I know that I benefited from having to write short, pithy sentences that said clearly—and startlingly if possible—exactly what they meant."

After a time in the advertising world the work began to seem trivial, and Phipson became a telegraphist for the Women's Auxiliary Australian Air Force. After the war, she found herself married to Colin Fitzhardinge and settled in the Australian countryside. She wrote stories, some of which were published in magazines or read on the radio. "I am lucky because my husband has always encouraged me and made circumstances easy when he could," Phipson related in *SAAS*. One day, she began writing her first children's story. She followed it up with the award–winning *Good Luck to the Rider*. "Once a door of this kind opens before you, it takes a strong and perverse mind not to step through it," the author continued.

Home on the Range

The author's ranch home was no writer's escape. She and Colin, and eventually their children, Anna and Guy, lived in a small cottage whose corrugated iron roof had holes in it. The outside walls were of clapboard coated with sump oil, and the inside walls were covered with bubbling newspaper. "We had no electricity, no gas, and our only water supply was from a small iron tank that caught the rainwater that drained off the roof," Phipson remembered in *SAAS*. Nothing grew in the garden except upside–down beer bottles. Phipson spent a half hour each day replacing gravel in the garden with soil, and discovered that water used to soak dirty diapers made a good fertilizer.

younger cousin while in India. "I certainly remember exhilarating fights with my two–year younger cousin, whose hair I enjoyed pulling. . . . All she ever did was to look solemnly at me out of very large brown eyes and say with much feeling, `I'll fwow you in the jungle.'" Joan's parents had no other children, but while Phipson says she always felt like an observer as a child, she was also content. "Nasty I may have been, but . . . I had, in fact, a happy and eventful childhood," she wrote in *SAAS*. Actually, she feels that her upbringing formed the character needed to become a successful writer, developing the ability to note action and detail.

Joan and her parents often vacationed near a small country town eighty–five miles from Sydney. "It was here that I first became acquainted with horses and began riding," Phipson remembered in *SAAS*. "Open paddocks surrounded the boarding

The Fitzhardinges were perhaps too close to nature on the ranch. There were rats in the ceiling and poisonous snakes in the summer. Phipson wrote in *SAAS* that "I imagine myself to be probably the only woman of seventy–two years old to have been given a shotgun for Christmas." On the ranch, she needed a gun. One day, years earlier, Phipson heard her daughter Anna screaming and pounding on the screen door. She looked "into the laundry door and was just in time to see a foot or so of snake's tail. . . . Fortunately my husband was within call, and after I had shrieked at him I returned our daughter to the bedroom, shut the door, and returned with quaking knees to do battle." It had gone under the house, her husband told her, where he had it jammed with a garden rake. He instructed her to poke a rifle behind the hinge, until she could feel the snake. "I still remember the rubbery, bouncy feeling of that rifle barrel on the snake. When I shot there was a slithering sound of writhing on the other side." She shot again and again. Eventually, the snake came "wavering in a bleary way out over the top of the bottom hinge." Colin struck its head with a rake and pulled it out. It was over six feet long.

The Fitzhardinges were fairly confined to life on the ranch, as gasoline was rationed, and Joan did most of her writing at night, while her husband read books and newspapers in front of the fire. "So I began to write stories about the countryside and of farm life as I had experienced it," Phipson related in *SAAS*. "The books I wrote at this period were *Good Luck to the Rider, Christmas in the Sun* (the little story I had begun with), *Six and Silver, The Family Conspiracy, Threat to the Barkers, Peter and Butch, The Boundary Riders,* and *Birkin,* all of which, with the exception of *It Happened One Summer,* have been published in the States."

Good Luck to the Rider revolves around the Barker family on their ranch. A shy girl falls in love with the clowning stray foal, Rosinante, and the process matures her. The Barkers also appear in *The Family Conspiracy* and *Threat to the Barkers.* In the latter, twenty–one–year–old Jack hopes to increase the family income by breeding sheep. But fourteen–year–old Edward runs into sheep rustlers, and they threaten to harm him, his family, and his dogs if he reveals their whereabouts. The theme involves how Edward deals with fear. In detailing

"Edward's inner turmoil," *Threat to the Barkers* "is a fine job," says Mary Louise Hector in the *New York Times Book Review*. The book's "style, understanding and humor" make Edward's "successive moods credible and logical."

A sheep farm is also the setting for *Six and Silver,* written for younger audiences. The little girl in *Six and Silver* must adapt to a New South Wales sheep station after city life. Similarly, in *Polly's Tiger,* Polly moves to the country after living in the city. When she is shunned by her new classmates, Polly imagines a proud tiger. "Wherever she goes, the tiger walks bravely at her side, giving her the courage to be alone," as a *Publishers Weekly* contributor describes. But Polly eventually earns the

In Phipson's 1985 novel, a bond develops between a young car thief and the constable who breaks his leg while chasing him.

BIANCA
Joan Phipson

Published in 1988, this work deals with trauma and memory loss.

children's respect by facing a frightening dog and its owner.

Courage is also in evidence in *Cross Currents* (published in Australia as *The Crew of the "Merlin"*), in which Phipson tells about a seventeen–year–old boy and his younger cousin in trouble at sea. "With this storm–tossed story," writes a *Publishers Weekly* contributor, the author "will add older readers to the already wide circle of Phipson enthusiasts." A less serious subject is exhibited in Phipson's *Horse with Eight Hands*. "Horse" is actually Horst, an immigrant "adopted" by a group of children. Horse and the children become friends, and the children help in fixing up his house and protecting him from wandering delinquents. Phipson's "perfectly delightful sparkle of dry humor" turns her relatively "ordinary" story into a tale "which

will keep readers chuckling right through to the end," writes a *Publishers Weekly* contributor.

Australian Setting Distinguishes Suspense Fiction

Phipson continued using Outback settings when she turned to suspenseful young adult novels in the 1970s. *The Cats* involves two boys whose parents have won the lottery. Local hoods Socker and Kevin kidnap them and take them to the countryside. Willy, the shy younger brother, knows the land, as well as the large feral cats that inhabit the region, but his abductors don't. In the end, the kidnapped boys save their captors, and make a secret pact to keep others from knowing about the cats. *New York Times Book Review* reviewer Susan Meyers finds the conclusion hard to believe. "I can buy the pact being made," she states, but can't imagine that the adults in the story "would accept the false explanations." She appreciates the setting, however, adding, "And you thought all they had down there were platypi and kangaroos and cuddly koalas!" *Fly into Danger*, "like *The Cats*, is rooted in cruel reality," notes a *Publishers Weekly* reviewer. When flying from Australia to London, thirteen–year–old Margaret suspects that the elderly German couple sitting with her are smuggling wild parrots. She proves their guilt and finds the stolen birds, some of which have died from drugs and airless quarters. "Phipson gives readers a rousing thriller, but she does more," notes the reviewer, adding that Phipson also reveals why the poor immigrants, Theo and Maria, stole the birds.

Others of Phipson's thrillers use an urban—but still Australian—setting. *When the City Stopped* leaves two children to survive on their own when a nationwide strike shuts down all city services in Sydney. Nick and Binkie's father is away and their mother is in the hospital. In trying to escape the city, the children face "danger from looters and other thugs who are liberated when all the rules are broken," explains a *Publishers Weekly* reviewer. A *Horn Book* contributor calls the book "frightening" and its style "poetic." *Fly Free* is likewise about being trapped. Two boys urgently want to make money to go on a school trip to an interesting offshore island. Johnny persuades Wilfred to join him trapping rabbits and selling the skins, but the boys become involved with two men who illegally trap birds for export, and learn for themselves what it is like to be trapped. The result is "a situation that jets Phipson's story into a stunning climax," writes a *Publishers Weekly* reviewer.

Inner Conflicts Characterize Later Works

As she has grown older, Phipson has enjoyed testing the limits of her craft. "That is why I wrote *A Tide Flowing, The Way Home,* and *The Watcher in the Garden,*" she stated in *SAAS.* "I feel more sense of achievement with them than with earlier books, even if they fall short of my original intention." Violence and danger play a part a part in these later works, as well. In *A Tide Flowing,* a boy is lost in the jungle of his own emotions after his mother's suicide. Mark goes to stay with his Australian grandparents, who "are kind and loving but unable to understand" Mark's pain, writes Karen Harris in *School Library Journal.* The boy remains apart from everyone who would help him until the day he sees a quadriplegic's wheelchair break loose from the woman pushing it, aiming toward the highway. He stops the wheelchair in time, but both he and Connie, the handicapped girl, are injured. As Mark and Connie recover, they become friends, and their friendship helps Mark deal with tragedy. "There is a strong sense of place and the plot is engrossing," Harris adds.

The Watcher in the Garden leads turbulent fifteen–year–old Kitty into a blind man's garden, where she finds temporary peace. She is drawn into conflict, however, when a teenaged hood attacks the older man. Through the power of the garden, the two teens become able to communicate telepathically and learn to overcome their differences. "The mental and physical upheavals of the climax are merged almost perfectly," praises Gale Eaton in *School Library Journal.* "This novel is serious, exciting and nearly a masterpiece."

A more outward adventure characterizes *Hit and Run,* an "unforgettable tale of survival set in the rough and inhospitable hinterlands of Australia," writes a *Horn Book* reviewer. Phipson tells the story in the second person so the reader can experience the characters' thoughts and feelings. Sixteen–year–old Roland steals a Ferrari when taunted by garage mechanics. He hits a baby carriage and panics when he sees a small bundle fly through the air. Pursuing Roland is Constable Gordon Sutton, who catches the boy. But when Sutton breaks his leg, Roland gets the chance to bolt. A *Publishers Weekly* reviewer finds that as *Hit and Run* "unfolds, readers come to experience the ben-

efits from the companionship that binds the two in a crucial time." The night that Roland and Sutton spend together forges a bond between them, although they only meet once more. Roland's crisis is one "from which he emerges to stand on his own, for the first time standing up to his father," says Cathi Edgerton in *Voice of Youth Advocates.* She adds, however, that while "his story, told with economy and insight, will interest many young adults, . . . its psychological focus may not." In contrast, Mary M. Burns of *Horn Book* remarks that "the book is also a sensitive and engrossing exploration of a boy's transition from childhood to maturity, told in a style commensurate with the painful dignity that marks such a passage."

In *Bianca,* Phipson stresses more psychological dangers. Emily and Hubert Hamilton find a strange girl rowing in the fog near a deserted dam. On two traumatic occasions, Bianca's mother has abruptly dismissed her daughter in order to protect her. But Bianca interprets this as rejection. "Not understanding . . . Bianca stumbles away through the darkness and suffers a total loss of memory," reports a *Horn Book* contributor. Bianca also fears contact with people. In the course of searching for her daughter and consulting about her anxiety attacks, Bianca's mother Frances meets Hubert's father, Dr. Hamilton. When Hubert confides in his father about the girl, the whole family tries to help Bianca regain her memory. Phipson's "understated depiction" of the security

of the Hamilton family "makes the horrors that befall Bianca seem all the more devastating," emphasizes a *Publishers Weekly* contributor. And Jane Van Wiemokly reports in *Voice of Youth Advocates* that "the story flows smoothly and reads like well–crafted suspense, one scene naturally leading on to the next, as the reader keeps page turning."

The Rewards of Writing

Now that her children are grown, Phipson enjoys travelling to schools and libraries and talking to her young audiences. She wrote in *SAAS* that "there is one question that is always asked . . . and it never fails to embarrass the teacher or librarian in charge. It is, `Please, Miss Phipson, how much do you MAKE?'" She finds the question difficult. Children want to know if they will "be wealthy beyond the dreams of avarice if they take to writing stories. They have to be disillusioned, and this is where I try to explain how great are the rewards for achieving something, however small, on one's own." Phipson equates writing with spinning and finds it "hard to equate the joy of this with actual money."

In *SAAS*, Phipson stated that "I am glad I write books for children." She likes working with people who all share "the same aim: to open a world of fun, pleasure, consolation, and wisdom to those who are beginning life and who will find life so much richer for being part of this ageless inheritance." She told *AAYA* in 1994 about another aim of her work: "It seems to me, now that I have stopped writing books for children and begin to look back on what I have written, that one thing stands out clearly. This is that through almost all of my stories runs one important theme—the relationship of my characters to the land they live in (or sometimes `off'). I know that I have always thought it important that people should think of themselves as part of the world around them, and not as a unique creation for whose convenience the world exists. Animals are important, trees are important, every living thing is important. Man is important, but only to himself is he more important than the rest of the world.

"If any of this belief has penetrated to any of the boys and girls who read my books I shall feel the writing of them has not been wasted."

■ Works Cited

Review of *Bianca, Horn Book,* January, 1989, p. 80.

Review of *Bianca, Publishers Weekly,* July 29, 1988, p. 234.

Burns, Mary M., review of *Hit and Run, Horn Book,* January/February, 1986, pp. 63–64.

Review of *Cross Currents, Publishers Weekly,* April 3, 1967, p. 56.

Eaton, Gale, review of *The Watcher in the Garden, School Library Journal,* November, 1982, p. 89.

Edgerton, Cathi, review of *Hit and Run, Voice of Youth Advocates,* April, 1986, pp. 33–34.

Review of *Fly Free, Publishers Weekly,* September 3, 1979, p. 96.

Review of *Fly into Danger, Publishers Weekly,* August 1, 1977, p. 116.

Harris, Karen, review of *A Tide Flowing, School Library Journal,* April, 1981, p. 130.

Hector, Mary Louise, review of *Threat to the Barkers, New York Times Book Review,* May 9, 1965, p. 18.

Review of *Hit and Run, Publishers Weekly,* November 15, 1985, pp. 56–57.

Review of *Horse with Eight Hands, Publishers Weekly,* July 29, 1974, p. 56.

Meyers, Susan, Review of *The Cats, New York Times Book Review,* November 21, 1976, p. 60.

Phipson, Joan, "Just a Silkworm," *Something about the Author Autobiography Series,* Volume 3, Gale, 1987, pp. 205–219.

Review of *Polly's Tiger, Publishers Weekly,* March 4, 1974, p. 76.

Van Wiemokly, Jane, review of *Bianca, Voice of Youth Advocates.* April, 1989, p. 30.

Review of *When the City Stopped, Horn Book,* May, 1986, p. 349.

Review of *When the City Stopped, Publishers Weekly,* October 2, 1978, p. 133.

■ For More Information See

BOOKS

Children's Literature Review, Volume 5, Gale, 1983.

PERIODICALS

Bulletin of the Center for Children's Books, November, 1985, p. 54; September, 1988, p. 17.

Christian Science Monitor, July 29, 1965, p. 7.

Horn Book, October, 1982, p. 522.

Saturday Review, April 22, 1967, p. 100.

School Library Journal, December, 1977, p. 62; October, 1978, p. 148; October, 1979, p. 161; November, 1988, p. 130.

Times Literary Supplement, September 20, 1974, p. 1005; December 6, 1974, p. 1376; October 1, 1976, p. 1242; March 28, 1980, p. 362; September 7, 1984, p. 1114.

—Sketch by Jani Prescott

Edgar Allan Poe

■ Personal

Born January 19, 1809, in Boston, MA; died October 7, 1849, in Baltimore, MD; buried in the Westminster Presbyterian Churchyard, Baltimore; son of David, Jr. (an actor) and Elizabeth (an actress; maiden name, Arnold) Poe; unofficially adopted, 1811, by John (a tobacco merchant) and Frances Allan; married Virginia Clemm, May 16, 1836 (died, 1847). *Education:* Attended the Manor House School, Stoke Newington, England, 1815–1820; University of Virginia, 1826; United States Military Academy at West Point, 1830– 1831 (dismissed).

■ Career

Poet, short– story writer, critic. *Southern Literary Messenger,* Richmond, VA, staff member, 1835–1837, assistant editor, 1936– 1837; *Burton's Gentleman's Magazine,* Philadelphia, PA, co– editor, 1939– 1840; literary editor, *Graham's Lady's and Gentleman's Magazine,* 1841– 1842; *Evening Mirror,* New York City, staff member, 1845; *Broadway Journal,* New York City, editor, 1845, owner, 1845– 1846. *Military service:* Enlisted in the United States Army under the name "Edgar A. Perry," 1827; became regimental sergeant– major, January, 1829; discharged, April, 1829.

■ Awards, Honors

First prize, *Baltimore Sunday Visiter* fiction contest, 1833, for "MS. Found in Bottle"; first prize, *Philadelphia Dollar Newspaper* fiction contest, 1843, for "The Gold Bug."

■ Writings

POETRY

Tamerlane and Other Poems. By a Bostonian (published anonymously), Calvin F. S. Thomas, 1827.
Al Aaraaf, Tamerlane, and Minor Poems, Hatch & Dunning, 1829.
Poems, by Edgar A. Poe, Second Edition, Elam Bliss, 1831.
The Raven and Other Poems, Wiley & Putnam, 1845.

FICTION

The Narrative of Arthur Gordon Pym, of Nantucket (published anonymously), Harper, 1838.
Tales of the Grotesque and Arabesque, 2 volumes, Lea & Blanchard, 1840.
The Prose Romances of Edgar A. Poe, No. I. Containing the Murders in the Rue Morgue, and The Man That Was Used Up, William H. Graham, 1843.
Tales by Edgar A. Poe, Wiley & Putnam, 1845.

Eureka: A Prose Poem by Edgar A. Poe, Putnam, 1848.

Most of Poe's stories first appeared in such periodicals as the *Southern Literary Messenger, Burton's Gentleman's Magazine, Graham's Lady's and Gentleman's Magazine,* the Philadelphia *Saturday Courier,* and the *Evening Mirror.*

COLLECTIONS

The Works of the Late Edgar Allan Poe, with a Memoir by Rufus Wilmot Griswold and Notices of His Life and Genius by N. P. Willis and J. R. Lowell, 4 volumes, edited by Griswold, J. S. Redfield, 1850– 1856.

The Works of Edgar Allan Poe, 10 volumes, edited by Edmund Clarence Stedman and George Edward Woodberry, Stone & Kimball, 1894– 1895.

The Complete Works of Edgar Allan Poe, 17 volumes, edited by James A. Harrison, Thomas Y. Crowell, 1902.

Selections from the Critical Writings of Edgar Allan Poe, edited by F. C. Prescott, Holt, 1909, reissued with new preface by J. Lasley Dameron and new introduction by Eric W. Carlson, Gordian Press, 1981.

The Complete Tales and Poems of Edgar Allan Poe, Modern Library, 1938.

The Letters of Edgar Allan Poe, edited by John Ward Ostrom, 2 volumes, Harvard University Press, 1948, published with three supplements, Gordian Press, 1966.

Selected Prose and Poetry, edited with an introduction by W. H. Auden, Holt, 1950, reprinted as *Selected Prose, Poetry, and Eureka,* 1968.

The Selected Poetry and Prose of Edgar Allan Poe, edited by Thomas Ollive Mabbott, Random House, 1951.

Literary Criticism of Edgar Allan Poe, edited by Robert L. Hough, University of Nebraska Press, 1965.

The Poems of Edgar Allan Poe, edited by Floyd Stovall, University Press of Virginia, 1965.

Collected Works of Edgar Allan Poe, 3 volumes, edited by T. O. Mabbott, Belknap Press of Harvard University Press, 1969– 1978.

Collected Writings of Edgar Allan Poe, edited by Burton R. Pollin, volume 1, *The Imaginary Voyages: The Narrative of Arthur Gordon Pym, The Unparalleled Adventure of one Hans Pfaall, The Journal of Julius Rodman,* G. K. Hall, 1981, volume 2, *The Brevities: Pinakidia, Marginalia, Fifty Suggestions and Other Works,* Gordian Press, 1985.

Edgar Allan Poe: Poetry and Tales, edited by Patrick F. Quinn, Library of America, 1984.

Edgar Allan Poe: Essays and Reviews, edited by G. R. Thompson, Library of America, 1984.

Dozens of collections of Poe's stories and poems have appeared, many of them illustrated. Poe's works have been translated into over a dozen languages.

OTHER

The Conchologist's First Book, Haswell, Barrington & Haswell, 1839.

Mesmerism "In Articulo Mortis" (pirated publication of Poe's story, "The Facts in the Case of M. Valdemar"), Short & Co. (London), 1846.

The Literati, J. S. Redfield, 1850.

Politan: An Unfinished Tragedy, George Banta, 1923.

Poe's Contributions to the Columbia Spy: Doings of Gotham, as described in a series of letters to the editors of the Columbia Spy, together with various editorial comments and criticisms by Poe now first collected, compiled by Jacob E. Spannuth, introduction by T. O. Mabbott, Jacob E. Spannuth, 1929.

■ Adaptations

MOVIES

The Raven, American Eclair Company, 1912, Essanay Film Manufacturing Company, 1915, Universal Pictures (starring Boris Karloff and Bela Lugosi), 1953, American International Pictures (starring Vincent Price, Peter Lorre, and Karloff), 1963, Texture Films, 1973.

The Bells, Thomas A. Edison, Inc., 1913.

The Murders in the Rue Morgue, Sol. A. Rosenberg, 1914, Universal Pictures (starring Lugosi), 1932, as *Phantom of the Rue Morgue,* Warner Brothers, 1954.

The Black Cat, Universal Pictures (starring Karloff and Lugosi), 1934, Universal Pictures (starring Broderick Crawford), 1941, University of Southern California, 1956, World/Selenia, 1984.

The Crime of Doctor Crespi (adaptation of "The Premature Burial"), Republic Pictures, 1935, as *The Premature Burial,* American International Pictures, 1962.

The Tell– Tale Heart, Metro– Goldwyn– Mayer, 1941, Learning Corporation of America, 1953, Columbia Pictures, 1953, CBS Films, 1958, Rothschild Film Corp., 1959, American Film Institute, 1971, as *Heartbeat,* General Television Enterprises, 1950.

The Mystery of Marie Roget, Universal Pictures, 1942.

Masque of the Red Death, American International Pictures, 1954, 1964, Contemporary Films/McGraw– Hill, 1970.

Manfish (adaptation of "The Gold Bug" and "The Tell– Tale Heart"), United Artists, 1956.

The Fall of the House of Usher, Brandon Films, 1959, American International Pictures, 1960, Encyclopaedia Britannica Educational Corp., 1976, Sunn Classic, 1980, as *The Haunted Palace,* American International Pictures, 1963.

Pit and the Pendulum, American International Pictures, 1961, Murray Cowell, 1966, as *The Pit,* British Film Institute, 1961 (released in the U.S. by Films Incorporated, 1971).

Tales of Terror (adaptations of "Morella," "The Black Cat," and "The Case of M. Valdemar"), American International Pictures (starring Price, Lorre, and Basil Rathbone), 1962.

The Haunted Palace, American International Pictures, 1963.

The Tomb of Ligeia, American International Pictures, 1965.

War– Gods of the Deep (adaptation of "City in the Sea"), American International Pictures, 1965.

The Oblong Box, American International Pictures, 1969.

Spirits of the Dead, American International Pictures, 1969.

Annabel Lee, Productions Unlimited, 1973.

PLAYS

Robert Brome, *Edgar Allan Poe's "Masque of the Red Death,"* Eldridge Publishing, 1963.

Brome, *Edgar Allan Poe's "The Tell– Tale Heart,"* Eldridge Publishing, 1966.

Brome, *Edgar Allan Poe's "The Cask of Amontillado,"* Eldridge Publishing, 1968.

Steven Berkoff, *The Fall of the House of Usher,* J. Calder, 1977.

Gip Hoppe, *The Fall of the House of Usher: A Play Based on the Short Story by Edgar Allan Poe,* Samuel French, 1991.

OTHER

Numerous recordings of Poe's stories have been made, including Caedmon Records' *The Gold Bug,* read by Vincent Price, 1974, *The Imp of the Perverse, and Other Tales,* read by Price, and *Edgar Allan Poe,* read by Basil Rathbone; American Forces Radio and Television Service's *The Black Cat,* 1972, *The Cask of Amontillado and The Scapegoat,* 1972, *The Cask of Amontillado,* 1974, *Hall of Fantasy: The Tell– Tale Heart,* 1974, and *Never Bet the Devil Your Head,* 1974; and *Selected Stories of Edgar Allan Poe,* Books on Tape.

Numerous filmstrips of Poe's works have been made for use in schools.

■ Sidelights

On Thursday, September 27, 1849, author Edgar Allan Poe left Richmond, Virginia by boat, heading for his home in New York. Poe never reached his destination. After visiting a friend in Baltimore on September 28, Poe disappeared and was not heard from again until October 3, when a friend received word that Poe was in "great distress" at a local tavern. This friend, Dr. J. E. Snodgrass, found Poe in a sorry condition, as Wolf Mankowitz reported in *The Extraordinary Mr. Poe:* "His face was haggard, not to say bloated, and unwashed, his hair unkempt and his whole physique repulsive." It was clear that Poe had been on an extended alcoholic binge. Poe was taken to a hospital and, hallucinating, he begged his friends "to blow out his miserable brains with a pistol." Nearing death, he muttered about his novel *The Narrative of Arthur Gordon Pym,* which ended with these lines: "And now we rushed into the embraces of the cataract, where a chasm threw itself open to receive us. But there arose in our pathway a shrouded human figure, very far larger in its proportions than any dweller among men. And the hue of the skin of the figure was of the perfect whiteness of the snow." Poe's death, on the morning of Sunday, October 7, 1849, must have seemed as awesome and inscrutable as the death he had long imagined.

When Poe died, many of his contemporaries believed that his death was of a piece with his life and his stories, for Poe had lived a life of remarkable tumult while creating stories that chronicled the bizarre twists and turns of the human subconscious. Though Poe's stories told of madness, Poe is now recognized as a genius who reinvented the Gothic tale of mystery and horror for his age. In stories like "The Tell– Tale Heart," "The Fall of the House of Usher," and "Ligeia," Poe placed the reader inside the tortured minds and lives of people confronting the supernatural.

Yet Poe was more than a writer of horror stories. Midway through his career, Poe literally invented the modern detective story. His character Inspector Dupin became the model for the greatest fictional detective of all time, Arthur Conan Doyle's

Vincent Price starred in the 1961 film version of Poe's chilling short story, "Masque of the Red Death."

Sherlock Holmes. Moreover, Poe's poetry is thought to have been the single most important influence on the Symbolist movement in European poetry at the end of the nineteenth century. A perfectionist in his own writing, Poe demanded perfection of others as well and was known in his time as a sophisticated though strident critic, an ambitious editor of literary journals, and a principled promoter of good American writing. Edmund Wilson, summing up Poe's career in 1942, wrote, "Intellectually, [Poe] stands on higher ground than any other American writer of his time."

From Squalor to Comfort

There was little glamour in the lives of David and Elizabeth Arnold Poe, actors travelling along the east coast of the United States in the early 1800s. Paid poorly and scorned by respectable society, the Poes scrounged what money they could to start a family. In 1807 they had a son, William Henry Leonard, but were so poor that they had to send him to live with David Poe's parents. On January 19, 1809, Elizabeth gave birth to her second son, Edgar. In order to keep her son, Elizabeth returned to the stage three weeks after his birth. The baby's

father was no help: he disappeared soon after Edgar's birth and was not heard of again until a newspaper clipping revealed his death, of tuberculosis (known then as consumption), in October of 1810.

The infant Poe accompanied his mother on her ceaseless theatrical tours, watching from the wings as Elizabeth recreated her favorite roles from Shakespeare. Poe later remembered her as a princess in flowing white robes, ethereal in her beauty. While Poe watched his mother act on stage, he watched her die off of it. Her tuberculosis had been exacerbated by her pregnancies, and by the end of 1811 she posted newspaper advertisements appealing to the sympathy of strangers for charity. On December 8, 1811, Elizabeth Poe, aged twenty–four, died. "The small fairy–like figure of his mother wearing her best gown, her face white as wax after the hectic colour of her last days, illuminated by candles, an ultimate dream–lady deep in her mysterious sleep, remained one of the most haunting images of Poe's childhood," wrote biographer Mankowitz.

Poe was adopted by John and Frances Allan, a childless couple from Richmond, Virginia. His circumstances could hardly have changed more dramatically, for John Allan was a prosperous merchant who dealt in tobacco, feed, farm animals, and slaves, and owned a spacious home in town. Adoption was Frances Allan's idea, not John's, and he was not eager to pass on the family inheritance to the son of "poor devils of actors." Though Frances Allan loved Edgar like her own child, the relationship between John Allan and Edgar was, as Mankowitz wrote, "of that fateful cut which makes tragic consequences inevitable."

Poe was an attractive and intelligent child, and he entertained his parents' guests by reciting long passages from poems. Though John Allan resisted the role of father, he was fiercely proud of the boy and took care to send him to the best schools money could buy. The Allan family moved to England to attend to business in 1815 and in 1818 Poe began to attend the Manor House boarding school in the village of Stoke Newington. Poe later described the school in the story "William Wilson": "My earliest recollections of a school life are connected with a large, rambling, Elizabethan house, in a misty-looking village of England, where a vast number of gigantic and gnarled trees stood, and where all the houses were excessively ancient. In truth, it was a dream- like and soothing place, that venerable old town."

Poe had gone to England a waiflike child, but the exercise regimen practiced by the English schools had made him strong. When he returned to Richmond with his family in 1820 he became a leader among his boyhood friends. "His athletic exploits became legendary," wrote biographer Suzanne LeVert. "He was able to broad–jump a distance of 21 feet 6 inches on a dead–level run of 20 yards. At the age of 15 he swam a distance of 7 1/2 miles against a strong tide." Poe succeeded in school as well, learning several languages and devoting himself to great literature and the written word. "His imaginative powers seemed to take precedence over all his other faculties," recalled the headmaster at one of Poe's schools, "he gave proof of this in his juvenile compositions, addressed to his young lady friends."

A Romantic Imagination

At the age of 14, Poe became devoted to Jane Stanard, the mother of a classmate. Idolizing her

as if she was a goddess, Poe was crushed to find that she was dying of a malignant brain tumor. Recasting Jane as Helen, Poe wrote one of his best early poems, called "To Helen," which began: "Helen, thy beauty is to me/ Like those Nicean barks of yore/ That gently, o'er a perfumed sea,/ The weary, way– worn wanderer bore/ To his own native shore." Jane represented to Poe the ideal woman—unattainable, beautiful, and doomed. "In Edgar's mind," wrote LeVert, "beauty was now forever linked with death."

As Poe became increasingly romantic, dedicating his life to reading and writing, his adoptive father grew ever more critical. Describing Poe in a letter as "miserable, sulky, and ill-tempered," Allan was cold to Poe and constantly reminded of him of the debt of gratitude he owed to the Allans. At the same time, Allan continued to provide for Poe, and in 1826 sent him to the University of Virginia at Charlottesville, where students regularly dined with the university's founder, President Thomas Jefferson. The University of Virginia "was the most idealistic and most dissolute college in America," wrote biographer Jeffrey Meyers in *Edgar Allan Poe: His Life and Legacy*. Poe revelled in what Meyers called the "rough male code of fighting, sports, drinking and gambling," and soon ran himself into debt.

Worse than Poe's gambling was his drinking, for Poe had a strange and disastrous relationship with alcohol. Poe did not drink for pleasure; rather, he rushed headlong into a stupor, gulping alcohol as quickly as he could until he reached the point of oblivion. Mankowitz related the words of a friend at college, Thomas Tucker, who described Poe's drinking: "He would always seize the tempting glass . . . and without the least apparent pleasure, swallow the contents, never pausing until the last drop had passed his lips. One glass at a time was all that he could take; but this was sufficient to rouse his whole nervous nature into a state of strongest excitement, which found vent in a continuous flow of wild, fascinating talk that irresistible enchanted every listener with siren– like power." Once the excitement of the drink passed, Poe would often pass out.

Poe's drinking plagued him throughout his life, and eventually led to his death. But it is uncertain whether Poe was in fact an alcoholic.

Following his youthful drinking binges, Poe drank only sporadically. Yet when he was depressed, as he was quite often in his life, he needed only a few drinks to push him over the edge. Most biographers agree that Poe was a "problem" drinker, whose tumultuous temperament simply could not bear the exciting affects of drink.

Cast Adrift

John Allan had had enough of his foster son's behavior in the winter of 1826 and 1827, and when he refused to pay Poe's debts, Poe was forced to withdraw from the university. Then, in March of 1827, Allan issued an ultimatum to Poe: live by my rules or leave. Poe left with only the clothes on his back and, as he later wrote in a letter begging for money, "not one cent in the world to provide any food." For the rest of his life, Poe would wander from job to job and city to city, looking for financial and emotional support, but also looking for some way to exercise his intellect and his churning imagination. It would be a long and frustrating journey.

Poe set off for Boston, the city in which his mother had had her greatest success as an actress. Poe was determined to become a great writer, yet becoming great would never guarantee him a living. There were no best seller lists in the early nineteenth century and publishers did not pay unknown writers for their manuscripts. Poe would have to attract attention on his own, and he set out to do so when he met the owner of a print shop named Calvin F. S. Thomas. Poe convinced Thomas to print 40 or 50 copies of his poems under the title *Tamerlane and Other Poems*; the author was cited as "A Bostonian." "Poe's first published poems reveal a sensitive young man with a strong musical sense, a good deal of technique, and a great inclination towards dreams and melancholy moods," wrote Mankowitz. But there is little evidence that anyone read the poems. Poe would need to find some other way to attract attention to his writing.

Burdened by the costs of publishing his poems, Poe decided to join the U.S. Army, under the name Edgar A. Perry. He made a surprisingly good soldier, and within two years had earned the rank of sergeant major. Seeing the military as a road to respect and stability, Poe decided that he must attend the United States Military Academy at West Point, New York, and become an officer.

Borrowing $50 from John Allan, with whom he had not spoken in two years, and paying a man to take his place in the army, Poe applied for and earned admission to West Point. "Poe entered the academy on July 1, 1830," wrote LeVert, "hoping for a good education, increased employment opportunities, and, of course, a chance to prove himself to his eternally distant foster father." In the meantime, he had also published his second book of poems, *Al Aaraaf, Tamerlane, and Minor Poems*, which earned Poe equal measures of praise and scorn for his still developing talent.

The life of an officer–in–training was not at all what Poe had expected. Instead of having leisure to read and write, Poe was kept busy from dawn to dusk, and he released his frustration by drinking large amounts of brandy. Miserable and again burdened by debts, Poe wrote to Allan and threatened to get himself ejected from West Point if he did not send money. Allan, again disgusted with Poe, sent no money and Poe made good on his word. He was court– martialed on January 28, 1831, on charges of gross neglect of duty and kicked out of the academy. Only 21 years old, Poe was on his own again and scrambling to make a living.

Also in 1831, Poe published his third book of poems, entitled *Poems by Edgar A. Poe, Second Edition*. The book was dedicated to his West Point classmates, whose subscriptions to the book gave Poe what little money he had. In the preface to this book, Poe began to develop a theory of poetry that would carry him for the rest of his life. "A poem . . . is opposed to a work of science by having, for its *immediate* object pleasure, not truth." Thus the job of the poet was to provide the reader with a glimpse beyond the reality of everyday human experience into the realm of pure emotional ecstasy. For Poe, that ecstasy need not always be beautiful, for emotions could be dark and disturbing as well as charming and joyful.

John Allan remarried in 1831, two years after the death of his first wife. Poe knew that his dreams of taking his place in the Allan family were dashed and he headed to Baltimore to live near what remained of his natural family. (Allan would die in 1834, making no mention of Poe in his will.) Poe's family—a paralyzed grandmother; an alcoholic, tubercular brother who soon died; and a hardy, loving aunt, Maria Clemm, and her two children, Henry, 13, and Virginia, 9—survived off the income left by Poe's grandfather's army pen-sion and the meager earnings of Maria Clemm. Poe did little to contribute, but instead plunged once more into writing poetry. But when the *Philadelphia Saturday Courier* offered $100 to the author of the best short story, Poe left his beloved poetry to write a series of stories he called "Tales of the Folio Club."

Grotesques and Arabesques

The "Tales of the Folio Club" consisted of two kinds of stories, grotesques and arabesques. The grotesques were outrageous comic tales, such as "The Duc de L'Omelette," which describes a man who dies of shock at being served food improperly and must play cards with the devil. The arabesques were tales of terror, wrote Meyers, "depicting pathological emotional states, subconscious criminal impulses and a poetic atmosphere that combined realistic and supernatural worlds." In the arabesques, Poe developed the terrifying emo-

A murderer is tortured by the sounds of his victim's still-beating heart in "The Tell-Tale Heart," illustrated by Arthur Rackham in *Tales of Mystery and Imagination.*

tions and gothic scenes that would become his trademark. One story, "Metzengerstein," is among Poe's most popular tales. It tells the story of a young German baron who kills an old family rival, only to find that the rival count's spirit takes possession of a wild horse come to life from one of the count's tapestries. "When the young baron rides the horse," wrote LeVert, "both horse and rider die in a fiery blaze created by their own hatred for each other." None of Poe's stories won the prize, but the judges liked them enough to publish each one over the course of the following year.

Poe's first published stories brought him little happiness, however, for he received no pay nor was he credited with authorship. For nearly two more years, Poe wrote poems and stories and grew to love the security and comfort of living with his family, despite their poverty. Poe especially grew to cherish the company of his young cousin Virginia, who bore a resemblance to his mother. In 1833, Poe entered another short story contest, sponsored by the Baltimore *Saturday Visiter,* and this time he won. His story "MS. Found in a Bottle" earned him the $50 first prize and the praise of the judges, who said of Poe's six submissions, "These tales are eminently distinguished by a wild, vigorous, and poetical imagination, a rich style, a fertile invention, and varied and curious learning." Poe cherished the praise as much as he did the money.

By 1835, Poe had begun to publish his stories in the *Southern Literary Messenger,* the South's most important literary journal, which was based in Richmond, Virginia, where Poe had spent his youth with the Allans. Thomas White, the owner of the journal, liked Poe's work so much that he offered him the job of editor. Finally, Poe would earn a salary and be able to exercise his critical facilities in shaping the tastes of the literary public. But his good luck did not last. Haunted by memories of his unhappy childhood and depressed at being so far from his family, Poe took to drinking, and his bouts left him unable to work or write. White fired Poe in disgust, and Poe returned to Baltimore.

Poe's bad luck did not last for long, however, as White rehired him on the condition that he remain sober. Realizing that his success depended on the support and love of others, Poe returned to Richmond with Virginia and her mother, Maria. According to Mankowitz, Poe made quite an impression: "His figure, black as a raven, shabbily but carefully dressed in Byronic style, his haunted blue– grey eyes superbly intelligent above a mouth twisted with pain and bitterness, was noteworthy upon the quiet streets of Richmond." Poe finally married Virginia on May 16, 1936, and though their wedding certificate claimed that she was 21 years old, in fact his little cousin was only 13.

Growing Reputation

Once again the editor of the *Southern Literary Messenger*, Poe enjoyed one of the best years of his life as he developed the talents that made him one of the first and finest literary critics in the United States. Reviewing hundreds of books, Poe was intent on creating serious standards for American literature and treated harshly those works he deemed second rate. *The Swiss Heiress*, Poe wrote, "should be read by all who have nothing better to do."; *Paul Ulric*, he intoned, "is too purely imbecile to merit an extended critique." Geoffrey O'Brien, writing in the *Voice Literary Supplement*, called Poe's efforts as a critic "heroic," noting that Poe "was the quintessential profes-

A twin brother and sister, the last descendants of a cursed family, spend their days in a mansion that seems possessed by evil in the 1839 tale, "The Fall of the House of Usher."

sional, a consummate literary hustler who delighted in all the Machiavellian tricks of self– promotion and reputation– mongering, the rituals of critical attack and rejoinder." Though his criticism earned him many enemies, Poe was later recognized as one of the most astute minds of his time.

Poe's controversial essays eventually offended so many readers that White felt compelled to fire him once again. This time, however, Poe was ready. He had established a name for himself, knew that he was underpaid for the work he did, and realized that, in LeVert's words, "to achieve true fame for his own writing he must establish a reputation in New York, Philadelphia, or Boston, the major literary centers in 19th– century America." After a short stint with the *New York Review*, Poe and his family moved to Philadelphia, where Poe was asked to join the staff of *Burton's Gentlemen's Magazine* in 1839. Despite being warned to curb his caustic tongue, Poe continued to challenge what he considered poor writing wherever he found it. At one point, he poked fun at America's most established literary figures: "Mr. [William Cullen] Bryant is not *all* a fool," wrote Poe. "Mr. [N. P.] Willis is not *quite* an ass. Mr. [Henry Wadsworth] Longfellow *will* steal, but, perhaps, he cannot help it." With such comments, Poe made more enemies than friends.

Poe had begun his longest work shortly after he left the *Southern Literary Messenger*, and it was published by Harpers in July of 1838. *The Narrative of Arthur Gordon Pym, of Nantucket* was presented as a true tale of adventure on the high seas, but Poe could not hold the fantastic and supernatural in check for long. The main character, Arthur Gordon Pym, undergoes a series of ocean voyages that take him ever closer to the South Pole. Along the way he is pinned by the neck to the hull of a boat, spends days in a coffinlike box in the hold of a ship where he is assailed by an unending nightmare of demons, bright– eyed serpents, and vacant deserts, encounters a ghost ship manned by chattering corpses, and lands on an island populated by cannibals. As the book ends, Pym drifts helplessly toward the South Pole, and as the water around him grows warm and milky there arises out of the vapor a huge human figure whose skin is "of the perfect whiteness of snow." For years, *The Narrative of Arthur Gordon Pym* was dismissed as a very minor work; Poe himself called it "a very silly book." Late in the twentieth century, however, critics began to reinterpret the book within the context of all of Poe's work and have expressed appreciation of its ambiguous and hallucinatory qualities. T. O. Mabbott, editor of the authoritative edition of Poe's works, once said that the book's chief importance was that "it is supposed to have inspired to some extent [Herman] Melville's *Moby–Dick*."

Poe's job with *Burton's,* which lasted until 1840, allowed him ample free time to pursue his own writing, and during his tenure there he published many of his very best stories. The best known of these are "Ligeia," "The Fall of the House of Usher," and "William Wilson." In "Ligeia," a man recounts the death of his beloved wife, his remarriage to a woman he grows to hate, and his first wife's resurrection in the dead body of that second wife, thus exploring the horrifying possibility that the human will can triumph over death. "The Fall of the House of Usher" is a beautifully fabricated tale of the last descendants, a twin brother and sister, of a cursed family disintegrating in a haunted mansion that seems to be alive with evil. The struggle between the forces of life and death is paralleled in the story by the struggle between the forces of reason and insanity, and these tensions eventually bring the mansion toppling in on itself, killing those inside. In "William Wilson," Poe explored similar tensions within the mind of a man who drives himself mad.

In 1839, a Philadelphia printer published all 25 of Poe's existing stories in a two volume set titled *Tales of the Grotesque and Arabesque.* Like all of Poe's works, it attracted little critical attention and sold very few copies. By 1840, however, Poe was busy with a venture he had long dreamed of: he was to edit and publish his own magazine, called the *Penn.* The *Penn* would be expensive and of high quality, unlike *Burton's,* from which Poe had departed, and he eagerly sought subscriptions at the cost of $5 per year. But money was hard to come by and Poe caught the flu. The *Penn* was never published, and Poe was forced to take a position as editor of *Graham's Magazine* in the spring of 1841. His dream of running his own magazine went unrequited.

The Birth of the Detective Story

In the year between leaving *Burton's* and joining *Graham's,* Poe had begun writing a kind of story unlike any attempted in the history of fiction. Featuring a brilliant detective named C. Auguste Dupin and his slow–minded companion to whom everything must be explained, "The Murders in

Poe's sense of melancholy and the macabre infused his poetry, as in the tragic "Lenore" from *Poems of Edgar Allan Poe,* illustrated by W. Heath Robinson.

the Rue Morgue" was the archetype for the modern detective story. Poe called his story a "tale of ratiocination," for it involved solving a crime through a rigorous process of rational thought and detection. For four years, between 1841 and 1845, Poe wrote permutations of the ratiocinative story which included "The Mystery of Marie Roget," "The Purloined Letter," and "The Gold Bug." In each of these stories, the detective sifts through the available clues to try to arrive at the solution to the mystery. He also included the techniques used in these stories in tales of horror such as "The Pit and the Pendulum" and "A Descent into the Maelstrom."

Poe's detective tales are among his most well known. Sir Arthur Conan Doyle, who created Sherlock Holmes, the most famous detective in fiction, once said that Poe "was the father of the detective tale, and covered its limits so completely that I fail to see how his followers can find any fresh ground which they can confidently call their

The haunting poem "The Raven," published in 1845, gave Poe his first taste of national celebrity.

own." In the twentieth century, many of Poe's detective stories were made into popular movies, for the suspense and the action of these stories transferred well to the screen. Poe himself thought less of these stories than of those that depended on creating and sustaining a mood, but these stories earned him an improved reputation and more money—$1200 a year—than he had ever earned before.

The Imp of the Perverse

All should have been well with Poe, but it was not. Poe had begun to drink again, and was seen so frequently in Philadelphia's taverns that his reputation as a drunk began to surpass his reputation as a writer. Furthermore, he indulged ever more frequently in opium, a drug that encouraged fantastic visions and unlikely associations but weakened Poe's heart. Poe's biographers have speculated that Poe's fervid imagination fed off such excesses, but it may also have been that only in a stupor could Poe avoid the undeniable fact that his wife, Virginia, was showing the first signs of the tuberculosis that had killed so many in Poe's family. Poe's own explanation for his irrational behavior is contained in the essay "The Imp of the Perverse," in which he describes his self-destructive impulses: "the assurance of the wrong or error of any action is often the one unconquerable *force* which impels us, and alone impels us to its prosecution." "His own unhappy life," wrote Meyers, "seemed dominated by this fatal principle."

Ever restless, Poe left *Graham's Magazine* after two productive years. As he left the magazine, Poe made an enemy of Rufus Griswold, another celebrated writer and editor of the period who took over Poe's position. Griswold spread rumors about Poe's drinking while Poe was alive, and after his death did what he could to keep Poe's reputation from overshadowing his own. Poe tried again to start his own literary magazine, but this magazine, called the *Stylus*, floundered for lack of money. In 1843, tired of trying to make a living as a writer, Poe travelled to Washington, D.C., where he tried to secure a government job with the help of a friend. But Poe got drunk at a party on the way to the White House to meet President John Tyler, and was sent home in disgrace.

To make matters worse, by the end of 1842 Virginia Poe's disease was reaching the lethal stage and the frail girl began coughing up blood. Poe drowned his despair in drink and melancholy, as this account written by Rufus Griswold and confirmed by others makes clear: "He walked the streets, in madness or melancholy, with lips moving in indistinct curses, or with eyes upturned in passionate prayers . . . and at night, with drenched garments and arms wildly beating the wind and rain, he would speak as if to spirits." Seeking to escape his sorrows, Poe moved himself and his family to New York to make a new start in the spring of 1944.

Starting Again . . . For the Last Time

Poe was by this time accustomed to pulling himself up from abject failure, and he did so in spectacular fashion by foisting a hoax upon the readers of the *New York Sun*. "ASTOUNDING NEWS!," trumpeted the headline of the paper on April 13, "BY EXPRESS VIA NORFOLK! THE ATLANTIC CROSSED IN THREE DAYS! Signal Triumph of Mr. Monck Mason's FLYING MACHINE!!!!!" The story told of an incredible journey by hot- air balloon, and helped the paper sell out two entire editions. The author of this fiction, Edgar Allan Poe, attracted much publicity and was soon hired to write a weekly column for the *Columbia Spy*, and later became an editor for the *New York Evening Mirror*. Poe also found enough money to purchase a small farmhouse on 84th Street where he lived with Maria Clemm and Virginia.

In January of 1845, Poe published the poem that would bring him his greatest fame, "The Raven." "An incantatory first– person narrative, with cunning internal rhyme, 'The Raven' portrays . . . the monomaniacal obsession of a melancholy man who is hovering on the edge of madness," wrote Meyers. This melancholy man asks a raven perched upon his windowsill if he will meet his dead lover, Lenore, in the afterlife: "'...Tell this soul with sorrow laden if, within the distant Aidenn,/ It shall clasp a sainted maiden whom the angels name Lenore—/ Clasp a rare and radiant maiden whom the angels name Lenore.'/ Quoth the Raven, 'Nevermore!'"

The poem created an immediate sensation and made Poe a minor celebrity. "Surpassing the popularity of any previous American poem," wrote Meyers, "'The Raven' was reprinted throughout the country and inspired a great number of imitations and parodies. In contrast to the hermit's existence he had led during his first nine months

In this illustration of "The Raven" by E. Dulac in *Poetical Works of Edgar Allan Poe*, the narrator--a man obsessed with grief over his dead lover--hears an ominous message from the black bird.

in New York, Poe frequently appeared, throughout 1845, as a literary lion in fashionable salons." James Russell Lowell published a biographical essay about Poe that was the kindest thing written about him during his lifetime. In it, he wrote: "Mr. Poe has two of the prime qualities of genius, a faculty of rigorous yet minute analysis, and a wonderful fecundity of imagination. . . . On the whole, it may be considered that Mr. Poe has attained an individual eminence in our literature, which he will keep. He has given proof of power and originality."

Poe's fame did not last long; like everything that went well in his life, it fell prey to his cruelty, his drunkenness, and his despair. The success of Poe's poem nearly won him a position as co–owner of a new publication called the *Broadway Journal,* but a feud with Longfellow persuaded his backers that he was a poor risk. Moreover, Poe was seen wandering drunkenly through the streets of New York and was believed to be drunk when he made an appearance in Boston to read "The Raven" to a prestigious literary society. But nothing ruined Poe like the slow, agonizing death of his beloved wife Virginia. By the end of 1846, the *New York Express* announced that "Edgar A. Poe and his wife are both dangerously ill with the consumption . . . they are so far reduced as to be barely able to obtain the necessaries of life." Virginia escaped the misery of her life on January 30, 1847, and Poe was left to face his demons alone.

Virginia's death left Poe in a deep depression for nearly a year. Yet he returned to life once again, in pursuit of a magazine of his own, a wife who had money, and a grand theory of the universe. He sought the latter by writing *Eureka,* an attempt, according to LeVert, "to sum up his theories about the origin, character, and future of the universe." Nearly everyone found the long essay incomprehensible, a problem Mankowitz attributed to the influence of both opium and morphine. *Eureka* remains the least understood of Poe's works. Poe pursued a wealthy wife and a magazine together, for he thought the former would make the latter possible. He engaged in extended flirtations with at least four different ladies, Louise Shew, Sarah Helen Whitman, Annie Richmond, and Sarah Elmira Shelton. Yet his deep despair, his drinking binges, and his encroaching insanity drove each of them away, just as it destroyed every chance he had ever had to publish a magazine of his own.

"Poe was extremely restless during the last year of his life," wrote biographer Meyers. "While courting, lecturing, fund– raising, visiting and drinking, he frequently moved up and down the East Coast between New York, Lowell, Philadelphia, Richmond, Norfolk and Baltimore." On one such trip he became convinced that some men were plotting to kill him and he bolted from the train on which he was riding. On other trips he drank himself into oblivion, collapsing into unconsciousness and hallucinating wildly. Such was probably the case when Poe disappeared in Baltimore between September 28 and October 3, 1849. When he was found, Poe was already too far gone to recover and he died on Sunday, October 7, at five in the morning. The cause of Poe's death remains unknown, and has been cited variously as alcoholic poisoning, brain fever, nervous prostration, cerebral epilepsy, apoplexy, and syphilis. Poe was buried in the Westminster Presbyterian Cemetery in Baltimore on October 8, in a ceremony that one observer called "cold– blooded and unchristianlike."

Poe's reputation has undergone many strange twists in the century and a half since his death. His literary executor, Rufus Griswold, succumbed to his own jealousy of Poe and did all he could to paint Poe as a vicious drunk who lacked moral principle. In his obituary of Poe, published anonymously, Griswold stated that "few will be grieved by" Poe's death because "he had few or no friends." Finally, in 1874, John Henry Ingram published a well– researched and positive life of Poe that began to set the record straight. In Europe, Poe was celebrated by French poets Charles Baudelaire and Paul Valery, and later by British novelist D. H. Lawrence and American expatriate T. S. Eliot. Russian writer Fyodor Dostoyevsky called Poe "a strange, though enormously talented writer."

By the second half of the twentieth century, Poe was recognized as one of the great geniuses of American letters, and was taught in schools and universities alongside Nathaniel Hawthorne, Herman Melville, Ralph Waldo Emerson, and Henry David Thoreau. It is Poe's achievement in the short story for which he is best remembered by critics, who applaud Poe's technique in making every element in the story come to bear on the conscious and unconscious responses of the reader. Yet Poe retains a popular audience rare among so– called "classic" authors, for his tales of terror contain a fascination and a mystery that

transcends critical comment about form and function. O'Brien explained Poe's appeal to romantic youths: "He was the outsider, the marginal man, the lonely and delirious genius: a perfect totem for the romantically self– destructive fantasies of adolescence." Whether they are published as comic books, released as movies, or read in their original versions, Poe's dark romances speak to the human desire to lift the smiling mask of consciousness and peer into the realm of the unknown and the unspeakable.

■ Works Cited

Anderson, Madelyn Klein, *Edgar Allan Poe: A Mystery*, Franklin Watts, 1993.

Carlson, Eric W., "Edgar Allan Poe," *Dictionary of Literary Biography*, Volume 74: *American Short Story Writers before 1880*, Gale, 1988, pp. 303–322.

Dameron, J. Lasley and Robert D. Jacobs, "Edgar Allan Poe," *Dictionary of Literary Biography*, Volume 59: *American Literary Critics and Scholars, 1800–1850*, Gale, 1987, pp. 257–275.

Lent, John A., "Edgar Allan Poe," *Dictionary of Literary Biography*, Volume 73: *American Magazine Journalists, 1741–1850*, Gale, 1988, pp. 235–251.

LeVert, Suzanne, *Edgar Allan Poe*, Chelsea House, 1992.

Mankowitz, Wolf, *The Extraordinary Mr. Poe*, Summit Books, 1978.

Meyers, Jeffrey, *Edgar Allan Poe: His Life and Legacy*, Scribner's, 1992.

O'Brien, Geoffrey, "The Secret Life of Edgar Allan Poe," *Voice Literary Supplement*, October 1984, p. 12.

Poe, Edgar Allan, *Collected Works of Edgar Allan Poe*, 3 volumes, edited by T. O. Mabbott, Belknap Press of Harvard University Press, 1969–1978.

Thompson, G. R., "Edgar Allan Poe," *Dictionary of Literary Biography*, Volume 3: *Antebellum Writers in New York and the South*, Gale, 1979, pp. 249–297.

■ For More Information See

BOOKS

Alexander, Jean, editor, *Affadavits of Genius: Edgar Allan Poe and the French Critics, 1847–1924*, Kennikat, 1971.

Alterton, Margaret, *The Origins of Poe's Critical Theory*, University of Iowa Press, 1925.

Bloom, Harold, editor, *Edgar Allan Poe*, Chelsea House, 1985.

Campbell, Killis, *The Mind of Poe and Other Studies*, Harvard University Press, 1933.

Carlson, Eric, editor, *Critical Essays on Edgar Allan Poe*, G. K. Hall, 1987.

Hoffman, Daniel, *Poe Poe Poe Poe Poe Poe Poe*, Doubleday, 1972.

Ingram, John H., *Edgar Allan Poe: His Life, Letters and Opinions*, 2 volumes, John Hogg, 1880.

Kennedy, J. Gerald, *Poe, Death, and the Life of Writing*, Yale University Press, 1987.

Krutch, Joseph Wood, *Edgar Allan Poe: A Study in Genius*, Knopf, 1926.

Lawrence, D. H., *Studies in Classic American Literature*, Seltzer, 1923.

Levin, Harry, *The Power of Blackness: Hawthorne, Poe, and Melville*, Knopf, 1958.

Moss, Sidney P., *Poe's Literary Battles: The Critic in the Context of His Literary Milieu*, Duke University Press, 1963.

Saliba, David R., *A Psychology of Fear: The Nightmare Formula of Edgar Allan Poe*, University Press of America, 1980.

Silverman, Kenneth, *Edgar A. Poe: Mournful and Never-ending Remembrance*, New York, 1991.

Symons, Julian, *The Tell-Tale Heart: The Life and Works of Edgar Allan Poe*, Harper, 1978.

Thomas, Dwight, and David Jackson, *The Poe Log: A Documentary Life of Edgar Allan Poe*, G. K. Hall, 1987.

Thompson, G. R., *Poe's Fiction: Romantic Irony in the Gothic Tales*, University of Wisconsin Press, 1973.

Wagenknecht, Edward, *Edgar Allan Poe: The Man Behind the Legend*, Oxford University Press, 1963.

Walker, I. M., *Edgar Allan Poe: The Critical Heritage*, Routledge & Kegan Paul, 1986.

Zayed, Georges, *The Genius of Edgar Allan Poe*, Schenkman, 1985.

PERIODICALS

New York Review of Books, June 28, 1979, p. 46; October 11, 1984, p. 23.

New York Times Book Review, July 9, 1978, pp. 15, 36; September 9, 1984, p. 3; February 8, 1987, p. 11.

Times Literary Supplement, January 22, 1971, p. 95.

Washington Post Book World, August 10, 1975, p. 4.*

—Sketch by Tom Pendergast

Harold Ramis

■ Personal

Full name, Harold Allen Ramis; born November 21, 1944, in Chicago, IL; son of Nathan and Ruth (Cokee) Ramis; married Anne Jean Plotkin, July 2, 1967 (divorced); married Erica Mann, May 7, 1989; children: (first marriage) Violet Isadora; (second marriage) Julian Arthur. *Education:* Washington University, B.A., 1966.

■ Addresses

Home—Brentwood, CA. *Office*—Ocean Pictures, c/o Sony Studios, 10202 West Washington Blvd., Culver City, CA 90232. *Agent*—Jack Rapke, Creative Artists Agency, 9830 Wilshire Blvd., Beverly Hills, CA 90212.

■ Career

Film actor, director, producer, and writer. *Playboy,* Chicago, IL, associate editor, 1968-70; Second City (comedy troupe), Chicago, writer and actor, 1970-73; *The National Lampoon Show,* New York City, writer and actor in *The National Lampoon Radio Hour,* 1974-75; Second City, head writer of thirty-nine episodes and actor in twenty-six episodes of *SCTV* (television series), 1976-78. Director of motion pictures, including *Caddyshack,* Orion, 1980; *National Lampoon's Vacation,* Warner Brothers, 1983; and *Goundhog Day,* Columbia, 1993. Executive producer of the television special *Will Rogers: Look Back in Laughter,* HBO, 1987. Actor in motion pictures, including *Stripes,* Columbia, 1981, *Heavy Metal,* Columbia, 1981, *Ghostbusters,* Columbia, 1984, *Baby Boom,* Metro-Goldwyn-Mayer, 1987, *Stealing Home,* Warner Brothers, 1988, and *Ghostbusters II,* Columbia, 1989; also appeared on television in specials, including *The Rodney Dangerfield Show: I Can't Take It No More,* ABC-TV, 1983, *Richard Lewis I'm in Pain Concert,* Showtime, 1985, *Second City Twenty-Fifth Anniversary Special,* HBO, 1985, *Comic Relief,* HBO, 1986, *Will Rogers: Look Back in Laughter,* HBO, 1987, and *Time Warner Presents the Earth Day Special,* ABC-TV, 1990. *Member:* American Federation of Television and Radio Artists, Writers Guild of America, Directors Guild of America, Screen Actors Guild, Academy of Motion Picture Arts and Sciences.

■ Awards, Honors

Academy of Canadian Television and Radio Artists (ACTRA) Award, best writer—variety (with others), 1978; distinguished alumni award, Washington University, 1988; honorary doctorate, Washington University, 1993.

■ Writings

SCREENPLAYS

(With Douglas Kenney and Chris Miller) *National Lampoon's Animal House,* Universal, 1978.

(With Dan Goldberg, Len Blum, and Janice Allen) *Meatballs,* Paramount, 1979.

(With Kenney and Brian Doyle-Murray; and director) *Caddyshack,* Orion, 1980.

(With Goldberg and Blum) *Stripes,* Columbia, 1981.

(With Dan Aykroyd) *Ghostbusters,* Columbia, 1984.

(With Peter Torokvei, Steven Kampmann, and Will Porter; and executive producer) *Back to School* (based on a story by Rodney Dangerfield, Greg Fields, and Dennis Snee), Orion, 1986.

(With Doyle-Murray; and director) *Club Paradise* (based on a story by Miller, Ed Roboto, Tom Leopold, and David Standish), Warner Brothers, 1986.

(With Aykroyd) *Ghostbusters II,* Columbia, 1989.

(With Danny Rubin; and director) *Groundhog Day,* Columbia, 1993.

TELEPLAYS

(With others) *Second City Television* (series), syndicated, 1976-78.

(With others) *Delta House* (pilot), ABC-TV, 1979.

(With others; and producer) *The Rodney Dangerfield Special: It's Not Easy Bein' Me,* ABC-TV, 1980.

(With others; and producer) *The Rodney Dangerfield Show: I Can't Take It No More* (special), ABC-TV, 1982.

PLAYS

(With John Belushi, Brian Doyle-Murray, Bill Murray, and Gilda Radner) *The National Lampoon Show,* produced at New Palladium, New York City, 1975.

OTHER

(With Aykroyd) *Making Ghostbusters: The Screenplay,* edited by Don Shay, New York Zoetrope, 1985.

Also author, with Rodney Dangerfield, of story "Rover Dangerfield"; contributor to periodicals, including *Premiere.*

■ Adaptations

Characters created by Ramis and Aykroyd in *Ghostbusters* and *Ghostbusters II* were adapted for animated television series *The Real Ghostbusters,* ABC-TV, 1986-88, and *Slimer! and the Real Ghostbusters,* ABC-TV, 1988—; "Rover Dangerfield" was adapted for film and released by Warner Brothers, 1991.

■ Sidelights

The mild-mannered brown-haired man wore wire-rimmed glasses as he sat down at his typewriter for the day. His fingers raced over the keys, pounding life into outlandish characters and side-splitting situations. A college fraternity full of nerds, food fights, and riotous parties sprang to life. Then came a summer camp with an oddball counselor, followed closely by a country club inhabited by a groundskeeper obsessed with doing in a bothersome gopher. Military life and its many disciplines were next to undergo his comic scrutiny before he moved on to the supernatural and the profession of ghostbusting. Leaving the marshmallow man melting in defeat, the writer's secret identity began to show as he leapt in a single bound to the stories of a less than glamorous resort island that opens for business a bit too early and a father and son who attend the same college. And from college, he moved on to Punxsutawney, Pennsylvania, focusing on an endless Groundhog Day that begins with the sounds of Sonny and Cher over and over again.

By this time, the average screenwriter's strength had reached its peak and the "S" beneath his shirt began to show as he pioneered a new generation of comedy. "More than anyone else," writes Paul Weingarten in the *Chicago Tribune Magazine,* "Harold Ramis has shaped this generation's ideas of what is funny. But he has done it quietly, with a disarming modesty. The 'Clark Kent of Comedy' is how the Los Angeles Times recently described him. 'He may be that,' says Dave Thomas, former SCTV star, 'but those studio guys can see the "S" under the shirt. And they know. All the other variables change, but the one name that's always there is Harold Ramis.'" And Ramis is always there because he continues to write box-office hits—hits that include *National Lampoon's Animal House, Caddyshack, Stripes, Ghostbusters, Back to School,* and *Groundhog Day.* "As an actor, writer or director, or all three, Ramis has been associated with a series of films that together form a nearly complete list of the major comedy box-office successes of the last two decades," observes Richard Christiansen in the *Chicago Tribune.*

Obedient Beginnings

Involved in comedy for most of his adult life, Ramis sees the responsibilities thrust upon him at an early age as one of the main factors that led to his later career. Growing up in Chicago, Ramis and his older brother were often in charge of such household duties as cooking while their parents worked long hours at the family store—Ace Food and Liquor Mart. And when they were old enough, the two brothers helped out by actually working in the store as well. By this time, however, the neighborhood was declining and Ramis's father bought another store in a better part of the city, moving his family at the same time. This venture ended in disaster. "My father opened his store and the next day 400 supermarkets opened around the city," explains Ramis in his interview with Weingarten. "The supermarkets were selling food cheaper than my father could buy it from his wholesaler. So he would say to me, 'Go to the Eagle and get me two dozen cantaloupes.' So I'd go to the Eagle and get two dozen cantaloupes and go through the checkout line, and they'd say, 'What, you having a party or something?' 'No, my dad just likes cantaloupe.'"

Despite these difficulties, Ramis did experience such normal childhood diversions as television, the medium which began his film education at an

John Belushi starred as a member of a nonconformist college fraternity in Ramis's first screenplay collaboration, *National Lampoon's Animal House.*

Head counselor Tripper, played by Bill Murray, cheers his campers to victory in the 1979 comedy *Meatballs*.

early age. "I was the kind of kid who would get up on Saturday morning and first I'd watch the snow on the screen, until the test pattern came on, then there was about 10 minutes of test pattern, then the first program," Ramis tells Weingarten. This television education continued on Saturday afternoons at the movies. Ramis admired a wide variety of stars, including the Marx Brothers, Errol Flynn, Sid Caesar, Ernie Kovacs and Steve Allen. "More than anything," remembers Ramis in his Weingarten interview, "I wanted to be a World War II fighter pilot. That's how I imagined myself. But because of my need for upward mobility, at five years old I decided to become a doctor. I took kindergarten very seriously because I knew it would be important on my permanent record."

From kindergarten on, Ramis stayed on the path of a good son and student. He began by running for the position of class president in the eighth grade, and in high school he was a National Merit Scholar, editor-in-chief of the yearbook, a member of the all-city chorus, and president of the senior honors club. "My parents trusted us, and we never abused it," comments Ramis in his *Chicago Tribune Magazine* interview. "We took our bar mitzvah money and bought carpeting for our parents. We were good boys. I mean I'm talking real guilt, major Jewish guilt."

College Corruption

1963 marked the turning point for Ramis's path of the straight and narrow. This was the year he entered Washington University on a full scholarship. It didn't take him long to notice that no one was taking attendance; he began to skip classes and quit pre-med by the third week of the semester. Sophomore year continued this downward spiral when Ramis moved into a fraternity house. "That was the year I think I started watching TV *a lot,"* points out Ramis in his Weingarten interview. "Like they would find me in the morning lying there in front of the TV. Sometimes I actually pinned a note to myself saying, 'Wake me for breakfast.'" Other aspects of fraternity living also became a part of Ramis's college experience. "Food fights. Throwing lit matches at each other. Looking through girls' dormitory windows. Trying to get beer with fake I.D.s. I'll never forget five guys going into a bar with the same I.D. We all had Xeroxes of the same draft card, and somehow we thought it would work. Five guys named Gary Chernin."

Junior year saw the upswing of Ramis's grades (he took mainly theatre and speech courses), and he graduated with a degree in English literature in 1967. Shortly following graduation, Ramis took a break and journeyed to San Francisco with a couple of friends for the "Summer of Love." While there he met Anne Plotkin, with whom he had a brief romance before entering a graduate program which would give him a Master of Arts and a teaching degree. By the end of the quarter, though, Ramis dropped out and sought work from the student employment service. "There were two jobs listed," he explains to Weingarten. "One was a collection agent in the worst ghetto in St. Louis. That seemed bad. The other was as a psychiatric orderly." Choosing the latter, Ramis learned a great deal about madness.

In the meantime, Anne returned to St. Louis and she and Ramis continued their romance. He proposed to her at a production of *The Mikado* just before the show began. Married on July 2, 1967, the couple moved to Chicago, where Ramis began working as a substitute teacher in a rough neighborhood. "We had to lock our doors while we taught," remembers Ramis in his interview with Weingarten. "We had armed Chicago police in the halls. . . . I was teaching kindergarten

Ramis exposed the lighter side of country clubs in 1980 as coauthor and director of *Caddyshack.*

through sixth. It would take half a day to take attendance. Then I realized that everyone had given me a phony name."

Ramis moved on to his next career by picking a name off the masthead of *Playboy* and calling to ask for a job. Hired as the jokes editor, Ramis was eventually promoted to an associate editor position which enabled him to interview such celebrities as Dick Cavett, Rowan and Martin, and Tiny Tim. At the same time, he free-lanced for the *Chicago Daily News.* It was during a 1968 visit to Second City that Ramis had his first inkling of a career in comedy. "I thought they were funny," he points out in his *Chicago Tribune Magazine* interview. "But at the same time I thought *I* could be doing this. I'm *that* funny." After a number of sessions in an acting workshop Ramis auditioned for the Second City touring company. He didn't get the spot, so he taught an improv workshop, and bided his time. It was when Michael Miller became director of Second City that Ramis finally joined the company.

Second City Superman

The touring company that Ramis was a part of went on to become the Second City regulars in 1969, and the critics hated them until the material gradually began to improve. "Harold was one of the fastest humans, just in terms of coming up with funny," recalls Bernie Sahlins (founder of Second City) in his interview with Weingarten. "They called him The Professor," Weingarten writes. "The resident intellectual. The one who could always save a floundering improvisation by skewing its point of view, or delivering a scene-ending punchline. Lightning-quick on the ad lib. His ensemble wrote many of the classics, scenes still performed by Second City troupes."

A year later, Ramis left Second City and travelled to Europe with his wife for a year. While there, he wrote his first film script; it wasn't a comedy and it didn't sell. Returning home, Ramis planned to return to his old job at *Playboy* until Sahlins offered to match this salary at Second City. Ramis found a few changes; "I had a favorite spot on the stage," he explains to Weingarten. "It was upstage. You get behind everyone and you can make faces, do whatever you want to get focus. But when I went for my spot, there was [John] Belushi, mugging it up." This time Ramis only lasted for two revues before he travelled to Europe again. But he was back for a television spe-

cial a year later before moving on to *The National Lampoon Comedy Show* revue with Belushi, Gilda Radner, Bill Murray, and Brian Murray in 1974. Within another year Ramis had left this behind to write and direct *Supervision,* an innovative serial for public television in Los Angeles. Belushi and Radner were signed for *Saturday Night Live,* and by the time Ramis was approached to be a writer for *SNL* he had already accepted the job of head writer and co-star of *SCTV.*

"Harold really helped in developing our structure and bringing out our comedic sense," asserts *SCTV* co-star John Candy in his Weingarten interview. "He taught us a lot of discipline. We were always writing long stage pieces. Harold would come in and just slash, slash, slash. Initially you thought it was something you did. Why does he hate me? But he was always explaining, 'There, this is what's funny right here. Cut right to it.' He always kept saying, 'Just think of yourself watching.' And Harold liked it if you took it one step beyond."

Famous Food Fights

While creating comic figures for *SCTV,* which became a quick success, Ramis was also working on a script with Chris Miller and Doug Kenney for a movie about college fraternity life. Based on the college experiences of its writers, *National Lampoon's Animal House* brought its creators instant success. Set in the 1960s at a fictional college, the film focuses on the members of the Delta fraternity, including John "Bluto" Blutarsky, played by Belushi. Food fights, failed exams, and toga parties abound in the disorderly and chaotic house. "The Deltas are the kind of guys who bash beer cans against their foreheads, wheel their dates home in shopping carts and think they know the words to 'Louie, Louie,' which they will sing in off-key unison at less than the slightest provocation," describes Janet Maslin in the *New York Times.* And Vincent Canby, film critic for the *New York Times,* points out that "the movie's fondness for sloth, mess, vulgarity, non-conformism (circa 1962, of course), as demonstrated by the members of an especially disorganized college fraternity, is frequently very, very funny. The targets of its humor (gung-ho fraternities, neatness, [Richard] Nixon, chastity, sobriety, Vietnam, patriotism, ceramics) are not exactly sacred at this point, but the gusto of this movie is undeniably appealing."

In his 1981 acting debut, Ramis wreaks havoc at an Army training camp with co-star Bill Murray in *Stripes.*

After the immediate success of *Animal House,* Ramis co-wrote and directed a string of equally successful films. "It's simple economics," explains Weingarten. "1. Only one out of 10 movies makes money. 2. Harold Ramis has never had a flop. Ergo, Harold Ramis *knows* something." Ramis's movies have never been a losing venture; they always make money. "That is also why people offer him new projects every day and why Ramis turns them down just as fast," continues Weingarten. "He can afford to be picky, which is one of the measures of success in Hollywood. For most, just working in the industry is a major achievement; working *steadily,* as Ramis does, is cause indeed for Hollywood's major spectator sport, envy."

Another Second City comedian, Bill Murray, is featured in Ramis's second co-writing venture, *Meatballs.* Murray plays Tripper, the head counselor at a summer camp lacking in both discipline and legitimate activities. The movie focuses on the relationship that builds between Tripper and Rudy, a home-sick camper who has a hard time fitting in with the other kids. Canby compares the film unfavorably to Ramis's early success: "With far fewer high spirits than *Animal House,* and only two characters of any interest, *Meatballs* reveals itself to be a loud, off-key cry for conformism of the most disappointing sort." Despite its tepid critical reception, *Meatballs* appealed to its young audience because of its many humorous gags and was one of the biggest hits of 1979.

Directorial Demands

The following year, Ramis made his directorial debut with another co-written film—*Caddyshack.* Set at a posh country club, *Caddyshack* features Murray as a grungy greenskeeper obsessed with killing a bothersome gopher, Chevy Chase as a suave playboy, and Rodney Dangerfield as a tactless millionaire. Among the more memorable scenes of this popular and critically acclaimed film are one in which swimmers frantically flee a pool when a Baby Ruth candy bar is found floating in it, and another in which a clergyman is struck by lightning as he thanks God for the best golf game of his life. Canby remarks in the *New York Times* that *Caddyshack* "tears the lid off the apparently placid life at a WASPy country club to expose bigotry, ignorance, lust and a common tendency to cheat on the golf course."

"After *Caddyshack*'s release," describes Christiansen, "Ramis, stressed from his directorial debut, found himself with 'a feeling of ashes,' partly, he says 'because I wanted more affirmation,' and because of the death under mysterious circumstances, of Kenney, his writing partner." In his interview with Weingarten, Ramis reveals: "Being close to Doug [Kenney] was a little terrifying. Just like being close to John [Belushi] must have been. The more we were together, the more my life started to unravel. I sort of lusted after that dissipated Hollywood bachelor lifestyle he was leading, the night life, the excessive drug use. And he in a way longed for the kind of family life I had."

Despite this personal loss, Ramis's career was back on track within a year, and 1981 saw the release of *Stripes*. The first film in which Ramis appears, *Stripes* also features Murray as John Winger, an oddball taxi driver who loses his cab, his apartment, and his girlfriend all at once. Convinced that the military is as glamorous as it is portrayed to be in a television commercial, Winger joins and persuades his friend Russell (played by Ramis) to enlist at the same time. The duo survive a tough basic training period in a platoon of comic characters before accidentally starting a minor war in Czechoslovakia. Maslin praises the screenplay in the *New York Times*, stating that it "is at its funniest when it gives Mr. Murray the chance to tell all his platoonmates how interesting they are, particularly the ones who grew up on farms." Maslin also applauds Ramis's portrayal of Russell, describing him as "a fine foil for Mr. Murray." And Canby observes that most of the "genuinely funny . . . moments" in the film are supplied by Ramis.

Acting and writing were both left behind in favor of directing for Ramis's next film. "I didn't think I would be a happy person if my life depended on whether I was acting or not," reveals Ramis in an interview with Diana Loevy for the *Washington Post*. "Fortunately, I had other work."

Ramis's "other work" was the popular 1983 comedy *National Lampoon's Vacation*, which stars Chevy Chase as a father (Clark Griswold) who tries to cram a year's worth of quality family time into a two-week vacation. The trip culminates at the arrival of the California amusement park Wally World. "I really saw Clark as a guy who's trying to live up to an image of what fatherhood is," remarks Ramis in his interview with Loevy. "He really doesn't even come close to satisfying that image in real life."

Marshmallow Man Makes History

The image of Ramis as a successful writer was given another boost in 1986 with the release of *Ghostbusters*, one of the largest grossing comedies in history. Written by Dan Aykroyd and Ramis, this tale of three scientists who go into the business of exterminating ghosts stars its authors as well as Bill Murray. When the storage area for the captured spirits malfunctions the ghostbusters are eventually faced with a climatic battle with a giant marshmallow man. *Ghostbusters* is "delightfully silly," sums up David Ansen in *Newsweek*, adding that the writers and the director "have the good sense to know that every round of a comedy doesn't have to end with a KO. They win on points: a hip feint here, a jab to the funnybone there, a bolo punch for surprise. Both as writers and co-stars, they also demonstrate amazing generosity, not to mention smarts, in recognizing who their prize-fighter is here: Bill Murray. . . . Aykroyd and Ramis perform excellently as his backup men."

Leaving the world of the supernatural for a few years, Ramis set his next two scripts (both released in 1986) on a college campus and an island resort. *Back to School* follows self-made millionaire Thornton Melon, played by Rodney Dangerfield, as he returns to college to set a good example for his son. "Not that many comedians have been as lucky as Rodney Dangerfield in getting a film tailored so knowingly to his talent, personality and blue-collar humor," points out Kevin Thomas in the *Los Angeles Times*. "Clearly, he and all those writers (including Harold Ramis, with whom he did *Caddyshack*) realized that in pulling out all the stops in the creation of Melon, the guy would have to have a day of reckoning—with his son, and with what education is all about." *Club Paradise*, which Ramis also directed, features Robin Williams as a retired firefighter who invests all his money in a ramshackle Caribbean resort. Corrupt politicians and real estate developers try to disrupt the venture while an odd cast of tourists cavort about the island. *Club Paradise* "is full of thoughtful, original humor that never relies on obscenity or cruelty and entertains its audience without pandering to it," maintains Ralph Novak in *People.*

Shortly after the release of *Club Paradise,* Ramis's personal life began to unravel and he eventually divorced his wife and began a relationship with Erica Mann. The two were married in 1989, the same year that Ramis reteamed with Aykroyd to co-write *Ghostbusters II,* a sequel to their 1984 hit. In this film, the ghostbusters are called out of retirement to rid New York City of a supernatural slime that is flowing beneath its streets. "*Ghostbusters II* is a sweet, cute, self-mocking comedy—it makes the supernatural safe for the whole family," describes Brian D. Johnson in *Maclean's.* Johnson goes on to conclude, however, that "despite some hilarious scenes, the sequel seems too

carefully contrived, celebrating the ghostbusters' populist appeal with the drumming insistence of a homecoming parade." "The concept is bigger than we are now," Ramis explains to Johnson. "And there is a great familiarity in putting on the uniforms—I've often felt like one of the *Star Trek* crew."

Maturity Meets Popularity

A touch of familiarity is also felt in Ramis's most recent film—1993's *Groundhog Day.* As both co-author and director, Ramis brings to life the cynical weatherman Phil Connors (played by Bill Murray), his ever cheerful producer Rita (played by Andie MacDowell), and the cameraman Larry (played by Chris Elliott). Covering the Groundhog Day Festival in Punxsutawney, Pennsylvania, Connors wakes the day after to discover that he must relive the previous day over and over again. Every day is the same, and Connors goes through a variety of reactions that include anger, reckless-

The 1986 film *Ghostbusters*—one of the highest grossing comedies of all time—starred Bill Murray and coauthors Ramis and Dan Aykroyd as spook exterminators.

ness, and eventually goodness. It is only when he is able to change as a person that the day finally ends and a new one begins.

"I like to think of *Groundhog Day* as a fairy tale, a kind of 'Frog Prince' story," describes Ramis in an interview with John Stanley for *Datebook*. "It's about making mistakes and lost opportunities and what we can do to change ourselves. In some ways it touches on the theme of *It's a Wonderful Life*, where a man is given a second chance." Jonathan Romney, writing in *New Statesman*, praises the film's cynicism: "*Groundhog Day* may be the purest nightmare movie Hollywood has ever produced—potentially endless repetition, just for its own sake—but it's also the most formalist. It's like a dare between Rubin and Ramis to see how many variants they can work on one theme before 101 minutes are up. The go about it with fiendish ingenuity, undercutting our expectations when we least expect it, but also confirming them just when we're getting as weary as Murray is of having them confirmed; they like to make sure that from time to time it feels like hell for us too." "Let's all cheer the emergence of *Groundhog Day*, a very original comedy about deja vu," directs Richard Corliss in *Time*.

Not all of Ramis's films are as well-received by critics as *Groundhog Day*, but he does seem to have a finger on the pulse of what mainstream America finds funny. And his films have progressed in their levels of maturity. Speaking of his earlier films, Ramis tells Stanley: "The raunchy films we made then were about raunchy people deliberately testing the edge of propriety. That's the very heart and soul of *Animal House* and *Caddyshack*—the upsetting of the social order. I guess you could say we were working off our adolescent need to pull society's beard. *Stripes* is also about an anarchic individual, but celebrates the personal qualities of duty, honor and courage. The success of *Ghostbusters* was a liberating force for all of us, a step up. And *Groundhog Day* is, I hope, a step closer to my own personal values."

Though Ramis's films may have matured over the years, he's not so sure that he has done the same. "I might never get past 13 [emotionally]," he reveals to Weingarten. "Most people are still hung up somewhere. Some people act like five-year-olds, some people will be college students for the rest of their lives, and some people are too old from the minute they can walk. I'm still trying to hold on to what made me happy as an adolescent . . . . A feeling that there was time to have fun before the real work began." And this feeling sometimes makes it hard for Ramis to believe that he's living such a successful life. "I really do suffer from the imposter syndrome," he explains in an interview with Steve Weinstein for the *Los Angeles Times*. "It's hard to believe that any of us deserve the life that some of us are living. I mean, I think I would have been happy being a production assistant. On the other hand, having been involved even tangentially in some of the films I've worked on, and given the public's deep love for some of them, I feel I've earned this little footnote in film history.

■ Works Cited

Ansen, David, review of *Ghostbusters, Newsweek*, June 11, 1984, p. 80.

Canby, Vincent, "What's So Funny about Potheads and Toga Parties?," *New York Times*, November 19, 1978, p. D17.

Canby, review of *Meatballs, New York Times*, July 3, 1979, p. C10.

Canby, review of *Caddyshack, New York Times*, July 25, 1980, p. C8.

Christiansen, Richard, "All Herald Ramis," *Chicago Tribune*, January 31, 1993, Section 13, pp. 16-17.

Corliss, Richard, "Bill Murray's Deja Voodoo," *Time*, February 15, 1993, pp. 63-64.

Johnson, Brian D., "Summer of Superheroes," *Maclean's*, June 26, 1989, pp. 50-52.

Loevy, Diana, "Harold Ramis and His 'Vacation,'" *Washington Post*, September 4, 1983, p. D3.

Maslin, Janet, review of *National Lampoon's Animal House, New York Times*, July 28, 1978, p. C7.

Maslin, review of *Stripes, New York Times*, June 26, 1981, p. C16.

Novak, Ralph, review of *Club Paradise, People*, July 28, 1986, p. 8.

Romney, Jonathan, "Endless Nightmare," *New Statesman*, May 7, 1993, pp. 34-35.

Stanley, John, "Frustrating Forecast: More of the Same," *Datebook*, February 7, 1993, pp. 39-40.

Thomas, Kevin, review of *Back to School, Los Angeles Times*, June 12, 1986.

Weingarten, Paul, "Tales of Uncle Ramis," *Chicago Tribune Magazine*, October 30, 1983, Section 9, pp. 12-14, 16-18, 20, 22-25.

Weinstein, Steve, "Happily Living on the Cranky Comic Edge," *Los Angeles Times*, February 12, 1993, p. F12.

■ For More Information See

PERIODICALS

Film News International, September, 1984, pp. 15-17.
Library Journal, February 1, 1992, p. 141.

Los Angeles Times, April 23, 1983, pp. 1, 5; July 11, 1986.
Newsweek, June 26, 1989, p. 68.
New Yorker, August 11, 1986, pp. 74, 77; February 22, 1993, p. 171.
People, July 3, 1989, p. 14.

—Sketch by Susan M. Reicha

Rod Serling

■ Personal

Full name, Edward Rodman Serling; born December 25, 1924, in Syracuse, NY; died of complications during coronary bypass surgery, June 28, 1975, in Rochester, NY; son of Samuel Lawrence (a wholesale butcher) and Esther (Cooper) Serling; married Carolyn Louise Kramer, July 31, 1948; children: Jodi, Anne. *Education:* Antioch College, B.A., 1950. *Religion:* Jewish.

■ Career

Television writer, producer, and narrator. WLW–Radio, Cincinnati, OH, network continuity writer, 1946–48; WKRC–TV, Cincinnati, television writer, 1948–53; free–lance television screenwriter, 1953–75. Writer, producer, and narrator of television series *The Twilight Zone,* Columbia Broadcasting System, Inc. (CBS–TV), 1959–64; producer, narrator, and contributing writer of television series *Rod Serling's Night Gallery,* National Broadcasting Company, Inc. (NBC–TV), 1969–73; free–lance television narrator. Teacher of dramatic writing, Antioch College, 1962–63, and Ithaca College, 1970–75. *Military service:* Paratrooper in Pacific theater, U.S. Army,

World War II. *Member:* National Academy of Television Arts and Sciences (member of board of governors of New York City chapter, 1956–57, and of California chapter, 1959; national president, 1965–66); Writers Guild of America West (member of council, 1965–67).

■ Awards, Honors

Emmy Awards, National Academy of Television Arts and Sciences, including Best Original Teleplay, 1955, for *Patterns,* Best Single Program of the Year, 1956, for *Requiem for a Heavyweight,* Best Teleplay Writing, 1959, for *The Comedian,* Outstanding Writing Achievement in Drama, 1960 and 1961, for *The Twilight Zone,* and Outstanding Writing Achievement in Drama, 1963, for "It's Mental Work"; Sylvania Awards, 1955 and 1956; Christopher Awards, 1956 and 1971; George Foster Peabody Award, University of Georgia, 1957, for *Requiem for a Heavyweight;* Hugo Awards, World Science Fiction Society, 1960, 1961 and 1962; Golden Globe Award, Hollywood Foreign Press Association, Best Male Television Star, 1962, and for Best Director, 1965; Writers Guild nomination, 1964, for *Seven Days in May;* D.H.L., Emerson College, 1971, Alfred University, 1972; Litt. D., Ithaca College, 1972.

■ Writings

Stories from the Twilight Zone, Bantam, 1960.
More Stories from the Twilight Zone, Bantam, 1961.
New Stories from the Twilight Zone, Bantam, 1962.

From the Twilight Zone, Doubleday, 1962.
Requiem for a Heavyweight: A Reading Version of the Dramatic Script, Bantam, 1962.
Rod Serling's The Twilight Zone, Grosset, 1963.
(Editor) *Rod Serling's Triple W: Witches, Warlocks, and Werewolves; A Collection,* Bantam, 1963.
Twilight Zone Revisited, Grosset, 1964.
The Season to Be Wary (novellas; includes "The Escape Route," "Color Scheme," and "Eyes"), Little, Brown, 1967.
(Editor and author of introduction) *Devils and Demons: A Collection,* Bantam, 1967.
Night Gallery, Bantam, 1971.
Night Gallery 2, Bantam, 1972.
Rod Serling's Other Worlds, Bantam, 1978.

PLAYS

Patterns: Four Television Plays with the Author's Personal Commentaries (includes *Patterns, The Rack, Requiem for a Heavyweight,* and *Old MacDonald Had a Curve*), Simon & Schuster, 1957.
Patterns: A Drama in Three Acts, Samuel French, 1959.
The Killing Season, produced on Broadway, 1968.

SCREENPLAYS

The Strike, United Artists, 1955.
Patterns, Metro–Goldwyn–Mayer (MGM), 1956.
The Rack, MGM, 1956.
(With Thomas Thompson) *Saddle the Wind,* MGM, 1958.
Incident in an Alley (based on Serling's television drama *Line of Duty*), United Artists, 1962.
Requiem for a Heavyweight, Columbia, 1962.
The Yellow Canary (based on novel *Evil Come, Evil Go,* by Whit Masterson), Twentieth Century–Fox, 1963.
Seven Days in May (based on novel by Fletcher Knebel and Charles W. Bailey II), Paramount, 1964.
Assault on a Queen, Paramount, 1966.
(With Michael Wilson) *Planet of the Apes* (based on *Monkey Planet,* by Pierre Boulle), Twentieth Century–Fox, 1968.
(With brother, Robert J. Serling) *The President's Plane Is Missing* (based on novel by Robert J. Serling), Commonwealth–United, 1969.
R.P.M., Columbia, 1969.
The Man (adapted from television drama; based on novel by Irving Wallace), Paramount, 1971.
A Time of Predators (based on novel by Joe Gores), Avco–Embassy, 1971.

The Salamander, ITC, 1982.

■ Adaptations

Twilight Zone—The Movie (includes "Kick the Can," "Nightmare at 20,000 Feet," "It's a Good Life," and "A Quality of Mercy"; directed by Steven Spielberg, George Miller, Joe Dante, and John Landis), Warner Bros., 1983.
The Twilight Zone (sound recording series; includes "The Midnight Sun," "The Mighty Casey," and "Walking Distance"), 1992.
The Twilight Zone: Rod Serling's Lost Classics (includes "The Theatre" and "Where the Dead Are"; directed by Robert Markowitz), CBS–TV, 1994.

■ Sidelights

"You're travelling through another dimension, a dimension not only of sight and sound but of mind; a journey into a wondrous land whose boundaries are that of imagination—next stop, the Twilight Zone!" With these words, Rod Serling introduced his best–known creation to millions of television viewers each week. Although *The Twilight Zone* ran for only five seasons—1959 to 1964—the science fiction–fantasy series renewed its hold over each succeeding generation through reruns. As a result, "Serling and his magic voice became a part of mass culture and modern folklore," Mark Olshaker explained in *New Times.*

Serling first gained prominence as a writer in 1955, when his play *Patterns* was broadcast on television to glowing reviews. Over the next twenty years he wrote numerous influential screenplays and won six coveted Emmy awards. *The Twilight Zone*—with its high–quality writing, startling twist endings, and stark commentary on social themes—stood apart from mainstream television of its time. Serling used his status as one of television's most gifted writers to challenge the prejudices he saw in American society. In fact, he eventually became known as "the angry young man" for his constant battles with network television censors.

Growth of a Writer

Serling was born on December 25, 1924. He spent most of his childhood years in the small city of Binghamton in upstate New York, where he lived with his parents and his brother, Robert. Serling was attractive, outgoing, and imaginative even as

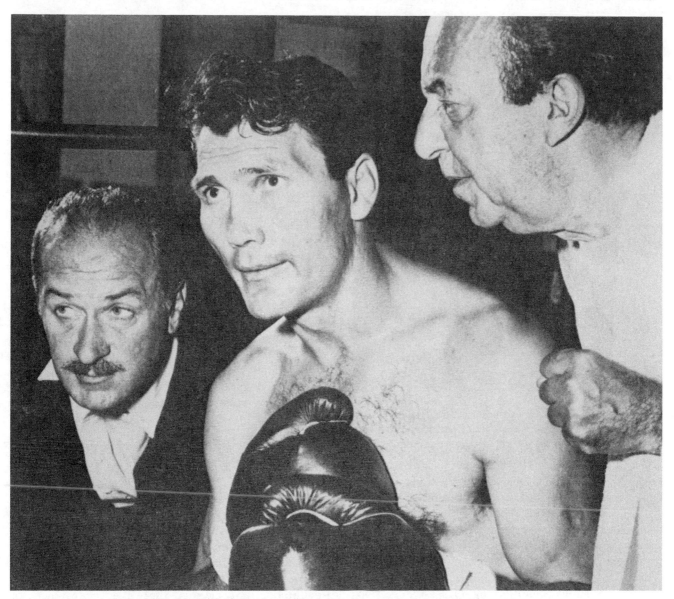

Requiem for a Heavyweight, Serling's Emmy and George Foster Peabody Award-winning screenplay, focuses on an aging boxer whose manager schemes to keep him in the ring past his prime.

a child, and this helped make him popular in the neighborhood. A favorite pastime in his youth was reading "pulp" magazines, such as *Amazing Stories* and *Weird Tales.* Serling also enjoyed going to the movies, and afterward acted out various parts with his brother.

Serling's family seemed to recognize and support his creative spirit from an early age. As Robert Serling told Marc Scott Zicree in *The Twilight Zone Companion:* "The big treat for the family was to drive from Binghamton to Syracuse, which was seventy miles away, and my father once tipped us off that nobody was to say a word from the start of the trip *until Rod stopped talking.* Now,

in those days it took approximately two and a half hours to drive the seventy miles and, so help me, he never stopped talking from the time he got into the car to the time we arrived in Syracuse. My mother and father were in absolute hysterics. He must have been six or seven years old. He was in a world all by himself. He'd sing, he'd act out dialogue, he'd talk to us without waiting for answers. He just kept talking."

After he graduated from high school, Serling's sense of adventure led him to join the U.S. Army 11th Airborne Division paratroopers. He fought in the Pacific during World War II and received the Purple Heart for shrapnel wounds to his wrist and

"To Serve Man," a 1962 episode of *The Twilight Zone,* Serling's acclaimed science fiction anthology series, featured Richard Kiel as an all-too benevolent alien.

knee. In some ways, Serling felt that his wartime experience contributed to his becoming a writer. As he once explained: "I was bitter about everything and at loose ends when I got out of the service. I think I turned to writing to get it off my chest."

In 1946, Serling began taking classes at Antioch College in Yellow Springs, Ohio. At first he majored in physical education, but he soon changed his emphasis to literature and began writing stories. He also wrote, directed, and acted in many productions for the campus radio station. While this provided Serling with a valuable learning experience, he later claimed that his work from this period was "pretty bad stuff." Another significant event that occurred during college was when Serling met fellow student Carolyn Kramer. Although Carolyn was reluctant to date Serling at first due to his reputation on campus as a ladies' man, the couple were married in 1948 and eventually had two daughters.

Serling took a job at WLW radio in Cincinnati following graduation, where he performed a variety of menial writing tasks—from scripts for a coun-

try musical–comedy duo to advertisements for high–alcohol–content patent remedies. In the meantime, Serling worked on his own stories every evening and collected forty rejection slips. Since he had a wife and family, he hesitated to take the financial risk of quitting his job to try to make a living as a free–lance writer. Eventually, however, Serling realized that writing was not something he could do part–time. "Writing is a demanding profession and a selfish one. And because it is selfish and demanding, because it is compulsive and exacting, I didn't embrace it. I succumbed to it," he once admitted.

Serling moved his family to Connecticut and began writing full–time. He had some success in selling scripts to the live "anthology" shows that dominated television in the 1950s, such as *Kraft Television Theater* and *Hallmark Hall of Fame.* On the whole, his writing seemed more thoughtful and relevant than typical television dramas at the time. In evaluating Serling's early scripts, Zicree noted: "Sometimes the situations were cliched, the characters two–dimensional, but always there was at least some search for an emotional truth, some attempt to make a statement on the human condition."

Serling's first major success came in early 1955, when his play *Patterns* was broadcast on *Kraft Television Theater.* In this compelling story of cut-throat corporate politics, a ruthless company president applies so much pressure to an aging executive that he eventually dies of a heart attack. In the *New York Times,* critic Jack Gould called *Patterns* "one of the high points in the TV medium's evolution," and claimed that "For sheer power of narrative, forcefulness of characterization and brilliant climax, Mr. Serling's work is a creative triumph that can stand on its own." *Saturday Review,* reviewer Robert Lewis Shayon stated that "In the years I have been watching television I do not recall being so engaged by a drama, nor so stimulated to challenge the haunting conclusions of an hour's entertainment." The public's reaction to *Patterns* was overwhelming, and the show became the first ever to be repeated by popular demand.

The success of *Patterns* elevated Serling to an elite position among writers. He received numerous requests for interviews, as well as offers to write television shows, movies, Broadway plays, and novels. In what he later looked back upon as a mistake, Serling took advantage of this newfound popularity to sell many of his old, lower–quality scripts and stories. After a couple of disappointing shows that led some critics to question whether Serling could duplicate what he had accomplished with *Patterns,* Serling came through in 1956 with *Requiem for a Heavyweight,* originally broadcast on *Playhouse 90.* The play tells the tragic story of a declining prize fighter whose devious manager pressures him to keep boxing so he can make money by betting against him. *Requiem for a Heavyweight* won five Emmy awards and was also made into a movie.

Entering the Twilight Zone

During the 1950s—when Serling was gaining prominence as a writer of realistic television dramas—the content of programs was largely determined by corporate sponsors. The television networks often allowed sponsors to have the final say over what programs aired, as well as over the tiniest details in individual scripts. Most corporate sponsors tried to avoid being associated with anything that could be considered controversial. The result, according to Serling, was that the most meaningful portions of many of his stories were changed or deleted.

The censorship he experienced ranged from trivial changes, such as deletion of the line "Got a match?" from *Requiem for a Heavyweight* at the request of sponsor Ronson lighters, to reworking of some scripts beyond recognition. Serling described his frustration in an interview with Mike Wallace: "I don't want to fight anymore. I don't want to have to battle sponsors and agencies. I don't want to have to push for something that I want and have to settle for second best. I don't want to have to compromise all the time, which in essence is what a television writer does if he wants to put on controversial themes."

The final straw for Serling occurred during production of his story *The Arena,* about the inner workings of the U.S. Senate, for the anthology show *Studio One.* "To say a single thing germane to the current political scene was absolutely prohibited," Serling recalled in his introduction to *Patterns.* "So, on television in April of 1956, several million viewers got treated to an incredible display on the floor of the United States Senate of groups of Senators shouting, gesticulating and talking in hieroglyphics about make–believe issues, using invented terminology, in a kind of prolonged, unbelievable double–talk." In explaining how this experience drove him toward science fic-

tion, Serling continued: "In retrospect, I probably would have had a much more adult play had I made it science fiction, put it in the year 2057, and peopled the Senate with robots."

In 1957, Serling submitted a script to CBS with the title "The Time Element," which he intended to be the pilot episode for a weekly science fiction–fantasy series called *The Twilight Zone.* Network executives, as well as fans of Serling's earlier work, were initially dismayed at his decision to "step down" from realism to science fiction. Many of Serling's friends, however, understood his belief that science fiction would allow him to continue his social commentary without fear of censorship. "I don't think it far–fetched that he should have been as impressed as he was by science fiction," producer Dick Berg explained in *The Twilight Zone Companion,* "particularly because he had much on his mind politically and in terms of social condition, and science fiction—and *Twilight Zone* specifically—gave him as much flexibility in developing those themes as he might have had anywhere else at that time."

CBS did not commit to *The Twilight Zone* at first, but did produce "The Time Element" for the *Westinghouse Desilu Playhouse* in 1958. "The Time Element" is the eerie story of a man who sees a psychiatrist to help him deal with vivid dreams about the bombing of Pearl Harbor. In the first of Serling's trademark twist endings, it turns out that the patient was actually killed at Pearl Harbor, and the psychiatrist is the one having the vivid dreams. The show received more viewer mail than any other episode of the *Westinghouse Desilu Playhouse,* which prompted CBS to let Serling proceed with a pilot for *The Twilight Zone.*

The original script Serling wrote for the pilot was called "The Happy Place," and dealt with a society where people are herded off and exterminated as soon as they turn sixty years old. CBS executives decided that the tale was too depressing, however, so Serling instead submitted "Where Is Everybody?" In this original episode of *The Twilight Zone,* aired October 2, 1959, a man walks around a spooky, deserted town and finds signs that all the people have just left. In the final scene, Serling reveals that the man has hallucinated the entire experience: he is actually the subject of a government isolation experiment who has finally cracked up after spending 484 hours alone.

Popular reaction to the pilot convinced CBS to give Serling the go–ahead for the first season of *The Twilight Zone.* He began by hiring a producer, Buck Houghton, to handle all the production details in order to free himself up for writing. (Although Serling was deeply committed to the series and had the final say in most matters, he trusted Houghton to smooth out the daily problems.) Next, Serling and Houghton hired several prominent directors, some with film backgrounds, to provide the show with its memorable camera work and eerie atmosphere. The duo also decided to film the series at Metro–Goldwyn–Mayer studios, since MGM offered access to the sets from hundreds of different movies. The familiar, haunting theme music for the show was composed by Marius Constant, although a different piece by Bernard Herrmann was used for most of the first season.

Serling's contract with CBS specified that he would provide 80 percent of the scripts for *The Twilight Zone.* For the other 20 percent, he at first decided to accept submissions from aspiring writers all over the country. When he received 14,000 manuscripts in the first week, he instead relied upon a few, well–known writers with a style and vision similar to his own. Richard Matheson and Charles Beaumont provided scripts for the majority of the remaining episodes of the series, although the show's contributors also included Montgomery Pittman, Earl Hamner Jr., and Ray Bradbury.

Serling and Houghton auditioned a number of well–known actors to narrate the show, including Orson Welles, but had so much difficulty settling on one that Serling finally decided to try it himself. Surprisingly, Serling was very nervous in front of the camera, and he frustrated several directors who tried to change his deadpan delivery style.

Serling wrote the screenplay for the sci-fi classic *Planet of the Apes,* with Charlton Heston as an twentieth-century astronaut who finds himself stranded on a world where apes rule and humans act like beasts.

Eventually, however, Serling's voice and presence became a trademark of *The Twilight Zone*. The writer's appearances also transformed Serling into a popular television personality in addition to his position as a writer.

When the first episode of *The Twilight Zone* finally aired in 1959, reactions were positive from critics and viewers alike. In *The Twilight Zone Companion*, Cecil Smith of the *Los Angeles Times* was quoted as calling the show "the finest weekly series of the season, the one clear and original light in a season marked by the muddy carbon copies of dull westerns and mediocre police shows." Tod Raper of the *Columbus Dispatch* described *The Twilight Zone* as "the hottest show that CBS–TV has come up with," and claimed that while watching it "we felt the hair on our neck rise, the skin on our back cringe, and our heart flop at the finish with a feeling of relief." *Variety* reviewer Helm stated that "the writing and narration of Serling . . . gave it an epic dimension of greatness." On top of the critical acclaim, the series generated over 500 letters per week from viewers. After the first season, Serling released a book of short stories based on the series, *Stories from the Twilight Zone*, which became a smash hit. He also authorized production of a board game, comic book, and record album based on the show.

Memorable Episodes

Although each episode of *The Twilight Zone* was different, they all drew a fine line between reality and fantasy and featured an intriguing twist ending. In addition—largely due to Serling's influence—the series often dealt with serious, current issues, such as racism, the persecution of suspected Communists during the Cold War, and the war in Korea. As Lawrence Venuti explained in *Western Humanities Review*, "Serling did not shrink from the social criticism which had characterized his previous work in television; he rather embodied his examination of American society in fantasy. Of course, his messages were not entirely explicit, and less sophisticated viewers, enthralled by the fantastic plot, might not always perceive its significance, yet his narrations before and after each episode often made his themes more obvious or at least pointed to the intention behind the fantastic surface. . . . Even though television censorship moved Serling to give up his commitment to social realism, *The Twilight Zone* shows that he did not surrender

his conception of the responsible writer's function in society."

One recurring theme in the series was an individual receiving a second chance, usually just for a brief time. In "Walking Distance," for example, a stressed–out advertising executive walks back to the town where he spent his childhood and nostalgically finds everything just the way it was when he was a kid. He even sees himself as a little boy, riding on a merry–go–round. When he confronts his parents, however, they tell him to leave, since there is "only one summer to a customer." As Serling concluded in his closing narration, the man was "Successful in most things, but not in the one effort that all men try at some time in their lives—trying to go home again."

"Time Enough at Last" provides a bleaker example of the same theme. A bookworm—who is henpecked by his wife and harassed by his boss at the bank where he works—just wants to be left alone to read. One day while Henry Bemis is eating lunch in the bank's vault, a nuclear war wipes out the rest of the world and leaves him as the sole survivor. Bemis is depressed until he finds the remains of a library; he then becomes excited at the prospect of reading in peace for the rest of his life. As soon as he sits down with his first book, however, Bemis breaks his glasses and can't see a thing. As Serling's narration noted: "The best–laid plans of mice and men––and Henry Bemis, the small man in the glasses who wanted nothing but time. Henry Bemis, now just a part of a smashed landscape, just a piece of the rubble, just a fragment of what man has deeded to himself."

Another of Serling's favorite themes involved people encountering death or the devil. In "The Hitchhiker," for example, a woman named Nan Adams drives alone across the country. After a minor accident in Pennsylvania, she repeatedly sees the same man standing at the side of the road and calling to her. Nan becomes more and more frightened each time he appears, especially when she realizes that no one else can see him. She finally calls home, only to learn that her family is mourning Nan's death in a car accident a few days earlier. Nan suddenly becomes calm as she understands that the man who has been following her is Death.

Serling also wrote a number of *Twilight Zone* episodes about aliens and space travel, and he often used these stories to make a statement about human nature. In "The Monsters Are Due on Maple Street," a group of people in a normal neighborhood see something strange fly overhead and then begin to experience strange power outages. As they search for an explanation, they gradually become hysterical and begin persecuting each other. When an all–out riot ensues, two small, unarmed aliens return to their spaceship, having proven how easy it is to take over the planet simply by turning people against each other. Serling's closing narration explained: "For the record, prejudices can kill and suspicion can destroy, and a thoughtless, frightened search for a scapegoat has a fallout all its own—for the children, and the children yet unborn. And the pity of it is that these things cannot be confined to the Twilight Zone."

"Eye of the Beholder" was another episode in which Serling made a forthright comment about human nature. In this story, a woman lies in a hospital with bandages covering her face following an operation that was her last chance to correct a terrible disfigurement. If the surgery fails, she will be sent away to live with other "freaks," since her society places a high value on conformity. When the bandages are removed, the woman is remarkably beautiful, but all the doctors and nurses in the operating room are hideously ugly––the norm in this society. A handsome man comes to take the patient away, reassuring her that she will be accepted among the other outcasts. In his closing narration, Serling stated: "Now the questions come to mind. Where is this place and when is it, what kind of world where ugliness is the norm and beauty the deviation from that norm? The answer is, it doesn't make any difference. Because the old saying is true. Beauty *is* in the eye of the beholder."

Serling also wrote several episodes considering the question of identity, in which things were not quite what they seemed. In "The After Hours," for example, a woman is locked in a department store after it closes, and becomes terrified when she finds that all the people she met there during the day have turned into mannequins. Gradually she remembers that she is also a mannequin, but became so caught up in her annual month as a human that she forgot to come back. Serling concluded the episode with: "It makes you wonder, doesn't it? Just how normal are we? Just who are the people we nod our hellos to as we pass on the street?"

Another favorite theme of Serling's was time travel, which he often mixed into an otherwise plausible situation. One of the best–remembered episodes with this theme was "The Odyssey of Flight 33." A jet plane on a routine flight across the Atlantic gets caught in a strange windstorm and picks up incredible speed. When the pilots get back on course, they descend toward New York City only to find dinosaurs roaming there. On their next try, they see the World's Fair of 1939, and they begin to worry that they are running low on fuel. Serling commented in his closing narration: "If some moment, any moment, you hear the sound of jet engines flying atop the overcast, engines that sound searching and lost, engines that sound desperate, shoot up a flare or do something. That would be Global 33 trying to get home—from the Twilight Zone."

Critics generally considered the first three seasons of *The Twilight Zone* to contain the best episodes in terms of writing and direction. In its prime, the show attracted top talent; in fact, many actors accepted half of their usual fees to appear, simply because they liked the show and the interesting characters it presented. The series did experience some difficulties during this time, however. For example, CBS pressured Serling to put some episodes on videotape rather than film during the second season in order to save money on production costs. This limited the range of camera angles and prevented shooting outdoors, so Serling soon abandoned the idea. Since the series received a huge number of unsolicited manuscripts from aspiring writers, Serling also became the target of several lawsuits in which people claimed he had used their story ideas without compensation. Most of these cases were dismissed or settled, but a lasting effect was that several outstanding episodes were never released for syndication because they were tied up in legal disputes at the time.

Fatigue started to take a toll on Serling during the third season. "I've never felt quite so drained of ideas as I do at this moment," he once explained. "You can't retain quality. You start borrowing from yourself, making your own cliches. I notice that more and more." At the end of the year, CBS had problems finding a sponsor, and for a while it looked like the series would not be renewed for 1963. As a result, Houghton accepted an attractive job offer from a movie production company and left the show. Then Serling quit to take a one–year teaching position at Antioch College. He continued to provide scripts and narra-

Danny Kaye starred in "Paladin of the Lost Hour," an episode from the revived *Twilight Zone* series, which returned to the airwaves only somewhat successfully from 1985-89.

tion for *The Twilight Zone* during the remaining two years of its run, but the extent of his involvement was considerably less than before. He offered three reasons for his decision: "First is extreme fatigue. Second, I'm desperate for a change of scene, and third is a chance to exhale, with the opportunity for picking up a little knowledge instead of trying to spew it out."

The Twilight Zone was expanded to an hour per episode during the fourth season, although everyone involved found it difficult to adapt the show to this format. During the fifth season the show returned to a half–hour format. Many of the episodes from these years shared the eerie mood and clever plot twists of the early series, although some were of considerably lower quality. CBS officially cancelled *The Twilight Zone* in January, 1964 after production of 156 episodes, 92 of which had been written by Serling. The president of the network claimed he cancelled the show because it was over budget and had begun to slip in the ratings. In evaluating his best–known work, Serling once stated: "We had some real turkeys, some fair ones, and some shows I'm really proud to have been a part of. I can walk away from this series unbowed."

Life outside the Zone

Serling stayed active following cancellation of *The Twilight Zone.* He wrote a number of television scripts and screenplays, hosted and narrated television and radio shows, appeared in commercials, and even acted as president of the National Academy of Television Arts and Sciences from 1965 to 1966. He also taught dramatic writing at Ithaca College in New York and made frequent public appearances to speak out about political issues. Although these activities were fulfilling for Serling, in some ways they seemed like a letdown after reaching the pinnacle of success a few years earlier.

In 1969 Serling participated in the creation of the television series *Rod Serling's Night Gallery,* which included short dramas with a slightly greater emphasis on horror than *The Twilight Zone.* The series ran until 1972 and garnered Serling two Emmy nominations, but on the whole he was disappointed with it. Serling also created *The Loner,* a western with an emotional rather than action–oriented flavor, but the series was cancelled after Serling entered into a dispute with CBS executives who wanted to make it more conventional. Serling's screenplays included *Doomsday Flight,* which told the story of a plane containing a bomb that would explode if its altitude dropped below 4,000 feet. (Although the film received high ratings on television, Serling was very disturbed when it also led to an increase in bomb threats against airlines.) In 1969, Serling co–wrote the screenplay for the popular film *Planet of the Apes,* based on the novel by Pierre Boulle.

Serling suffered a mild heart attack in May of 1975, then entered the hospital again a month later for a heart bypass operation. He died of complications during surgery on June 25, 1975, at the age of fifty. His brother attributed Serling's death at such a young age to a family history of heart disease, his intense personality, and the fact that he smoked four packs of cigarettes per day. The television world mourned one of its greatest writers and personalities. In recognition of Serling's contribution to the medium, he was given a posthumous Emmy award in 1975.

Remembering Serling in *The Twilight Zone Companion, Star Trek* creator Gene Roddenberry said: "The fact that Rod Serling was a uniquely talented writer with extraordinary imagination is not our real loss. These merely describe his tools and the level of his skill. Our loss is the man, the intelligence and the conscience who used these things for us. No one could know Serling, or view or read his work, without recognizing his deep affection for humanity, his sympathetically intense curiosity about us, and his determination to enlarge our horizons by giving us a better understanding of ourselves."

Although Serling's contributions were many and varied, he would be remembered mainly as the creator of *The Twilight Zone.* Many elements of the show became firmly entrenched in American popular culture. The term "Twilight Zone" became synonymous with any strange situation or occurrence, while its haunting theme song remains instantly recognizable. In summing up the series' impact, Zicree stated: "If, in his darkest moments, Rod

Serling felt his accomplishments on *The Twilight Zone* were of a transient nature, these were only the passing fears of every writer that his life's work has been of no consequence. The shining product of his imagination still flourishes, reborn each time a person turns on a television and sits before the glowing screen, caught in the spell. To those already acquainted, each new meeting is a reunion filled with delight. To those coming at it fresh, it is a revelation full of wonder and mystery and awe."

■ Works Cited

Gould, Jack, review of *Patterns, New York Times,* January 13, 1955.

Helm, review of *The Twilight Zone, Variety,* October 5, 1959.

Olshaker, Mark, "Requiem for a Heavyweight: Final Tribute," *New Times,* July 25, 1975.

Raper, Tod, "*The Twilight Zone* Is Hottest CBS Series," *Columbus Dispatch,* August 23, 1959.

Serling, Rod, *Patterns: Four Television Plays with the Author's Personal Commentaries,* Simon & Schuster, 1957.

Shayon, Robert Lewis, "The Efficient Murderer," *Saturday Review,* February 26, 1955.

Venuti, Lawrence, "Rod Serling, Television Censorship, *The Twilight Zone,*" *Western Humanities Review,* Winter 1981.

Zicree, Marc Scott, *The Twilight Zone Companion,* Bantam Books, 1982.

■ For More Information See

BOOKS

Contemporary Literary Criticism, Volume 30, Gale, 1984, p. 352.

Dictionary of Literary Biography, Volume 26: *American Screenwriters,* Gale, 1984, p. 285.

Peter Nicholls, editor, *Encyclopedia of Science Fiction,* Granada, 1979, p. 536.

Twentieth–Century Science–Fiction Writers, St. Martin's, 1981, p. 480.

—*Sketch by Laurie Collier Hillstrom*

Leslie Marmon Silko

■ Personal

Born March 5, 1948, in Albuquerque, NM; daughter of Lee H. Marmon; children: Robert and Cazimir. *Education:* University of New Mexico, B.A. (summa cum laude), 1969; attended American Indian Law Program at University of New Mexico.

■ Addresses

Home—8000 West Camireo Del Cerro, Tucson, AZ 85705. *Office*—Department of English, University of Arizona, Tucson, AZ 85721.

■ Career

Writer. Instructor at Navajo Community College, Tsaile, AZ, and University of New Mexico, Albuquerque, NM; University of Arizona, Tucson, AZ, assistant professor of English since 1978. Writer-in-residence at University of Montana and Vassar College; visiting professor of fiction, University of Washington, 1979.

■ Awards, Honors

National Endowment for the Arts (NEA) grant, 1971, for "The Man to Send Rain Clouds"; NEA fellowship, 1974; *Chicago Review* poetry award, 1974; Pushcart Prize for poetry, 1977; MacArthur fellow, John D. and Catherine T. MacArthur Foundation, 1983 (some sources say 1981 or 1982); Woodrow Wilson fellow.

■ Writings

Laguna Woman: Poems, Greenfield Review Press, 1974.
Ceremony (novel), Viking, 1977.
Storyteller (poems and stories), Seaver Books, 1981.
(With James A. Wright) *The Delicacy and Strength of Lace: Letters between Leslie Marmon Silko and James A. Wright,* edited by Anne Wright, Graywolf Press, 1986.
Almanac of the Dead: A Novel, Simon & Schuster, 1991.

Author, with Frank Chia, of the one-act play *Lullaby* (adapted from a story by Silko), produced by the American Bicentennial Theater Project, San Francisco, CA, 1976; also author of *Estoyehmuut and the Kunideeyah* (screenplay based on a Laguna narrative; title means "Arrowboy and the Destroyers"), 1979. Contributor of stories to anthologies, including *The Man to Send Rainclouds: Contemporary Stories by American Indians,* edited by Kenneth Rosen, Viking, 1974; *Come to Power,* edited by Dick Lourie, Crossing Press, 1974; *The Remem-*

bered Earth: An Anthology of Native American Literature, edited by Gerry Hobson, University of New Mexico Press, 1981; and *Earth Power Coming,* edited by Simon J. Ortiz, Navajo Community College Press, 1983.

A collection of Silko's manuscripts are housed at the University of Arizona in Tucson.

■ Sidelights

In a contest of witchery among an assembly of Native American witches, one tells the group about white–skinned people who will come across the ocean. The storyteller explains how the newcomers will "grow away from the earth," pollute the land and water, bring diseases, and kill the native people out of fear. When the witch reveals that the events of the story will begin to happen as he tells it, the other witches ask him to take back the tale and its destructive spell. "But the witch just shook his head . . . . *It's already turned loose./It's already coming./It can't be called back."* This story, published in both the books *Ceremony* and *Storyteller* by Leslie Marmon Silko, illustrates one of Silko's main themes as a writer: the direct impact that storytelling has on life and history. "It's a whole way of being," Silko told Kim Barnes in an interview published in *Yellow Woman.* "When I say `storytelling,' I don't just mean sitting down and telling a once–upon–a–time kind of story. I mean a whole way of seeing yourself, the people around you, your life, the place of your life in the bigger context, not just in terms of nature and location, but in terms of what has gone on before, what's happened to other people."

Silko was born in 1948 in Albuquerque, New Mexico. She grew up "in the house at Laguna where my father was born," she related at the end of her poetry collection *Laguna Woman.* Laguna is one of several Indian pueblos, or villages, that have existed in the American Southwest for centuries, most of them in New Mexico. The pueblo is located 150 miles from Trinity Site, where the first atomic bomb test took place on July 16, 1945. The largest open pit uranium mine in the world is on land there belonging to the Laguna people, and it extends to Mt. Taylor, a mountain peak considered sacred to the Laguna, who know it by the name Tse–pi'na.

Silko is of Laguna, white, and Mexican ancestry, and she shares her family's stories and background in her prose and verse collection *Storyteller.* The

A half-breed named Tayo recovers from his traumatic World War II experiences with the help of a Navajo medicine man and a mysterious woman in this 1977 novel.

book delineates how her great–grandmother from the village of Paguate, Marie Anaya, married Robert G. Marmon, a white man from Ohio who came to Laguna in 1872, learned the language, and settled there. In the late nineteenth century, white settlers and missionaries came to the area, and their presence disrupted in profound ways the lifestyles of the people who had been there. According to Silko, her great–grandfather, along with his older brother, Walter, were responsible "for all kinds of factions and trouble at Laguna—They came on the heels of a Baptist preacher named Gorman who also must have upset Laguna ceremonialism."

While growing up at Laguna, Silko felt the tensions of being a Marmon, a family which was part white. In the autobiographical note at the end of *Laguna Woman* she revealed, "The Marmons are very controversial, even now; but I think that people watch us more closely than they do full bloods or white people." According to Per Seyersted in his book, *Leslie Marmon Silko,* Silko's family, whose house was situated on the outskirts of Old Laguna, "was included in clan activities, but not to the same extent as full bloods, and . . . the young Leslie helped out at ceremonial dances, but did not dance herself." As Silko noted in one interview, though, the genetic or blood measure of belonging to a race or community of people means nothing if one is not raised in that community and brought up with their culture. In the autobiographical note concluding *Laguna Woman,* Silko calls her upbringing mixed—neither fully white nor fully Laguna. Seyersted quotes Silko in a note about herself which appeared in a collection of stories: "I am of mixed–breed ancestry, but what I know is Laguna." And that knowledge began to enter her consciousness early. During her first year of life, her mother kept her on a cradle board, a custom which involves believing that the child will be protected while strapped on the board.

Laguna Culture and Home

The language of the Laguna people is Keresan, though the use of English is widespread. Silko learned some of the Keresan language from her great–grandmother, Marie Anaya, but at school English was mandatory, and students using their own languages were punished. Silko attended the Laguna Day School, a Bureau of Indian Affairs (BIA) institution, through the fourth grade. In "Language and Literature from a Pueblo Indian Perspective," a talk she gave at Harvard University's English Institute, Silko described those schools as "so terrible that we never heard of Shakespeare. There was Dick and Jane, and I can remember reading that the robins were heading south for winter, but I knew that all winter the robins were around Laguna—I worried for quite a while about the robins because they didn't leave in the winter, not realizing that the textbooks were written in Boston," where the robins do migrate south in the winter.

The BIA schools did not educate students past the fourth grade, so beyond that, most children would attend boarding school. Until she was sixteen, Silko went to a private school in Albuquerque, Manzano Day School, which required a hundred–mile round trip drive every day. There, in the fifth grade, she started writing. In a classroom assignment, the teacher handed out a list of words and

instructed the students to use them in sentences. Silko wrote a story. Her talents were nurtured in a home environment that was rich in the telling of stories about neighbors, family members, history, and the land. Silko's Aunt Susie was a major influence. In *Storyteller,* Silko writes that her aunt belonged to "the last generation here at Laguna,/that passed down an entire culture/by word of mouth/an entire history/an entire vision of the world/which depended upon memory/and retelling by subsequent generations." But her aunt also belonged to one of the first generations to have their lives changed by the influence of the European settlers. "She was a brilliant woman," Silko goes on, "a scholar of her own making" who studied at Dickinson College.

Her father, Lee Marmon, played an important encouraging role in Silko's life as well. He employed himself with various unfulfilling jobs to support his family, but what he really loved was landscape photography. He took many of the photographs which appear in *Storyteller.* In that volume, Silko remembers, "He used to wait for the cumulus clouds to come give him the sky he needed for his photographs. When I was a girl I could tell by the clouds whether I'd find him working at the store" or out among the mesas she calls his "second home." Lee Marmon imparted to his daughter a love for the land around them and encouraged her to possess a sense of freedom about living, particularly about living at Laguna. "As I got older he said I should become a writer because writers worked their own hours and they can live anywhere and do their work. `You could even live up here in these hills if you wanted' [he told her]."

One of the most significant differences between the Laguna culture in which Silko grew up and mainstream American culture is that the Laguna adhere to a matrilineal system, in which children trace their lineage from their mother rather than their father. In addition, women own and maintain the houses and hold much of the decision–making power in the family, ranging from disciplining children to outside business matters. In the *Yellow Woman* interview, Silko explained to Barnes that the activities of Laguna men and boys were not kept separate from those of the women and girls, and that "labor wasn't divided into men's work and women's work. When I was a kid," she continued, "I got to hang around wherever I wanted to hang around—Nobody shooed me away, no one told me girls couldn't watch men build a shed." While she grew up, Silko saw a work crew of women replaster their house. She was allowed to go on her first deer hunt when she was eight. At thirteen she was permitted to carry a rifle on the hunts.

Silko attended the University of New Mexico and majored in English. During her sophomore year, she had her first baby, Robert, named after her first husband. Shortly after, she took her first creative writing class. She told interviewer Laura Coltelli in *Winged Words* that this was at the suggestion of her first husband, who asked her one day, "how would you like to take a class where you could get an easy A?" Silko remembers that "I would like that, you know, because having this baby and all, it would be nice to bring up my grade–point average." Grades proved to be no problem for Silko; even with a small child to care for, she graduated summa cum laude in 1969. That year she also published her first story, "The Man to Send Rain Clouds," in the *New Mexico Quarterly*. She then began attending law school in a program for Native Americans at the University of New Mexico in order to learn about filing land claims. In 1971, while attending the program, she gave birth to her second son and also won a National Endowment of the Arts Discovery grant for "The Man to Send Rain Clouds." She dropped out of law school and began writing and teaching. Silko taught first at Navajo Community College, then at the University of Arizona and the University of New Mexico. She has taught at other universities, such as the University of Montana, Vassar College, and the University of Washington as a visiting professor and writer–in–residence. She currently holds an assistant professorship at the University of Arizona and lives in the hills near Tucson.

In 1974 *Laguna Woman* was published. This small volume, containing poems which had previously been published in the *Chicago Review* and the *Greenfield Review,* earned Silko a *Chicago Review* poetry award and the Pushcart Prize for poetry. Many of the poems in *Laguna Woman* appear again in *Storyteller.* Also in 1974, many of her stories appeared in an anthology edited by Kenneth Rosen entitled *The Man to Send Rain Clouds: Contemporary Stories by American Indians.* Silko's writing often straddles the genres of prose and poetry. The author told Barnes that making distinctions between the two forms is not important to her.

"What I'm interested in is getting a feeling or an idea that's part of the story. Getting the story across."

Storytelling

For a year and a half, from September 1978 to March 1980, Silko had a correspondence with the poet James A. Wright, in which they frequently discussed the nature of storytelling and writing. These letters were published by Wright's wife, Anne, after his death in March 1980, as *The Delicacy and Strength of Lace: Letters between Leslie Marmon Silko and James A. Wright.* In one letter, Silko wrote that "through stories from each other we can feel that we are not alone, that we are not the first and the last to confront losses—At Laguna whenever something happens (happy or sad or strange), that vast body of remembered stories is brought forth by people who have been listening to the account of this recent event. Immediately the listeners, in turn, begin telling stories about the other times and other people from the area who have enjoyed or suffered the same luck." Just as the old stories serve a function in helping people in the present, Silko continued that "if something very sad and difficult comes to you, you know that it will take its place with the other stories and that somehow, as a story, it will, from that time on, be remembered and told to others who have suffered losses."

This idea that stories are dynamic parts of life is at the core of Silko's writing. Stories come from events in people's lives and people's lives create more stories, and both the stories and the lives influence each other. In that sense, stories are made real in the telling of them. As Silko told Barnes, "the stories have a life of their own—The old folks at Laguna would say, `If it's important, you'll remember it.' If it's really important, if it has a kind of substance that reaches to the heart of the community life and what's gone before and what's gone later, it will be remembered. And if it's not remembered, the people no longer wanted it, or it no longer had its place in the community." It is this phenomenon that Silko captures in her first novel, *Ceremony*.

Silko finished *Ceremony* while living for two years in Ketchikan, Alaska. The novel established her reputation as an important writer.

Underscoring Silko's philosophy about storytelling, the novel begins as a story that will happen as it is told, or, in this case, thought: "Ts'its'tsi'nako, Thought–Woman,/is sitting in her room/and whatever she thinks about/appears—She is sitting in her room/thinking of a story now/I'm telling you the story/she is thinking." In an interview with Dexter Fisher appearing in *The Third Woman*, Silko described how the process of writing *Ceremony* was a ceremony for her and how that influenced her choice of the novel's title: "I was having migraine headaches all the time and horrible nausea that went on and on. I kept writing and all of a sudden it occurred to me that he [Tayo] was very sick and I was wondering if he was going to get well, because of those who came back, some made it and some didn't—I was trying to figure out how some stay sane and some don't, and then I realized that the one thing that kept me going at all was writing. And as Tayo got better, I felt better."

The novel tells the story of the struggle of a young half–breed, Tayo, to recover from his traumatizing experiences while serving in the Philip-

In her 1981 work, Silko, who is of mixed ancestry, reveals the history of her family, beginning with her great-grandparents, Robert G. Marmon and Marie Anaya Marmon.

pines during World War II. He eventually finds his way to a Navajo medicine man who helps create a modern ceremony to cure Tayo's spiritual illness. He is helped also by a mysterious woman, who teaches him about nurturing the land. Silko paints a very detailed picture of what this war meant to Tayo and other characters in the novel. Tayo recalls an incident where the men in his troop killed some Japanese soldiers, but in a semi–hallucination, he saw in the fallen men members of his own family. As Toni Flores put it in an essay in *Frontiers: A Journal of Women Studies*, Tayo "perceives an identity between the Japanese and his own people (a correct racial identity, of course), and he recoils in horror at his own complicity, willed or not, with both sides in this slaughter." To his friends, or rather, former friends, the war was an opportunity for them to reap what they thought of as benefits for themselves– white women would date them, and white people in general seemed to treat them better when they wore the uniform. When they return from the war, they spend their time getting drunk, telling war stories, and reminiscing about going out with blondes. By the time the novel ends, Tayo has had to confront his old friends, himself, and the vast difference between them during a ghastly incident.

In Silko's introduction to the book she states: "This novel is essentially about the powers inherent in the process of storytelling—The chanting or telling of ancient stories to effect certain cures or protect from illness and harm have always been part of the Pueblo's curing ceremonies—My book tells the story of an Indian family, but it is also involved in the search for a ceremony to deal with despair, the most virulent of diseases—the despair which accounts for the suicide, the alcoholism, and the violence which occur in so many Indian communities today." Silko told Seyersted that she wanted to get *Ceremony* published during 1976, the United States' bicentennial anniversary year, because "I just want to make sure that . . . Americans can be reminded that there are different ways to look at the past 200 years."

The ceremony the Navajo medicine man, Betonie, devises for Tayo recognizes the realities of life at Laguna and deals with the "witchery" going on. In the witchery story, Betonie shows Tayo how the coming of Europeans led up to the war he experienced. Betonie, in creating the new ceremony, even deals with the uranium found in the Laguna hills that was used to make the atomic bomb: "Up here in these hills they will find the rocks, rocks with veins of green and yellow and black. They will lay the final pattern with these rocks they will lay it across the world and explode everything."

Critics have commented on how Silko intersperses sections of poetry—such as Betonie's witchery story—within the novel. However, to Silko, those sections serve more to blend the oral tradition with the literary form of the novel. As she told Barnes, the sections that are written in verse form are the parts "that ideally you would hear rather than read." Reed Way Dasenbrock, in *Genre*, points out that Silko's technique challenges the way we define a coherent story. He notes that she does "precisely the opposite of the Western tradition of closure and boundedness." In *Ceremony*, "stories are valued for their overlap, for the way they lead to new stories in turn." Even though they may seem to not directly link up with the novel as a whole, the narratives suggest that other ideas and traditions are present and exist in the current events being told.

Numerous critics applauded the scope and themes of *Ceremony*. B. A. St. Andrews, in an essay in *Arizona Quarterly*, wrote that the novel "is a round and classical work which examines identity on a cosmic level." Charles R. Larson, in *Washington Post Book World*, lauded *Ceremony* as "powerfully conceived." In the *New York Times Book Review*, Frank MacShane called *Ceremony* "one of the most realized works of fiction devoted to Indian life that has been written in this country, and it is a splendid achievement."

Tradition and Innovation

Silko's next book, *Storyteller*, is part autobiography, part family and pueblo history, part previously published stories and poems, and part testament to and continuation of the oral tradition that Silko grew up with. She dedicated it "to the storytellers as far back as memory goes and to the telling which continues and through which they all live and we with them." While putting the book together, Silko looked back on family photographs kept in "a tall Hopi basket," as she wrote in *Storyteller*, and decided to include some. Most were taken by either her father or her grandfather. In a letter to James Wright, Silko described a discovery she made about the relationship between photos and memory: "much of what I `remember' of places and people is actually a memory of the photograph of the place and person, but that I had forgotten the photograph and remembered it

as if I had been told about it." Bernard A. Hirsch commented in *Yellow Woman* that the photographs "are important because they reveal something of the particular landscape and community out of which Laguna oral tradition is born." He also noted that they "involve the reader more fully in the storytelling process itself."

Some of Silko's best–known stories appear in *Storyteller*, including "Yellow Woman," "Lullaby," "Storyteller" (her personal favorite), "Tony's Story," "The Man to Send Rain Clouds," and "Toe'osh: A Laguna Coyote Story." "Yellow Woman" has garnered so much attention that an entire book, *Yellow Woman*, has been published about it. The work includes a collection of critical essays on the story "Yellow Woman," as well as on *Storyteller*.

The Yellow Woman story is an old one and has been told many times. It tells of a young, often married, woman who meets a kachina, a powerful mountain spirit, when she goes to get water. The kachina kidnaps her, takes her to his home, and makes her perform impossible feats under threat of death. In many versions the woman is killed, and in some she gives birth to the mountain spirit's twin children before her death. Often, the pueblo would benefit in some way or another from Yellow Woman's abduction. Silko told Barnes that "what's operating in [the Yellow Woman] stories is this attraction, this passion, this connection between the human world and the animal and spirit worlds."

Silko modifies the story by bringing it into a modern setting and exploring the boundary between legend and real life. In Silko's version, the story begins with a modern pueblo woman waking up next to the river with a man she had met the day before. He calls her Yellow Woman, implying that she is the mythical character, but she initially doubts this. She insists that she cannot be the woman of the legend: she has her own name, she comes from a particular pueblo, and his "name is Silva and you are a stranger I met by the river yesterday afternoon." "Silva," however, is Spanish for forest, and the man seems convinced that they somehow embody the old legend. When the woman tells him that she doesn't believe that things like that can happen in their modern world, Silva replies, "But someday they will talk about us, and they will say, `Those two lived long ago when things like that happened'." Unlike the traditional story, she has not been kidnapped, but she does fall under this man's power of seduction.

Silko explores the paradoxical relationship between myth and reality in this woman who wonders "if Yellow Woman had known who she was—if she knew that she would become part of the stories."

Silko's version ends with "Yellow Woman" alive. After Silva is confronted by an angry white man, she leaves him and returns home. Approaching the house, "I could hear their voices inside—my mother was telling my grandmother how to fix Jell-O and my husband, Al, was playing with the baby. I decided to tell them that some Navajo had kidnapped me, but I was sorry that old Grandpa wasn't alive to hear my story because it was the Yellow Woman stories he liked to tell best." Silko's inclusion of other variations of the Yellow Woman story in *Storyteller* drive home the point that there is no one true version—the stories can be written and rewritten, told and retold, and each has its own significance. In this way, Melody Graulich asserted in her introduction to *Yellow Woman*, Silko "suggests that different stories reflect different interpretations of the same experience, even when told from the same point of view." Bernard A. Hirsch, in *Yellow Woman*, called *Storyteller* a book which "lovingly maps the fertile storytelling ground from which her art evolves and to which it is returned—an offering to the oral tradition which nurtured it." In an essay in the same book, Linda Danielson wrote that *Storyteller* is "a testimony to verbal art as a survival strategy."

A Monumental Story

Silko won a MacArthur Foundation fellowship in 1981, which allowed her to devote herself full-time to writing her next novel. The resulting book, *Almanac of the Dead,* is an epic-like conclusion of sorts to the story of European domination of the Western hemisphere that began with Christopher Columbus's arrival in the Americas. The novel was published in 1991, the same year as the quincentennial anniversary of the explorer's landfall. The story follows a multitude of Native American characters who are involved in a revolutionary plot to reclaim their land. On the inside cover of the hardcover edition is a five hundred year map outlining the myriad characters in their respective locations—Tucson, New Jersey, Mexico City, among others. It also presents the Prophecy: "When Europeans arrived, the Maya, Azteca, Inca cultures had already built great cities and vast networks of roads. Ancient prophe-

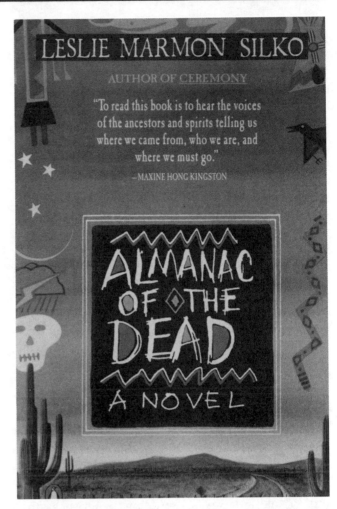

Ancient prophecies foretell a revolution in which Native Americans will attempt to reclaim the Americas in this 1991 work.

cies foretold the arrival of Europeans in the Americas. The ancient prophecies also foretell the disappearance of all things European."

Silko brings to life a large cast of revolutionaries, some directly involved in the revolutionary plans, including drug and arms dealers and some local officials, and some people whose lives brush the fringes of the imminent "invasion." Behind all the action is the almanac, a five-part document which is believed to foretell wars and famine, as well as serve as a guide on planting crops. In reality, there are four Mayan fragments of the almanac; in her novel, Silko invented a fifth fragment which two of her characters possess. Zeta and Lecha are twin sisters who receive the fragment from their grandmother. Zeta and Lecha's grandmother "and others believed the almanac had living power within it, a power that would bring all the tribal people of the Americas together to retake the land." Twins are significant in Pueblo mythology, and in this novel. The keepers of the fragment are twins, as are the two men who will lead the army of native peoples north from Mexico.

Almanac of the Dead was well received by critics. Elizabeth Tallent, writing in the *New York Times Book Review,* asserted that "This wild, jarring, graphic, mordant, prodigious book embodies the bold wish to encompass in a novel the cruelty of contemporary America, a nation founded on the murder and deracination of the continent's native peoples." In *Time,* John Skow thought some of the characters could have been more fully developed and was distracted by the fact that many of the characters in the first part of the book are inebriated or deranged. But, he concluded, "angry prophets can't be expected to write neat, button-down denunciations," and Silko's "success [with the novel] is far more troubling than her failure." Malcolm Jones, Jr. in *Newsweek* felt that the novel "is guaranteed to make you mad and just as sure to make you squirm."

In a talk at the English Institute at Harvard University, published as "Language and Literature from a Pueblo Indian Perspective," Silko eloquently summed up the importance of storytelling: "The stories are always bringing us together." Though one's impulse might usually be to run off and be alone after a troubling experience, the storytelling tradition she continues says, "'Don't go away, don't isolate yourself, but come here, because we have all had these kinds of experiences'—Inherent in this belief is the feeling that one does not recover or get well by one's self, but it is together that we look after each other and take care of each other."

■ Works Cited

Barnes, Kim, "A Leslie Marmon Silko Interview," *Yellow Woman,* Rutgers University Press, 1993, pp. 49–50.

Coltelli, Laura, *Winged Words: American Indian Writers Speak,* University of Nebraska Press, 1990.

Danielson, Linda, "The Storytellers in *Storyteller,*" *Yellow Woman,* edited by Melody Graulich, Rutgers University Press, 1993.

Dasenbrock, Reed Way, "Forms of Biculturalism in Southwestern Literature: The Work of Rudolfo Anaya and Leslie Marmon Silko," *Genre,* fall, 1988, pp. 307–19.

Fisher, Dexter, "Stories and Their Tellers—A Conversation with Leslie Marmon Silko," *The Third*

Woman: Minority Women Writers of the United States, edited by Dexter Fisher, Houghton, 1980.

Flores, Toni, "Claiming and Making: Ethnicity, Gender, and the Common Sense in Leslie Marmon Silko's *Ceremony* and Zora Neale Hurston's *Their Eyes Were Watching God,*" *Frontiers: A Journal of Women Studies,* Volume X, number 3, 1989, p. 53.

Graulich, Melody, "Introduction," *Yellow Woman,* edited by Melody Graulich, Rutgers University Press, 1993.

Hirsch, Bernard A., "'The Telling Which Continues': Oral Tradition and the Written Word in Leslie Marmon Silko's *Storyteller,*" *Yellow Woman,* edited by Melody Graulich, Rutgers University Press, 1993.

Jones, Malcolm, Jr., review of *Almanac of the Dead, Newsweek,* November 18, 1991. p. 84.

Larson, Charles R., review of *Ceremony, Washington Post Book World,* April 24, 1977, p. E4.

MacShane, Frank, review of *Ceremony, New York Times Book Review,* June 12, 1977, p. 15.

St. Andrews, B. A., "Healing the Witchery: Medicine in Silko's *Ceremony,*" *Arizona Quarterly,* spring, 1988, p. 87.

Seyersted, Per, *Leslie Marmon Silko,* Boise State University, 1980.

Silko, Leslie, *The Almanac of the Dead: A Novel,* Simon & Schuster, 1991.

Silko, Leslie, *Ceremony,* Viking, 1977.

Silko, Leslie, and James A. Wright, *The Delicacy and Strength of Lace: Letters between Leslie Silko and James A. Wright,* edited by Anne Wright, Graywolf Press, 1986.

Silko, Leslie, *Laguna Woman: Poems,* Greenfield Review Press, 1974.

Silko, Leslie, "Language and Literature from a Pueblo Indian Perspective," *English Literature: Opening up the Canon,* edited by Leslie Fiedler and Houston A. Baker, Johns Hopkins University Press, 1981.

Silko, Leslie, *Leslie,Storyteller,* Seaver Books, 1981.

Skow, John, "People of the Monkey Wrench," *Time,* December 9, 1991, p. 86.

Tallent, Elizabeth, "Storytelling with a Vengeance," *New York Times Book Review,* December 22, 1991, p. 6.

■ For More Information See

BOOKS

Four American Indian Literary Masters, University of Oklahoma Press, 1982.

Studies in American Indian Literature: Critical Essays

and *Course Designs*, edited by Paula Gunn Allen, Modern Language Association of America, 1983.

PERIODICALS

American Indian Quarterly, Volume 5, number 1, 1979; summer, 1988, pp. 213–20; fall, 1988, pp. 313–28.
American Studies in Scandinavia, Volume 13, 1981, pp. 17–33.
Arizona Quarterly, spring, 1988, pp. 78–85.
Book Forum: An International Interdisciplinary Quarterly, Volume 5, number 3, 1981, pp. 383–88.

Journal of Ethnic Studies, spring, 1981, pp. 53–8.
Journal of the Southwest, autumn, 1988, pp. 325–55.
Melus, summer, 1988, pp. 281–316.
Minority Voices: An Interdisciplinary Journal, spring/fall, 1981, pp. 1–10.
Notes on Contemporary Literature, September, 1985, pp. 11–12.
Sun Tracks: An American Indian Literary Magazine, fall, 1976, pp. 28–33.
Wikazo Sa Review: A Journal of Indian Studies, fall, 1989, pp. 22–5.

—*Sketch by Helene Henderson*

Timothy Zahn

■ Personal

Born September 1, 1951, in Chicago, IL; son of Herbert William (an attorney) and Marilou (an attorney; maiden name, Webb) Zahn; married Anna L. Romo (a computer programmer), August 4, 1979; children: Corwin. *Education:* Michigan State University, B.A., 1973; University of Illinois at Urbana–Champaign, M.A., 1975, graduate study, 1975–1980. *Hobbies and other interests:* Listening to classical music (particularly nineteenth–century romantic era), crossword puzzles, and martial arts.

■ Addresses

Home—Oregon. *Agent*—Russell Galen, Scott Meredith Literary Agency, 845 Third Ave., New York, NY 10022.

■ Career

Writer, 1980—. *Member:* Science Fiction Writers of America.

■ Awards, Honors

Hugo Award nomination for best short story, World Science Fiction Convention, 1983, for "Pawn's Gambit"; Hugo Award for best novella, 1984, for *Cascade Point;* Hugo Award nomination for best short story, 1985, for "Return to the Fold."

■ Writings

SCIENCE FICTION

The Blackcollar, DAW, 1983.
A Coming of Age, Bluejay Books, 1984.
Cobra, Baen, 1985.
Spinneret (first published serially in *Analog,* July–October, 1985), Bluejay Books, 1985.
Blackcollar: The Backlash Mission, DAW, 1986.
Cobra Strike, Baen, 1986.
Cascade Point and Other Stories, Bluejay Books, 1986, title novella published singly (bound with *Hardfought* by Greg Bear), Tor Books, 1988.
Triplet, Baen, 1987.
Cobra Bargain, Baen, 1988.
Deadman Switch, Baen, 1988.
Time Bomb and Zahndry Others (stories), Baen, 1988.
Warhorse, Baen, 1990.
Heir to the Empire (Star Wars Trilogy, Vol. 1), Bantam, 1991.
Distant Friends and Others (stories), Baen, 1992.
Cobras Two, Baen, 1992.
Dark Force Rising (Star Wars Trilogy, Vol. 2), Bantam, 1992.

The Last Command (Star Wars Trilogy, Vol. 3), Bantam, 1993.

Work included in anthologies, including *The 1983 Annual World's Best SF*, edited by Donald A. Wollheim, DAW, 1983, and *Alien Stars*, edited by Elizabeth Mitchell, Baen, 1985. Contributor of numerous stories and novelettes to magazines, including *Analog Science Fiction/Science Fact, Ares, Fantasy and Science Fiction, Fantasy Gamer, Isaac Asimov's Science Fiction Magazine, Rigel,* and *Space Gamer.*

■ Adaptations

Star Wars: Heir to the Empire, read by Denis Lawson, is available on cassette from Bantam, 1991.

■ Sidelights

When Timothy Zahn decided to try his hand at writing, he had no idea how successful he would become: he just knew he enjoyed making up entertaining stories. Working towards a Ph.D. in physics at the University of Illinois, Zahn began writing science fiction as a hobby. When he sold "Ernie," his first story, in 1978, he considered taking a year off after he got his degree in order to write fiction full- time. Zahn's plans changed completely in mid- 1979, when his thesis advisor died suddenly and unexpectedly. The then- graduate student was faced with the prospect of beginning a new project with another professor, and decided to take time off to write instead. The nine stories he sold that year convinced him to stick with writing science fiction. Since then Zahn has become known for tales of complicated characters who often face moral dilemmas, generally involving conflicts between human and alien cultures. As well, he often focuses on seemingly impossible situations—inhabitable planets, tyrannical alien rulers—and shows how ingenious, inventive and determined individuals manage to find solutions. He presents readers with tightly constructed stories whose energy rarely flags, and his tales have earned him both respect and popularity. Zahn has become a prolific and esteemed force in the science fiction field.

Initially, Zahn limited himself to short stories, publishing many of them in the early 1980s. He became one of *Analog Science Fiction/Science Fact* magazine's regular contributors. In one of his early stories, "Hollow Victory," an alien ambassador has fallen seriously ill and two human biomedics must discover the cause of his sickness. To do this, they use clues about the Thrulmodi physiology and the Thrulmodi planet, where the first human–Thrulmodi conference is taking place. It was an early incidence of a common theme in Zahn's work, that of two cultures—generally human and alien—coming to terms with each other.

The Blackcollar, his debut novel, combined science fiction with martial arts adventure and was published in 1983. The book centers on the conflict between the Ryqril, a conquering alien race who have vanquished Earth and its worlds. By carefully training humans and exerting total control over them, they guarantee complete loyalty from their subjects—until a group of their human subjects decide to rebel. Among these revolutionaries are several people who remember a time when the humans had their own superwarriors, the Blackcollars, who were well–trained fighters whose lives were extended by drugs. Despite the fact that the Blackcollars were dissolved after the war with the Ryqril, a small band of them is known to still exist. Allen Caine leaves the Earth to seek them out, highlighting one of Zahn's ongoing themes of the limits and strengths of human potency. *Analog Science Fiction/Science Fact* reviewer Tom Easton complimented Zahn for not allowing the predictable triumph of humans to be total. He also made special mention of *Blackcollar's* "originality": "There is more realism here, and hence more satisfaction." The writer used the scenario again in another book, *Blackcollar: The Backlash Mission.*

From Military Strength to Mind over Matter

Once a writer has established a following and knows his strengths in a particular area—militaristic science fiction for Zahn—it can be difficult to take a new tack. But this is exactly what the writer did. Three stories that the former physicist published in the early eighties revealed his interest in the universe of the mind and the psychological difficulties that can result from working at a higher mental level. "Dark Thoughts at Noon" tells the story of two telepaths who are kidnapped by a technician in an attempt to mechanically duplicate their abilities for profit. And in "The Final Report on the Lifeline Experiment" researchers have devised a telepathic experiment to determine at what point a human fetus transforms into a "real person." Their work becomes a rallying point for pro- and anti- abortion activists and precipitates a political crisis. Similarly, "The

The issue of capital punishment is examined in this 1988 science fiction novel about an interstellar society that explores the world of Solitaire, where only the dead may travel.

Cassandra" begins with a mutation that endows the human colonists of one planet with the ability to foretell death, and ends with the hypothesis that the death of any sentient creature may influence the structure of the universe.

Telekinesis and social questions play key roles in Zahn's second novel *A Coming of Age.* Again, Zahn played with the idea of a mutation whose effects bring both good and evil to humans. Because of a mutation some two hundred years before the novel begins, children on the planet Tigris develop psychic powers at five years of age. These powers enable them to fly and move objects with their minds, among other telekinetic skills—but the abilities disappear at the onset of puberty. During this eight- year interval, the children are more powerful than adults. At a certain period of the planet's early

history, the children ruled Tigris. However, during this time, recordkeeping and institutions fell apart and the society realized it had to get adopt a new strategy to deal with the children's abilities. Therefore, the society has developed several means by which to control the potent pre- teens and harness their powers for itself. Children are raised in hives and given very little education; they are even deprived of reading. Industry profits from them by tapping into their skills as an energy source. Once they reach puberty and lose their powers, they are allowed to go to school and are streamlined into adult society. The characters include a 13- year- old girl who dreads the loss of her special facility, an adult detective and his preteen assistant who are looking into a kidnapping, a scientist who is researching the biology of the telekinetic phenomenon and a criminal who plans to use this research. By using the universal experience of adolescence and the accompanying gains and losses that everyone feels, Zahn showed that his concerns range beyond hard science and speculation of technological development to include social and psychological questions. *Analog's* Easton said he found *A Coming of Age* "a warm and sympathetic story very suitable for a broad range of ages," being "complex" enough to entertain older readers. *Publishers Weekly* commended Zahn for writing "an entertaining science fiction police procedural that should especially appeal to teenagers."

While Zahn was branching out into more psychological themes, he still maintained his ability to interest his readers with space adventures. Despite the fact that Earth vessels can travel beyond the stars, no habitable worlds remain within reach as the author's 1985 novel *Spinneret* opens. All the potentially habitable areas have been colonized by other starfaring races. In what Hal Hoover, writing in *Voice of Youth Advocates,* described as a "first class sci-fi novel," Zahn follows Colonel Lloyd Meredith's attempt to colonize Astra, a world no one wants because it has no metals—or so everyone thinks until its dormant volcano spews a metal thread into orbit shortly after Meredith's expedition lands. One *Publishers Weekly* reviewer pronounced this one of "Zahn's best novels," while another admired it as a "light, brisk and entertaining yarn." And *Booklist's* Roland Green remarked on the novel's "excellent narrative technique, clear prose, and intelligent characterization."

A Superwarrior Trilogy

Cobra, Cobra Strike and *Cobra Bargain* deal with the theme of superhuman warriors Zahn began to explore in the Blackcollar books. The Cobras (Computerized Body Reflex Armament) are technologically souped– up soldiers programmed to react lethally to anything their reflexes read as an attack. They are created after one of the colony worlds of the Dominion of Man is conquered by the Troft forces, whom they manage to subdue. Because the Cobras' indiscriminate responses make them dangerous for civilian life, they are sent to protect the colonists on the far side of Troft territory. Zahn focuses on Jonny Moreau, a twenty– year– old from a backwater planet who is one of the first people to sign up for the Cobra program. Moreau changes from a naive, idealistic young man into a savvy politician as he becomes a leader on his new home.

In *Cobra Strike,* second in the series, Jonny Moreau's three sons must contend with another threat. On the distant planet of Quasama, a paranoid race of humans lives in a mutually beneficial and dependent relationship with predatory birds called mojos. The formerly adversarial Trofts, now trading partners with the humans, want to use the Cobras as mercenaries to destroy this race, in return for five new worlds that can support human life. The last installment of the "Cobra" series, *Cobra Bargain,* takes place after Jonny Moreau has passed away. Jonny's granddaughter, Justine, decides to buck the all–male tradition of the Cobras and join their ranks—she's a Moreau, after all. She successfully completes the training and proves herself to be a resourceful and independent young woman, whose diplomatic and warrior abilities mirror or surpass those of her male predecessors.

Writing in *Voice of Youth Advocates* about the ways in which Zahn manages to avert war throughout the series, Diane G. Yates noted that "the moral questions that [the Moreaus] struggle with are those that concern us all, and to find a character in a military SF novel who agonizes over ethical questions is a refreshing change, and a welcome one." *Analog*'s Easton lauded *Cobra Bargain* especially for its heroine, noting that Jasmine is "smart, empathetic, energetic, [and] determined" and that by the end "a number of males have had their consciousness suit-ably broadened or their egos ventilated."

More Interstellar Explorations

Zahn gathered thirteen short stories for *Cascade Point and Other Stories,* including the Hugo Award–winning title work. *Booklist* reviewer Green praised Zahn's "consistent intelligence in both the presentation and the resolution" of his stories, concluding that despite the traditional nature of Zahn's science fiction it is "certainly high–quality work." Gregory Frost of the *Washington Post Book World* remarked that "every story of Zahn's contains a novel idea" and that the stories center on scientific theories or pos-

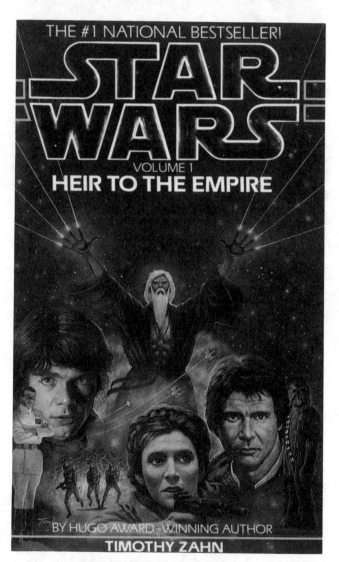

Zahn continued the famous "Star Wars" saga with this 1991 novel which traces the adventures of Luke Skywalker, Han Solo, and Princess Leia as they battle Grand Admiral Thrawn, a former warlord of the Evil Empire.

sible advances in science. Frost did, however, take Zahn to task for failing to handle his ideas in an unusual way. He said that "Zahn is what is referred to as an 'idea' writer," someone whose stories "are often extrapolations from hard scientific data." In *Voice of Youth Advocates* Yates cautioned readers that both "The Energy Crisis of 2215," in which scientists try to bring about a total matter conversion from a black hole in order to meet the Earth's energy needs, and "Cascade Point," about a spaceship that ends up in an alternative universe, "provide heavy going for non-scientific types."

The other selections in *Cascade Point* include "The Giftie Gie Us," about two handicapped people who discover that love is not weakened by physical deformities, "Job Inaction," about what happens when computers do the hiring and firing, and "Teamwork" in which a man with a multiple personality disorder may have cured himself—but by doing so, he destroys an alien structure. Yates notes that Zahn's stories are "decidedly upbeat" in feeling, though "the tone is wry and ironic." In another issue of *Voice of Youth Advocates,* reviewer Joni Bodart emphasized the fact that the collection was "well written, with believable situations, witty dialogue and engaging characters." Describing the collection, Zahn said in the introduction that it would give readers "five years of story development as I've slowly grown from a semi– rank amateur to at least journeyman status in this field."

Triplet takes its title from a strange planetary system where travelers from the Twenty Worlds land on Threshold in order to journey through a tunnel to reach the Hidden Worlds. These include Shamsheer, a world where technology is at such a high level that it appears like magic, and Karyx, where magic actually works but is dependent on summoning demons. Zahn's heroine is Danae mal ce Taeger, an heiress who uses her influence to get assigned to Ravagin, the most experienced courier to these worlds. Despite the fact that these worlds are full of danger and that very little is known about them, Danae is fearless, believing that by entering them she can escape her father's influence. Danae learns the spells that force spirits to do as she commands—and she also that one mistake and these demons will turn on her. Danae has worked hard to accomplish something for herself, to free herself of all the advantages that her father's wealth has afforded her, but ultimately she discovers that these too have their part in her

In this 1992 sequel to *Heir to the Empire,* Grand Admiral Thrawn seeks to destroy the New Republic with the aid of a traitorous Jedi Master.

success and that she can use them to her advantage. *Analog* reviewer Easton faulted *Triplet* for being "hackneyed, cliched, and unexciting" and wondered whether Zahn felt an obligation to "rationalize fantasy and fit it into the science fiction mold." And while a *Publishers Weekly* writer similarly criticized the novel as one of Zahn's less successful efforts, the reviewer also said that "as usual he scores with a progressively enlarging perspective and gradual revelation of the hidden logic behind" his ideas.

Zahn explored possible permutations of the death penalty in his 1988 work *Deadman Switch.* The galactic society the novel describes uses its convicts as pilots for space travel to the world of Solitaire, which is surrounded by a mysterious cloud that can only be navigated by corpses. Ships that seek to enter or exit the system must kill a member of their crew to create a "zombi" pilot. When Gilead Benedar, who works for the magnate Lord Kelsey– Ramos as a human lie detector, is sent on an inspection tour of Kelsey– Ramos's newly acquired Solitaire–licensed ships, he discovers that one of the ship's two intended zombis is innocent. Benadar discovers that she, like Benedar, belongs to the Watchers, a Christian sect that is one of the last remnants of organized religion left in the galaxy. Watchers are trained to accurately, truly and deeply observe the universe. Benedar's recognition—and subsequent search for a replacement zombi—leads to all sorts of problems with Solitaire's elite as well as the executives whose company his boss has taken over. *Analog* reviewer Easton chided the story for its "elementary" structure and theme, adding that the "plot is too largely predictable."

THE GRIPPING CONCLUSION TO THE #1 BESTSELLING SAGA!

STAR WARS

VOLUME 3 OF A THREE-BOOK CYCLE

THE LAST COMMAND

BY THE HUGO AWARD–WINNING AUTHOR
TIMOTHY ZAHN

The Republic's soldiers, led by Luke Skywalker, must invade the stronghold of Grand Admiral Thrawn and defeat his devastating clone soldiers in this 1993 work, the final book in Zahn's "Star Wars" trilogy.

In 1990's *Warhorse,* the author imagines a conflict between an outwardly mobile human race and an alien species of sophisticated biological engineers. The "Tampies" have decided that all life is valuable and should be protected, a philosophy which often clashes with the often violent realities of human society. Among the Tampies' weapons are living, genetically–engineered spaceships called "warhorses," which are more powerful than anything humanity has produced—and could be used to destroy mankind if proven a threat. Writing in *Booklist,* Roland Green deemed *Warhorse* "Zahn at his best," making special mention of the author's mix of "hard science and social science extrapolation."

Successfully Adopting the Star Wars Clan

Sometimes a writer decides to rework a classic—a play by William Shakespeare, for example, or a myth—but very few do what Zahn did in 1991: take a popular and celebrated film series and resume the story where the creators left off. With *Heir to the Empire,* the author picked up the *Star Wars* story five years after *The Return of the Jedi,* the last of George Lucas's three films. Han Solo and Princess Leia are married and expecting twins. Luke Skywalker continues to learn the secrets of the Jedi, as well as to train Leia in the Jedi arts. Darth Vader and the Evil Empire have been defeated and the Republic is at peace. All appears to be well—until Grand Admiral Thrawn, former warlord of the empire, shows up and attacks the Republic. John Lawson noted in *School Library Journal* that while *Heir to the Empire* is "not on a par with Zahn's creative, powerful works" it was "well written." The book reached the top of the *New York Times* best seller list.

Dark Force Rising, the second book in the series, joined *Heir to the Empire* on the best seller list. The same characters are back, along with Grand Admiral Thrawn, who is preparing to crush the New Republic. To this end, he has enlisted the help of unsavory smugglers, political rivals, a well– placed snitch and an insane Jedi Master. *Booklist's* Green termed Zahn's adoption of the Star Wars characters "one of the more remarkable pastiches of recent years." He also praised Zahn's "real flair" for incorporating elements of science fiction into the *Star Wars* saga, while *Library Journal* contributor Jackie Cassada complimented Zahn's "snappy prose and cinematic style." *Dark Force Rising* reached the number two position on the *New York Times* bestseller list.

In the final volume of Zahn's trilogy, *The Last Command,* Grand Admiral Thrawn has been quite successful and is preparing to mount a final siege against the Republic using his new technology: clone soldiers. As Han and Leia struggle to keep up resistance—and await their twins at any moment—it becomes clear that the Empire has too many ships and clones for the rebels to have a chance in face–to–face combat. The only solution is the infiltration of Thrawn's stronghold by a small band of fighters, led by Luke. Naturally, further dangers await the fighters at Thrawn's headquarters. Writing in *Voice of Youth Advocates,* Lisa Prolman described the novel as "a thoroughly mesmerizing and satisfying continuation of the *Star Wars* saga." She applauded Zahn's sensitive extension of the original characters, noting that they had achieved a new depth in his trilogy. "*The Last Command* is a must read for anyone who has followed the George Lucas series from the beginning," she stated, adding that "Zahn's handling of the characters and plot create a work that readers will enjoy and is a good read." Clearly, quite a few readers agreed with her: the book spent 12 weeks on the *New York Times* best–seller list and managed to reach third place.

But Zahn's popularity is not limited to readers; he is a favorite among critics as well. Green of *Booklist* has praised Zahn's "generally excellent military novels" as well as his "consistently acute eye for detail." And *Analog*'s Easton has pointed out that in the vein of most traditional science fiction, Zahn deals with a vast interplanetary system in his work. However, according to Easton, like many of his contemporaries, Zahn's ideas are "smaller, of lesser sweep" than those of older writers. But in Zahn's case, he concluded, "this is a consequence of more attention to character, to individuals, to matters of soul instead of destiny."

Zahn himself professes no deep motives to his writing other than to tell a good tale. "I consider myself primarily a storyteller and as such have no major pulpit–thumping 'message' that I always try to insert into each story or book," he once commented. "If any theme crops up more than any other, it is my strong belief that there is no prison—whether physical, social, or emotional—that can permanently trap a person who truly wishes to break free of the bonds."

■ Works Cited

Review of *A Coming of Age, Publishers Weekly,* December 14, 1984, p. 41– 42.

Bodart, Joni, review of *Cascade Point and Other Stories, Voice of Youth Advocates,* June, 1986, pp. 91– 92.

Review of *Cascade Point and Other Stories, Publishers Weekly,* March 21, 1986, p. 77.

Cassada, Jackie, review of *Dark Force Rising, Library Journal,* April 15, 1992, p. 125.

Easton, Tom, review of *A Coming of Age, Analog Science Fiction/Science Fact,* November, 1985, pp. 182– 183.

Easton, Tom, review of *The Blackcollar, Analog Science Fiction/Science Fact,* February, 1984, pp. 167– 168.

Easton, Tom, review of *Cascade Point and Other Stories, Analog Science Fiction/Science Fact,* November, 1986, p. 182.

Easton, Tom, review of *Cobra Bargain* and *Triplet, Analog Science Fiction/Science Fact,* April, 1988, pp. 181– 182.

Easton, Tom, review of *Deadman Switch, Analog Science Fiction/Science Fact,* May, 1989.

Frost, Gregory, "Hard Tech," *Washington Post Book World,* May 25, 1986, p. 8.

Green, Roland, review of *Cascade Point and Other Stories, Booklist,* May 1, 1986, p. 1288.

Green, Roland, review of *Dark Force Rising, Booklist,* April 1, 1992, p. 1413.

Green, Roland, review of *Spinneret, Booklist,* January 1, 1986, p. 662.

Green, Roland, review of *Triplet, Booklist,* August, 1987, p. 1722.

Green, Roland, review of *Warhorse, Booklist,* March 15, 1990, p. 1420.

Hoover, Hal, review of *Spinneret, Voice of Youth Advocates,* June, 1986, p. 92

Lawson, John, review of *Heir to the Empire, School Library Journal,* February, 1992, p. 122.

Prolman, Lisa, review of *The Last Command, Voice of Youth Advocates,* October, 1993, p. 237.

Review of *Spinneret, Publishers Weekly,* October 25, 1985, p. 61.

Review of *Triplet, Publishers Weekly,* July 3, 1987, p. 58.

Yates, Diane G., review of *Cascade Point and Other Stories, Voice of Youth Advocates,* August/ October, 1986, pp. 167– 168.

Yates, Diane G., review of *Cobra* and *Cobra Strike, Voice of Youth Advocates,* June, 1986, p. 92.

Zahn, Timothy, introduction to *Cascade Point and Other Stories,* Bluejay Books, 1986.

■ For More Information See

BOOKS

Chute, John and Peter Nicholls, *The Encyclopedia of Science Fiction,* St. Martin's, 1993.
Twentieth– Century Science Fiction Writers, 3rd edition, St. James Press, 1992.

PERIODICALS

Analog Science Fiction/Science Fact, October, 1985, p. 182; August, 1986, pp. 178–179.
Christian Science Monitor, January 3, 1986, p. 18.
Fantasy Review, April, 1985, p. 31; May, 1985, p. 22; December, 1985, p. 26; March, 1986, p. 25.
Publishers Weekly, March 23, 1992, p. 64.
School Library Journal, September, 1985, p. 155.
Voice of Youth Advocates, August, 1985, p. 196; February, 1987, p. 294; February, 1989, p. 296.*

—Sketch by Megan Ratner

Acknowledgments

Acknowledgements

Grateful acknowledgement is made to the following publishers, authors, and artists for their kind permission to reproduce copyrighted material.

ANSEL ADAMS. Photographs by Ansel Adams copyright © 1994, by the Trustees of the Ansel Adams Publishing Rights Trust. All Rights Reserved. Photograph of Ansel Adams with Joseph Le Conte and members of the Le Conte family in Giant Forest, Kings Canyon, California, c.1925, by the Trustees of the Ansel Adams Publishing Rights Trust. All Rights Reserved. Ansel Adams holding his Box Brownie camera on his first visit to Yosemite National Park, California, in 1916, by the Trustees of the Ansel Adams Publishing Rights Trust. All Rights Reserved./ Photograph by Jim Alinder.

DAVE BARRY. Cover of *Dave Barry Turns 40,* by Dave Barry. Copyright © 1990 by Dave Barry. Cover photos by Bill Wax. Cover design by James K. Davis. Reprinted by permission of Ballantine Books, a division of Random House, Inc./ Cover of *Dave Barry Does Japan,* by Dave Barry. Copyright © 1992 Random House, Inc. Reprinted by permission of Random House, Inc./ Cover of *Dave Barry Slept Here: A Sort Of History Of The United States,* by Dave Barry. Copyright © 1989 by Dave Barry. Cover photograph by Bill Wax. Reprinted by permission of Ballantine Books, a division of Random House, Inc./ Cover of *Dave Barry's Greatest Hits,* by Dave Barry. Copyright © 1988 by Dave Barry. Cover photograph by Bill Wax. Reprinted by permission of Ballantine Books, a division of Random House, Inc./ Photograph courtesy of Dave Barry.

ROBERT BENCHLEY. Cover of *White Shark,* by Peter Benchley. Copyright © 1994 Random House, Inc. Reprinted by permission of Random House, Inc./ Cover of *Jaws,* by Peter Benchley. Copyright © 1974 by Peter Benchley. Reprinted by permission of Ballantine Books, a division of Random House, Inc./ Cover of *Beast,* by Peter Benchley. Copyright © 1991 by Peter Benchley. Reprinted by permission of Ballantine Books, a division of Random House, Inc./ Photograph courtesy of Tracy Benchley.

TIM BURTON. Photograph by Zade Rosenthal, with Tim Burton on the set of *Batman.*/ Movie still by Joel Fletcher, from *The Nightmare Before Christmas.*/ Movie still from *Batman,* courtesy of Warner Bros./ Photograph of Tim Burton, by R. Brown/ONYX./ Movie still from *Frankenweenie,* courtesy of Walt Disney Studios.

BARBARA CORCORAN. Cover of *A Dance To Still Music,* by Barbara Corcoran. Illustrated by Charles Robinson. Reprinted by permission of Charles Robinson./ Cover of *The Potato Kid,* by Barbara Corcoran. Copyright © 1989 by Barbara Corcoran. Reprinted by permission of Avon Books./ Jacket of *The Person In The Potting Shed,* by Barbara Corcoran. Copyright © 1980 by Judith Gwyn Brown. Reprinted by permission of Atheneum Books for Young Readers, an imprint of Simon & Schuster Children's Publishing Division./ Jacket of *Face The Music,* by Barbara Corcoran. Reprinted by permission of Michael Garland./ Cover of *Which Witch Is Which?,* by Barbara Corcoran. Cover illustration copyright © 1992 by Renee Grant. Cover design by Rebecca Tachna. Reprinted by permission of Renee Grant.

RICHIE TANKERSLEY CUSICK. Cover of *The Lifeguard,* by Richie Tankersley Cusick. Copyright © 1988 by Richie Tankersley Cusick. Reprinted by permission of Scholastic Inc./ Cover of *April Fools,* by Richie Tankersley Cusick. Copyright © 1990 by Richie Tankersley Cusick. Reprinted by permission of Scholastic, Inc./ Cover of *Fatal Secrets,* by Richie Tankersley Cusick. Cover copyright © 1992 by Simon & Schuster, Inc. Cover art by Gerber Studio. Reprinted by permission of Pocket Books, a division of Simon & Schuster, Inc./ Cover of *Trick Or Treat,* by Richie Tankersley Cusick. Copyright © 1989 by Richie Tankersley Cusick. Reprinted by permission of Scholastic Inc./ Photograph by Kathleen Casey, courtesy of Richie Tankersley Cusick.

FRANK DEFORD. Jacket of *Love And Infamy,* by Frank Deford. Copyright © 1993 by Frank Deford. Jacket design by Neil Stuart. Illustration by Will Williams, Wood, Ronsaville, Harlin Inc. Photograph copyright © 1993 Comstock Inc. Reprinted in the USA and Canada by permission of Viking Penguin, a division of Penguin Books USA Inc./ Cover of *The Best American Sports Writing 1993,* by Frank Deford. Cover design copyright © Carin Gordberg. Reprinted by permission of Houghton Mifflin Company./ Photograph of Deford and Price, by John S. Abbott./ Photograph by Chris Sanders.

ARTHUR CONAN DOYLE. Cover of *The Memoirs of Sherlock Holmes,* by A. Conan Doyle. Copyright © 1975 by A & W Publishers, Inc. Cover illustration by Sidney Paget. Jacket design: Trezzo/Braren Studio./ Illustration from *The Memoirs of Sherlock Holmes,* by A. Conan Doyle. Copyright © 1975 by A & W Publishers, Inc. Illustrations by Sidney Paget./ Movie still from *Young Sherlock Holmes,* copyright © MCMLXXXL by Paramount Pictures Corporation and Amblin Entertainment, Inc./ Movie still from *The Hound of the Baskervilles,* courtesy of Twentieth Century-Fox.

RODDY DOYLE. Cover of *The Van,* by Roddy Doyle. Copyright © 1991 by Roddy Doyle. Cover design by Michael

245

Ian Kaye and Melissa Hayden. Reprinted by permission of Viking Penguin, a division of Penguin Books USA Inc./ Cover of *The Snapper*, by Roddy Doyle. Copyright © 1990 by Roddy Doyle. Cover clouds and design by Melissa Jacoby. Cover photographs: baby: The Image Bank; the River Liffey in the center of the business district of Dublin, Ireland: copyright © Don Klumpp/The Image Bank. Reprinted by permission of Penguin, a division of Penguin Books USA Inc./ Cover of *The Commitments*, by Roddy Doyle. Vintage Contemporaries, 1989. Copyright © 1987 by Roddy Doyle. Reprinted by permission of Vintage Books, a division of Random House, Inc./ Photograph by David Appleby, of the cast from *The Commitments*./ Photograph of Doyle by Derek Speirs.

DANNY ELFMAN. Photograph of Warren Beatty as Dick Tracy, the Kobal Collection./ Film clip by Bo Henry, from *The Nightmare Before Christmas*./ Film clip from *Batman Returns*, courtesy of Warner Bros./ Photograph of Elfman by Dennis Keeley, copyright © 1990 MCA Records, Inc.

FRANK FRAZETTA. Illustration by Frank Frazetta from his *Frank Frazetta: The Living Legend*. Copyright © 1981 by Frank Frazetta. Reprinted by permission of Frazetta Prints./ Cover illustration by Frank Frazetta from *Back To The Stone Age*, by Edgar Rice Burroughs. Copyright © 1936, 1937 by Edgar Rice Burroughs, Inc. Cover painting by Frank Frazetta. Reprinted by permission of Edgar Rice Burroughs./ Illustration by Frank Frazetta from *Frank Frazetta: Book Two*, with introduction by Betty Ballantine. Copyright © 1977 by Frank Frazetta. Reprinted by permission of Frazetta Prints./ Illustration by Frank Frazetta from his *Small Wonders: The Funny Animal Art Of Frank Frazetta*, Compilation copyright © 1991 by Kitchen Sink Press, Inc., and Pure Imagination, Inc. Reprinted by permission of Kitchen Sink Press, Inc., and Pure Imagination, Inc./ Photograph courtesy of Frank Frazetta.

JOHN GRISHAM. Cover of *A Time To Kill*, by John Grisham. Copyright © 1989 by John Grisham. Reprinted by permission of Doubleday, a division of Bantam Doubleday Dell Publishing Group./ Cover of *The Firm*, by John Grisham. *The Firm* copyright © 1994 by Paramount Pictures. All Rights Reserved. Reprinted courtesy of Paramount Pictures and Tom Cruise./ Photograph from the movie *The Client*, courtesy of Warner Bros./ Movie still by Ken Regan/Camera 5, from *The Pelican Brief*.

JAMES HASKINS. Jacket of *Black Music In America*, by James Haskins. Jacket copyright © 1987 by Harper & Row, Publishers, Inc. Jacket design by Patricia Parcell Watts. Jacket photos, clockwise from upper left: Louis Armstrong (Institute of Jazz Studies, Rutgers University), Billie Holiday (Haskins Collection), Scott Joplin (Haskins Collection), Duke Ellington (Haskins Collection), James Reese Europe and band (Frank Driggs Collection), Aretha Franklin (Frank Driggs Collection). Reprinted by permission of HarperCollins Publishers Inc./ Cover photograph from *The Life And Death Of Martin Luther King, Jr.*, by James Haskins. Cover photograph by Lynn Pelham, LIFE Magazine, copyright © Time Warner, Inc., reprinted by permission. Cover reprinted by permission of Beech Tree Books, an imprint of William Morrow & Company, Inc./ Cover of *Scott Joplin*, by James Haskins with Kathleen Benson. Copyright © 1978 by James Haskins with Kathleen Benson. Cover design by Douglas Bergstreser. Reprinted by permission of Doubleday, a division of Bantam Doubleday Dell Publishing Group, Inc./ Photograph of Haskins at lectern by Conway-Atlantic Photography./ Photograph of Haskins by Teddy R. Ancrum, Jr.

WILL HOBBS. Cover of *Bearstone*, by Will Hobbs. Copyright © 1989 by Will Hobbs. Reprinted by permission of Avon Books./ Cover of *Downriver*, by Will Hobbs. Cover art copyright © 1992 by Robert McGinnis. Reprinted by permission of Bantam Books, a division of Bantam Doubleday Dell Publishing Group, Inc./ photographs courtesy of Will Hobbs.

DOROTHEA LANGE. Photographs by Dorothea Lange from *Dorothea Lange: Life Through The Camera*, by Milton Meltzer. Text copyright © 1985 by Milton Meltzer. Reprinted by permission of Viking Penguin, a division of Penguin Books USA Inc./ Photograph of Irish couple by Dorothea Lange and photograph of Lange on hood of car taking pictures. Copyright © the Dorothea Lange Collection, The Oakland Museum, The City of Oakland. Gift of Paul S. Taylor./ Photograph of young girl and photograph of gas station air hose, courtesy of The Library of Congress.

H. P. LOVECRAFT. Jacket of *Tales Of The Cthulhu Mythos*, by H. P. Lovecraft and Divers Hands. Copyright © 1990 by Arkham House Publishers, Inc. Illustrations copyright © 1990 by Jeffrey K. Potter. Jacket by Jeffrey K. Potter. Reprinted by permission of Jeffrey Potter./ Jacket of *H. P. Lovecraft: Dagon and Other Macabre Tales*, selected by August Derleth, with texts edited by S.T. Joshi. Copyright © 1939, 1943, by August Derleth and Donald Wandrei. Copyright © 1965 by August Derleth. Jacket by Raymond Bayless. Reprinted by permission of Raymond Bayless./ Cover of *The Best of H. P. Lovecraft: Bloodcurdling Tales Of Horror And The Macabre*, introduction by Robert Bloch. Cover art copyright © 1981 by Michael Whelan. Reprinted by permission of Ballantine Books, a division of Random House, Inc./ Cover of *Herbert West Re-Animator*, by H.P. Lovecraft. Copyright © 1977, 1985 by Necronomicon Press. Cover art by Robert H. Knox. Reprinted by permission of Necronomicon Press.

PATRICIA A. MCKILLIP. Jacket of *Harpist In The Wind*, by Patricia A. McKillip. Atheneum, 1979. Copyright © 1979 by Patricia A. McKillip. Jacket painting by Michael Mariano. Reprinted by permission of Atheneum Publishers, an imprint of Macmillan Publishing Company./ Cover of *The House on Parchment Street*, by Patricia A. McKillip. Cover illustration copyright © 1991 by Jeffrey Lindberg. Cover design by Rebecca Tachna. Reprinted by permission of Jeffrey Lindberg./ Jacket of *The Forgotten Beasts Of Eld*, by Patricia A. McKillip. Atheneum, 1974. Copyright © 1974 by Patricia A. McKillip. Jacket painting by Peter Schaumann. Reprinted by permission of Atheneum Publishers, an imprint of Macmillan Publishing Company./ Photograph by Carol McKillip.

ANDRE NORTON. Cover of *Catfantastic*, edited by Andre Norton & Martin H. Greenberg. Copyright © 1989 by Andre Norton and Martin H. Greenberg. Cover art by Braldt Bralds. Reprinted by permission of DAW Books, Inc./ Cover of *Witch World*, by Andre Norton. Copyright © 1963 by Ace Books, Inc. Reprinted by permission of The Putnam Berkley Publishing Group./ Jacket of *Moon Mirror*, by Andre Norton. Copyright © 1988 by Andre Norton Limited. Cover art by Yvonne Gilbert. Reprinted by permission of Tom Doherty Associates./ Jacket of *Forerunner: The Second Venture*, by Andre Norton. Copyright © 1985 by Andre Norton. Cover art by Victoria Poyser. Cover design by Carol Russo. Reprinted by permission of Tom Doherty Associates./ Photograph by Jay Kay Klein.

JOAN PHIPSON. Cover of *Hit And Run*, by Joan Phipson. Cover illustration copyright © 1989 by Gary Lang. Cover design by Rebecca Tachna. Reprinted by permission of Gary Lang./ Jacket of *Bianca*, by Joan Phipson. Jacket illustration copyright © 1988 by Deborah Chabrian. Reprinted by permission of Deborah Chabrian./ Jacket of *Fly Into Danger*, by Joan Phipson. Copyright © 1977 by Joan Phipson. Jacket painting by Kinuko Craft. Reprinted by permission of Margaret K. McElderry Books, an imprint of Macmillan Publishing Company./ Photographs of Phipson as a young girl, courtesy of Joan Phipson.

EDGAR ALLAN POE. Illustrations from *The Poetical Works Of Edgar Allan Poe*, by Edgar Allan Poe. Weathervane, 1978. Illustrations by Edmund Dulac. Reprinted by permission of Hodder & Stoughton Limited./ Illustrations from *Tales of Mystery & Imagination*, by Edgar Allan Poe. Copyright © MCMXXXV by George G. Harrap & Co. Ltd. Illustrations by Arthur Rackham./ Movie still from *The Masque of the Red Death*, courtesy of American International Pictures./ Photograph courtesy of Brown University Library.

HAROLD RAMIS. Movie still from *Animal House*, courtesy of Universal Pictures./ Movie still from *Caddyshack*, courtesy of Orion Pictures./ Movie still from *Meatballs*, copyright © MCMLXXIX by Haliburton Films Ltd./ Movie still from *Ghostbusters*, courtesy of Columbia Pictures./ Movie still from *Stripes*, courtesy of Columbia Pictures./ Photograph courtesy of Columbia Pictures Industries, Inc.

ROD SERLING. Movie clip from *To Serve Man*, courtesy of Bob Burns./ Movie clip from *Requiem for a Heavyweight*, courtesy of Sony Fox Productions./ Photograph courtesy of the Estate of Rod Serling.

LESLIE MARMON SILKO. Photograph from *Storyteller*, by Leslie Marmon Silko. Copyright © 1981 by Leslie Marmon Silko. Reprinted by permission of Leslie Marmon Silko./ Cover of *Ceremony*, by Leslie Marmon Silko. Copyright © 1977 by Leslie Silko. Cover art: Portrait by Bennie Buffalo, 1976, Tribal Arts Gallery and Dr. M. A. Shapiro, Oklahoma. Reprinted by permission of Viking Penguin, a division of Penguin Books USA Inc./ Cover of *Almanac Of The Dead*, by Leslie Marmon Silko. Copyright © 1991 by Leslie Marmon Silko. Cover design and painting copyright © 1991 by Wendell Minor. Reprinted by permission of Viking Penguin, a division of Penguin Books USA Inc./ Photograph courtesy of Leslie Marmon Silko.

TIMOTHY ZAHN. Jacket of *Star Wars: Dark Force Rising*, by Timothy Zahn. Jacket copyright © 1993 by Tom Jung. Reprinted by permission of Bantam Books, a division of Bantam Doubleday Dell Publishing Group, Inc./ Jacket of *Star Wars: The Last Command*, by Timothy Zahn. Jacket art copyright © 1993 by Tom Jung. Reprinted by permission of Bantam Books, a division of Bantam Doubleday Dell Publishing Group, Inc./ Cover of *Star Wars: Heir To The Empire*, by Timothy Zahn. Cover art copyright © 1991 by Tom Jung. Reprinted by permission of Bantam Books, a division of Bantam Doubleday Dell Publishing Group, Inc./ Cover of *Deadman Switch*, by Timothy Zahn. Copyright © 1988 by Timothy Zahn. Cover art by David Mattingly. Reprinted by permission of Baen Publishing Enterprises./ Photograph, copyright © by Bill Morrow/Gliessman Studios.

Cumulative Index

Author/Artist Index

The following index gives the number of the volume in which an author/artist's biographical sketch appears.

Adams, Ansel 1902-1984 14
Adams, Douglas 1952- 4
Adler, C. S. 1932- 4
Adoff, Arnold 1935- 3
Aiken, Joan 1924- 1
Alcock, Vivien 1924- 8
Alexander, Lloyd 1924- 1
Allen, Woody 1935- 10
Anderson, Poul 1926- 5
Andrews, V. C. ?-1986 4
Angell, Judie 1937- 11
Angelou, Maya 1928- 7
Anthony, Piers 1934- 11
Archie Comics 9
Ashabranner, Brent 1921- 6
Asimov, Isaac 1920-1992 13
Atwood, Margaret 1939- 12
Auel, Jean M. 1936- 7
Avi 1937- 10
Baldwin, James 1924-1987 4
Ballard, J. G. 1930- 3
Bambara, Toni Cade 1939- 5
Barker, Clive 1952- 10
Barry, Dave 1947- 14
Barry, Lynda 1956- 9
Benchley, Peter 1940- 14
Bennett, Jay 1912- 10
Block, Francesca Lia 1962- 13
Blume, Judy 1938- 3
Bochco, Steven 1943- 11
Bonham, Frank 1914- 1
Boorman, John 1933- 3
Bradley, Marion Zimmer 1930- 9
Brancato, Robin F. 1936- 9
Breathed, Berke 1957- 5
Bridgers, Sue Ellen 1942- 8
Brooks, Bruce 1950- 8
Brooks, Mel 1926- 13
Brown, Claude 1937- 7
Bunting, Eve 1928- 5
Burroughs, Edgar Rice 1875-1950 11
Burton, Tim 1958(?)- 14
Cameron, James 1954- 9
Campbell, Joseph 1904-1987 3

Cannell, Stephen J. 1941- 9
Card, Orson Scott 1951- 11
Carpenter, John 1948- 2
Chatwin, Bruce 1940-1989 4
Childress, Alice 1920- 8
Christie, Agatha 1890-1976 9
Cisneros, Sandra 1954- 9
Clancy, Tom 1947- 9
Clark, Mary Higgins 1929?- 10
Clarke, Arthur C. 1917- 4
Cleary, Beverly 1916- 6
Cleaver, Vera 1919-1993 12
Cohen, Daniel 1936- 7
Collier, Christopher 1930- 13
Collier, James Lincoln 1928- 13
Colman, Hila 1
Conford, Ellen 1942- 10
Connell, Evan S. 1924- 7
Conroy, Pat 1945- 8
Cooney, Caroline B. 1947- 5
Cooper, J. California 12
Cooper, Susan 13
Corcoran, Barbara 1911- 14
Cormier, Robert 1925- 3
Craven, Wes 1939- 6
Crichton, Michael 1942- 10
Crutcher, Chris 1946- 9
Cusick, Richie Tankersley 1952- 14
Daly, Maureen 1921- 5
Danziger, Paula 1944- 4
Davis, Jim 1945- 8
Deford, Frank 1938- 14
Deighton, Len 1929- 6
Delton, Judy 1931- 6
Dickinson, Peter 1927- 9
Dillard, Annie 1945- 6
Doyle, Arthur Conan 1859-1930 14
Doyle, Roddy 14
Duncan, Lois 1934- 4
Dygard, Thomas J. 1931- 7
Eiseley, Loren 1907-1977 5
Elfman, Danny 1953- 14
Ellis, Bret Easton 1964- 2
Erdrich, Louise 1954- 10

Faulkner, William 1897-1962 7
Feiffer, Jules 1929- 3
Fleischman, Paul 1952- 11
Follett, Ken 1949- 6
Forster, E. M. 1879-1970 2
Fox, Paula 1923- 3
Francis, Dick 1920- 5
Frank, Anne 1929-1945 12
Frazetta, Frank 1928- 14
Freedman, Russell 1929- 4
Friesner, Esther M. 1951- 10
Fuentes, Carlos 1928- 4
Garcia Marquez, Gabriel 1928- 3
Garfield, Leon 1921- 8
George, Jean Craighead 1919- 8
Gibson, William 1948- 12
Godden, Rumer 1907- 6
Golding, William 1911- 5
Goudge, Eileen 1950- 6
Gould, Chester 1900-1985 7
Grafton, Sue 1940- 11
Greenberg, Joanne 1932- 12
Greene, Bette 1934- 7
Greene, Constance C. 1924- 7
Grisham, John 1955- 14
Groening, Matt 1954- 8
Guest, Judith 1936- 7
Guisewite, Cathy 1950- 2
Guy, Rosa 1925- 4
Hall, Lynn 1937- 4
Hamilton, Virginia 1936- 2
Haskins, James S. 1941- 14
Hawking, Stephen 1942- 13
Heat-Moon, William Least 1939- 9
Hentoff, Nat 1925- 4
Herriot, James 1916- 1
Highwater, Jamake 1942?- 7
Hildebrandt, Greg 1939- 12
Hildebrandt, Tim 1939- 12
Hillerman, Tony 1925- 6
Hinton, S. E. 1950- 2
Hobbs, Will 1947- 14
Holland, Isabelle 1920- 11
Hoover, H. M. 1935- 11
Howard, Ron 1954- 8
Howker, Janni 1957- 9
Hughes, John 1950?- 7
Hughes, Langston 1902-1967 12
Hunter, Mollie 1922- 13
Huxley, Aldous 1894-1963 11
Irving, John 1942- 8
Irwin, Hadley 13
Jackson, Shirley 1919-1965 9
Janeczko, Paul B. 1945- 9
Johnston, Lynn 1947- 12

Johnston, Norma 12
Jones, Chuck 1912- 2
Jones, Diana Wynne 1934- 12
Jordan, June 1936- 2
Kane, Bob 1916- 8
Kaufman, Bel 4
Keillor, Garrison 1942- 2
Kennedy, William 1928- 1
Kerr, M. E. 1927- 2
Kincaid, Jamaica 1949- 13
King, Stephen 1947- 1
Kingston, Maxine Hong 1940- 8
Kinsella, W. P. 1935- 7
Klein, Norma 1938-1989 2
Knowles, John 1926- 10
Koertge, Ron 1940- 12
Konigsburg, E. L. 1930- 3
Koontz, Dean R. 1945- 9
Korman, Gordon 1963- 10
Kundera, Milan 1929- 2
Kurosawa, Akira 1910- 11
Lackey, Mercedes 1950- 13
Lange, Dorothea 1895-1965 14
Larson, Gary 1950- 1
Lee, Harper 1926- 13
Lee, Spike 1957- 4
Lee, Stan 1922- 5
Le Guin, Ursula K. 1929- 9
Leibovitz, Annie 1949- 11
L'Engle, Madeleine 1918- 1
Lester, Julius 1939- 12
Letterman, David 1947- 10
Levitin, Sonia 1934- 13
Lewis, C. S. 1898-1963 3
Lipsyte, Robert 1938- 7
Lloyd Webber, Andrew 1948- 1
London, Jack 1876-1916 13
Lopez, Barry 1945- 9
Lovecraft, H. P. 1890-1937 14
Lowry, Lois 1937- 5
Lucas, George 1944- 1
Ludlum, Robert 1927- 10
Lustig, Arnost 1926- 3
MAD Magazine 13
Mahy, Margaret 1936- 8
Mamet, David 1947- 3
Marshall, Garry 1934- 3
Marshall, Penny 1943- 10
Martin, Ann 1955- 6
Mason, Bobbie Ann 1940- 5
Mathabane, Mark 1960- 4
Mathis, Sharon Bell 1937- 12
Matthiessen, Peter 1927- 6
Mazer, Harry 1925- 5
Mazer, Norma Fox 1931- 5

McCaffrey, Anne 1926- 6
McKillip, Patricia 1948- 14
McKinley, Robin 1952- 4
Meltzer, Milton 1915- 8
Michaels, Lorne 1944- 12
Miklowitz, Gloria 1927- 6
Mohr, Nicholasa 1935- 8
Momaday, N. Scott 1934- 11
Montgomery, L. M. 1874-1942 12
Monty Python 7
Morrison, Toni 1931- 1
Mowat, Farley 1921- 1
Myers, Walter Dean 1937- 4
Naylor, Gloria 1950- 6
Naylor, Phyllis Reynolds 1933- 4
Neufeld, John 1938- 11
Nixon, Joan Lowery 1927- 12
Norton, Andre 1912- 14
O'Brien, Robert 1918-1973 6
O'Connor, Flannery 1925-1964 7
O'Dell, Scott 1898-1989 3
Oneal, Zibby 1934- 5
Pascal, Francine 1938- 1
Paterson, Katherine 1932- 1
Paton Walsh, Jill 1937- 11
Paulsen, Gary 1939- 2
Peck, Richard 1934- 1
Peck, Robert Newton 1928- 3
Pfeffer, Susan Beth 1948- 12
Phipson, Joan 1912- 14
Picasso, Pablo 1881-1973 10
Pierce, Meredith Ann 1958- 13
Pike, Christopher 13
Pini, Richard 1950- 12
Pini, Wendy 1951- 12
Pinkwater, Daniel Manus 1941- 1
Plath, Sylvia 1932-1963 13
Platt, Kin 1911- 11
Poe, Edgar Allan 1809-1849 14
Pratt, Jane 1963?- 9
Quin-Harkin, Janet 1941- 6
Ramis, Harold 1944- 14
Rand, Ayn 1905-1982 10
Reid Banks, Lynne 1929- 6
Reiner, Rob 1945- 13
Rice, Anne 1941- 9
Roberts, Willo Davis 1928- 13
Roddenberry, Gene 1921-1991 5
Rylant, Cynthia 1954- 10
Sachs, Marilyn 1927- 2
Sagan, Carl 1934- 2
St. George, Judith 1931- 7
Salinger, J. D. 1919- 2

Saul, John 1942- 10
Scoppettone, Sandra 1936- 11
Scott, Ridley 1939- 13
Sebestyen, Ouida 1924- 8
Seinfeld, Jerry 1954- 11
Serling, Rod 1924-1975 14
Shange, Ntozake 1948- 9
Shepard, Sam 1943- 1
Sherburne, Zoa 1912- 13
Siegal, Aranka 1930- 5
Silko, Leslie Marmon 1948- 14
Sleator, William 1945- 5
Sondheim, Stephen 1930- 11
Soto, Gary 1952- 10
Spiegelman, Art 1948- 10
Spielberg, Steven 1947- 8
Spinelli, Jerry 1941- 11
Steinbeck, John 1902-1968 12
Stine, R. L. 1943- 13
Stolz, Mary 1920- 8
Strasser, Todd 1950- 2
Sutcliff, Rosemary 1920-1992 10
Tan, Amy 1952- 9
Taylor, Mildred D. 1943- 10
Taylor, Theodore 1921- 2
Thomas, Joyce Carol 1938- 12
Thompson, Julian F. 1927- 9
Tolkien, J. R. R. 1892-1973 10
Townsend, John Rowe 1922- 11
Trudeau, Garry 1948- 10
Vallejo, Boris 1941- 13
Voigt, Cynthia 1942- 3
Vonnegut, Kurt 1922- 6
Walker, Alice 1944- 3
Warhol, Andy 1928?-1987 12
Watterson, Bill 1958- 9
Wayans, Keenan Ivory 1958?- 11
Wells, Rosemary 1943- 13
Wersba, Barbara 1932- 2
Westall, Robert 1929-1993 12
White, Edmund 1940- 7
Wiesel, Elie 1928- 7
Wojciechowska, Maia 1927- 8
Wolfe, Tom 1930- 8
Wolitzer, Meg 1959- 6
Wrede, Patricia C. 1953- 8
Wright, Richard 1908-1960 5
Wrightson, Patricia 1921- 5
Yep, Laurence 1948- 5
Yolen, Jane 1939- 4
Zahn, Timothy 1951- 14
Zelazny, Roger 1937- 7
Zindel, Paul 1936- 2